The Fun is Inside!

Dear Friend,

You can always count on Wilton to add fun to your celebrations. If you want to serve something out of the ordinary, there is no better way to spark your imagination than by looking through the amazing cakes and desserts inside the 2006 Yearbook.

For 2006, the big news is in small party treats. Take a look at the delightful jungle scene depicted on the front cover, to see how much fun decorated cupcakes can bring to your celebration. When displayed on our new Cupcakes 'N More™ Dessert Stands, cupcakes create a great deal of excitement.

In this edition, our "Dazzling Displays" special section will show you how to present fun cupcakes and other small party foods on a grand scale. Imagine greeting your guests with a terrific dessert table filled with shimmering gelatin "cupcakes" and candy-filled cookies that look like stained glass. It's just one of the many coordinated party scenes you'll find, in exciting themes like smiley faces and circus clowns.
As an extra, we're sharing some of our favorite party recipes—tempting tastes like Spicy Asian Cheeseballs, Chicken Italiano Appetizers and colorful holiday truffles in 4 incredible flavors.

In addition to all the great single-serving desserts, the Yearbook is also packed with hundreds of new, exciting full size cake designs. Poker is hot and we have the perfect cake for a birthday party—a classic poker table complete with fondant chips and cards. Boys and girls are sure to love our piñata fiesta cake, topped with cookie kids. You'll also enjoy the fun themes we've chosen for holiday cakes, candies and cookies in 2006. Look for wacky witches and spiders for Halloween, brilliant Christmas ornaments and Valentine message hearts. These treats capture the spirit of each season for everyone!

Decorating is even more fun with all the great new products in our Yearbook. Be sure to see our new Ultimate 3-in-1 Caddy™, the easy-to-use Checkerboard Cake Pan Set and the Incredible Ice Cream Machine™ for delicious homemade ice cream. As always, you'll also find the essential Wilton products decorators have come to count on for great results.

Use the 2006 Yearbook throughout the year to make your party planning more enjoyable. I wish you and your family a wonderful year of celebrations.

Vince Naccarato

Vince Naccarato
Chairman and CEO
Wilton Industries, Inc.

Wilton Cake Decorating!
2006 WILTON YEARBOOK

Bolder Birthdays .... *p. 4*

Cakes that leave no doubt who the day's all about! Kids will know they're in for some serious fun when they see a wild piñata, colorful gumball machine or cool convertible at the party. See lots of great looks for adults, too—from a candy-filled barbeque grill to a poker table cake stacked with chips and a full deck of cards made with fondant.

Famous Friends .... *p. 26*

You'll love these characters as much as your kids do—because they make everyone feel part of the celebration! We make it easy to "toon" up your party, with designs built around our fun licensed shaped pans, toppers, candles and baking cups.

The Holidays Are Here! . . . . *p. 40*

You'll look forward to all 4 seasons! Want to make them scream this Halloween? A monster castle and a witch's cauldron cake are waiting for you. Building the perfect Christmas buffet? Mold 3 savory party spreads in festive ornament shapes. Don't forget our Valentine chocolate and cherry cheesecake!

CREATIVE DIRECTOR
Daniel Masini

ART DIRECTOR/CAKE DESIGNER
Steve Rocco

DECORATING ROOM SUPERVISOR
Mary Gavenda

SENIOR CAKE DECORATOR
Susan Matusiak

CAKE DECORATORS
Debbie Friedman
Ana Johnson
Diane Knowlton
Mark Malak
Judy Wysocki
Anne Christopher

EDITOR/WRITER
Jeff Shankman

WRITERS
Mary Enochs
Marita Seiler
Jessica Radzak

PRODUCTION MANAGER
Challis Yeager

ASSOCIATE PRODUCTION MANAGER
Mary Stahulak

GRAPHIC DESIGN/PRODUCTION
Alena Sokoloski
Deborah Casciato
RNB Graphics
Quebecor World Premedia

PHOTOGRAPHY
Peter Rossi - PDR Productions
Dale DeBolt Photography
Black Box Studios

PHOTO STYLIST
Carey Thornton

ADMINISTRATIVE ASSISTANT
Sharon Gaeta

IN U.S.A.
Wilton Industries, Inc.
2240 West 75th Street
Woodridge, IL 60517
www.wilton.com

Retail Customer Orders:
Phone: 800-794-5866
Fax: 888-824-9520

Website: www.wilton.com
Class Locations:
Phone: 800-942-8881
Website: www.wilton.com

IN CANADA
Wilton Industries, Canada, Ltd.
98 Carrier Drive
Etobicoke, Ontario M9W5R1 Canada
Retail Customer Orders:
Phone: 416-679-0798
Class Locations:
Phone: 416-679-0790 x200
E-mail: classprograms@wilton.ca

¡SE HABLA ESPAÑOL!
Para mas informacion, marque 800-436-5778

Times of Your Life . . . . p. 68

*Make life's biggest events even more meaningful.
Some of the distinctive theme looks you'll see—cute
umbrellas for bridal and baby showers, fondant and
cookie diplomas for grads and beautiful fondant
cross accents for communion cakes.*

The Wedding Party . . . . p. 80

*Special effects for the cake of a lifetime. Thin lines
of icing create a delicate curtain look. Cool pastels
brighten the day on cakes accented with color flow
panels and gently curled fondant plumeria blossoms.*

Dazzling Displays! . . . . p. 90

*How do you make smaller party treats look as
exciting as a large decorated cake? Fill our
Cupcakes 'N More™ Dessert Stands with the
fun and colorful designs we've cooked up for
you! You'll find shimmering gelatin "cupcakes,"
a mini-cake bridal court, holiday truffles in
4 wonderful flavors and a complete party buffet
with appetizers, sandwiches, strawberry mousse
and molten chocolate cakes.*

Decorating Guide . . . . p. 106

*It's easy to find the help you need! Includes step-
by-step techniques, luscious recipes, construction
guides and cutting charts, cookie and candy tips.*

The Wilton School . . . . p. 122

*The world's leading experts on cake decorating are
waiting to teach you! Get class descriptions and
schedules for courses throughout the year.*

Product Shops . . . . . p. 123

*Everything you need to create the exciting ideas
in this Yearbook! From decorating tips to famous
Wilton bakeware, from character candles to elegant
wedding ornaments, find it all here.*

Index . . . . p. 223

BOLDER BIRTHDAYS!

You wouldn't think of giving someone the same birthday gift year after year. Why not mix up their cake too? Try something wild and unpredictable like this supercharged neon fondant cake with candy stars and balloons bursting from the top! Or create a great theme cake to delight that special child or adult—from piñatas to poker, there's a great look for every birthday on your calendar.

Instructions for projects shown on these two pages are on page 6.

The Power to Surprise!

Pans: 8, 12 x 2 in. Square, p. 148; Mini Tiered Cakes, p. 150; Non-Stick Large Cookie/Jelly Roll, p. 146
Tip: 1M (2110), p. 139
Fondant: Ready-To-Use Rolled Fondant in White (24 oz. needed), Pastel Green and Pastel Yellow (48 oz. each); Primary and Neon Colors Fondant Multi Packs, p. 126; Star Cut-Outs™, p. 128; Ribbon Cutter/Embosser Set, p. 127; Brush Set, p. 129; Rolling Pin, Roll & Cut Mat, p. 130; Easy-Glide Fondant Smoother, p. 131
Candy: White Candy Melts®† (2 pks. needed), p. 218; Garden and Primary Candy Color Sets, p. 219; 11¾ in. Lollipop Sticks, p. 221
Recipe: Buttercream Icing, p. 112
Also: Circle Metal Cutter, p. 214; Parchment Triangles, p. 137; Assorted Celebration Candles, p. 188; Wooden Dowel Rods, p. 167; 8 in. Cookie Treat Sticks, p. 217; Cake Boards, Fanci-Foil Wrap, p. 169; ruler, curling ribbon

In advance: Make candy cake, balloons and stars. For cake, pour melted white candy ¼ in. thick into Mini Tiered Pan cavity. Refrigerate until firm; unmold. Divide remaining melted candy into five 3 oz. portions. Using candy colors, tint portions pink, violet, yellow, green (with a small amount of yellow and blue). Position round cutters and medium star Cut-Outs on non-stick pan, fill with assorted colors to make stars and balloons; refrigerate until firm, unmold. Pipe zigzag garland and outline trims on candy cake using melted candy in cut parchment bag. Attach cookie treat stick and candle to back of candy cake and lollipop sticks to backs of stars and balloons with melted candy. Set aside.

To lighten neon fondant, add 1½ oz. white fondant to 1 oz. blue, 2 oz. yellow fondant to 1 oz. green, 2 oz. white fondant to 2 oz. violet and 2 oz. white fondant to 1 oz. pink. Prepare 3-layer 8 in. cake (bake two 2 in. layers and one 1 in. layer to make a 5 in. high cake) and 1-layer 12 in. cake for stacked construction (p. 110). Prepare cakes for rolled fondant by icing lightly in buttercream. Cover cakes with pastel green and yellow fondant (p. 111); smooth with Fondant Smoother. Roll out colors ⅛ in. thick. For 8 in. cake, use various cutting wheels from Ribbon Cutter/Embosser (without spacers) to cut approximately forty 5 x ¼ in. wide fondant strips in various colors. Attach to cake sides, ½ in. apart, with damp brush. On 12 in. cake, use straight-edge cutting wheels with 1 striped embossing wheel to cut four 4 x 1 in. wide strips; attach with damp brush. Roll out colors ¹⁄₁₆ in. thick. Cut dots using wide end of tip 1M; randomly attach to cake with damp brush. Insert candies on sticks. Position curling ribbon on cake top. Serves 44.

Party Faces

Pan: Standard Muffin, p. 149
Tips: 3, 4, p. 138
Colors: Copper (skin tone), Brown, Black, p. 133
Candy: White Candy Melts®†, p. 218; Primary, Garden Candy Color Sets, p. 219; Party Time Candy Mold, p. 220
Recipe: Buttercream Icing, p. 112
Also: Party Hats Standard Baking Cups, p. 184; Decorator Brush Set, p. 219; cornstarch

Tint portions of melted white candy blue, yellow, green and violet using candy colors. Mold candy party hats using painting method (p. 121). Refrigerate until firm; unmold. Ice cupcakes smooth. Pipe tip 3 outline mouth, eyelids and eyelashes. Pipe tip 4 dot cheeks and nose (flatten and smooth with finger dipped in cornstarch). Pipe tip 4 swirl or pull-out hair, add tip 3 bows. Position candy hats. Each serves 1.

Cakes That Crunch

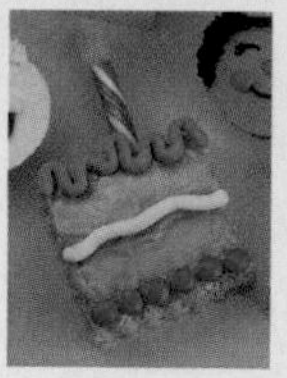

Pan: 10½ x 15½ in. Jelly Roll, p. 149
Candy: White Candy Melts®†, p. 218; Primary and Garden Candy Color Sets, p. 219; Kandy Clay™ Multi-Color Packs in Primary and Bright Colors, p. 222
Recipe: Your favorite crisped rice cereal treats
Also: Square Crinkle Comfort Grip™ Cutter, p. 214; Round Cut-Outs™, p. 128; Rolling Pin, Roll & Cut Mat, p. 130; Tapered Spatula, Disposable Decorating Bags, p. 137, spice drops, stick candy, candy-coated chocolate dots, granulated sugar, scissors, paring knife

Prepare cereal treats recipe and press into pan, even with top edge. Let cool. Cut into squares using crinkle cutter.

Divide candy into 4ths. Using candy colors, tint melted candy pink, yellow, green (with a small amount of yellow), and blue. Using spatula, spread melted candy on top of treats separating colors at center; let set. For squares with swag roll out lime green Kandy Clay from Bright Multi-Color Kit ⅛ in. thick. Cut 2 circles using medium Cut-Out, then re-cut each at bottom end to form 2 swags ⅛ in. deep. For other squares, roll a ¼ in. rope of Kandy Clay and position in a curving line. Attach candy-coated chocolates at swag points and both bottom borders with melted candy. Roll a ¼ in. rope of Kandy Clay and attach in a zigzag at top border with melted candy. Cut candy stick to 2¼ in. long. Cut spice drop into a flame shape; roll in sugar. Attach flame to stick using melted yellow candy. With craft knife, cut a small hole at top of square and insert stick. Each serves 1.

▼ A Horn Blast!

Everyone loves pop music! With these lollipop-filled, candy-coated party horns at every plate, you'll hear the sound of cheers from your guests!

Pans: Cookie Sheet, Cooling Grid, p. 149
Candy: White Candy Melts®† (3 pks. needed to make approximately 8 favors), p. 218; Primary and Garden Candy Color Sets, Decorator Brush Set, p. 219; Stars Candy Mold, p. 220; 4 in. Lollipop Sticks, p. 221
Recipes: Candy Clay, p. 120; favorite crisped rice cereal treats
Also: Rolling Pin, Roll & Cut Mat, p. 130; sugar cones, vegetable shortening, curling ribbon (18 in. needed for each star), corn syrup, waxed paper

In advance: Make 3 candy stars for each favor. Tint a portion of melted white candy yellow using candy color. Mold candy (p. 121). Refrigerate to set; unmold. Attach lollipop sticks to back with melted candy; let set.

Prepare cereal treats recipe and immediately fill cones with mixture. Tint 1 pk. candy green using candy color; thin with a small amount of vegetable shortening. Cover cones with melted candy (p. 120). Tap to remove excess candy and stand cone wide end down on waxed paper to dry.

Prepare one candy clay recipe; divide into thirds and tint blue, orange and violet. For mouthpieces, roll out clay ⅛ in. thick; cut 1 x 1½ in. long strips. Mold strips around narrow end of cone and attach with brush dipped in corn syrup (if needed). For stripes, roll out clay ¹⁄₁₆ in. thick; cut ¼ x 8 in. long strips; wind around cone and attach with brush dipped in corn syrup if (if needed). Let set. Attach curling ribbon to star lollipops and insert in cones at staggered heights. Each serves 1.

† Brand confectionery coating.

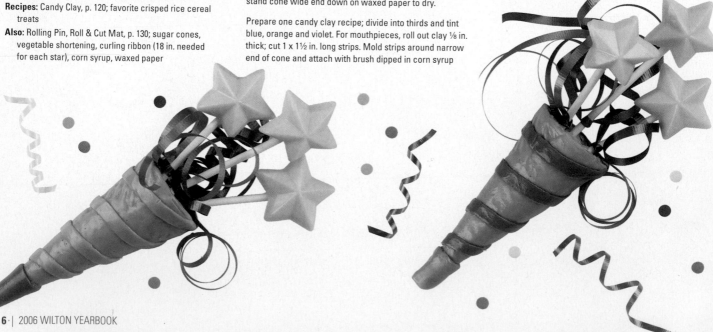

◄ The Crowd's in the Clouds!

Pan: 9 x 13 x 2 in. Sheet, p. 148
Tip: 21, p. 139
Color: Royal Blue, p. 133
Fondant: White Ready-To-Use Rolled Fondant (24 oz. needed); Primary Colors Fondant Multi Pack, p. 126; Alphabet/Number, Round Cut-Outs™, p. 128; Fine Tip Primary Colors FoodWriter™ Edible Color Markers, Brush Set, p. 129; Rolling Pin, Roll & Cut Mat, p. 130;
Recipe: Buttercream Icing, p. 112
Also: Blue Color Mist™, p. 133; Cake Board, Fanci-Foil Wrap, p. 169; paper towels, craft knife

Ice 1-layer cake smooth. Make cloud and sky effect (p. 117) on cake top using Color Mist and paper towels. Roll out primary colored fondant ⅛ in. thick. Cut 3 balloons in each color, using medium round Cut-Out™; position on cake. For eyes, roll ¼ in. white fondant balls; attach with damp brush. Draw pupils and mouths with black FoodWriter™. Cut message from primary blue fondant, using alphabet Cut-Outs™; position on cake. For balloon ties, cut small fondant triangles with craft knife; position. For balloon strings, cut ⅛ in. wide fondant strips; position. Add tip 21 zigzag puff bottom border. Serves 22.

► One Colossal Cupcake

Pan: Cupcake, p. 151
Tips: 4, 8, p. 138
Colors: Violet, Black, p. 133
Fondant: Primary Colors Fondant Multi Pack, p. 126; Star and Alphabet/Number Cut-Outs™, p. 128; Brush Set, p. 129; Rolling Pin, Roll & Cut Mat, p. 130; Cutter/Embosser, p. 131
Recipe: Buttercream Icing, p. 112
Also: Yellow Cake Sparkles™, p. 134; Spatula, p. 137; Cake Board, Fanci-Foil Wrap, p. 169; Plastic Dowel Rod, p. 167; thick spaghetti, ruler

In advance: Roll out yellow fondant ⅛ in. thick. Cut large star using large Cut-Out; brush with water and sprinkle with Cake Sparkles. Let dry.

Ice bottom half of cake smooth. Cut 4½ x ½ in. strips of yellow fondant ⅛ in. thick and position on bottom half of cake. Ice top half of cake fluffy with spatula. Roll out all fondant colors ⅛ in. thick. Cut confetti dots using small opening of tip 8. Cut stars using small and medium Cut-Outs; brush with water and sprinkle with Cake Sparkles. Position dots and stars on cake top. For candle, cut dowel rod to 4 in. long; using damp brush, cover outside and fill inside of dowel rod with yellow fondant. Cut a ⅜ x 5 in. strip of red fondant and wrap around candle; attach with damp brush. Pipe tip 4 melted wax effect on top end of candle. Cut a piece of spaghetti to 4 in. long. Attach to large star with damp brush; add a small piece of fondant for support. Paint top 1 in. of spaghetti with black icing color for wick; insert in candle and let set. Insert candle in cake. Cut fondant name using alphabet Cut-Outs; position on cake. Serves 12.

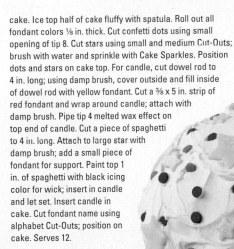

message on crown using pink FoodWriter. Brush edges of wand heart with water and sprinkle with Cake Sparkles. Attach wand heart to lollipop stick with thinned fondant adhesive (p. 111); let dry. For bow, roll out dark pink fondant ⅛ in. thick. Cut two 4 in. long loop strips and two 3 in. long streamer strips, all ½ in. wide. Attach loop ends together with damp brush; let dry on side on cornstarch-dusted surface. Let streamer strips dry on dowel rod. Roll ½ in. ball for bow knot. Reserve remaining fondant.

Bake and cool Animal Crackers and 1-layer heart cakes. On Animal Crackers cake, trim off muzzle and eyes, trim portion of ears to flatten (crown will rest on remaining ear areas). Prepare cakes for rolled fondant (p. 111). Tint 28 oz. fondant skin tone, 6 oz. yellow combination and 2 oz. black. Cover heart cake with dark pink and Animal Crackers cake with skin tone fondant; smooth with Fondant Smoother. On heart cake, use straight-edge wheel of Cutter/Embosser to imprint diagonal lines from bottom of dress to top; space 1 in. apart at bottom, tapering to top center. Do not cut through fondant. Place cakes on foil-wrapped double-thick board, cut to fit assembled cakes.

Roll out light pink fondant ⅛ in. thick and cut dress using pattern; attach to heart cake with damp brush. Trim excess if needed. For sleeves, roll two 2½ in. balls of light pink. Press dowel rod in sides to create arm openings. For arms, cut dowel rods in two 3 in. lengths. Roll out copper fondant ⅛ in. thick. Cut a 2½ in. square for each arm and attach around dowel rod with damp brush, leaving ½ in. open at top. Attach arm in sleeve with damp brush. For hands, roll two 2 in. copper balls; flatten to ½ in. thick and cut notch for thumb. Shape into left and right hands, then cut ½ in. wide slits for fingers. Wrap right hand fingers around wand. Attach hands to arms with damp brush. For bracelets, roll twelve ¼ in. dark pink balls; attach with damp brush. For shoes, roll two 3¼ x 1½ in. wide dark pink logs; flatten to ¾ in. thick. Cut notch for heel and shape rounded toes. Attach shoes and crown to cakes with damp brush. For hair, roll out yellow fondant ⅛ in. thick. Cut ¼ x 6 in. strips and wrap around lollipop sticks; slide off sticks and let dry 10 minutes. Attach to cake with damp brush; work from bottom side up towards top center, overlapping curls. For eyes, roll two ½ in. black balls; flatten and attach. For mouth, roll out black fondant ⅛ in. thick, cut and attach. For cheeks, roll two ¾ in. light pink balls; flatten and attach. For eyelashes, roll out black fondant ⅛ in. thick. Cut ⅜ in. strips, taper ends and attach with damp brush. For ribbon, roll out dark pink fondant ⅛ in. thick; cut a ½ x 8½ in. long strip. Attach ribbon and bow to cake with damp brush. Position hearts around cake. Serves 24.

*Note: Combine Lemon Yellow and Golden Yellow for yellow shown.

▲ The Magical One

Pans: Animal Crackers, p. 151; 10 x 2 in. Heart, p. 147

Colors:* Rose, Lemon Yellow, Golden Yellow, Copper (skin tone), Black, p. 133

Fondant: White Ready-To-Use Rolled Fondant (120 oz. needed), p. 126; Fine Tip Neon Colors FoodWriter™ Edible Color Markers, p. 129; Rolling Pin, Roll & Cut Mat, p. 130; Cutter/Embosser, Easy-Glide Fondant Smoother, p. 131

Recipe: Buttercream Icing, p. 112

Also: 2006 Pattern Book (Princess Crown, Dress), p. 124; Plastic Nesting Hearts Cutter Set, p. 202; Pink Cake Sparkles™, p. 134; 6 in. Lollipop Sticks, p. 221; Plastic Dowel Rods, p. 167; Gum-Tex™, p. 130; Fanci-Foil Wrap, p. 169; ½ in. foamcore board (20 x 24 in. needed), paring knife, cornstarch

Several days in advance: Make fondant crown, points, hearts and bow. Tint 36 oz. fondant dark pink and 48 oz. light pink using rose icing color. For crown, knead ½ teaspoon Gum-Tex into 5 oz. light pink fondant. Roll out ¼ in. thick. Using pattern, cut crown. Let dry on cornstarch-dusted surface. For points of crown, roll 5 dark pink balls, ½ in. diameter; attach to crown with damp brush. For hearts, roll out dark pink fondant ⅛ in. thick. Cut wand heart using 3rd largest heart cutter. Cut several hearts using smallest and 2nd smallest cutter; brush with water and sprinkle with Cake Sparkles. Let all hearts dry on cornstarch-dusted surface. Print name on wand heart and

◄ 2 For 1 Special!

Boy or girl, the smiles come easily with these party face cakes. Just put a round cake together with our new Party Hat for a quick-to-complete design that simply states the fun of turning 1!

Pans: Party Hat, p. 151; Decorator Preferred™ 9 x 2 in. Round, p. 147

Tips: 3, 16, p. 138-139

Colors: Copper (skin tone), Black, Rose (or Royal Blue), p. 133

Recipe: Buttercream Icing, p. 112

Also: 2006 Pattern Book (Number 1), p. 124; Cake Boards, Fanci-Foil Wrap, p. 169, cornstarch, toothpick

Decorate boy or girl cake following same instructions. Cut 3 in. off top of 1-layer 9 in. round cake. Position below Party Hat cake. Ice cakes smooth; trace number 1 pattern with toothpick. Pipe tip 3 string mouth. Outline and pipe in tip 3 eyes, nose, cheeks and #1 (pat smooth with finger dipped in cornstarch). Add tip 3 pull-out eyelashes on girl cake and a rose or blue outline to each #1. Pipe tip 3 swirls on hat. Add tip 16 pull-out star pompom and hat band. Each cake serves 24.

◄ Crawling with Gifts!

Pans: Stand-Up Cuddly Bear, p. 152; 8 x 2 in. Square (2 pans needed), p. 148; Cooling Grid, p. 149

Tips: 3, 5, 16, p. 138-139

Colors: Copper (skin tone), Red-Red, Royal Blue, Black, Lemon Yellow, p. 133

Recipe: Buttercream Icing, p. 112; favorite crisped rice cereal treats (3 batches needed)

Candy: White Candy Melts®† (3 pks. needed), p. 218; Primary, Garden Candy Color Sets, p. 219

Also: Plastic Dowel Rods, p. 167; Cake Boards, Fanci-Foil Wrap, p. 169; sugar cone, ½ in. wide white ribbon (5 ft. needed per package), toothpick, cornstarch

Prepare cereal treat recipes; press into 2 square pans, 1¾ in. high. Unmold and cut into eight 3½ in. squares for gifts; reserve excess treats to use for hands.

Bake and cool bear cake using firm-textured batter such as pound cake. Trim off ears, muzzle and arms. For arms, cut dowel rods to 4 in. long; insert at shoulder level. Using reserved cereal treats, form hands at ends of dowel rods and insert. Lightly ice face area and mark facial features with toothpick. Outline and pipe in mouth, tongue and eyes with tip 3. Build up nose, fingers and toes with tip 5. Cover face, body, arms, legs and overalls with tip 16 stars. Outline and pipe in 1 in. diameter buttons with tip 3 (smooth with finger dipped in cornstarch). Overpipe rim and add dot buttonholes with tip 3. For party hat, cut sugar cone to 3 in. high and ice smooth. Attach on head with dots of icing. Add tip 16 pull-out star pompom and brim. Pipe tip 3 number.

Using candy colors, tint portions of melted white candy pink, green, violet, blue and yellow. Cover cereal treat gifts with melted candy (p. 120); let set. Cut 24 in. ribbon to wrap around each gift; make bows using 36 in. ribbon; Attach with melted candy. Position gifts around baby. Cake serves 12; each gift serves 1.

† Brand confectionery coating.

▲ Piñata Fiesta

One of the most popular kids' party games comes to birthday cakes! The cookies give kids an extra treat in case someone else takes home the real piñata goodies.

Pans: 11 x 15 x 2 in. Sheet, p. 148; Cookie Sheet, Cooling Grid, p. 149

Tips: 2, 4, 6, 13, 21, p. 138-139

Colors: Copper (skin tone), Black, Lemon Yellow, Leaf Green, Orange, Royal Blue, Christmas Red, Brown, Violet, p. 133

Recipes: Buttercream and Royal Icings, Roll-Out Cookie, p. 112

Also: 13 x 19 in. Cake Boards (2 needed), Fanci-Foil Wrap, p. 169; Bold Tip Primary Colors FoodWriter™ Edible Color Markers, p. 129; 4 in. and 11¾ in. Lollipop Sticks, p. 221; Plastic Dowel Rods, p. 167; Circus Balloons Set, p. 186; Gingerbread Boy Metal Cutter, p. 214; Animal Pals 50 pc. Cookie Cutter Set, p. 216; Meringue Powder, p. 132; Rolling Pin, p. 130; large spice drops, candy-coated chocolates, hot glue gun, curling ribbon in yellow (4 yds. needed), green, red and blue (1 yd. each needed), craft knife, plastic drinking straw, cornstarch

In advance: Make cookies. Roll out plain dough and cut out 1 horse; cut hole in top of horse with straw. Tint remaining dough skin tone and cut 6 children. For child hitting piñata, trim off right arm. Bake and cool cookies. Decorate cookies using royal icing. Pipe tip 2 outline and dot facial features; add tip 13 curlique or pull-out hair. Outline and pipe in clothes with tip 4 (smooth with finger dipped in cornstarch). Pipe tip 4 ball hand and dot fingers. On child hitting piñata, pipe tip 4 string blindfold; trim lollipop stick to 3½ in. and attach to back of hand with icing. For hats, slightly trim spice drops and attach. Add tip 2 dot pompom. Attach 4 in. sticks to backs of children. Draw stripes on horse with FoodWriter markers.

Ice 1-layer cake smooth in buttercream. Divide front and back of cake into six 2½ in. wide sections; divide sides into four 2¾ in. wide sections. Pipe tip 6 zigzag garlands, ¾ in. deep. Attach 3 candy-coated chocolates with tip 4 dots of icing at each division point. For piñata stand, cut 2 dowel rods 9 in. long. With knife, poke a hole ½ in. from top of each dowel rod. Attach a spiral of yellow ribbon on dowel rods with hot glue, stopping 2¼ in. from bottom. At top, with hot glue, attach 6 in. pieces of curled ribbon in various colors. Cut a lollipop stick to 11¼ in. long and insert into holes. Insert dowel rods in cake 1½ in. from sides and back of cake. Tie horse to stick with ribbon. Insert balloon toppers into tops of dowel rods. Print tip 4 message. Insert children in cake top. Pipe 21 shell bottom border. Cake serves 30; each cookie serves 1.

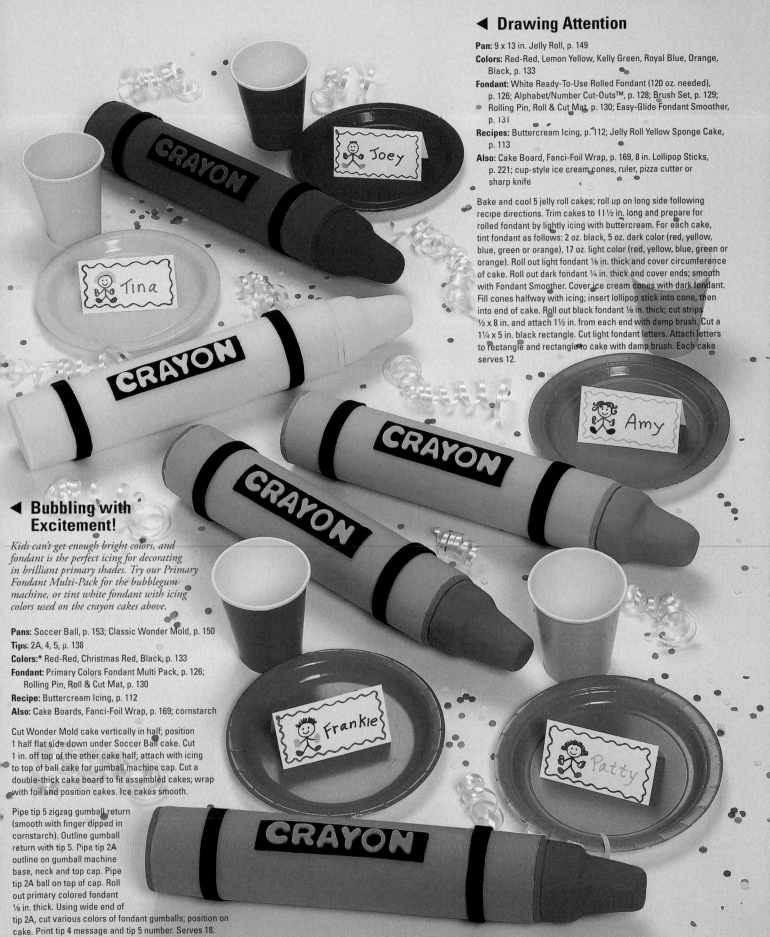

◀ Drawing Attention

Pan: 9 x 13 in. Jelly Roll, p. 149

Colors: Red-Red, Lemon Yellow, Kelly Green, Royal Blue, Orange, Black, p. 133

Fondant: White Ready-To-Use Rolled Fondant (120 oz. needed), p. 126; Alphabet/Number Cut-Outs™, p. 128; Brush Set, p. 129; Rolling Pin, Roll & Cut Mat, p. 130; Easy-Glide Fondant Smoother, p. 131

Recipes: Buttercream Icing, p. 112; Jelly Roll Yellow Sponge Cake, p. 113

Also: Cake Board, Fanci-Foil Wrap, p. 169, 8 in. Lollipop Sticks, p. 221; cup-style ice cream cones, ruler, pizza cutter or sharp knife

Bake and cool 5 jelly roll cakes; roll up on long side following recipe directions. Trim cakes to 11½ in. long and prepare for rolled fondant by lightly icing with buttercream. For each cake, tint fondant as follows: 2 oz. black, 5 oz. dark color (red, yellow, blue, green or orange), 17 oz. light color (red, yellow, blue, green or orange). Roll out light fondant ⅛ in. thick and cover circumference of cake. Roll out dark fondant ¼ in. thick and cover ends; smooth with Fondant Smoother. Cover ice cream cones with dark fondant. Fill cones halfway with icing; insert lollipop stick into cone, then into end of cake. Roll out black fondant ⅛ in. thick; cut strips ½ x 8 in. and attach 1½ in. from each end with damp brush. Cut a 1¼ x 5 in. black rectangle. Cut light fondant letters. Attach letters to rectangle and rectangle to cake with damp brush. Each cake serves 12.

◀ Bubbling with Excitement!

Kids can't get enough bright colors, and fondant is the perfect icing for decorating in brilliant primary shades. Try our Primary Fondant Multi-Pack for the bubblegum machine, or tint white fondant with icing colors used on the crayon cakes above.

Pans: Soccer Ball, p. 153; Classic Wonder Mold, p. 150

Tips: 2A, 4, 5, p. 138

Colors:* Red-Red, Christmas Red, Black, p. 133

Fondant: Primary Colors Fondant Multi Pack, p. 126; Rolling Pin, Roll & Cut Mat, p. 130

Recipe: Buttercream Icing, p. 112

Also: Cake Boards, Fanci-Foil Wrap, p. 169; cornstarch

Cut Wonder Mold cake vertically in half; position 1 half flat side down under Soccer Ball cake. Cut 1 in. off top of the other cake half; attach with icing to top of ball cake for gumball machine cap. Cut a double-thick cake board to fit assembled cakes; wrap with foil and position cakes. Ice cakes smooth.

Pipe tip 5 zigzag gumball return (smooth with finger dipped in cornstarch). Outline gumball return with tip 5. Pipe tip 2A outline on gumball machine base, neck and top cap. Pipe tip 2A ball on top of cap. Roll out primary colored fondant ⅛ in. thick. Using wide end of tip 2A, cut various colors of fondant gumballs; position on cake. Print tip 4 message and tip 5 number. Serves 18.

***Note:** Combine Red-Red and Christmas Red for red shown. Add a small amount of Black to white icing for gray shown.

◀ To Serve Her Majesty

Pans: Decorator Preferred™ 8, 10 x 3 in. Round, p. 147

Colors: Royal Blue, Leaf Green, Lemon Yellow, p. 133

Fondant: Ready-To-Use Rolled Fondant in White (24 oz. needed), Pastel Pink and Pastel Yellow (48 oz. each needed), Fondant Multi Packs in Natural and Neon Colors, p. 126; People Cut-Outs™, p. 128; Fine Tip Neon Colors FoodWriter™ Edible Color Markers, Brush Set, p. 129; Rolling Pin, Roll & Cut Mat, p. 130; Easy-Glide Fondant Smoother, p. 131

Recipe: Buttercream Icing, p. 112

Also: 2006 Pattern Book (Crown), p. 124; 101 Cookie Cutters Set, p. 216; Cake Boards, 12 in. Round Silver Cake Base, p. 169; 8 in. Lollipop Sticks, p. 221; Plastic Dowel Rods, p. 167, cornstarch, craft knife

In advance: Make fondant message. For purple letters, combine 2 oz. of white with 3 oz. of neon purple fondant. For green letters, tint 4 oz. of white fondant with Leaf Green and Lemon Yellow Icing Colors. For blue letters, tint 4 oz. of white fondant with Royal Blue Icing Color. Roll out these colors, plus neon yellow and pink ⅛ in. thick; cut letters with cookie cutters; let dry on cornstarch-dusted surface. Make crown. Roll out neon yellow fondant ⅛ in. thick and cut crown using pattern and knife. Attach crown to letter "R" with thinned fondant adhesive (p. 111); let dry completely. Cut 4 lollipop sticks to 5 in.; attach cut sticks to "RULE" letters and whole sticks to "GIRLS" letters with thinned fondant adhesive; attach stick on letter "R" high enough to support crown). Reserve remaining colored fondant for use on cake.

Prepare 1-layer 10 in. cake (3 in. high) and 2-layer 8 in. cake (bake two 2½ in. layers to create a 5 in. high cake) for stacked construction (p. 110). Prepare cakes for rolled fondant (p. 111); cover cakes and smooth with Fondant Smoother. Assemble cakes on base.

For 10 in. cake, make 18 various fondant shapes (p. 118). Attach all shapes to cake with damp brush. For bottom border, roll ⅝ in. pastel yellow balls; attach with damp brush. For 8 in. cake, make 10 girls using people Cut-Outs and reserved and multi pack fondant. Roll out colors ⅛ in. thick. For shirts, pull sleeves upward to make extended arms. For hands, use shoe Cut-Out, trim in half and use rounded end. For skirts, trim ¼ in. off bottom and a little off sides for a narrower, mini-skirt look. For legs, use shoe Cut-Out, trim in half and use square end. Cut shoes and boots with shoe Cut-Out; for platforms, add a small square of fondant for heel and a small rectangle for sole; attach with damp brush. For boots, attach another small rectangle vertically. Attach pieces to cake with damp brush. Attach thin strips for belts, small ball for buckle. Draw facial features, shirt polka dots and heart with FoodWriter Markers. For frizzy hair, cut a ¼ x 1 in. strip of black fondant, cut slits almost to edge and attach with damp brush; add a few rows for fullness. For other hair, cut thin strips of fondant and attach in ponytail or pageboy style. For bows, form two ⅜ in. triangles and attach; add a small ball center. Write messages with FoodWriters. Insert letters. Serves 48.

▶ Snappy Satchels

Pans: 10½ x 15½ in. Jelly Roll, Mini Loaf, p. 149

Colors: Royal Blue, Leaf Green, p. 133

Fondant: White Ready-To-Use Rolled Fondant (24 oz. needed), Neon and Pastel Colors Fondant Multi Packs (1 pk. each needed), p. 126; Heart and Flower Cut-Outs™, p. 128; Brush Set, p. 129; Rolling Pin, Roll & Cut Mat, p. 130; Cutter/Embosser, p. 131

Recipe: Buttercream Icing, p. 112

Also: Heart and Round Comfort Grip™ Cutters, p. 214; Cake Board, Fanci-Foil Wrap, p. 169; paring knife, ruler

Bake and cool 1 in. high mini loaf and sheet cakes. Cut sheet cakes with round and heart cookie cutters. For heart, trim 1 in. off pointed end of heart. For round, trim ½ in. off bottom. For Mini Loaf, trim sides at an angle, tapering off ½ in. on top sides. Position on foil-wrapped boards, cut to fit. Prepare cakes for rolled fondant (p. 111).

Tint fondant for all cakes: Reserve a 1 in. ball of pastel green. For green purse, combine remaining pastel green with ½ pk. of neon yellow fondant. For green stripe used on yellow purse, add Leaf Green Icing Color to the reserved green ball. For purple, combine ½ in. neon purple ball with a 1 in. white ball. For light pink, combine ½ in. neon pink ball and 1½ in. white ball. (For dark pink, use straight neon pink fondant). For orange, combine ½ in. neon orange ball and 1½ in. white ball. For blue, add a little Royal Blue Icing Color to a 1½ in. pastel blue ball.

Cover all cakes with fondant. For handles, roll 5¾ x ⅜ in. diameter rope in matching color; attach to cakes with damp brush. For clasps, roll ⅜ in. balls (2 each for green and yellow purses, 1 for pink); attach with damp brush. Roll out colors ⅛ in. thick and cut various decorations; attach all with damp brush. Cut flowers with smallest Cut-Out; roll and attach ¹⁄₁₆ in. yellow ball centers. Cut ⅛ in. wide stems with paring knife. For leaves, cut a heart with smallest Cut-Out; cut heart in half with knife. For stripes on yellow purse, cut ¼ in. strips with straight-edge wheel of Cutter/Embosser; attach ½ in. apart. Cut hearts on pink purse with smallest Cut-Out. Each serves 1.

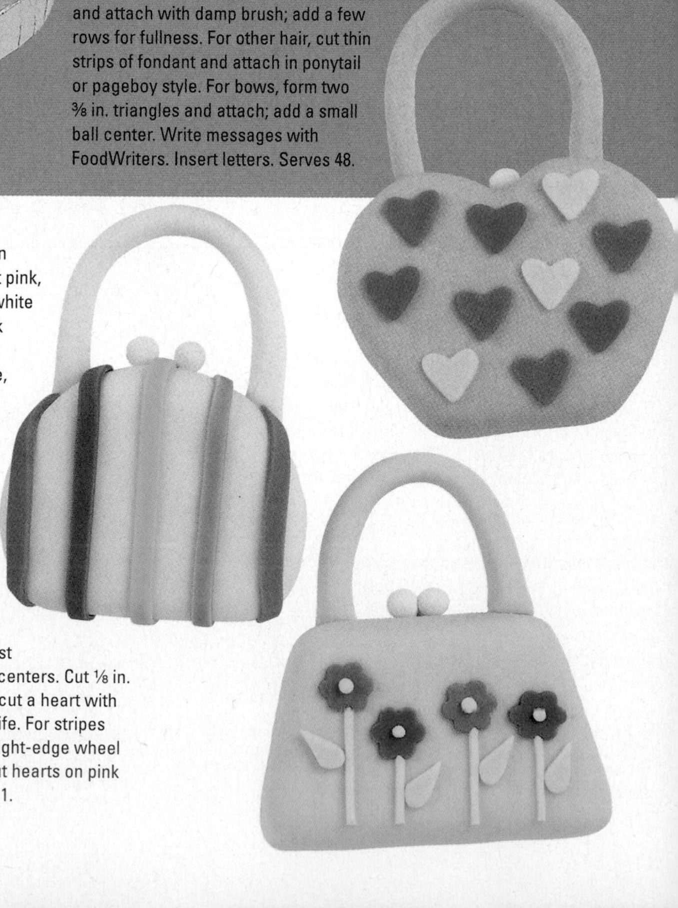

◄ Daisies Are Dancing!

Pan: 8 x 2 in. Round, p. 148

Colors:* Rose, Leaf Green, Lemon Yellow, p. 133

Fondant: White Ready-To-Use Rolled Fondant (24 oz. needed), Neon Colors Fondant Multi Pack, p. 126; Round Cut-Outs™, p. 128; Fine Tip Primary Colors FoodWriter™ Edible Color Markers, Brush Set, p. 129; Rolling Pin, Roll & Cut Mat, p. 130

Recipe: Buttercream Icing, p. 112

Also: Flower Plastic Cookie Cutter, 101 Cookie Cutters Set, p. 216; Cake Board, Fanci-Foil Wrap, p. 169; 11¾ in. Lollipop Sticks, p. 221; cornstarch

In advance: Make fondant flowers. For violet flower, combine a 2 in. ball of white with a 1 in. ball of violet fondant. For green flowers, knead Leaf Green and Lemon Yellow Icing Colors into 8 oz. of white fondant. Roll out violet and green fondant ⅛ in. thick. Cut 1 violet and 2 green flowers using cutter; reserve remaining fondant. For flower centers, roll 1½ in. neon yellow fondant balls, slightly flatten and attach to flowers with damp brush. Let flowers dry on cornstarch-dusted surface. When completely dry, attach lollipop sticks to backs with thinned fondant adhesive (p. 111). Draw facial features with black FoodWriter.

Ice 2-layer cake smooth. For orange circles, combine a 1 in. ball of white with a 1½ in. ball of neon orange fondant. Roll out orange and yellow ⅛ in. thick. Cut circles using small and medium Cut-Outs; attach to cake with damp brush. Roll out reserved violet fondant ⅛ in. thick. Cut name using alphabet cutters from set. For bottom border, roll ¾ in. balls of green fondant; attach with damp brush. Cut lollipop sticks for flowers at various lengths and insert in cake. Serves 20.

► Happy Bee-Day!

Pan: Lady Bug, p. 151

Tips: 3, 12, 16, p. 138-139

Colors:* Rose, Orange, Violet, Black, Lemon Yellow, Leaf Green, p. 133

Cookie: Heart Copper Cookie Cutter, p. 203; Cookie Sheet, Cooling Grid, p. 149

Recipes: Buttercream and Royal Icings, Roll-Out Cookie, p. 112

Also: Meringue Powder, p. 132; 6 in. Lollipop Sticks, p. 221; Cake Board, Fanci-Foil Wrap, p. 169; Decorator Brush Set, p. 219; craft block, waxed paper

In advance: Make cookie wings. Roll out dough and cut 2 wings using heart cutter. Trim 1¼ in. from pointed end of each heart; bake and cool. Cover cookies with thinned royal icing (p. 120); let dry. Pipe tip 3 dots on wings using full-strength royal icing. Paint three lollipop sticks with brush dipped in black icing color; insert in craft block to dry. Make ends for stinger and antennae. On waxed paper pipe tip 12 balls, 1 in. diameter, in royal icing; let dry. Top each ball with tip 3 swirls in royal icing. Attach balls to black lollipop sticks with royal icing; let dry.

Position cake on foil-wrapped board, cut to fit. Pipe tip 3 mouth and pipe in eyes (smooth with finger dipped in cornstarch). Ice feet smooth. Cover face and body with tip 16 stars. Insert plain lollipop sticks on cake sides for wing supports; position wings on top. Insert antennae and stinger. Cake serves 12; each cookie serves 1.

***Note:** Combine Leaf Green and Lemon Yellow for green shown. Combine Violet and Rose for violet shown.

◄ Happy Landings

Cookie: Bug Buddies Metal Cutter Set, p. 214; Cookie Sheet, Cooling Grid, 6 in. Cookie Treat Sticks, p. 217

Tips: 2, 3, 8, p. 138

Colors: Royal Blue, Orange, Rose, Lemon Yellow, Leaf Green, Violet, p. 133

Recipes: Buttercream Icing, Roll-Out Cookie, p. 112

Also: White Candy Melts®†, p. 218; Rolling Pin, p. 130; black shoestring licorice, mini candy-coated chocolates

Tint cookie dough yellow. Roll out dough; cut bee and butterfly cookies. Bake and cool. For butterflies, pipe tip 8 bead body and ball head. Pipe tip 2 dot and string facial features and stripes on body. Add tip 3 bead hearts on wings. Cut licorice in 1 in. lengths; insert in head and attach mini chocolates with melted candy. For bee, ice wing area smooth. Add tip 8 ball head, tip 2 dot and string facial features. Pipe tip 3 zigzag stripes on body. Insert licorice antenna and stinger; attach mini chocolates with melted candy. Attach cookies to sticks with melted candy. Each serves 1.

† Brand confectionery coating.

◄ Dragon Cookie Pops

Cookie: Heart Plastic Cutter, p. 216; 8 in. Cookie Treat Sticks, Cookie Sheet, Cooling Grid, p. 217

Tips: 2, 4, 6, 8, 352, p. 138-139

Colors:* Violet, Lemon Yellow, Leaf Green, Black, Rose, p. 133

Recipes: Color Flow Icing, Roll-Out Cookie, p. 112

Also: 2006 Pattern Book (Dragon Mouth), p. 124; White Candy Melts®†, p. 218; Color Flow Mix, p. 132; Parchment Triangles, p. 137; waxed paper, sharp knife

In advance: Roll out dough and cut cookies using heart cutter; bake and cool. Trace Mouth Pattern with sharp knife. Outline mouth and tongue areas with tip 2 and full-strength color flow; flow in mouth, tongue and face with tip 2 and thinned color flow (p. 120). Let dry overnight.

Decorate cookies using full-strength color flow: Pipe tip 352 pull-out leaf spikes, tip 8 ball nose and eyes, tip 4 dot nostrils and pupils. Add tip 6 pull-out teeth. Attach cookie stick to cookie with melted candy. Each serves 1.

***Note:** Combine Leaf Green and Lemon Yellow for green shown. Combine Violet and Rose for violet shown.

▲ There'll Be a Hot Time!

Pan: 8 x 2 in. Heart, p. 147

Tips: 5, 10, 18, 366, p. 138-139

Colors:* Leaf Green, Lemon Yellow, Rose, Black, Violet, p. 133

Cookie: Mini Geometric Crinkle Cutters, p. 214; Cookie Spatula, Cookie Sheet, Cooling Grid, p. 217

Recipes: Buttercream Icing, Roll-Out Cookie, p. 112

Also: 2006 Pattern Book (Flame, Top Leg, Foot, Arm, Tail, Belly, Mouth), p. 124; Lavender Colored Sugar, p. 134; 15 in. Parchment Triangles, p. 137; Rolling Pin, p. 130; Fanci-Foil Wrap, p. 169; markers in orange, yellow and black, scissors, ruler, knife, 20 in. cake circle, toothpick, cornstarch

Tint a portion of cookie dough violet; roll out and cut spikes using triangle cookie cutter; sprinkle with lavender sugar. Roll out plain dough; trace top leg, foot, tail and arm patterns with toothpick. Cut cookies with knife. For eyes, form two 2 in. balls of dough; flatten at bottom edge. Bake and cool all cookies.

Bake and cool two 1-layer heart cakes. Position top heart horizontally, pointed end facing left. Position bottom heart at an angle, with its pointed end against the lower rounded side of the top heart. Join cakes together with icing to form head and body, then lightly ice both cake tops. Using patterns, mark mouth and belly areas with toothpick. Pipe in tip 5 mouth and tongue (pat smooth with finger dipped in cornstarch). Pipe in belly area with tip 10 lines. Cover cakes with tip 18 stars in light green with dark green spots; overpipe head for dimension. Cover all cookies except spikes with tip 18 stars. Position cookies; insert spikes.

Add tip 366 leaf teeth. Pipe tip 5 dot nose and nostrils. Ice eye cookies smooth and position; pipe tip 18 stars on eye lids; add tip 5 dot pupils.

Trace flame pattern on parchment; cut out with scissors. Using markers, draw flame lines and print message. Position over cake. Cakes serve 18; each cookie serves 1.

***Note:** Combine Leaf Green and Lemon Yellow for light and dark green shown. Combine Violet and Rose for violet shown.

Hunting For A Bir

▶ Victory Lap

Pans: 3-D Cruiser, Mini Ball, p. 153

Tips: 3, 4, 8, 12, 13, 16, p. 138-139

Colors:* Red-Red, Christmas Red, Lemon Yellow, Golden Yellow, Copper (skin tone), Royal Blue, Black, Brown, p. 133

Candy: White Candy Melts®† (1 pk. needed), p. 218; Garden Candy Color Set, p. 219; 4 in. Lollipop Sticks, p. 221

Recipe: Buttercream Icing, p. 112

Also: 2006 Pattern Book (Windshield, Hand), p. 124; Round Cut-Outs™, p. 128; Circus Balloons Set, p. 186; Flower Nail No. 7, p. 137; Flower Spikes, Plastic Dowel Rods, p. 167; Cake Boards, Fanci-Foil Wrap, p. 169; waxed paper, 1½ in. wide x 4 in. long x 1 in. high craft block, curling ribbon in red, blue, orange, yellow and green (2 yds. each), cornstarch

In advance: Make candy tires and hands. Using candy color, tint portion of melted candy black. Position large Cut-Out on waxed paper-covered board and fill with candy, ¼ in. deep; refrigerate until firm and unmold. Repeat to make 4 tires. Cover hand pattern with waxed paper. Outline and fill in pattern with white candy; refrigerate until firm. Reverse pattern and repeat to make opposite hand.

Bake and cool car and 2 mini ball cakes. Trim off top of car. Position car on foil-wrapped double cake board, cut to fit. Wrap craft block with foil and position under car. Trace windshield pattern on cake board and cut out; wrap with foil. Attach lollipop sticks to windshield with melted candy; let set. Attach candy tires with melted candy. Outline and pipe in tip 3 hubcaps and axles (pat smooth with finger dipped in cornstarch). Ice passenger area smooth. Outline car with tip 4. Cover car with tip 16 stars; overpipe wheel wells for dimension. Pipe tip 8 outline trim and numbers; add tip 8 ball lights (flatten and smooth with finger dipped in cornstarch). Pipe tip 12 band bumpers and running boards. Insert flower nail for steering wheel; cover with tip 13 stars.

Ice mini ball cakes together for head; position. Outline eyes and pipe in mouth with tip 3. Cover face with tip 13 stars; overpipe nose for dimension. Add tip 16 pull-out star hair. Cut dowel rods to 4½ in. and 2½ in. long for arms. Attach hands with candy. Insert arms in cake, leaving 2¼ in. extended for left arm, 1 in. extended for right arm. Cover hands with tip 13 stars and arms with tip 16 stars. Insert windshield and cover with tip 16 stars. Fill 3 flower spikes with icing and insert in cake; insert balloons in spikes. Position curling ribbon. Serves 14.

***Note:** Combine Red-Red and Christmas Red for red shown. Combine Lemon Yellow and Golden Yellow for yellow shown.

◀ Paradise Found

Pans: 12 x 18 x 2 in. Sheet, p. 147; First and Ten Football, p. 153

Tips: 2B, 3, 12, 21, p. 138-139

Colors:* Brown, Red-Red, Royal Blue, p. 133

Candy: Treasure Chest and Funny Faces Candy Making Kits, p. 222; Party Time Candy Mold, p. 220; White Candy Melts®† (1 pk. needed in addition to candy included in kits), p. 218; Primary Candy Color Set (may be needed for additional candies), p. 219; 11¾ in. Lollipop Sticks, p. 221

Recipe: Buttercream Icing, p. 112

Also: 2006 Pattern Book (Sails), p. 124; Circus Balloons Set, p. 186, Rainbow Jimmies Sprinkle Decorations, p. 134, Cake Board, Fanci-Foil Wrap, p. 169; Piping Gel, p. 132; Flower Spikes, p. 167; Parchment Triangles, p. 137; scissors, cellophane tape, curling ribbon in red, blue, green and yellow, granulated brown sugar

In advance: Make candy using Candy Melts in kits and a portion of white. For skin tones, combine melted white candy with a little melted orange candy or combine melted Light Cocoa candy with a little white candy. Mold heads on lollipop sticks and treasure chest following kit directions. Mold party hats and gifts using painting method (p. 121). If additional candies are needed, tint melted white candy with candy colors as desired. Refrigerate until firm; unmold. Pipe hair and facial features using melted candy in cut parchment bag. Attach party hats to faces with melted candy. Refrigerate until firm.

Ice sides of 1-layer sheet cake smooth in white. Ice top left of cake with light brown icing and cover with granulated brown sugar. Add piping gel to light blue icing and ice right side of cake fluffy. Pipe tip 21 shell bottom border in white. Position football cake boat, round side down, on sheet cake. Ice top of boat smooth; cover sides with tip 2B stripes, smooth side up. Pipe tip 12 outline around top edge of boat. Pipe tip 3 message.

Trace sail patterns on parchment paper; cut out and tape to lollipop sticks. Insert sail into back of boat. Insert candy heads in boat, trimming sticks as needed. Position treasure chest and position with candy gifts; add curling ribbon to boat. Fill 3 flower spikes with icing and insert in cake; insert balloons in spikes. Cakes serve 48; candies each serve 1.

***Note:** Combine Brown and Red-Red for brown shown on boat.

† Brand confectionery coating.

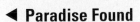

◄ You Passed Every Test!

Cookie: 101 Cookie Cutters Set, p. 216; Cookie Sheet, Cooling Grid, 8 in. Cookie Treat Sticks, p. 217

Tips: 2, 349, p. 138-139

Colors:* Copper (skin tone), Brown, Kelly Green, Royal Blue, Lemon Yellow, Golden Yellow, Red-Red, Christmas Red, Violet, Rose, Black, p. 133

Recipes: Roll-Out Cookie, Color Flow Icing, p. 112

Also: Color Flow Mix, p. 132; 11¾ in. Lollipop Sticks, p. 221; Fanci-Foil Wrap, p. 169; White Candy Melts®†, p. 218; Rolling Pin, p. 130; cornstarch, ruler, paring knife, 8 x 2 in. round craft block, ¼ in. wide curling ribbon in red, yellow, blue, green (2 yds. each needed)

One day in advance: Make cookies. Roll out dough; use cutters from set to cut ABC; cut 6 hearts with smallest heart cutter. Cut off ¼ in. from bottom of hearts to resemble apples. For skin tones, tint ⅓ of remaining dough copper and ⅓ copper/brown combination; roll out and cut a variety of children using gingerbread boy cutter. Tint remaining dough brown and cut a 4 x 6 in. wide rectangle for chalkboard. Bake and cool all cookies; decorate with color flow (p. 120). Outline and flow in black area of chalkboard with tip 2, ½ in. from edges. Also outline and flow in ABCs and apples with tip 2. Outline and pipe in kids' clothes with tip 2 (smooth with finger dipped in cornstarch). Add tip 2 outline arms, hands, faces, eyes, mouths and dot hair. Let all cookies dry overnight.

Using full-strength color flow, pipe tip 2 outline stem on apples; add tip 349 pull-out leaf. Write tip 2 message on chalkboard. Let dry. Turn over cookies; attach lollipop sticks to backs of ABC cookies and cookie treat sticks to backs of children and apples with melted candy; let set. Wrap craft block with Fanci-Foil. Trim sticks to staggered lengths and insert in craft block. Position curling ribbon between cookies. Each cookie serves 1.

*Note: Combine Lemon Yellow and Golden Yellow for yellow shown, Red-Red and Christmas Red for red shown and Violet and Rose for violet shown.

► Best Feet Forward

Pan: Standard Muffin, p. 149

Colors:* Golden Yellow, Lemon Yellow, Leaf Green, Rose, Violet, Orange, p. 133

Recipe: Buttercream Icing, p. 112

Also: Colored Sugars in Yellow, Pink, Lavender, Light Green, and Orange p. 134; White Standard Baking Cups, p. 184; black shoestring licorice, candy coated chocolates, spice drops, white gumballs

Ice cupcakes smooth with spatula. Sprinkle with matching colored sugars. Cut licorice into two 3 in. lengths for each cupcake. Insert spice drops into licorice to make feet and antennae; insert into cupcakes. For head cupcake, insert white gumball eyes; attach brown candy-coated chocolate pupils with buttercream. Position red candy-coated chocolate nose and licorice mouth. Each serves 1.

*Note: Combine Golden Yellow and Lemon Yellow for yellow shown and Violet with a little Rose for violet shown.

◄ A Lively Brew

Pan: Small Non-Stick Cookie, p. 146

Tip: 32, p. 139

Candy: White Candy Melts®†, p. 218; Primary, Garden Candy Color Sets, p. 219; Cordial Cups Candy Mold, p. 221

Recipe: White Chocolate Mousse, p. 113

Also: Round Cut-Outs™, p. 128, Parchment Triangles, p. 137

Prepare White Chocolate Mousse recipe. Melt candy; divide into 3rds and tint portions pink, blue and green. Mold candy shells (p. 121) ⅛ in. thick in Cordial Cups Mold. For saucers, place largest round Cut-Out on non-stick pan. Spoon in melted candy ⅛ in. thick; tap to remove air bubbles, refrigerate to set. For handles, pipe a question mark shape, ¾ x ⅜ in. wide, directly on cookie sheet. Refrigerate until firm, turn over candy and overpipe on back; refrigerate until firm. Attach handles to cups with melted candy. Fill cups with mousse using tip 32 swirl motion. Position cups on saucers. Each serves 1.

† Brand confectionery coating.

▶ Sundae Surprise

Pan: Mini Wonder Mold, p. 150

Candy: White Candy Melts®† (4 pks. needed; 3 pks. will yield 4 sundaes with the 4th pk. used for candy clay), p. 218; Garden Candy Color Set, p. 219

Recipes: Candy Clay, p. 120; favorite crisped rice cereal treats

Also: 2006 Pattern Book (Sundae Triangle), p. 124; Disposable Decorating Bags, p. 137; Cake Dividing Set, p. 136; Rainbow Jimmies Sprinkle Decorations, p. 134; Rolling Pin, Roll & Cut Mat, p. 130; stick candy, candy-coated chocolate dots, red sour candy balls, waxed paper, paring knife

For bowl section, make a ¼ in. thick candy shell (p. 121) using pan and melted white candy. For base section, make a ¾ in. deep candy plaque in pan (p. 121); reserve any leftover candy. Divide bowl in 8ths using cake divider. Tint 1 recipe of candy clay pink using candy color. Roll out candy clay ⅛ in. thick and cover base. Using pattern, cut 8 triangles for each bowl. Attach at division marks using melted candy; trim as needed. Prepare cereal treats and form mound shapes to cover top of bowls; let cool. Cover treats with reserved melted white candy (p. 120); sprinkle with jimmies and attach sour ball and stick candy; let set. Attach bowl to base using melted candy; let set. Fill bowl with chocolate dots and position cereal treat on top. Each serves 1.

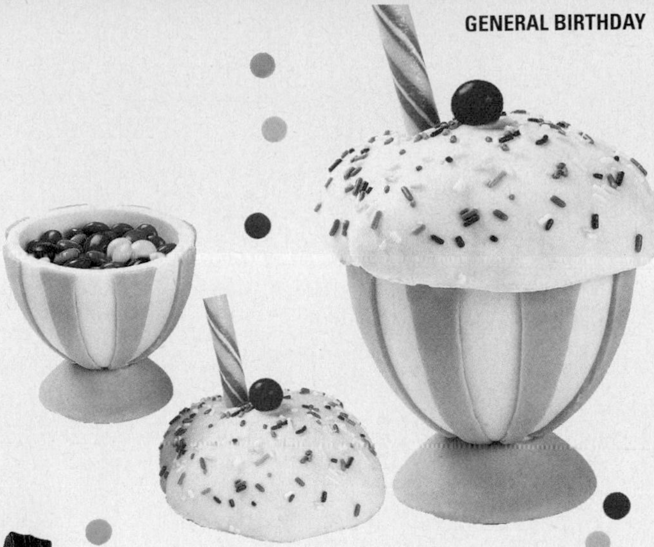

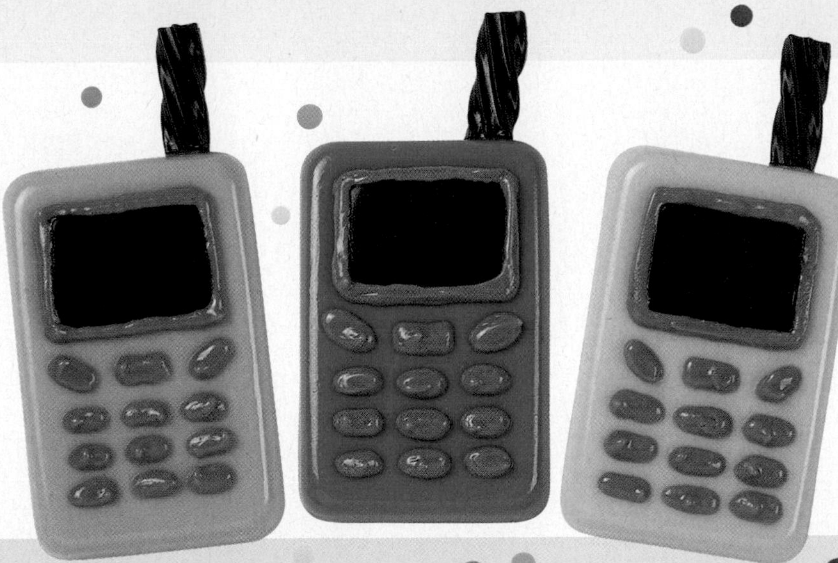

◀ A Strong Signal

Pan: Petite Loaf, p. 149

Candy: White Candy Melts®† (1 pk. needed), p. 218; Garden and Primary Candy Color Sets, p. 219

Also: Parchment Triangles, p. 137; black twist licorice, scissors

Divide melted candy into 4ths; tint ¼ pink, ¼ blue, ¼ yellow using candy colors. Divide remaining candy in half and tint black and gray (use a small amount of black candy color for gray). Using pan, make ¼ in. deep candy plaques (p. 121) in pink, blue and yellow; refrigerate until firm and unmold. With melted black candy in cut parchment bag, outline and fill in display area; refrigerate until firm. With melted gray candy in cut parchment bag, outline display area and pipe buttons. Cut licorice in 1 in. pieces; attach for antenna with melted candy. Each serves 1.

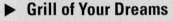

▶ Grill of Your Dreams

Here's the perfect birthday treat for your family's boss of the BBQ! It's a candy shell grill, topped with candy clay burgers and dogs resting on a grate of foil wrapped lollipop sticks. The inside's also well done, filled with licorice bits.

Pan: Sports Ball, p. 153

Tip: 2A, p. 138

Candy: Candy Melts®† in Red (3 pks. needed) and White (1 pk. needed), p. 218; Garden Candy Colors Set, p. 219; 6 in. Lollipop Sticks, p. 221

Recipe: Candy Clay, p. 120

Also: 101 Cookie Cutters Set, p. 216; Fine Tip Primary Colors FoodWriter™, Edible Color Markers, p. 129; Disposable Decorating Bags, p. 137; Cake Boards, Silver Fanci-Foil Wrap, p. 169; Plastic Dowel Rods, p. 167; glue stick, paring knife, black licorice bits

Make a ¼ in. thick candy shell (p. 121) using Sports Ball Pan half and melted red candy. Make 2 recipes of candy clay, one using 14 oz. of red candy remaining from preparing shell, the other using white candy. Divide white candy clay and tint black, gray and yellow using candy colors (use a small amount of black color for gray). Divide red candy clay and tint brown for hamburgers (add green) and red for hot dogs (add a little white); reserve remaining red for trim on grill.

For grate, lay lollipop sticks ½ in. apart on waxed paper-covered 6 in. cake circle. Trim sticks to fit. Wrap each stick with Fanci-Foil, attaching with glue stick. Reposition sticks on cake circle. Roll a ⅜ in. diameter rope of red candy clay, place over sticks on inside edge of cake circle, press down to cover ends of sticks. Attach sticks to bottom of grate rim with melted candy; Let dry. For legs, cut plastic dowel rods into three 3½ in. lengths. Trim ends on an angle to fit against grill base. Wrap in Fanci-Foil, attaching with glue stick. To assemble grill, turn candy shell upside down. Shape three 1 in. diameter balls from red candy clay; flatten bottoms and attach with melted candy. Insert legs, attaching with melted candy; let dry before turning upright. Roll out black candy clay ⅜ in. thick; cut 2 wheels using smallest round cutter from set. Roll out gray candy clay ⅛ in. thick; cut 2 hubcaps using large end of tip 2A. Attach hubcaps to wheels, then wheels to legs with melted candy; let set.

Shape hot dogs, 2½ x ½ in. thick. Score casing lines at ends using paring knife. Draw grill marks using black FoodWriter. Shape hamburgers 1¾ x ¼ in. thick. Score edges using paring knife. Roll out yellow candy 1⁄16 in. thick and cut 1½ in. squares for cheese; position on burgers. Fill candy shell grill with licorice bits. Position grate, arrange food on top.

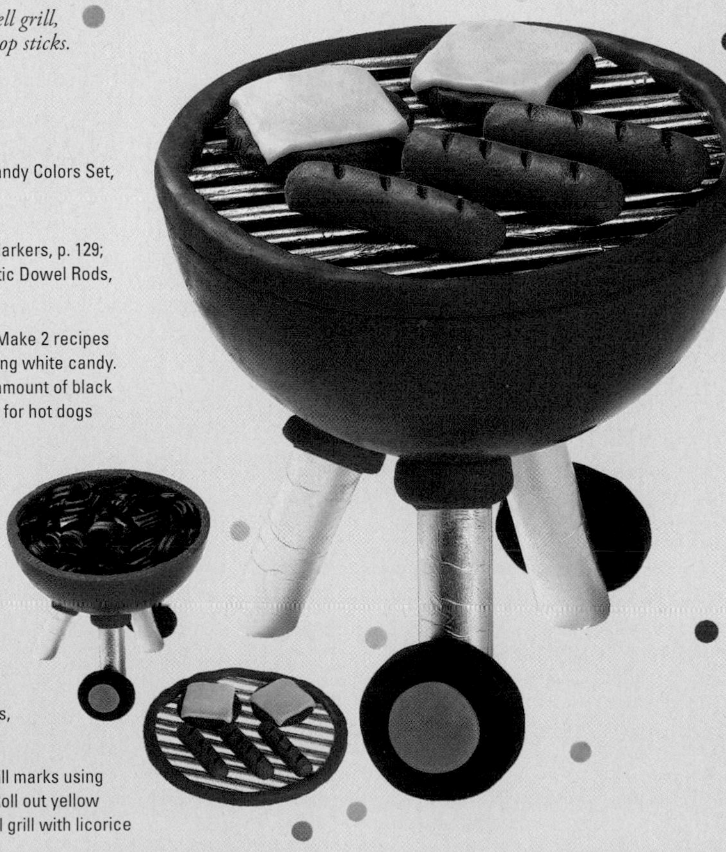

▼ Streaming a Message

The school of fish spells out a birthday greeting, while the bobbling fisherman nods his appreciation. The easy-to-make fondant boat and trees help set the scene.

Pan: 8 x 2 in. Round, p. 148

Tips: 2, 3, 10, 16, p. 138-139

Colors:* Royal Blue, Orange, Red-Red, Christmas Red, Golden Yellow, Lemon Yellow, Brown, Kelly Green, Black, p. 133

Fondant: White Ready-To-Use Rolled Fondant (24 oz. needed), p. 126; Brush Set, p. 129; Rolling Pin, Roll & Cut Mat, p. 130; Cutter/Embosser, p. 131

Recipe: Buttercream Icing, p. 112

Also: Fisherman Bobbling Topper, p. 185; 101 Cookie Cutters Set, p. 216; White Candy Melts®†, p. 218; Gum-Tex™, p. 130; Wooden Dowel Rods, p. 167; Cake Board, Fanci-Foil Wrap, p. 169; cornstarch, ruler, tissue

Several days in advance: Make fondant boat and trees. For boat, tint 6 oz. fondant brown; add ½ teaspoon Gum-Tex. Roll out ⅜ in. thick and cut 2 strips 1¼ x 5 in. using straight-edge wheel of Cutter/Embosser. Score lines ¼ in. apart using Cutter/Embosser. Shape the strips into an oval, attaching short ends with damp brush; on a cake board, position topper inside oval and adjust width as needed. Let dry on cornstarch-dusted surface, supporting with crushed tissue. For 4 trees, tint 6 oz. fondant green; add ½ teaspoon Gum-Tex. Roll out ⅜ in. thick and cut with tree cutter from set. Trim off bottom stem and let dry on cornstarch-dusted surface.

Ice smooth 2-layer cake. For bottom border, pipe tip 10 ball rocks in various shapes using gray buttercream. For fish, pipe tip 10 oval bodies; add tip 3 bead lips and fins. Pipe tip 2 dot eye. Pipe tip 2 dot message and rising bubbles. Cut dowel rods to 8 in. long; attach trees with melted candy. For motor, make a 1 in. white fondant ball; flatten and shape into an "L." Attach to boat with damp brush. Pipe tip 2 lines on motor. With spatula, ice top back portion of cake in green. Insert trees. Pipe tip 16 pull-out star grass around trees. Position boat and topper. Serves 20.

***Note:** Combine Red-Red and Christmas Red for red shown, Golden Yellow and Lemon Yellow for yellow shown and Brown and Red-Red for brown shown.

† Brand confectionery coating.

▲ Hunting Birdies

Pans: 6, 10 x 2 in. Round, p. 148

Fondant: Ready-to-Use Rolled Fondant in Pastel Green (24 oz. needed) and Pastel Blue (72 oz. needed), Primary Fondant Multi Pack, p. 126; Fine Tip Primary Colors FoodWriter™ Edible Color Markers, Brush Set, p. 129; Rolling Pin, Roll & Cut Mat, p. 130; Easy-Glide Fondant Smoother, p. 131

Recipe: Buttercream Icing, p. 112

Also: 2006 Pattern Book (Cake Top Flag, Cake Side Flag), p. 124; Golfer Bobbling Topper, p. 185; 12 in. Silver Cake Base, 6 in. Cake Circle, p. 169; 8 in. Lollipop Sticks, p. 221; Wooden Dowel Rods, p. 167; Gum-Tex™, p. 130; paring knife, construction paper in red, blue and yellow, cellophane tape, cornstarch

A few hours in advance: Make fondant trees and flags for cake sides. For trees, add ½ teaspoon Gum-Tex to primary green fondant. Roll out ⅛ in. thick and cut 22 triangles in various heights from 1 in. to 1½ in. high and from 1 in. to 1¼ in. wide. Cut slits for branches; let dry until firm on cornstarch-dusted surface. For flags on cake sides, add ½ teaspoon Gum-Tex to primary yellow, blue and red. Cut 15 flags using pattern; let dry until firm on cornstarch-dusted surface.

Prepare 2-layer cakes for stacked construction (p. 110). Prepare cakes for rolled fondant (p. 111); cover cakes with pastel blue fondant and smooth with Easy-Glide Smoother. Roll out pastel green fondant ⅛ in. thick; cut wavy strips for hills in various heights from 1¼ to 2½ in. and lengths from 10 to 12 in. Attach 1 group of hills for background with damp brush; attach 2nd group for foreground. Add more strips as needed. Attach side flags and trees to cake with damp brush; trim flag poles as needed. Draw holes with black FoodWriter. Trace Cake Top Flag pattern on construction paper; cut out flags and write message with black FoodWriter. Tape flags to sticks and insert in cake top. Position topper. Serves 40.

◄ You Goal Girl!

Your soccer star deserves a stellar cake. A burst of star lollipops puts her name in lights, while the fun bobbling topper and royal icing goal make everyone feel part of the action.

Pan: Decorator Preferred™ 8 x 3 in. Round, p. 147

Tips: 2, 16, p. 138-139

Color: Kelly Green, p. 133

Candy: White Candy Melts®†*, p. 218; Stars and Alphabet Candy Molds, p. 220; Primary Candy Color Set, p. 219; 11¾ in. Lollipop Sticks, p. 221

Recipes: Buttercream, Royal Icings, p. 112

Also: 2006 Pattern Book (Soccer Net Back, Top and Sides), p. 124; Female Soccer Bobbling Cake Topper, p. 185; Parchment Triangles, p. 137; Meringue Powder, p. 132; Cake Board, Fanci-Foil Wrap, p. 169; waxed paper

Several days in advance: Make net sections using royal icing. Place patterns on cake board and cover with waxed paper. Pipe tip 2 outlines over pattern lines; overpipe outlines with tip 2. Make extras to allow for breakage and let dry at least 24 hours. **One day in advance:** Carefully peel off waxed paper from net sections. Assemble and pipe tip 2 outline seams; let dry.

Divide candy in half. Using candy colors, tint ½ yellow, ⅛ red and ⅛ black (combine red and blue candy colors for black); reserve ¼ white. Mold letters (p. 121). For name, fill letter molds ½ full with red candy; for message, fill mold completely with white candy. Mold a full-depth yellow star for each letter in name plus 8 half-depth stars. Refrigerate all candy until firm. Using melted black and white candy in cut parchment bags, overpipe letters; refrigerate until firm. Attach lollipop sticks and name letters to full-depth stars with melted candy.

Ice 1-layer cake (3 in. high) smooth in buttercream. Pipe tip 16 pull-out star grass bottom border. Attach message and half-depth stars with icing. Position topper and net sections. Trim sticks as needed and insert star lollipops in cake. Serves 20.

Shake Things Up!

New Bobbling Toppers, in great sports designs, add fun to your cake in seconds. That's using your head!

► Play A Bobble Header!

This cake decorates faster than a 1-2-3 inning! Thanks to our fun Baseball Mitt decorations and the Bobbling Topper, there's enough fun to rally any party.

Pan: 8 x 2 in. Square, p. 148

Tips: 47, 233, p. 138-139

Color: Kelly Green, p. 133

Recipe: Buttercream Icing, p. 112

Also: Softball Bobbling Topper, p. 185; Alphabet/Numerals Icing Decorations, Baseball Mitt Icing Decorations (2 pks. needed), p. 184; cornstarch

Ice 1-layer cake smooth. For diamond, pipe tip 47 bands (smooth side up) on cake top, 1 in. from edge of cake. For bases, pipe a square at each corner (pat smooth with finger dipped in cornstarch). Pipe tip 233 pull-out grass bottom border. Attach 3 mitt icing decorations on each side with dots of icing. Position name letters on cake top. Position topper. Serves 10.

They've Come of Age

It's the birthday which marks a new beginning. Celebrate La Quinceañera and Bar or Bat Mitzvah with majestic cakes which portray your family's pride and love of tradition.

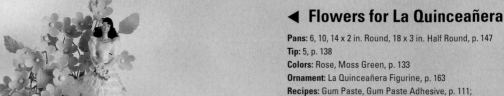

◀ Flowers for La Quinceañera

Pans: 6, 10, 14 x 2 in. Round, 18 x 3 in. Half Round, p. 147
Tip: 5, p. 138
Colors: Rose, Moss Green, p. 133
Ornament: La Quinceañera Figurine, p. 163
Recipes: Gum Paste, Gum Paste Adhesive, p. 111; Buttercream Icing, p. 112
Also: Floral Collection Flower Making Set, Confectionery Tool Set, p. 131; Gum Paste Mix (2 pks. needed), p. 130; Meringue Powder, p. 132; White Ready-To-Use Rolled Fondant (24 oz. needed), p. 126; Decorator Brush Set, p. 219; 8, 12, 16 in. Plates from Crystal-Clear Cake Divider Set; 9 in. Twist Legs (3 pks. needed), p. 165; Cake Boards, Fanci-Foil Wrap, p. 169; Flower Spikes, p. 167; Candy Melting Plate, p. 219; Flower Former Set, p. 131; Tulle Spool, p. 157; Rolling Pin, Roll & Cut Mat, p. 130; 24-gauge florist wire (6 in. lengths, 220 needed), 26-gauge florist wire (6 in. lengths, 122 needed), glue gun, floral tape, triple-thick 20 in. round heavy-duty cardboard, ⅜ in. pink satin ribbon (63 in. needed), craft blocks for drying flowers and leaves, cornstarch

Several weeks in advance: Make 220 flowers and 110 leaves using gum paste (p. 119). Prepare 2 recipes gum paste. Tint one recipe rose. Divide 2nd recipe in 3rds; tint ⅓ moss green and reserve remaining white. Make 12 tulle puffs. Cut 12 strips of tulle 12 in. long. Gather in center and twist wire around center to secure.

Assemble sprays. Gather flowers and leaves in small bunches. Assemble wires with floral tape. Arrange in flower spikes using the quantities that follow for each tier size: For 6 in. cake, use 45 flowers, 20 leaves, 2 spikes, 3 tulle puffs. For 10 in. cake, use 50 flowers, 25 leaves, 2 spikes, 2 tulle puffs. For 14 in. cake, use 60 flowers, 30 leaves, 2 spikes, 3 tulle puffs. For 18 in. cake, use 60 flowers, 30 leaves, 3 spikes, 4 tulle puffs.

Prepare triple-thick 20 in. base board, wrapped in foil. Attach ribbon to side with glue gun. Ice smooth 2-layer cakes (you will need four 18 in. half rounds, each 2 in. high). Prepare 10, 14 and 18 in. cakes for push-in pillar construction (p. 110). Pipe tip 5 bead bottom borders on all cakes. Roll out fondant ⅛ in. thick; cut flowers using pansy and apple blossom cutters from Flower Making Set. Position on cake top and sides. Roll small balls of fondant and attach for flower centers with damp brush. Randomly position small fondant balls on cake.

At reception, assemble cakes, insert flower spikes and position figurine*. Serves 213.

*Note: Always place a separator plate or cake board cut to fit, on the cake before you position any figurine or ornament. This protects both the cake and your keepsake. For extra stability, secure your figurine to the plate with double-stick craft tape.

▶ Life's Inspiration

Pans: 8, 10 x 3 in. Round, 18 x 3 in. Half Round, p. 147; Sports Ball, p. 153

Tips: 2, 3, 5, 12, 14, 18, 32, p. 138-139

Color: Royal Blue (for Bar Mitzvah), Rose Petal Pink (for Bat Mitzvah), p. 133

Recipes: Buttercream and Color Flow Icings, p. 112

Also: 2006 Pattern Book (Scrolled Panel), p. 124; Decorator Favorites Pattern Press Set, p. 142; 6 Pt. Star Plastic Cutter, p. 199; Cake Dividing Set, p. 136; Plastic Dowel Rods (3 pks. needed), p. 167; Color Flow Mix, p. 132; 8, 10, 14, 18 in. Cake Boards, White and Silver Fanci-Foil Wrap, p. 169; 6 in. Lollipop Sticks, p. 221; Fine Tip Neon Colors FoodWriter™ Edible Color Markers, p. 129; Disposable Decorating Bags, p. 137; 27 in. diameter plywood board, 8 x 3 in. round craft block or wood block, tracing paper, waxed paper

At least 48 hours in advance: Make 7 color flow stars and 6 scrolled panels (p. 120). Prepare 3 recipes of color flow; reserve 1 full-strength for outlining and decorating. For stars, trace cutter on paper; for panels, trace pattern. Outline with tip 3, let dry, then flow in with thinned color flow in cut disposable bag; let dry 48 hours. On stars, pipe tip 2 fleurs de lis and dots; edge with tip 2 beads. On 6 stars, pipe in tip 12 pull-out spike on back, let dry. Attach remaining star to lollipop stick with full-strength color flow; let dry. On panels, pipe tip 5 scrolls; overpipe with tip 3. Edge panel opening with tip 3 beads. Make extras to allow for breakage and let dry.

In buttercream, ice smooth seven 1-layer 8 in. (each 3 in. high) and two 1-layer 10 in. cakes (each 3 in. high). Ice sides of 10 in. cakes in blue (or pink). Ice smooth four 1-layer 18 in. Half Round cakes to make one 4 in. high cake and one half Sports Ball cake. To make

plywood base, use 8 in. cake circles to trace arrangement of six 8 in. cakes around a center 8 x 3 in. round craft block, extending 1 in. beyond each tracing; cut plywood following tracing and wrap with silver foil. Prepare cakes for stacked construction (p. 110). On base, position center craft block, wrapped in silver Fanci-Foil, with six 8 in. cakes around it. Position 18 in. cake on triple-thick foil-wrapped boards. Divide 18 in. cake in 6ths; imprint vine pattern press facing left and right from each division. Pipe a tip 32 elongated shell, 2 in. long, where imprints meet. Pipe tip 18 scrolls over imprint; add a longer scroll and a tip 18 upright shell, 1½ in. long, to connect. Overpipe scrolls with tip 14; add tip 3 dots. Imprint small C-scroll on top edge of cake. Pipe tip 14 scrolls over imprint. Position 18 in. cake on 8 in. cakes; pipe tip 18 shell bottom borders. On 8 in. cakes, pipe tip 32 crown border; add tip 3 dot at base of crowns. This bottom portion of cake will be carried separately to reception for final assembly and decorating.

Cut triple-thick 14 in. boards in a 13 in. hexagon. Wrap with white foil. Mark board for placement of scrolled panels (p. 120). Position stacked 10 in. cakes on hexagon board. Pipe tip 5 bead bottom border and tip 3 bead top border. Position remaining 8 in. cake on 10 in. cake. Pipe tip 32 crown border with tip 3 dots; add tip 3 overlapping double drop strings, 1 in. deep, from points of crowns. Pipe tip 18 shell bottom border. Divide half ball cake in 6ths. Pipe tip 14 scrolls from top to bottom at division points; pipe tip 3 scrolls between tip 14 scrolls; add tip 3 dots. Position on 8 in. cake; add tip 18 shell bottom border.

At reception: Position hexagon board with cakes on 18 in. cake. Attach color flow panels (p. 120). Using full-strength color flow, pipe tip 3 beads on all panel edges; add tip 5 beads at bottom edge of hexagon board. Insert spiked stars in cake sides and star on stick in cake top. Serves 214.

◄ Tile Style!

Exciting mosaic detail and cool shades of blue and violet make this a refreshing choice for a man's birthday cake. Cut perfect fondant "tiles" using our Square Cut-Outs™.

Pan: Oval Set (13½ x 9⅞ in. used), p. 148
Colors: Rose, Violet, Royal Blue, p. 133
Fondant: White Ready-To-Use Rolled Fondant (24 oz. needed), p. 126: Square Cut-Outs™, p. 128; Rolling Pin, Roll & Cut Mat, p. 130
Recipe: Buttercream Icing, p. 112
Also: A-B-C and 1-2-3 50 Pc. Cutter Set, p. 216; White Celebration Candles, p. 188; Cake Boards, Fanci-Foil Wrap, p. 169

Ice 2-layer cake smooth. Divide fondant in 4ths and tint dark violet (combine violet with rose), light violet (combine violet with a little rose), dark blue and light blue. Roll out fondant ⅛ in. thick and cut approximately 70 squares in each color using smallest Cut-Out. Press squares onto cake sides, alternating colors. Using dark violet fondant and alphabet cutters, cut out message. Position on cake top. Roll out remaining fondant ½ in. thick. Lightly grease the inside of smallest Cut-Out and cut candleholders. Flatten sides and insert candles. Position on cake top. Serves 30.

► Give Her a Garden

Simple apple blossoms say so much on this pretty oval cake. You can make the royal icing flowers weeks in advance, so you'll have minimal decorating to do on her birthday.

Pan: Oval Set (13½ x 9⅞ in. used), p. 148
Tips: 2, 5, 16, 101, 349, p. 138-139
Colors:* Violet, Rose, Moss Green, p. 133
Recipes: Buttercream, Royal Icings, p. 112
Also: White Celebration Candles, p. 188; Flower Nail No. 7, p. 137; Cake Board, Fanci-Foil Wrap, p. 169; Meringue Powder, p. 132; waxed paper squares

In advance: Using royal icing, make 100 tip 101 apple blossoms with tip 2 dot centers. Make extras to allow for breakage; let dry.

Ice 2-layer, 3 in. high cake smooth. Pipe tip 5 bead bottom border. Position flowers for "MOM" message and bottom border. Pipe tip 2 dots randomly on cake top and sides. Pipe tip 349 leaves on flowers. Pipe tip 16 rosette candleholders. Insert candles. Serves 30.

*****Note:** Combine Violet with a little Rose for light violet flowers shown.

◄ You've Turned 21!

Pan: 9 x 13 x 2 in. Sheet, p. 147

Fondant: Primary and Natural Fondant Multi Packs, p. 126; Heart Cut-Outs™, p. 128; Rolling Pin, Roll & Cut Mat, p. 130

Recipe: Buttercream Icing, p. 112

Also: Decorating Comb, p. 136; 10 x 14 in. Cake Boards, Silver Fanci-Foil Wrap, p. 169

Ice two 1-layer cakes smooth. Comb sides using small-tooth edge of decorating comb. Roll out red and black fondant ⅛ in. thick. For large spades, cut 10 hearts using medium Cut-Out; position on cake. For bases of spades, cut 10 hearts using small Cut-Out; shape into a "T" and position. For number 10, roll ⅛ in. wide ropes and position. For small spades, cut 2 hearts using small Cut-Out; position. Shape small spade bases using small pieces of fondant; position. Cut large heart using large Cut-Out; position. For letter A, roll ⅛ in. wide ropes and position. For small hearts, cut 2 hearts using small Cut-Out; position. Each cake serves 22.

◄ Cash In Your Chips

Cookies: Cookie Sheet, Cooling Grid, p. 217

Candy: White Candy Melts®† (2 pks. needed), p. 218; Primary and Garden Candy Color Sets, p. 219

Recipe: Roll-Out Cookie, p. 112

Also: Round Cut-Outs™, p. 128; Rolling Pin, p. 130; Parchment Triangles, p. 137

Use largest round Cut-Out to cut 30 cookies; bake and cool. Tint ⅓ pk. candy each red, green, and blue; ½ pk. black; reserve ½ pk. white. Cover 6 cookies in each color with melted candy (p. 120); let set. Pipe designs on cookies using melted white or black candy in cut parchment bag; let set. Each serves 1.

† Brand confectionery coating.

► Show Your Full House!

They'll see your poker table cake and you'll raise your decorating profile! Rolled fondant is the hands-down winner for creating detailed decorations like cards and chips with ease.

Pan: Hexagon Pan Set (12 x 2 in. needed), p. 148

Colors:* Kelly Green, Black, Christmas Red, Red-Red, Royal Blue, p. 133

Fondant:* White Ready-To-Use Rolled Fondant (48 oz. needed), p. 126; Round Cut-Outs™, p. 128; Fine Tip Primary Colors FoodWriter™, Edible Color Markers, Brush Set, p. 129; Rolling Pin, Roll & Cut Mat, p. 130; Cutter/Embosser, Easy-Glide Fondant Smoother, p. 131

Recipe: Buttercream Icing, p. 112

Also: 12 in. Cake Circles (3 needed), Fanci-Foil Wrap, p. 169; 3 in. Grecian Pillars, p. 166; hot glue gun; ruler

Tint 24 oz. fondant green, 2 oz. blue, 2 oz. red, 12 oz. black; reserve remaining white. Position 1-layer cake on double-thick cake circles trimmed to cake size. Prepare cake for rolled fondant (p. 111); cover top with green fondant and smooth with Fondant Smoother. Roll out black fondant ⅛ in. thick, cut two strips 19 x 3 in. wide and attach to cake sides and ½ in. over top edge with damp brush. Blend edge into tabletop with rounded end of Fondant Smoother. Roll out white, red, blue and black fondant ⅛ in. thick; cut 50 poker chips in each color using smallest round Cut-Out. For 30-35 cards, roll out white fondant ⅛ in. thick; cut ¾ x 1¼ in. rectangles using straight-edge wheel of Cutter/Embosser. Draw details on cards with FoodWriter markers.

For leg assembly, wrap 3rd cake circle, cut 1 in. smaller than cake, with Fanci-Foil. Cover four Grecian pillars with black fondant and hot glue to bottom of cake circle; let set. Position cake on top of cake board with legs. Position cards and poker chips. Serves 17.

***Note:** Combine Red-Red and Christmas Red for red shown.

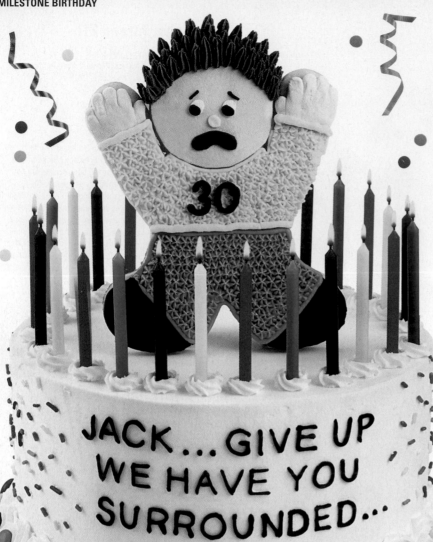

◀ **In the Line of Fire**

For those who won't go quietly into their 30s, this cake will bring them to justice. A ring of rainbow candles and a shower of sprinkles suggest that life will be more colorful than ever.

Pan: 8 x 2 in. Round, p. 148

Tips: 2, 3, 16, 21, p. 138-139

Colors: Royal Blue, Golden Yellow, Black, Brown, Copper (skin tone), p. 133

Cookie: 101 Cookie Cutters Set, p. 216; 8 in. Cookie Treat Sticks, Cookie Sheet, Cooling Grid, p. 217

Recipes: Buttercream Icing, Roll-Out Cookie, p. 112

Also: Rainbow Colors Round Candles (2 pks. needed), p. 188; White Candy Melts®†, p. 218, Rainbow Jimmies Sprinkle Decorations, p. 134; Rolling Pin, p. 130; Cake Board, Fanci-Foil Wrap, p. 169; candy-coated chocolates, cornstarch

Roll out dough and cut cookie using largest gingerbread boy cutter from set. Move arms and place in raised position, adding a ¾ in. piece of dough at end of hand to extend length. Bake and cool. Outline and pipe in head and hands with tip 3 (pat smooth with finger dipped in cornstarch). Outline shirt and pants with tip 3. Cover shirt, pants and shoes with tip 16 stars. Pipe tip 16 pull-out star hair. Using tip 2, pipe dot eyes, pupils, nose (smooth with finger dipped in cornstarch). Outline and pipe in mouth and string eyebrows with tip 2. Pipe tip 2 number.

Ice 2-layer cake smooth. Immediately press jimmies on sides, leaving 7 in. at front of cake clear. Pipe tip 2 message. Pipe tip 21 rosette bottom border; position candy-coated chocolates in centers. Attach cookie to sticks with melted candy, let set. Pipe tip 16 rosette candleholders on top edge of cake; insert cookies and candles. Serves 20.

▶ A Head Start on 40!

Pan: Party Hat, p. 151

Colors:* Lemon Yellow, Golden Yellow, Violet, Leaf Green, Royal Blue, p. 133

Fondant: White Ready-To-Use Rolled Fondant (48 oz. needed), p. 126; Alphabet/Number and Round Cut-Outs™, p. 128; Brush Set, p. 129; Rolling Pin, Roll & Cut Mat, p. 130; Cutter/Embosser, Easy-Glide Fondant Smoother, p. 131

Recipe: Buttercream Icing, p. 112

Also: Cake Board, Fanci-Foil Wrap, p. 169; craft knife, small plastic ruler

Prepare cake for rolled fondant (p. 111). Tint 8 oz. fondant blue and cover hat body area of cake; smooth with Fondant Smoother. Tint 6 oz. fondant violet. Roll out ⅛ in. thick and cut 1 in. wide strips using wavy-edge wheel of Cutter/Embosser. Attach diagonally to cake with damp brush, 1 in. apart; trim off excess. Tint a 2 in. ball of fondant green. Roll out ⅛ in. thick and cut 9 circles using medium Cut-Out. Inlay circles in violet strips, using medium round Cut-Out to remove portions of strips; attach circles with damp brush. Tint 24 oz. fondant yellow. Cover hat brim and top pompom area with yellow fondant; smooth. Roll out a portion ⅛ in. thick and cut nine "40" messages using number Cut-Outs. Attach to circles with damp brush. For fringe, roll out yellow fondant ⅛ in. thick and cut 1 x 1½ in. rectangles. Cut slits along 1½ in. side, ¾ in. deep. Roll up rectangles from short ends, pinching together at bottom edge; attach the uncut end of each roll to brim and pompom areas with damp brush, placing close together. Cut enough rectangles to cover areas completely. Serves 12.

***Note:** Combine Leaf Green and a little Lemon Yellow for green shown. Combine Lemon Yellow and a little Golden Yellow for yellow shown.

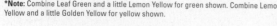

◀ The Bifocal Folks!

Cookie: Round Cookie Treat Pan, 8 in. Cookie Treat Sticks, Cooling Grid, p. 217
Candy: Candy Melts®† in White and Yellow (1 pk. each), p. 218; Primary Candy Color Set, p. 219
Also: Parchment Triangles, p. 137; sweetened coconut

Mold candy face lollipops (p. 121) in treat pan cavities using melted yellow candy; refrigerate until firm, unmold. Tint portions of melted white candy black (add red and blue candy colors) and blue. Using black candy in cut parchment bag, pipe dot eyes and string glasses frames, eyelashes and smiles. Pipe lenses with melted white candy in cut parchment bag. For hair, mix coconut with blue candy; immediately add hair to candy head; refrigerate until firm. Each serves 1.

▶ Rude Awakening

Pans: Over The Hill Tombstone, p. 152; 9 x 13 x 2 in. Sheet, p. 148; Sports Ball, p. 153
Tips: 3, 5, 16, p. 138-139
Colors: Copper (skin tone), Black, Brown, p. 133
Fondant: Ready-To-Use Rolled Fondant in White (48 oz. needed) and Pastel Blue (24 oz. needed), p. 126; Cutter/Embosser, p. 131; Rolling Pin, Roll & Cut Mat, p. 130
Candy: White Candy Melts®† (4 pks. needed), p. 218; Primary and Garden Candy Color Sets (2 Garden Sets needed), p. 219
Recipe: Buttercream Icing, p. 112
Also: 13 x 19 in. Cake Boards (2 needed), Fanci-Foil Wrap, p. 169; Parchment Triangles, p. 137; heavy duty aluminum foil, warming tray, sharp knife, ruler

In advance: Make candy plaque (p. 121) headboard, footboard and 2 bedstands. For headboard, tint 4 oz. each of melted white candy red, yellow, blue and dark gray using candy colors (use black to make gray). Pipe in letters and border in Tombstone Pan, using melted candy in cut parchment bags. Refrigerate until firm. Tint 40 oz. white candy light gray. Fill pan ¼ in. thick. Refrigerate until firm and carefully unmold. Trim headboard to 11½ in. high, then slide trimmed bottom across warming tray to create a straight edge. For footboard, mark 6 in. from top of pan with a dot of candy; make an aluminum foil dam to separate area below mark and fill top of pan ¼ in. thick with light gray candy. Refrigerate until firm and unmold. For bedstands, make a foil dam at bottom of pan to create a 9 x 1 in. wide area. Fill ¾ in. thick with light gray candy; refrigerate until firm and unmold. Repeat for 2nd bedstand. Attach stands at right angle to backs of headboard and footboard with melted candy; let set.

Wrap double-thick 13 x 19 in. cake boards with Fanci-Foil; set aside. Ice smooth 2-layer sheet cake (bake two 1½ in. high layers for a 3 in. high cake). Also bake and cool ½ Sports Ball cake for head; trim to 2½ in. high and ice smooth. Pipe tip 5 ball nose and eyes (flatten and smooth with finger dipped in cornstarch). Add tip 3 dot pupils, outline eyebrows and comma-shaped ears. Pipe tip 16 pull-out star hair. For pillow, shape 12 oz. white fondant into a 6 x 3½ x 1½ in. high wedge. For body under blanket, shape 24 oz. white fondant into a 7 x 4 x 1½ in. high oval. For each arm, shape 2½ oz. white fondant into a 3 x 1½ x 1¼ in. high oval. Position body, arms, pillow and head on sheet cake. For blanket, roll out blue fondant ¼ in. thick; cut an 13 x 16 in. rectangle and position on cake, folding back the top. Pipe tip 3 dot fingers. Attach candy plaques with melted candy. Serves 51.

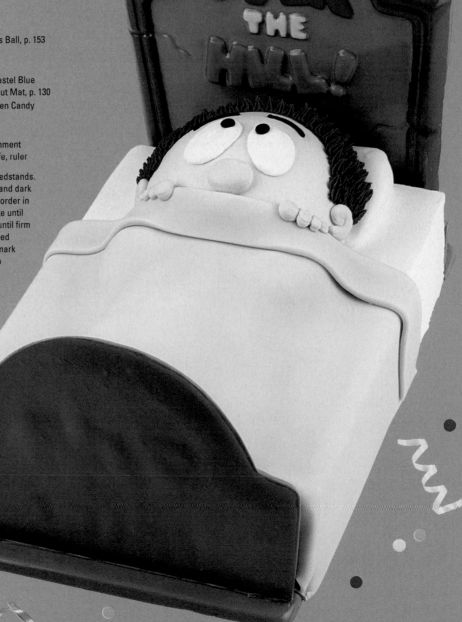

† Brand confectionery coating.

Famous Friends!

Remember when you counted the days until your birthday?
Kids do it every year—because it's the one day that's all about them.
There's no better way to give kids star status than bringing friends
like *Care Bears*™, *SpongeBob SquarePants*™ and *Spider-Man*™ to the party.
We have lots of fun ways to set the scene at your celebration,
from easy-to-make *Winnie the Pooh*™ cookies and cupcakes to
Strawberry Shortcake's™ candyland cottage cake.

Instructions for projects shown on these two pages are on page 28.

A Rainbow for Wishing

Pans: 8 x 2 in. Round, p. 148; Cookie Sheet, p. 149
Tips: 1, 2, 3, p. 138
Colors: *Care Bears™* Icing Color Set (teal, blue, yellow, orange), p. 174, Black, Rose, Violet, p. 133
Fondant: Ready-To-Use Rolled Fondant in White (72 oz. needed) and Pastel Blue (48 oz. needed), p. 126; Heart and Star Cut-Outs™, p. 128; Brush Set, p. 129; Rolling Pin, Roll & Cut Mat, p. 130; Easy-Glide Fondant Smoother, p. 131
Recipes: Buttercream, Royal Icings, p. 112
Also: 2006 Pattern Book (Rainbow, Sun, Large and Small Star Faces), p. 124; *Care Bears* Candle, p. 174; Confectionery Tool Set, p. 131; Gum-Tex™, p. 130; 10 in. (2 needed), 6 in., and 12 in. Cake Circles, Fanci-Foil Wrap, p. 169; 11¾ in. Lollipop Sticks, p. 221; Piping Gel, Meringue Powder, p. 132; pizza wheel, ruler, cornstarch, waxed paper

In advance: Make fondant rainbow, stars, sun, hearts and border clouds (p. 118). Set all pieces on cornstarch-dusted cookie sheet to dry.

Attach lollipop sticks to backs of rainbow, sun, and 3 largest hearts using royal icing. Let dry. Prepare 2-layer and 1-layer 8 in. rounds for rolled fondant (p. 111). Cover with blue fondant; smooth. Make 4 cloud formations for cake tops; roll white fondant balls ½ in. to 2 in. diameter. Roll out fondant thin and cover as for border clouds.

Insert rainbow in cake tops, trimming ends of sticks if necessary. Arrange cake top cloud formations, positioning against each side of the rainbow for support. Insert sun at back of rainbow. Pipe tip 1 string stars and dots on cakes using buttercream. Position clouds around bottom border. Insert hearts on sticks. Attach small stars, hearts and stars with faces, with dots of icing. Position candle. Serves 30.

Portable Rainbows!

Pan: Standard Muffin, p. 149
Tips: 3, 8, p. 138
Colors:* Lemon Yellow, Rose, Royal Blue, Sky Blue, Teal, p. 133
Recipe: Buttercream Icing, p. 112
Also: *Care Bears™* Icing Decorations, *Care Bears™* Baking Cups, p. 174; White Cake Sparkles™, p. 134

Ice cupcakes smooth. Pipe tip 3 lines in a rainbow pattern beginning at outer edge of cupcake and moving inward. Position icing decoration. Pipe tip 8 ball clouds, sprinkle with Cake Sparkles. Each serves 1.

*Note: Combine Royal Blue with a little Sky Blue for rainbow blue shown.

Care Bears™ Stars

Cookie: Plastic Star Cutter, p. 216; Cookie Sheet, Cooling Grid, p. 217
Color: Lemon Yellow, p. 133
Recipes: Royal Icing, Roll-Out Cookie, p. 112
Also: *Care Bears™* Icing Decorations, p. 174; Meringue Powder, p. 132

Roll out dough and cut 3 star cookies using 2nd smallest cutter; bake and cool. Cover cookies with thinned royal icing (p. 120); let set. Attach icing decorations with full-strength royal icing. Each serves 1.

Care Bears™ ©2005 Those Characters From Cleveland, Inc. Used under license by Wilton Industries, Inc. www.care-bears.com

---

CareBears™

Heart's Delight

Pans: Standard Muffin, p. 149; Non-Stick Cookie Sheet, p. 146
Candy: Candy Melts®† in Light Cocoa and White, p. 218; Garden and Primary Candy Color Sets, Decorator Brush Set, p. 219; 4 in. Lollipop Sticks, p. 221
Also: *Care Bears™* Icing Decorations, p. 174; Nesting Heart Cutter Set, p. 216; White Standard Baking Cups, p. 184; Mini Hearts, p. 160; 8 in. Straight Spatula, p. 137; spice drops

Using candy colors, tint 2 oz. each of white candy pink, yellow and teal (combine blue and green for teal). Mold heart candy plaques (p. 121), placing 2nd smallest cutter on cookie sheet and filling ⅛ in. thick. Refrigerate until firm; carefully unmold. Mold candy shell in baking cup (p. 121) using light cocoa candy mixed with a small amount of white. Refrigerate until firm. Carefully remove baking cup.

Attach pink candy heart to lollipop stick with melted candy; let set. Attach teal and yellow hearts to pink heart with melted candy; let set. Insert stick into spice drop for base; attach spice drop to shell, toward back edge, with melted candy. Attach another spice drop near front edge of shell, then attach icing decoration to spice drop with melted candy; let set. Fill candy shell with mini hearts. Each serves 1.

Share Bear™ Surprise

Pans: *Care Bears™*, p. 174; Cookie Sheet, Cooling Grid, p. 217
Tips: 2, 3, 6, 16, 21, p. 138-139
Colors: *Care Bears™* Icing Color Set (teal, blue, yellow, orange), p. 174; Violet, Rose, Black, p. 133
Recipes: Buttercream Icing, Roll-Out Cookie, p. 112
Also: 2006 Pattern Book (Cake, Party Hat), p. 124; Nesting Heart Cutter Set, p. 216; Colored Sugars in Yellow, Blue, Orange, Pink, Lavender, Light Green, p. 134; Rainbow Colors Round Candles, p. 188; Cake Board, Fanci-Foil Wrap, p. 169; Rolling Pin, p. 130; curling ribbon in violet, pink, orange, yellow, green, blue (2 ft. each color), paring knife, toothpick, cornstarch

Roll out cookie dough; trace cake and hat patterns with toothpick and cut cookies using knife. Cut 6 heart cookies using 3rd smallest cutter. Bake and cool all cookies. Cover heart cookies with thinned buttercream (p. 120); sprinkle with colored sugars and let set.

Ice cake sides, tummy and background areas smooth. Outline body, snout, mouth and eyes with tip 3. Cover bear with tip 16 stars. Pipe in eyes, nose and mouth with tip 3 (smooth with finger dipped in cornstarch); add tip 2 string eyelids and dot freckles. Outline and pipe in lollipops on tummy with tip 3; add tip 3 string confetti on cake sides. Pipe tip 21 shell bottom border.

Cover hat cookie with tip 6 stripes; position on cake. Add tip 3 zigzag brim and pull-out string pompom. Ice cake cookie smooth. Pipe tip 6 stripe bottom border. Add tip 3 dot and string garland. Ice top of cookie fluffy with spatula; add tip 3 dot drips of icing. On round candle, insert tip 16 over wick and pull out icing flame. Insert candle in iced cake cookie top, position in hand area of cake. Attach curling ribbon to heart cookies with dots of icing; position around cake. Attach ribbon ends at top of hand and shorter ribbon strips at bottom with icing. Cake serves 12; each cookie serves 1.

▲ *Dora's* Only Way to Travel

Cookie: Animal Pals 50-Pc. Cutter Set, p. 216; Cookie Sheet, Cooling Grid, p. 217
Tips: 2, 4, 6, p. 138
Colors:* *Dora the Explorer™* Icing Color Set (red, brown, skin tone needed), p. 179; Black, Leaf Green, Royal Blue, Orange, Violet, Rose, Lemon Yellow, p. 133
Recipes: Royal and Color Flow Icings, Roll-Out Cookie, p. 112
Also: Color Flow Mix, Meringue Powder, p. 132; *Dora the Explorer™* Icing Decorations, p. 179; Cake Board, p. 169; Parchment Triangles, p. 137; cornstarch, waxed paper

Use horse cutter from set to cut unicorn cookies; turn cookie over so that unicorn faces to the right; bake and cool. Using color flow, outline with tip 2 and flow in (p. 120); let dry on waxed paper. Figure pipe *Dora* body on unicorn using tips 2 and 6 (p. 117). Pipe tip 2 swirl horn on unicorn. Pipe tip 4 pull-out mane and teardrop shapes on tail. Outline and pipe in eyes with tip 2. Add tip 4 dot iris and tip 2 dot pupil. Pipe tip 2 eyebrow, mouth and ears. Outline and pipe in tip 2 hooves (smooth). Pipe tip 2 bead flower on hat with tip 2 dot center. Each serves 1.

*Note: Combine Violet with a small amount of Rose for lighter violet shown.

▶ Munchable Maracas

Pan: Mini Ball, p. 153
Also: Candy Melts®† in Orange, Yellow, Green, p. 218; Parchment Triangles, p. 137; *Dora the Explorer™* Party Toppers, p. 179; Decorator Brush Set, p. 219; orange-striped candy sticks, candy-coated chocolates, craft knife

For each maraca, make 2 candy shells in mini ball pan (p. 121); unmold. Using melted yellow and green candy in cut parchment bags, pipe zigzag design on outside of maracas; let set. Fill one shell with candies and party topper. Attach top shell to bottom shell with melted candy in cut parchment bag; let set. Use craft knife to carefully cut hole in bottom of shell to fit candy stick. Insert candy stick into hole and secure with melted candy; let set. Each serves 1.

† Brand confectionery coating.

©2005 Viacom International Inc. All Rights Reserved. Nickelodeon, Nick Jr., *Dora the Explorer* and all related titles, logos and characters are trademarks of Viacom International Inc.

▶ Fairytale *Dora*

Pan: *Dora the Explorer*, p. 179
Tips: 2, 3, 16, 17, p. 138-139
Colors: *Dora the Explorer* Icing Color Set (red, pink, brown, skin tone), p. 179; Violet, Lemon Yellow, Golden Yellow, Black, Leaf Green, p. 133
Fondant: Ready-To-Use Rolled Fondant in White, Yellow (24 oz. each needed), p. 126; Brush Set, p. 129; Rolling Pin, Roll & Cut Mat, p. 130
Recipe: Buttercream Icing, p. 112
Also: 2006 Pattern Book (Ponytail), p. 124; 13 x 19 in. Cake Board, Fanci-Foil Wrap, p. 169; Gum-Tex®, p. 130; Disposable Decorating Bags, p. 137; sugar cone, cornstarch, sharp knife, ruler, pizza cutter, scissors

In advance: Make ponytail (p. 120). Trim off backpack area and slightly trim down waist on *Dora* cake. Ice cake smooth. Using tip 3, outline *Dora*, outline and pipe in eyes, pupils, irises, mouth and tongue; smooth with finger dipped in cornstarch. Add tip 2 dot eye highlight. Cover *Dora's* face, neck and hair with tip 16 stars.

Add Lemon Yellow color to 18 oz. yellow fondant for yellow shade shown; roll out white and yellow fondant ⅛ in. thick. Follow pan dimensions to cut and position yellow fondant sleeves. Cut white triangle for center bodice with white scalloped ruffle at top edge, trim yellow fondant to form bodice areas. Shape and attach shoulder puffs with damp brush. Tint a 1 in. yellow fondant ball with Golden Yellow; roll five ¼ in. balls for bracelet and attach with damp brush.

Tint a 1 in. yellow fondant ball with Leaf Green. Roll six ¼ in. balls for necklace and a small strip for ring; position. For folds in skirt, roll five 1 x 6 in. white fondant logs; taper at one end and position 3 on body and 1 on each side, with narrower end at top. Cut a 12 x 6 in. yellow piece for dress and position; trim to fit. Taper top 12 in. edge for waist. Shape skirt over logs with fingers. Cut ⅛ in. wide yellow strips and position in lattice fashion in open bodice area.

Tint 1½ oz. portions of white fondant red, dark pink, violet and light violet. Roll out ⅛ in. thick; cut 12 in. strips in various widths and attach for hem with damp brush. For hat, moisten sugar cone with water and trim off back side with scissors. Cover cone with yellow fondant and position hat. Attach light violet strip with damp brush. For flower, roll ¼ in. dark pink balls; flatten and attach with damp brush. For bottom border, roll ⅜ in. white fondant balls; attach with damp brush. Position ponytail. Serves 12.

◀ Cowgirl *Dora*

Pans: *Dora the Explorer*, p. 179; Cooling Grid, Cookie Sheet, p. 217
Tips: 3, 8, 16, p. 138-139
Colors:* *Dora the Explorer* Icing Color Set (red, pink, brown, skin tone), p. 179; Royal Blue, Sky Blue, Violet, Orange, Black, Lemon Yellow, p. 133
Recipes: Royal and Buttercream Icings, Roll-Out Cookie, p. 112
Also: 2006 Pattern Book (Cowgirl Hat, Boots), p. 124; Meringue Powder, p. 132; Cake Boards, Fanci-Foil Wrap, p. 169; Rolling Pin, p. 130; cornstarch

Cut out hat and boot cookies using patterns. Bake and cool. Decorate cookies using royal icing. Outline shoes with tip 3; pipe in with thinned royal icing. Outline hat with tip 3. Cover hat with tip 16 stars.

Trim down left hand from *Dora* cake. Ice cake sides and background areas smooth in buttercream. Using tip 3, outline *Dora*; outline and pipe in eyes, pupils, irises, mouth and bracelet; smooth with finger dipped in cornstarch. Add tip 3 dot eye highlight. Cover *Dora* and clothes with tip 16 stars. Pipe tip 3 dot flower over bracelet. Position cookie hat and shoes. Build up left hand, outline with tip 3 and overpipe tip 16 star fingers slightly over hat. Cover tops of shoes with tip 16 stars. Pipe tip 8 ball bottom border. Serves 12.

*Note: Combine Skin Tone with a little Brown and Orange for tan shown; combine Royal Blue with Sky Blue for blue flower shown.

◀ His Biggest Bone-anza!

Pans: *Scooby-Doo!*, p. 180; Cookie Sheet, Cooling Grid, p. 217

Tips: 2, 3, 16, 21, p. 138-139

Colors:* Brown, Red-Red, Christmas Red, Teal, Leaf Green, Lemon Yellow, Violet, Rose, Creamy Peach, p. 133

Recipes: Buttercream and Color Flow Icings, Roll-Out Cookie, p. 112

Also: 2006 Pattern Book (Gift Box, Lid), p. 124; 101 Cookie Cutters Set, p. 216; Color Flow Mix, p. 132; 13 x 19 in. Cake Boards, Fanci-Foil Wrap, p. 169; curling ribbon in blue, pink, yellow (18 in. each color), large marshmallows, cornstarch

In advance: Make cookies. Cut 6 dog bone cookies using cutter from set; cut 1 cookie in half. Cut gift box and lid cookies using patterns. Bake and cool all cookies. Outline and flow in bone cookies using color flow (p. 120) and tip 2. Place gift box and lid cookies on cooling grid over cookie sheet and cover with color flow (leave bow area of lid uncovered). Let dry overnight. Pipe in lid bow area and ribbon with tip 3 and full-strength color flow. Let dry.

Trim hamburger and upper paw areas off cake. Ice cake sides and background areas smooth. Outline body, facial features, collar and dog tag with tip 3. Pipe in inside ears, nose, inside mouth, tongue, whites of eyes, dog tag ring and dog tag with tip 3 (smooth with finger dipped in cornstarch). Outline and pipe in letters on dog tag with tip 2 (smooth with finger dipped in cornstarch). Cover fur, spots and collar with tip 16 stars. Add tip 21 star bottom border. Position cookie package on cake; tuck ½ bone cookie under package. Randomly position dog bone and lid cookies, propping some on marshmallows. Curl ribbon and position around cookies. Cake serves 12; each cookie serves 1.

*Note: Combine Brown with a little Red-Red for brown shown. Combine Leaf Green and Lemon Yellow for green shown. Combine Violet with Rose for violet shown.

▶ *Scooby-Doo!* Stands Guard!

Pan: Standard Muffin, p. 149

Tips: 3, 4, 6, p. 138

Colors:* Lemon Yellow, Golden Yellow, Leaf Green, Orange, Violet, Rose, p. 133

Recipe: Buttercream Icing, p. 112

Also: Cupcakes 'N More Standard Dessert Stand, p. 143; *Scooby-Doo!* Party Toppers (4 pks. needed), p. 180; *Scooby-Doo!* Baking Cups, p. 181; Angled Spatula, Disposable Decorating Bags, p. 137, cornstarch

Ice cupcakes smooth. Pipe various designs: tip 3 or tip 6 swirls, tip 4 dots (flatten and smooth with finger dipped in cornstarch), wavy lines and outline and pipe-in flowers and flower centers (smooth with spatula). Place cupcakes on stand; position toppers. Each serves 1.

*Note: Combine Lemon Yellow and Golden Yellow for yellow shown. Combine Leaf Green and Lemon Yellow for green shown. Combine Orange and Golden Yellow for orange shown. Combine Violet with a little Rose for violet shown. Combine Rose with a little Violet for rose shown.

SCOOBY-DOO and all related characters and elements are trademarks of and © Hanna-Barbera. (s05)

◀ It's *Scooby*-delic!

Pans: 8 x 3 in. Round, p. 147; *Scooby-Doo!* Mini Treats Cake Pan, p. 180

Tips: 13, 16, p. 139

Colors:* Orange, Rose, Royal Blue, Lemon Yellow, Golden Yellow, Leaf Green, Violet, p. 133

Candy: Candy Melts®† in White, Light Cocoa, p. 218; Primary and Garden Candy Color Sets, Decorator Brush Set, p. 219

Recipe: Buttercream Icing, p. 112

Also: Flower Cut-Outs™, p. 128; 10 in. Cake Circles, Fanci-Foil Wrap, p. 169

In advance: Make a *Scooby-Doo!* candy plaque (p. 121) in Mini Treats Pan. Tint portions of melted white candy blue, yellow, pink and black using candy colors; mold plaque using painting method (p. 121); refrigerate until firm and unmold.

Position 2-layer cake on foil-wrapped board; ice smooth. Using largest Cut-Out, imprint flowers on cake top and sides. Cover flowers with tip 13 stars, beginning at flower centers and working to edges. Pipe tip 16 zigzag garland on cake board. Position candy plaque on cake top. Serves 20.

*Note: Combine Leaf Green and Lemon Yellow for green shown.

† Brand confectionery coating.

SCOOBY-DOO!™

◄ *Scooby's* Square Meal

Pans: 8 x 3 in. Square, p. 147; *Scooby-Doo!* Mini Treats Cake Pan, p. 180
Colors:* Violet, Royal Blue, Leaf Green, Lemon Yellow, p. 133
Fondant: White Ready-To-Use Rolled Fondant (72 oz. needed), p. 126; Cut-Outs™ in Oval, Alphabet/Number shapes, p. 128; Brush Set, p. 129; Rolling Pin, Roll & Cut Mat, p. 130; Cutter/Embosser, Easy-Glide Fondant Smoother, p. 131
Candy: Candy Melts®† in White, Light Cocoa, p. 218; Primary, Garden Candy Color Sets, p. 219
Recipe: Buttercream Icing, p. 112
Also: Cake Boards, Fanci-Foil Wrap, p. 169; Piping Gel, p. 132

In advance: Make a *Scooby-Doo!* candy plaque (p. 121) in Mini Treats Pan. Tint portions of melted white candy blue, yellow, pink and black using candy colors; mold plaque using painting method (p. 121); refrigerate until firm and unmold.

Tint 20 oz. fondant light blue and 28 oz. green. Tint 12 oz. light violet, 6 oz. dark violet and 3 oz. each dark blue and yellow. Spread a thin layer of Piping Gel on an 11 in. square cake board; cover board with light blue fondant and smooth with Fondant Smoother. On covered board, prepare 2-layer cake for rolled fondant (p. 111); cover with green fondant and smooth. Roll out dark blue fondant ⅛ in. thick. Cut approximately 28 ovals using medium Cut-Out; cut out centers using small oval Cut-Out. Attach to board with damp brush. Roll out light violet fondant ⅛ in. thick and cut a 6½ in. square. Roll out dark violet fondant ¹⁄₁₆ in. thick; cut into ⅜ x 7 in. strips using wavy-edge wheel of Cutter/Embosser. Brush backs lightly with water and position strips about 1 in. apart on light violet square; roll out until smooth. Cut into a 6½ in. square; attach to cake top with damp brush. Roll out yellow fondant ⅛ in. thick; cut message using alphabet Cut-Outs. Position candy plaque and message on cake top. Serves 20.

***Note:** Combine Leaf Green and Lemon Yellow for green shown.

◄ The Man with a Crayon

Pan: 9 x 13 x 2 in. Sheet, p. 148
Tips: 3, 16, 18, p. 138-139
Colors: Kelly Green, Royal Blue, Lemon Yellow, Red-Red, p. 133
Fondant: White Ready-To-Use Rolled Fondant (24 oz. needed), p. 126; Bold Tip Primary Colors FoodWriter™ Edible Color Markers, p. 129; Rolling Pin, Roll & Cut Mat, p. 130
Recipe: Buttercream Icing, p. 112
Also: 101 Cookie Cutters Set, p. 216; Icing Sculptor™, p. 136; Cake Board, Fanci-Foil Wrap, p. 169; Crayons Candles, p. 188; *Elmo* with Crayons Candle, p. 181; cornstarch

In advance: Make fondant name and cake side decorations. Roll out fondant ⅛ in. thick; cut out 16 stars using smallest star cutter, 16 circles using the centers from the letter "O" cutter, and name using other letter cutters. Let set on cornstarch-dusted surface, at least 2 hours. Using FoodWriter markers, outline and zigzag fill in letters, outline and color in stars, and add swirls to circles. Set aside.

Ice 1-layer cake smooth in buttercream, icing sides about ½ in. thick. Immediately comb sides with pale pink (W-shaped) blades from Icing Sculptor. Pipe tip 3 e-motion on inside border of cake top; add tip 3 message. Position fondant name. Pipe tip 18 shell bottom border; attach fondant stars and circles with dots of icing. Pipe tip 16 rosettes on cake top and insert crayon candles. Position *Elmo* candle. Serves 22.

► *Elmo* Electricity!

Pan: Standard Muffin, p. 149
Tip: 3, p. 138
Colors: Red-Red, Royal Blue, Kelly Green, Lemon Yellow, p. 133
Recipe: Buttercream Icing, p. 112
Also: *Elmo* Icing Decorations, *Elmo* Baking Cups, p. 181

Ice cupcakes smooth. Pipe tip 3 e-motion around top edge of cupcakes. Position icing decorations. Each serves 1.

▼ *Barbie*™ Has Blossomed

Pans: Ring Mold, p. 148; Cookie Sheet, Cooling Grid, p. 217
Tips: 2, 3, 6, 190, 224, 352, p. 138-139
Colors*: *Barbie*™ Icing Color Set (pink, yellow, violet) , p. 176;
Creamy Peach, Leaf Green, Lemon Yellow, p. 133
Recipes: Buttercream and Royal Icings, Roll-Out Cookie, p. 112
Also: *Barbie*™ Candle, p. 176; Daisy and Flower Cut-Outs™,
p. 128; White Candy Melts®† (1 pk.), p. 218; Meringue Powder,
p. 132; Cake Board, Fanci-Foil Wrap, p. 169; Parchment
Triangles, p. 137; Wooden Dowel Rods, p. 167; 18-gauge
green cloth-covered florist wire (18 needed, 18 in. long),
light pink curling ribbon (10 yds.), 2 x 3¾ in. diameter craft
block, ruler, toothpicks

In advance: Make cookie flower bouquet using Cut-Outs
(p. 117). Make drop flowers using royal icing in peach,
violet, pink and yellow. Make 24 tip 190 drop flowers, 6 in
each color, with tip 3 white dot centers. Make 72 tip 224
drop flowers, 18 in each color, with tip 2 white dot centers.
Make extras of each to allow for breakage and let dry.

Ice cake smooth. Mark 2 in. wide divisions on top and
bottom of cake sides with toothpick. Pipe 3 tip 3 vertical lines
at division points. Add tip 3 bead top and tip 6 bead bottom
borders. Attach drop flowers with tip 3 dots of icing. Pipe tip 3
C-motion curls above flowers; add tip 352 leaves. Wrap craft
block with foil and position in center of cake. Insert cookies on
wires at staggered lengths into craft block. Wrap some single

▼ Springtime *Barbie*™

Pan: *Barbie*™, p. 176
Tips: 1, 2, 4, 6, 67, 349, p. 138-139
Colors:* Royal Blue, Orange, Violet, Rose,
Leaf Green, Lemon Yellow, Golden
Yellow, p. 133
Recipe: Buttercream Icing, p. 112
Also: Cake Board, Fanci-Foil Wrap,
p. 169

Trim flower background areas on
top section of cake to level. Ice
cake smooth. Position facemaker
(included with pan) on cake. Pipe tip 2 curving vines and swirl
tendrils on skirt. Pipe tip 4 teardrop flowers with tip 2 dot
centers. Add tip 67 leaves on vines. Pipe tip 4 zigzag butterfly
wings, tip 2 outline bodies and tip 1 pull-out string antennas.
Pipe a cluster of tip 4 teardrop flowers in hands; add tip 2
pull-out stems and tip 349 leaves. Add tip 6 bead bottom
border. Serves 12.

*Note: Combine Leaf Green and Lemon Yellow for green shown.
Combine Lemon Yellow and Golden Yellow for yellow shown.

18 in. wires around wooden dowel rods to form tight spirals;
twist other wires into large spirals by hand, cut as needed
and insert in craft block. Curl ribbon and place around base of
cookies. Position candle. Cake serves 18; each cookie serves 1.

*Note: Combine Leaf Green and Lemon Yellow for green shown.

† Brand confectionery coating.

◀ Sunny *Strawberry* Day

Pans: *Strawberry Shortcake™*, p. 175; Mini Loaf, Cooling Grid, p. 149

Tips: 1, 2, 3, 4, 5, 10, 16, 67, 352, p. 138-139

Colors: *Strawberry Shortcake™* Color Set (red, brown, green, skin tone), p. 175; Lemon Yellow and Golden Yellow, Orange, Royal Blue, Kelly Green, Rose, Violet, p. 133

Recipes: Buttercream, Royal and Color Flow Icings, Roll-Out Cookie, p. 112; favorite pound cake recipe (for mini loaves)

Also: 2006 Pattern Book (Cloud, Sun), p. 124; Cake Boards, Fanci-Foil Wrap, p. 169; 4 in. Lollipop Sticks, p. 221; Meringue Powder, Color Flow Mix, p. 132; Parchment Triangles, p. 137; Decorator Brush Set, p. 219; craft block, cornstarch

In advance: Prepare flowers and cookies. Roll out dough, cut out sun and cloud cookies using patterns, bake and cool. Outline and flow in cookies using color flow (p. 120). Let dry overnight. Outline and pipe in facial features on sun using tip 2; add tip 3 cheeks. Using royal icing and tips 1, 3, 4, 5 and 10, make 3 tulips, 2 spiral flowers, 5 swirl flowers, 2 ice cream flowers and 17 various size dot flowers (p. 117). Make extras to allow for breakage; let dry. Make 11 stems using lollipop sticks. Paint sticks with thinned royal icing; insert ends in craft block to dry. Attach 3 tulips and 2 each spiral flowers, swirl flowers, ice cream flowers and dot flowers to stems using royal icing. Let dry.

Bake *Strawberry Shortcake* and 6 mini loaves. Cut cake board to fit Strawberry Shortcake plus loaves stacked 2 cakes high x 3 wide. Trim loaves to 1 in. high, stack. Position all cakes on board. Using tip 3, outline face and facial features, hands, neck, shirt, hat and bow; pipe in eyes. Add tip 1 dot eye highlights. Pipe in tip 3 bow (smooth with finger dipped in cornstarch), collar, lines on bow and shirt. Cover face, neck, hands, hat and strawberry on bow with tip 16 stars. Add tip 2 dots on strawberry and tip 67 pull-out leaves. Pipe tip 3 dot nose. Pipe tip 16 pull-out star hair. Insert flowers on sticks into cake. Attach remaining flowers using dots of buttercream. Using royal icing, pipe tip 352 leaves on stick flowers. Using buttercream, pipe tip 352 leaves on cake flowers. Pipe tip 352 leaf bottom border in buttercream, attach flowers. Add tip 4 message. Position cookies. Cake serves 18; each cookie serves 1.

*Note: Combine Lemon Yellow and Golden Yellow for yellow shown. Combine *Strawberry Shortcake* Green with a little Kelly Green for green shown on cakes and lollipop stick stems.

Strawberry Shortcake™
©2005 Those Characters From Cleveland, Inc.
Used under license by Wilton Industries, Inc.

▼ Visit the *Shortcake* Estate

Pans: Oval Set, 6, 8 x 2 in. Round, p. 148

Tips: 2, 3, p. 138

Colors: Rose, Lemon Yellow, Golden Yellow, Violet, Leaf Green, Royal Blue, Red-Red, Christmas Red, p. 133

Fondant: White Ready-To-Use Rolled Fondant (144 oz. needed), p. 126; Fine Tip Primary Colors FoodWriter™ Edible Color Markers, p. 129; Rolling Pin, Roll & Cut Mat, p. 130; Easy-Glide Fondant Smoother, p. 131

Candy: *Strawberry Shortcake™* Lollipop Making Kit (includes molds, red, white, blue Candy Melts®†, disposable decorating bags, decorating brush, 6 in. lollipop sticks), p. 175; White Candy Melts®† (1 pk. additional needed), p. 218; Primary and Garden Candy Color Sets, p. 219

Recipe: Buttercream Icing, p. 112

Also: 2006 Pattern Book (Door, Bottom Tier Window, Middle Tier Window, Top Tier Dormer), p. 124; Parchment Triangles, p. 137; Cake Boards, Fanci-Foil Wrap, p. 169; 6 in. Lollipop Sticks (1 pk. additional needed), p. 221; Confectionery Tool Set, p. 131; 101 Cookie Cutters Set, p. 216; Cake Dividing Set, p. 136, Plastic Dowel Rods, p. 167; paring knife, craft block, scissors

In advance: Mold candies (p. 121). Tint white fondant: 38 oz. yellow, 36 oz. rose, 24 oz. green, 17 oz. violet, 4 oz. red, 3 oz. royal blue; reserve 4 oz. white. Make fondant sundaes and pinwheels on lollipop sticks (p. 118).

Bake and cool 1-layer 13½ x 9⅞ oval (1 in. deep), 2-layer 8 in. round (4 in. deep) and two 6 in. rounds (2 in. deep). Using largest round cutter from set as a pattern, cut a circle from one 6 in. round cake with paring knife. Prepare cakes for stacked construction (p. 110) and position on double-thick foil-wrapped boards. Prepare for rolled fondant (p. 111); cover oval with green and remaining cakes with yellow fondant. Smooth with Fondant Smoother. After cutting fondant decorations, attach with damp brush. Roll out rose fondant ¼ in. thick; cut into scalloped circles 1½ in. larger than cake tops and attach to cake tops for dripping icing effect. Divide 0 in. cake into 0ths. For swags, roll out rose fondant ⅛ in. thick; cut 3½ x 1⅝ in. rectangles and gather ends into pleats. Taper ends with scissors. Attach at division points. Roll ¾ in. diameter red balls and attach at division points. For front door, roll out white fondant ⅛ in. thick; cut door using pattern and attach. Cut another door using blue fondant and using pattern, cut frame pieces; attach. Pipe tip 2 lattice. Roll and attach ⅛ in. blue balls for doorknobs. Cut 2 bottom tier windows using pattern and blue fondant rolled ⅛ in. thick; attach. Pipe tip 3 string frame and windowpanes. For 6 in. cake, cut 8 middle tier windows using pattern and violet fondant rolled ⅞ in. thick; attach. Cut window insets using middle tier window pattern and blue fondant rolled ⅛ in. thick; attach. For window arches, roll ¼ in. diameter violet logs; attach. Pipe tip 3 string windowpanes. Roll ⅝ in. diameter red balls and attach between windows. For small top cake, cut 2 dormers using pattern and yellow fondant rolled ¾ in. thick; attach. For dormer roofs, roll out violet fondant ⅛ in. thick; cut 2 x 1 in. rectangles and attach. Trim eaves with ¼ in. diameter violet fondant logs. Using pattern and blue fondant rolled ⅛ in. thick, cut dormer window area; attach. For rectangle window, roll out white fondant ⅛ in. thick; cut a 2 x ⅞ in. rectangle and attach. Pipe tip 3 string window panes.

For front steps, roll out violet fondant ¼ in. thick. Cut 2¾ x 1 in. rectangle for top stair and 3 x ½ in. rectangle for bottom stair. For side steps, roll out violet fondant ⁷⁄₁₆ in. thick. Cut two 3 x ⅝ in. rectangles; attach. For step fronts, roll ¼ in. diameter violet and white ropes; twist together and cut to 3 in. long; attach. For sidewalk, roll out yellow fondant ⅛ in. thick; cut 3 x 2 in. rectangle and attach with damp brush. For sidewalk border, roll out yellow fondant ⅛ in. thick; cut ⅜ x 2 in. long strips and attach. For stones on border, roll ¼ in. diameter rose balls, slightly flatten and attach. For stones on steps, roll ¾ in. diameter rose balls; attach. For bushes, roll green balls from 1 to 1½ in. diameter; indent with ball tool and attach. Cut lollipop sticks to staggered lengths and insert candies, sundaes, and pinwheel disks in cake. Cake serves 48; each candy serves 1.

*Note: Combine Lemon Yellow with a little Golden Yellow for yellow shown. Combine Rose with a little Lemon Yellow for rose shown. Combine Leaf Green with a little Lemon Yellow for green shown. Combine Violet with a little Rose for violet shown. Combine Red-Red with Christmas Red for red shown.

▼ Hang Ten With *SpongeBob*

Pan: *SpongeBob SquarePants™*, p. 178
Tips: 2, 3, 4, 6, 16, 21, p. 138-139
Colors: *SpongeBob SquarePants* Icing Color Set (yellow, red, blue, brown), p. 178; Black, Red-Red, Royal Blue, p. 133
Fondant: White Ready-To-Use Rolled Fondant (24 oz. needed), p. 126; Brush Set, p. 129; Rolling Pin, Roll & Cut Mat, p. 130; Cutter/Embosser, p. 131
Recipes: Buttercream, Royal Icings, p. 112
Also: 2006 Pattern Book (Surfboard Body and Surfboard Bottom Tip, Surfboard Fin, Fingers), p. 124; 13 x 19 in. Cake Board, Fanci-Foil Wrap, p. 169; Gum-Tex™, p. 130; Meringue Powder, p. 132; 11¾ in. Lollipop Sticks, p. 221; marshmallows, cornstarch, craft knife

At least 3 days in advance: Make fondant surfboard. Knead ½ teaspoon Gum-Tex into 7 oz. of fondant. Tint 5 oz. of fondant brown and 2 oz. red. Roll out brown fondant ¼ in. thick and use pattern to cut surfboard body and fin. Roll out red fondant ⅛ in. thick and cut ⅞ in. wide strip to length of surfboard body; attach with damp brush. Reserve remaining brown and red fondant. Let dry 48 hours on cornstarch-dusted surface. When completely dry, position pattern on surfboard body and trace flower patterns with craft knife. Outline flowers with royal icing and tip 2; pipe in with tip 3 and thinned royal icing; let dry. Using pattern, trace finger area on surfboard with knife. Pipe fingers with tip 6. Outline fingers with tip 3, fill in with tip 16 stars. Attach 2 lollipop sticks to back of surfboard body with royal icing.

Trim off necktie, right arm and heel areas from cake. Ice sides and background areas smooth. Using buttercream, outline *SpongeBob*, spots, facial features, arm, hand, trunks, legs and feet with tip 3; outline tongue with tip 4. Pipe in tip 3 spots, eyes, irises, pupils, inside of mouth, teeth, cuff on sleeve; pipe in tongue with tip 4 (smooth all with finger dipped in cornstarch). Cover head, trunks, legs, arm and sleeve with tip 16 stars. Pipe tip 3 drawstring bow on trunks and string eyelashes. Roll out reserved brown and red fondant ⅛ in. thick. Using pattern, cut surfboard tip in brown and a ⅞ in. wide red strip to fit. Attach strip with damp brush. Outline flowers with royal icing and tip 2; pipe in using tip 3 and thinned royal icing. Pipe tip 21 C-motion bottom border. Insert surfboard body into cake side; position surfboard tip behind right leg and fin under surfboard; support surfboard body with marshmallows. Serves 12.

Stephen Hillenburg

▲ *SpongeBob* Takes the Field

Pans: *SpongeBob SquarePants™*, p. 178; Mini Ball, p. 153; Cookie Sheet, Cooling Grid, p. 217
Tips: 2, 3, 12, 16, p. 138-139
Colors: *SpongeBob SquarePants™* Icing Color Set (blue, red, yellow, brown), p. 178; Terra Cotta, Black, p. 133
Recipes: Buttercream Icing, Roll-Out Cookie, p. 112
Also: 2006 Pattern Book (Baseball Mitt), p. 124; Circle Metal Cutter, p. 214; Cake Board, Fanci-Foil Wrap, p. 169; paring knife, cornstarch

Roll out cookie dough; cut mitt using pattern and paring knife. Cut circle cookie. Bake and cool. Outline mitt with tip 3 and cover with tip 16 stars. Pipe tip 12 ball in mitt; add tip 2 stitching lines; set aside.

Ice cake sides and background areas smooth. Outline *SpongeBob*, sponge spots, facial features, hand, arms, shirt, pants, shoes, socks and spikes on shoes with tip 3. Pipe in tip 3 sponge spots, whites of eyes, irises, pupils, inside of mouth, tongue and teeth (smooth with finger dipped in cornstarch). Cover sponge, arms, hands, pants, shirt with tip 16 stars. Pipe tip 3 string eyelashes and dot freckles. For cap, trim off 1 in. from Mini Ball cake; pipe tip 3 lines and cover hat with tip 16 stars. For brim, cut circle cookie in half and ice smooth. Attach hat, brim and mitt with icing. Pipe tip 16 pull-out star grass bottom border. Cakes serve 13; cookie mitt serves 1.

SPIDER-MAN

◄ *Spidey's* City

Pans: *Spider-Man*, p. 177; 12 x 2 in. Square, p. 148

Tips: 3, 6, 21, p. 138-139

Colors: Royal Blue, Black, p. 133

Candy: Candy Melts®† in White (3 pks. needed) and Red (1 pk. needed), p. 218; Garden, Primary Candy Color Sets, Decorator Brush Set, p. 219

Recipe: Buttercream Icing, p. 112

Also: 2006 Pattern Book (Buildings), p. 124; Plastic Dowel Rods, p. 167; Cake Boards, Fanci-Foil Wrap, p. 169; Parchment Triangles, p. 137; freezer paper, sharp knife

In advance: Make *Spider-Man* and Building candy plaques (p. 121). For *Spider-Man*, tint 3½ oz. melted white candy each in black and dark blue using candy colors. Paint white eyes and blue area of suit; refrigerate until firm. Fill in remaining areas using 14 oz. melted red candy; refrigerate until firm and unmold onto board cut to fit. Using melted black candy in cut parchment bag, pipe black suit and mask lines; refrigerate until firm. For buildings, melt 35 oz. of white candy. Tint ½ cup medium blue using candy color. Divide remaining melted candy in 3rds and tint yellow, orange and violet. Place patterns on cake board and cover with freezer paper, shiny side up. Using melted candy in cut parchment bags, outline and flow in each building. Refrigerate until firm and turn over, trimming with knife as needed. Tint remaining violet candy with additional violet color for darker shade. Outline edges of buildings and pipe string windows with melted candy in cut bag; refrigerate until firm.

Ice smooth 1-layer square cake (2 in. high) in light blue. Add tip 21 star bottom border. Position buildings on cake, securing with buttercream. Cut dowel rods to 3 in. long and insert in cake to support *Spider-Man* plaque. Position *Spider-Man*. In buttercream, pipe tip 3 string web and strand; add tip 6 name. Serves 24.

† Brand confectionery coating.

▼ Patrick's Grand Opening

Pan: Petite Loaf, p. 149; Cookie Sheet, Cooling Grid, p. 217

Candy: *SpongeBob SquarePants* Lollipop Making Kit (includes mold, yellow, pink and white Candy Melts®†, disposable bags), p. 178; Primary and Garden Candy Color Sets, p. 219; White Candy Melts® (1 pk. additional needed), p. 218

Also: waxed paper, marshmallow

Using candy colors, tint portions of white candy blue, violet, red and black. Combine yellow candy from kit with a portion of white for yellow shown. For green, combine yellow candy mixture with a little green candy color. For pink body, use pink candy from kit and add a little pink candy color. Mold candy plaques (p. 121) ¼ in. deep in pan cavities. Mold Patrick without stick following kit directions. For gift, trim marshmallow into a square using scissors. Cover with blue candy (p. 120); refrigerate until firm. For wrapping paper, make a pattern using a narrow strip of waxed paper cut same height as the marshmallow square and long enough to wrap around. Cut a jagged edge on one side. Spread pattern with a thin coat of violet candy, let partially set, and wrap around the marshmallow, paper side out. Refrigerate until firm. Carefully peel away waxed paper and trim excess candy if necessary. Attach Patrick and gift to plaque using

dots of melted candy. Pipe red ribbon strings. Make torn paper by piping a violet candy dot on waxed paper. Using a toothpick, pull out points from center of dot, chill to set. Attach torn paper to Patrick's hand using dot of melted candy. Each serves 1.

▶ Web Surfing *Spidey*

Pan: Standard Muffin, p. 149

Tip: 4, p. 138

Color: Black, p. 133

Recipes: Buttercream and Royal Icings, p. 112

Also: 2006 Pattern Book (Web), p. 124; Cupcakes 'N More™ Standard Dessert Stand, p. 143; Flower Former Set, p. 131; *Spider-Man™* Standard Baking Cups, Party Toppers (4 pks. needed), p. 177; Meringue Powder, p. 132

At least 24 hours in advance: Make 13 webs. Tape patterns to outside of large Flower Formers, cover in waxed paper. Outline with tip 4 and royal icing. Make 4 full webs; make 9 webs without bottom web line. Make extras to allow for breakage and let dry.

Ice cupcakes smooth and position on stand. Position full webs on 3rd tier from top; position partial webs on 2nd and 4th tiers. Position toppers. Each cupcake serves 1.

◀ **Birthday Hugs from *Mickey***

Pans: *Mickey* Face, p. 183; Classic Wonder Mold, p. 150; Mini Egg, p. 204; 9, 14 x 2 in. Round, p. 147; Non-Stick Cookie Sheet, Cooling Grid, p. 217

Tips: 3, 5, 12, 16, 20, p. 138-139

Colors: *Mickey* Icing Color Set {black, *Mickey* peach, copper (skin tone)}, p. 183; Lemon Yellow, Red-Red, p. 133

Candy: White Candy Melts®†, (4 pks. needed), p. 218; Primary Candy Color Set, p. 219; 4 in., 11¾ in. Lollipop Sticks, p. 221

Fondant: White Ready-To-Use Rolled Fondant (24 oz. needed), Primary Fondant Multi Pack, p. 126; Round Cut-Outs™, p. 128; Cutter/Embosser, p. 131; Rolling Pin, Roll & Cut Mat, p. 130

Recipes: Buttercream, Royal Icings, Roll-Out Cookie, p. 112

Also: 2006 Pattern Book (Hands, Shoe Support), p. 124; 16 in. Tall Tier Plate, Glue-On Legs (6 needed), 7¾ in. Columns (2 needed) from Tall Tier Cake Stand Set, p. 164; Plastic, Wooden Dowel Rods, p. 167; Cake Circles, p. 169; Parchment Triangles, p. 137; Meringue Powder, p. 132; Cake Corer, p. 164; balloons, glue gun, cornstarch, toothpicks, cellophane tape

In advance: Make *Mickey* candy plaque (p. 121). Using patterns, make cookie hands. For hand holding balloons, reverse pattern, cut dough; position wooden dowel rod in palm and fold over fingers about 2½ in. Bake; immediately remove dowel rod and let cool. Cover cookies with thinned royal icing (p. 120); let dry. Outline hands with tip 3 and royal icing.

Bake and cool Wonder Mold cake and 1-layer 9 in. round cake (both using firm-textured batter such as pound cake) plus 2-layer 14 in. round cake and 2 mini egg cakes. Prepare cake boards for center column opening and 16 in. tall tier plate by gluing on legs. Center core for Wonder Mold cake will be cut slightly off center, toward front of cake to allow dowel rod arms to be inserted toward back of body; cut cake board accordingly. Prepare Wonder Mold cake and 9 in. and 14 in. round cakes for center column and stacked construction (p. 110). Line up hole in cake board with core in Wonder Mold cake. Insert a wooden dowel rod horizontally behind center column core to support arms. For arms, cut 2 plastic dowel rods to 7 in. long; insert 2 in. of each rod into cake, positioning over wooden dowel rod. Attach cookie hands to dowel rods with melted candy.

Ice round cake smooth; position on cake plate along with center columns. For body, position 9 in. cake, then Wonder Mold cake over columns. Mark shorts and button areas on Wonder Mold cake with toothpick. Cover body, arms, and shorts with tip 16 stars. Pipe in buttons with tip 5 (smooth with finger dipped in cornstarch). Cut shoe supports from cake board using pattern; wrap with foil and insert into base of round cake. For shoes, position mini egg cakes; cover with tip 20 stars, filling in gap between back of shoes and 14 in. round cake. For legs, tint 9 oz. of fondant black; roll two 1 x 6 in. logs.

For leg openings, roll out red fondant ½ in. thick; cut 2 circles using largest round Cut-Out. Trim ¼ in. from bottom and position on cake top. Position legs; trim to fit. Cover leg openings with tip 16 stars. Cover ankles with tip 20 stars; overpipe for dimension. For balloons on cake, roll out fondant colors ⅛ in. thick; cut circles using medium round Cut-Out and position. Pipe tip 12 ball bottom border. Cut ⅛ in. wide fondant balloon strings; position. Attach head to column with melted candy. Tape balloons to 11¾ in. stick; insert in hand. Serves 89, each cookie serves 1.

▶ **Can't Miss *Mickey!***

Pans: Cupcake, p. 151; Standard Muffin, p. 149

Tips: 2A, 3, 8, 352, p. 138-139

Colors:* Red-Red, Christmas Red, Royal Blue, Kelly Green, Lemon Yellow, Golden Yellow, Orange, p. 133

Recipe: Buttercream Icing, p. 112

Also: *Mickey Mouse* Candle, Icing Decorations (2 pks. needed), Standard Baking Cups, p. 183; White Candy Melts®†, p. 218; 6 in. Cookie Treat Sticks, p. 217; Flowerful Medley Sprinkles Decorations, p. 134; Cake Board, Fanci-Foil Wrap, p. 169; black shoestring licorice, waxed paper

A day in advance: Make arms. Cut two 1 in. lengths of licorice for each cupcake. Position on waxed paper-covered cake board. Using buttercream and tip 3, pipe a ball on one end of each licorice piece; add tip 3 bead fingers and thumb. Let set.

Ice cupcakes smooth. For bursting effect, pipe tip 352 pull-out leaves in an oval pattern. Insert licorice arms and position icing decoration in oval area.

For large cake, bake, cool and level 2 cakes using firm-textured batter such as pound cake (two 18.25 oz. mixes per cake recommended). Place one cake back into pan. Melt candy; cover back of cake with ¾ package of melted candy. Position the 2nd cake on top so backs meet. For support, insert 2 cookie sticks, angled from top to bottom of cakes to form an "x" at upper half of cake. Refrigerate 30-45 minutes until firm. Unmold cake from pan. Level bottom and attach upright to foil-wrapped board using remaining melted candy. Refrigerate until firm. Pipe tip 2A vertical stripes from bottom to top. Ice cake top fluffy; position confetti sprinkles. Pipe tip 8 message. Position candle and arrange cupcakes around main cake. Cake serves 24, each cupcake serves 1.

*****Note:** Combine Red-Red and Christmas Red for red shown. Combine Lemon Yellow and Golden Yellow for yellow shown.

† Brand confectionery coating.

©Disney

Disney **MICKEY MOUSE**

◀ Her Royal Ride

Pan: Mini Loaf, p. 149

Tips: 2, 3, 5, p. 138

Colors:* Rose, Violet, Royal Blue, Lemon Yellow, Golden Yellow, p. 133

Cookie: Round Comfort Grip™ Cutter, Circle Metal Cutter, p. 214, Cookie Sheet, Cooling Grid, p. 217

Recipes: Color Flow Icing, Roll-Out Cookie, p. 112

Also: White Candy Melts®†, p. 218; Garden Candy Color Set, p. 219; *Disney Princess* Party Toppers, p. 183; Color Flow Mix, p. 132; Rolling Pin, p. 130; waxed paper

In advance: Make candy plaque base (p. 121). Tint melted white candy pink using candy color; fill mini loaf cavities ¼ in. thick. Refrigerate until firm; unmold. Also in advance: Make cookies. Roll out dough. For coach, cut 1 cookie using Comfort Grip cutter; for wheels, cut 2 cookies using circle metal cutter. Bake and cool. Using full-strength color flow, outline wheels with tip 2 and coach with tip 3. Flow in areas with thinned color flow (p. 120); let set overnight.

Using full-strength color flow, pipe tip 2 swirl on wheels. Place coach cookie on waxed paper and pipe tip 5 fleur de lis against top of cookie; pipe in tip 2 curtains and let dry completely. Attach coach and wheel cookies to candy plaque base with melted candy; let set. Position topper. Each serves 1.

*****Note:** Combine Lemon Yellow and Golden Yellow for yellow shown. Combine Violet with a little Rose for violet shown.

©Disney

▶ *Princess* For A Day!

Pans: *Disney Princess*, p. 183; 12 x 18 x 2 in. Sheet, p. 148

Tips: 1, 2, 3, 4, 5, 12, 16, 44, 352, p. 138-139

Colors: *Disney Princess* Icing Color Set (blue, yellow, pink needed), p. 183; Violet, Black, Brown, p. 133

Fondant: White Ready-To-Use Rolled Fondant (48 oz. needed), p. 126; Cutter/Embosser, p. 131; Brush Set, p. 129; Rolling Pin, Roll & Cut Mat, p. 130;

Candy: White Candy Melts®† (2 pks. needed), p. 218; Primary Candy Color Set, p. 219

Recipes: Buttercream and Royal Icings, Color Flow Icing, p. 112

Also: 2006 Pattern Book (Crown, Swirl, Scallop), p. 124; *Disney Princess* Icing Decorations (2 pks. needed), p. 183; Color Flow Mix, Meringue Powder, p. 132; Parchment Triangles, Angled Spatula, p. 137; Fanci-Foil Wrap, p. 169; 14 x 20 in. cardboard or plywood sheet, plastic ruler, miniature marshmallows, waxed paper, cornstarch

Two days in advance: Make color flow crown and swirls (p. 120) using waxed paper-covered patterns. Let dry overnight. Carefully remove crown from waxed paper; turn over and pipe zigzags on back using full-strength color flow in cut parchment bag to reinforce; let dry. Make and decorate initial using royal icing. On waxed paper, pipe initial with tip 5; let set. Pipe a tip 44 band ribbon around initial in spiraling fashion; let dry. On waxed paper, pipe tip 4 bead flowers with tip 1 yellow dot centers; let dry. Attach flowers to initial and add tip 352 leaves; let dry.

One day in advance: Make candy plaque *Princess* (p. 121). Fill banner area of pan with melted white candy; refrigerate until firm. Tint remainder of candy light orange using candy color and pour into pan to form face and upper body; refrigerate until firm. Cut cardboard to fit exactly inside pan. Place cardboard directly on plaque and gently turn pan over to unmold, resting plaque on cardboard. Decorate plaque with royal icing. Use tip 3 to outline gloves, dress, sleeves, hair, headband and earring. Cover dress, sleeves and glove with tip 16 stars; pipe in tip 12 hair. Outline neckband and pipe in with tip 4 (smooth with finger dipped in cornstarch). Pipe in tip 3 headband and earring (smooth with finger dipped in cornstarch). Outline eyes, eyebrows and mouth with tip 2. Pipe in tip 2 eyes, mouth, teeth and lips. Add tip 1 dot eye highlights and string eyelashes; set aside.

Ice 2-layer sheet cake smooth (bake two 1½ in. layers to form a 3 in. high cake). Tint 24 oz. fondant pink, 8 oz. violet; reserve remainder white. Roll out violet fondant ⅛ in. thick; cut into ½ in. wide strips and position around top edges of cake, cutting corners at an angle to fit. Using pattern, cut 24 violet scallops and attach to cake sides with buttercream.

Roll out pink fondant ⅛ in. thick; cut four 1½ in. wide strips; position 1½ in. apart on cake top. For bottom border, roll ½ in. diameter pink fondant logs to fit each side and position around cake. Roll ⅛ in. diameter white fondant balls, flatten and attach with damp brush, ¾ in. apart on bottom border. Position candy plaque on cake; attach initial to banner and pipe tip 3 name with royal icing. Position crown on cake, supporting with mini marshmallows; position scrolls. Attach icing decorations to cake sides between scallops with buttercream icing. Pipe tip 2 outline stars on cake. Serves 72.

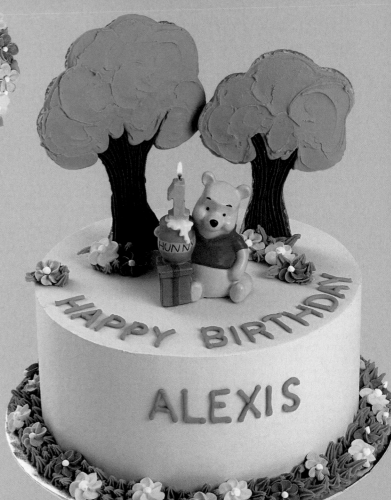

◀ A Gentleman Caller

Pan: *Pooh*, p. 182

Tips: 2, 3, 6, 16, 21, 101, 124, 349, 352, p. 138-139

Colors: *Pooh* Icing Color Set (*Pooh* gold, red, black needed), p. 182; Kelly Green, Lemon Yellow, Violet, Rose, p. 133

Recipes: Buttercream and Royal Icings, p. 112

Also: Cake Board, Fanci-Foil Wrap, p. 169; Flower Former Set, p. 131; Flower Nail No. 7, p. 137; Meringue Powder, p. 132; cornstarch

In advance: Make flowers using royal icing. Make 8 tip 124 wild roses (2 rose and 3 each yellow and violet) with tip 6 yellow dot centers (p. 116). Make extras to allow for breakage and let dry on medium flower formers. Make 60 tip 101 apple blossoms (20 each yellow, violet and rose) with tip 2 white dot centers. Make extras to allow for breakage and let dry on small flower formers.

Ice cake sides and background areas smooth. Outline *Pooh* and pipe in facial features with tip 3 (smooth nose and eyes with finger dipped in cornstarch). Cover *Pooh* and shirt with tip 16 stars. Position wild roses for bouquet and pipe tip 3 stems; add tip 352 leaves. Pipe tip 21 shell bottom border. Attach apple blossoms to border with dots of icing; add tip 349 leaves. Serves 12.

▶ *Pooh's* Park Party

Pans: 8 x 2 in. Round, p. 148; Cookie Sheet, Cooling Grid, p. 149

Tips: 3, 4, 16, 131, p. 138-139

Colors: Kelly Green, Brown, Rose, Violet, Lemon Yellow, p. 133

Recipes: Buttercream, Royal Icings, Roll-Out Cookie, p. 112

Also: 2006 Pattern Book (Large Tree and Small Tree), p. 124; *Pooh* #1 Hunny Pot Candle, p. 182; 8 in. Cookie Treat Sticks, p. 217; Meringue Powder, p. 132; Cake Board, Fanci-Foil Wrap, p. 169; waxed paper, paring knife, toothpick

In advance: Using royal icing, make 45 tip 131 drop flowers (15 each yellow, pink and violet) with tip 3 white dot centers. Make extras to allow for breakage and let dry. Roll out dough and trace tree patterns with toothpick; cut, bake and cool cookies. Using royal icing, pipe tip 16 trunk lines. Ice leaf areas fluffy with spatula; let set. Attach cookie sticks to backs of trees with royal icing, leaving 4 in. extended; let set.

Ice 2-layer cake smooth in buttercream. Insert trees. Pipe tip 16 pull-out star grass at bottom border and randomly on cake top; position flowers. Print tip 4 message; position candle. Cake serves 20; each cookie serves 1.

◀ Hunnysuckle Cookies

Cookie: Cookie Sheet, Cooling Grid, p. 149; Flower Plastic Cookie Cutter, p. 216; 8 in. Cookie Treat Sticks, p. 217

Colors: Rose, Violet, Orange, Lemon Yellow, p. 133

Recipes: Royal Icing, Roll-Out Cookie, p. 112

Also: *Pooh* Icing Decorations, p. 182; Parchment Triangles, p. 137; Meringue Powder, p. 132; Rolling Pin, p. 130

Cut, bake and cool cookies. Using thinned royal icing in cut parchment bag, pipe a 1½ in. diameter flower center; let set. Move cookies to cooling grid and cover petals with thinned royal icing (p. 120); let set. Attach cookie stick to back and icing decoration to front of cookie with full-strength royal icing. Each serves 1.

*Note: Combine Violet and a little Rose for violet shown.

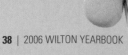

◄ Let *Pooh* Pile Up the Presents!

Pan: 8 x 2 in. Round, p. 148
Tip: 12, p. 138
Fondant: Fondant Multi Packs in Neon and Primary Colors, p. 126; Alphabet/Number Cut-Outs™, p. 128; Cutter/Embosser, p. 131; Brush Set, p. 129; Rolling Pin, Roll & Cut Mat, p. 130
Recipe: Buttercream Icing, p. 112
Also: *Pooh* and Presents Candle, p. 182; Cake Board, Fanci-Foil Wrap, p. 169; paring knife

Ice 2-layer cake smooth. Roll out fondant ⅛ in. thick. For balloons, use wide end of tip 12 to cut circles; randomly position on cake sides. For balloon strings, roll ⅛ in. diameter ropes of fondant and position. For party hats, use straight-edge wheel of Cutter/Embosser to cut various size triangles and position on cake sides. For hat brims, roll ⅛ in. diameter ropes and shape in a tight zigzag; attach with damp brush. For confetti, cut thin fondant strips into squares and attach. Roll ⅝ in. diameter fondant balls and position for bottom border.

For packages on cake top, shape various sizes of fondant balls; turn and flatten sides to form squares. For ribbons, roll fondant ⅛ in. thick and cut ¼ in. wide strips; attach with damp brush. For each bow, form two ⅜ in. fondant balls, flatten and shape into teardrops. For knot, make a ¼ in. ball; attach with damp brush. For name, roll out fondant ⅛ in. thick; cut letters with Cut-Outs. Position name, packages and candle. Serves 20.

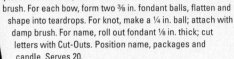

► Wish Along With *Pooh*

Pans: *Pooh*, p. 182; Cookie Sheet, Cooling Grid, p. 149
Tips: 2, 3, 6, 10, 16, 21, p. 138-139
Colors: *Pooh* Icing Color Set (*Pooh* gold, red, black), p. 182; Royal Blue, Lemon Yellow, Violet, Kelly Green, Rose, p. 133
Recipes: Buttercream, Royal Icings, Roll-Out Cookie, p. 112
Also: 2006 Pattern Book (Cake, Table), p. 124; 6 in. Lollipop Sticks, p. 221; Meringue Powder, p. 132; Flowerful Medley Sprinkle Decorations, p. 134; Parchment Triangles, p. 137; Rolling Pin, p. 130; Cake Boards, Fanci-Foil Wrap, p. 169; sugar ice cream cone, candy stick, cornstarch, toothpick, paring knife

In advance: Make table and cake cookies. Roll out dough, trace patterns with toothpick and cut out cookies. Bake and cool. Using royal icing, decorate cookies. Ice cake cookie smooth; add tip 6 zigzag frosting. Ice top of table cookie smooth; heavily ice, then imprint pleated tablecloth using large spatula edge. Divide side of table into 5ths. Pipe tip 2 drop strings from ½ to 1¼ in. deep; add tip 2 ball balloons at division points. Let set. For candle, cut candy stick to 1¼ in. and lollipop stick to 3 in. long. Attach lollipop stick to back of candy, then to back of cake cookie with royal icing; let set. Attach cookies with dots of icing. **Also in advance:** Make hat. Trim ice cream cone to 3 in. Ice smooth. Pipe tip 6 diagonal stripes in royal icing (pat smooth with finger dipped in cornstarch); let set.

Ice sides and background areas of cake smooth in buttercream. Position confetti sprinkles on cake sides. Outline *Pooh* and pipe in facial features with tip 3 (smooth nose with finger dipped in cornstarch). Pipe in balloon with tip 10 (smooth with finger dipped in cornstarch). Cover shirt and *Pooh* with tip 16 stars. Insert lollipop stick into top of head and position hat over stick. Using tip 3, pipe pull-out string fringe pompom and brim, message on balloon, and balloon string. Pipe tip 21 star bottom border. Spatula stripe (p. 107) a parchment bag fitted with tip 6 and pipe pull-out flame on candle. Cake serves 12; each cookie serves 1.

◄ Your Bear Buddy

Pan: Standard Muffin, p. 149
Tip: 3, p. 138
Colors: Royal Blue, Rose, Kelly Green, Lemon Yellow, p. 133
Recipe: Buttercream Icing, p. 112
Also: *Pooh* Standard Baking Cups, *Pooh* Icing Decorations, p. 182; cornstarch

Divide cupcake top in 4ths; outline and pipe in sections in various colors with tip 3 (smooth with finger dipped in cornstarch). Position icing decoration. Each serves 1.

©Disney
Based on "Winnie the Pooh" works by A.A. Milne and E. H. Shepard.

The Holidays Are Here!

Put your spin on each season. While we all enjoy sharing the tastes of the holidays, it's even more fun to give your celebration its own festive look. Nothing does it better than the cakes and treats here! Some of the great things you'll see—a spider web tower and this scary staircase cake for Halloween, a menu of wonderful Christmas appetizers molded in traditional shaped pans and a fun bunny family egg hunt for Easter. Mark your calendar!

Instructions for projects shown on these two pages are on page 42.

Every Body's Welcome!

Trick or treaters will love the cookie creatures who are creeping up the fondant stone staircase of our castle tower. And what a wicked view through the color flow windows!

Pans: 6, 8, 10, 12 x 2 in. Round, p. 148
Tips: 1s, 2, 3, 6, 8, 15, 44 and any large tip with a 1 in. bottom opening (such as 2B), p. 138-139
Colors:* Brown, Burgundy, Red-Red, Black, Orange, Leaf Green, Lemon Yellow, Violet, Royal Blue, Kelly Green, Golden Yellow, p. 133
Cookie: Spooky Shapes Cutter Set, p. 193; Boy Plastic Cookie Cutter, p. 216; Cookie Sheets, Cooling Grid, p. 217
Candy: White Candy Melts®†, p. 218; Garden Candy Color Set, p. 219; 8 in. Lollipop Sticks, p. 221
Fondant: White Ready-To-Use Rolled Fondant (162 oz. needed), p. 126; Brush Set, Rolling Pin, Roll & Cut Mat, p. 130; Cutter/Embosser, p. 131
Recipes: Buttercream, Royal, Color Flow Icings, Roll-Out Cookie, p. 112
Also: 2006 Pattern Book (5 Windows, Cape Wings, Window and Cookie Support), p. 124; Fine Tip Primary FoodWriter™ Edible Color Markers, p. 129; Confectionery Tool Set, p. 131; Color Flow Mix, Meringue Powder, Piping Gel, p.132; Parchment Triangles, p. 137; Wooden Dowel Rods, p. 167; Cake Circles, Fanci-Foil Wrap, p. 169; triple-thick 18 in. cardboard circles or foamcore for base, sharp knife, waxed paper, ruler, non-toxic chalk in black, gray and white, tea strainer, thin pretzel stick, candy-coated oval mints (35 needed), toothpicks, cardboard, cellophane tape, cornstarch, plastic ruler, plastic wrap

Begin 4 days in advance: Make 5 color flow windows (p. 120) using patterns. Let windows dry 48 hours.

When dry, draw diagonal windowpanes, 1 in. apart, with black FoodWriter, using ruler to guide. In gray royal icing, pipe a tip 8 outline on frame, inside original tip 3 frame outline. Pipe another tip 3 outline inside tip 8 outline; let dry overnight. Attach a lollipop stick to the back of windows 1 to 4 with royal icing; leave 2 in. extending at bottom. For window 5 (bottom window), use pattern to cut 2 supports from cardboard; attach to back of window with royal icing; let dry.

At least one day in advance: Make 7 candelabra (p. 118) using 6 oz. of medium gray-tinted fondant and melted candy tinted gray using black candy color.

One day in advance: Make cookies. Roll out dough. Using patterns, cut cape wings and 8 cookie supports. Also cut 3 boy cookies and 3 ghosts. Before baking, turn 1 ghost over for Witch. Bake and cool all cookies. Place cookies on waxed paper-covered cake boards and decorate with royal icing. For all piped-in areas, pat smooth with finger dipped in cornstarch. For wings, spatula ice smooth, then outline with tip 6. For all character cookies except Mummy, pipe tip 3 faces, hands and clothes. Add tip 2 facial features. For witch and Mrs. Frankenstein, spatula ice dresses smooth. Pipe witch hat with tip 6. Add tip 44 hatband and waistband. Position pretzel for broom; add tip 3 pull-out bristles and tip 44 band. Pipe Mrs. Frankenstein's hair with tip 3 zigzags, extending onto waxed paper; overpipe twice. For Mummy, pipe tip 44 band wrappings. Let all cookies dry overnight. Attach cookie sticks to backs of Witch and Dracula with melted candy; let dry. Attach 2 cookie supports to back of each remaining cookie with melted candy. Let set.

Make "wood" floor base. Tint 48 oz. fondant brown with a small amount of black added. Roll out ⅛ in. thick. Cover 18 in. cardboard or foamcore circle with foil; brush with piping gel and cover with fondant. Using straight-edge wheel of Cutter/Embosser and ruler, score horizontal lines for wooden planks, ⅝ in. apart from end to end, on base. Divide planks every 4½ to 5 in. with knife. Use small opening of tip 1s to imprint 3 nail holes in each plank. Use narrow end of veining tool from confectionery set to score wood grain lines. Randomly cut through corner of several boards and curl up slightly to resemble warped wood. Set aside.

Prepare four 1-layer cakes for rolled fondant (p. 111). Prepare cakes for stacked construction (p. 110) and position on same-size cake boards. Tint 84 oz. of fondant gray. Roll out fondant ¼ in. thick and individually cover each cake. Stack cakes together so that backs are flush.

Mark staircase area (p. 118). Cover cakes with plastic wrap to keep fondant soft as you carve stones on other tiers. Lightly carve stones with small end of veining tool. Press smallest ball tool between stones for grout lines. Blend stones from one layer to the next. Position all cakes on floor base.

Make stairs using remaining gray and carpet using 24 oz. of fondant tinted red (p. 110). Roll a ½ in. diameter gray fondant ball for all candelabra. Attach a ball to alternating stairs with damp brush. Insert candelabra sticks through balls and into cake.

Grate colored chalks separately onto waxed paper with tea strainer. Lightly brush on stones; brush dark shades between grout lines. Insert windows along side of stairs. Position bottom window on floor base. Insert Dracula and witch cookies in cake and position remaining cookies on floor base. Cake serves 50; each cookie serves 1.

*Note: Combine Leaf Green and Lemon Yellow for green faces and hands shown. Combine Red-Red, Black and Burgundy for red shown.

Phunny Phantoms

Pan: Mini Ghost, p. 190
Tip: 3, p. 138
Colors:* Leaf Green, Lemon Yellow, p. 133
Recipe: Buttercream Icing, p. 112
Also: Tube Decorating Icing in Black and Red, Coupler Ring Set, p. 133; Disposable Decorating Bags, p. 137; Just Batty, Jack-O-Lantern Lollipop Molds, p. 191; Candy Melts®† in Light Cocoa, Orange, Yellow, Dark Green, p. 218; pretzel sticks, sugar cones, spice drops, scissors, waxed paper

In advance: Make hats. Cut sugar cones to 2½ in. Dip cone into melted cocoa candy; refrigerate to set. For hat brim, using melted cocoa candy in cut disposable bag, pipe 2 in. circle on waxed paper; refrigerate until firm. Attach hat to brim with melted candy. Using melted orange and yellow candy, pipe zigzag hat band and outline buckle. Refrigerate until firm. Mold jack-o-lantern and "eek!" candies using painting method (p. 121)

Ice ghost cakes smooth in buttercream. Pipe tip 3 dot eyes, pupils, nose and cheeks. With tube icing, outline and pipe in tip 3 mouth and bead tongue. Add tip 3 dot tooth in white. For broom, flatten a spice drop and cut slits for bristles. Attach to pretzel stick with buttercream. Position broom, hat and candies. Each serves 1.

*Note: Combine Leaf Green and Lemon Yellow for green eye color shown.

† Brand confectionery coating.

◄ How Candy Corn is Born

Pan: Checkerboard Cake Set, p. 146
Tip: 16, p. 138
Colors: Orange, Lemon Yellow, p. 133
Recipe: Buttercream Icing, p. 112
Also: Petite Ghosts Icing Decorations, p. 191; assorted Halloween candy, white cake mix

Place Divider Ring in one 9 x 2 in. pan from set. Tint 1 cup of white batter orange and 1⅓ cup yellow; reserve ⅓ cup white. Fill inside small center ring with white batter, inside medium ring with orange batter and inside large outer ring with yellow batter. Carefully remove Divider Ring before baking. Bake and cool 1-layer cake.

Divide cake top: mark 2 inner circles, one 1 in. and one 2½ in. from edge of cake. Cover sides and top to 1 in. mark with yellow tip 16 stars, cover area to 2½ in. mark with orange tip 16 stars, fill in center with white tip 16 stars. Attach icing decorations to cake sides. Position candies around cake. Serves 6.

▼ Here's My Mummy!

Pans: Standard Muffin, p. 149; Stand-Up Jack-O-Lantern, p. 190

Tips: 1A, 2B, 4, p. 130

Colors: Black, Lemon Yellow, p. 133

Cookie: Hand and Foot Plastic Cutters, p. 216; Cookie Sheet, Cooling Grid, p. 217

Recipes: Buttercream Icing, Roll-Out Cookie, p. 112

Also: 2006 Pattern Book (Mummy's Tummy), p. 124; Cake Board, Fanci-Foil Wrap, p. 169; Spooky Ghost Baking Cups, p. 191; large marshmallows, paring knife

Bake and cool only front half of Jack-O-Lantern cake. Trim off stem area and position cake on foil-covered cake board. Bake and cool 11 cupcakes. Roll out cookie dough and cut 1 tummy using pattern, 2 hands and 2 feet using cutters (turn over 1 cut hand and foot before baking to create left hand and foot); bake and cool. Ice 2 cupcakes smooth. Pipe tip 2B band wrappings on cookies and remaining cupcakes. On cake, ice eye area smooth and add tip 2B bands to cover remaining areas, crossing and overpiping for dimension. Pipe tip 1A ball eyes; add tip 4 dot pupils and outline eyebrows. Position tummy cookie on 2 smooth-iced cupcakes; position remaining cupcakes and head cake. Position hand and foot cookies on large marshmallows. Cake serves 6; each cupcake and cookie serves 1.

▲ Jumpin' Jack

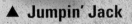

Pans: Standard Muffin, p. 149; Stand-Up Jack-O-Lantern, p. 190

Tips: 1A, 1M (2110), 4, 16, p. 138-139

Colors:* Orange, Red-Red, Black, Leaf Green, Violet, p. 133

Cookie: Hand and Foot Plastic Cutters, p. 216; Cookie Sheet, Cooling Grid, p. 217

Recipes: Buttercream Icing, Roll-Out Cookie, p. 112

Also: 2006 Pattern Book (Pumpkin Tummy, Bowtie, Bowtie Knot), p. 124; Colored Sugars in Light Green, Lavender, Orange, p. 134; Cake Board, Fanci-Foil Wrap, p. 169; Just Batty Baking Cups, p. 191; large marshmallows, paring knife, cornstarch

Bake and cool only front half of Jack-O-Lantern cake and position on foil-wrapped cake board. Bake and cool 11 cupcakes. Prepare cookie dough and divide into thirds; tint ⅓ green and ⅔ violet. Roll out green dough and cut 2 hands and feet (turn over 1 cut hand and foot before baking to create left hand and foot); sprinkle with light green sugar. Roll out violet dough; using patterns, cut tummy, bowtie and knot; sprinkle lower half of tummy and bowtie pieces with lavender sugar. Bake and cool all cookies.

Ice top half of tummy cookie smooth with green icing. Pipe tip 4 outline suspenders (smooth with finger dipped in cornstarch). Add tip 16 rosette buttons. Attach knot to bowtie with icing. Ice 2 cupcakes smooth. Pipe tip 1M swirls on remaining cupcakes and sprinkle with orange sugar. On cake, outline and pipe in tip 4 mouth (smooth with finger dipped in cornstarch). Cover remainder of face with tip 16 stars. Pipe tip 16 lines on stem; top stem with tip 16 swirl. Pipe tip 1A ball eyes, nose and cheeks. Cover nose and cheeks with tip 16 stars. Add tip 4 dot pupils (smooth with finger dipped in cornstarch). Position tummy cookie on 2 smooth-iced cupcakes. Position remaining cupcakes and head cake. Position hand and foot cookies on large marshmallows. Position bowtie. Cake serves 6; each cupcake and cookie serves 1.

***Note:** Add a small amount of Red-Red to Orange for orange shown.

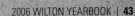

◄ 8-Legged Lollipops

Pan: Mini Muffin, p. 149
Candy: Just Batty Lollipop Mold, Candy Melts®† in Dark
   Cocoa and Yellow, p. 191; Garden Candy Color Set,
   4 in. Lollipop Sticks, p. 219
Also: Parchment Triangles, p. 137; black shoestring licorice

Using melted yellow candy in cut parchment bag, pipe eyes
in mold. Refrigerate until firm. Tint melted cocoa candy
black. To complete head, fill rest of mold with black candy;
refrigerate until firm. For bodies, fill pan cavities ⅓ full with
black candy; refrigerate until firm, unmold. Cut eight 2 in.
lengths of licorice for legs. Attach legs and lollipop stick
to back of body with melted candy; refrigerate until set.
Attach head to body with melted candy and add dot pupils
with melted candy in cut bag; refrigerate until firm. Each
serves 1.

▲ Covering Lots of Ground

Pans: Soccer Ball, Mini Ball, p. 153
Tip: 16, p. 139
Colors: * Black, Lemon Yellow, Leaf Green, p. 133
Recipe: Buttercream Icing, p. 112
Also: Neon Colors Fondant Multi Pack, p. 126;
   10 in. Cake Boards (2 needed), Fanci-Foil Wrap, p. 169;
   6 x 6 x 1 in. high craft block, candy corn, candy-coated
   chocolates, black twist licorice, yellow gumballs, ruler,
   toothpick

Cut double-thick cake boards to fit body and head cakes.
Wrap both boards and craft block with foil. Lightly ice
soccer ball body cake smooth with spatula; divide in half,
marking center of cake with toothpick. Starting from center,
mark seven 1 in. divisions for stripes, leaving any excess
width on ends. Cover stripe areas with tip 16 pull-out
stars. For head, generously ice mini ball with spatula and
attach to body; cover with tip 16 pull-out stars. Position
gumball eyes and attach candy-coated chocolate pupils
with tip 16 dots of icing. Roll a ¾ in. ball of neon orange
fondant for nose; position. Attach candy corn mouth with
icing. Position cake on foil-covered craft block to raise and
support spider's body. For front and back sets of legs, cut
four 2 in. and four 3½ in. licorice sections. For middle sets
of legs, cut four 2½ in. and four 3½ in. licorice sections.
Tint neon purple fondant black with icing color and roll
into eight ¾ in. balls to be used for joints on legs.
   For feet, roll eight neon orange fondant pieces into
1½ in. x 1¼ in. shapes. Insert joint pieces on ends
of short leg sections, then insert long leg sections
in joints. Insert feet into end of long leg
sections. Insert legs 1¼ in. apart in cake.
Serves 13.

*Note: Combine Lemon Yellow and
Leaf Green for green shown.

▶ Spin Control

Pans: Just Batty, p. 190; Mini Ball, p. 153
Tips: 1, 3, 6, 8, 16, 21, p. 138-139
Colors: * Black, Red-Red, Orange, Violet, Leaf Green,
   Lemon Yellow, p. 133
Recipe: Buttercream Icing, p. 112
Also: Cake Board, Fanci-Foil Wrap, p. 169; cornstarch

Bake and cool Just Batty cake and 1 mini
ball cake. Turn bat cake so that wings are
upside down; ice smooth. Pipe tip 1 outline
web on top and sides. Cover body area of
spider with tip 21 stars. Pipe tip 8 outline
legs and ball feet. On mini ball head,
pipe tip 6 ball eyes, tip 3 outline and
pipe-in mouth, dot cheeks and nose
(smooth all with finger dipped in
cornstarch). Add tip 3 dot pupils
and tongue. Position mini ball
head on Just Batty cake; cover
head with tip 16 stars. Pipe
tip 21 star bottom border.
Serves 13.

*Note: Combine Red-Red and
Orange for orange shown.
Combine Leaf Green and Lemon
Yellow for green shown.

† Brand confectionery coating.

◄ Web Weavers

Pans: 6, 8 x 2 in. Round, p. 148

Colors: Lemon Yellow, Black, p. 133

Fondant: Ready-To-Use Rolled Fondant in White (24 oz. needed) and Pastel Green (48 oz. needed), Neon Colors Fondant Multi Pack, p. 126; Green Brush-On Color™, Color Tray, Brush Set, p. 129; Rolling Pin, Roll & Cut Mat, p. 130; Easy-Glide Fondant Smoother, p. 131

Candy: White Candy Melts®†, p. 218; 8 in. Lollipop Sticks, p. 219

Recipe: Buttercream Icing, p. 112

Also: Cake Dividing Set, p. 137; 7½ in. Twist Legs (1 pk. needed) and 6 in. Plate from Crystal-Clear Cake Divider Set (sold separately), p. 164; 3 in. Grecian Pillars (1 pk. needed), 8 in. Decorator Preferred® Separator Plates (2 needed), p. 166; Spooky Cookie Cutter Set, p. 193; waxed paper, cornstarch, sharp knife

In advance: Make fondant spiders and words. Tint 12 oz. of white fondant black; reserve remainder. Roll out black fondant ⅛ in. thick and use cutter from set to cut 11 spiders; place spiders on board dusted with cornstarch. Make fondant details. Roll ¼ in. purple and orange balls for feet, 1¼ in. orange strip for mouth, ¼ in. white balls for eyes, ⅛ in. black balls for pupils, 1/16 in. yellow balls for noses, shape small white teardrops for teeth. Attach details with damp brush. For words: Roll out neon yellow fondant ⅛ in. thick; cut 2 yellow "EEK" pieces using cutter from set. To enlarge, carefully re-roll pieces to 1/16 in. thick, making sure that the letters do not lose their shape. Roll out neon orange fondant 3/16 in. thick; cut 2 "EEK" pieces. Use knife to cut out and remove void areas; attach to yellow pieces with damp brush. Let dry on cornstarch-dusted surface. When completely dry, attach lollipop sticks to "EEK" pieces and to 1 spider with melted candy; let set.

Combine Lemon Yellow color with Pastel Green fondant and any remaining white fondant for shade shown on cakes and pillars. Cover pillars, top 4 in. of twist legs and one 8 in. separator plate with fondant, ⅛ in. thick. Prepare 2-layer cakes (bake two 1½ in. high layers for 3 in. high cakes) for pillar construction (p. 110). Prepare for rolled fondant (p. 111). Position cakes on same-size separator plates; cover cakes and plates as one piece with fondant; smooth with Easy-Glide Smoother. Divide each cake and bottom plate into 8ths. Using Brush-On Color™, paint web center lines at division points; add connecting curves between lines. Position Grecian pillars and 8 in. cake on bottom plate. Position 6 in. cake on twist legs. Roll ⅛ in. rope of yellow fondant and wrap around base of twist legs. Insert words and spider on sticks into cake top at various heights. Attach spiders to pillars and cake sides with melted candy. Serves 32.

▶ Spider-licious Brownies

Pan: Petite Jack-O-Lantern, p. 190

Candy: Candy Melts®† in Light Cocoa, Red and Yellow, p. 218; Garden Candy Color Set, 4 in. Lollipop Sticks, p. 219

Recipe: Favorite brownies

Also: Parchment Triangles, p. 137; Cooling Grid, p. 217; malted milk balls, spice drops, black shoestring licorice, scissors, paring knife, waxed paper

Bake brownies in pan cavities; let cool. Position on cooling grid over waxed paper and cover with melted cocoa candy (p. 120). Let set. With paring knife, trim excess from bottom of brownies. Using melted candy in cut parchment bag, attach malted milk ball head. Pipe dot eyes and string mouth. Tint a small amount of melted cocoa candy black and pipe dot pupils. Cut eight 2¼ in. lengths of licorice for legs. Cut 8 spice drops horizontally in half; insert legs in center.

Insert end of lollipop stick into brownie sides to make leg holes. Pipe a small amount of melted candy into each hole and insert legs. Let set. Each serves 1.

▼ Shocking Warlock

It's easy to create a spellbinding sorcerer using rice cereal treats, shaped in our Jack-O-Lantern Pan. They're tinted with a special Halloween glow and topped with a fun fondant face.

Pan: Iridescents! Jack-O-Lantern, p. 190

Colors:* Orange, Red-Red, Black, Violet, Rose, Lemon Yellow, p. 133

Fondant: Ready-To-Use Rolled Fondant, p. 126; Brush Set, p. 129; Rolling Pin, Roll & Cut Mat, p. 130

Recipe: Favorite crisped rice cereal treats (4 batches needed)

Also: 2006 Pattern Book (Hat, Facial Features), p. 124; Cake Board, p. 169; Mini Geometric Crinkle Cutter Set, p. 214; craft knife

Using pan and hat pattern, cut a board to hold assembled treats. Prepare 2 batches of cereal treats for face. Melt butter and marshmallows, stirring until smooth, tint using icing colors, then stir in cereal. Press mixture into pan; unmold onto prepared board. Prepare 2 batches of cereal treats for hat; tint butter/marshmallow mixture, then stir in cereal (color will lighten when cereal is added). Mold treats on board in hat area; form brim portion by hand, pressing over top of face.

Tint fondant for trims: 3 oz. yellow, 4 oz. orange, 3 oz. black. Roll out yellow fondant ⅛ in. thick and, using patterns, cut mouth and eye areas; position on face. Roll 2 x 1½ x ¾ in. thick white ovals for eyes; attach with damp brush. Roll ½ in. balls for pupils; attach with damp brush. Roll 2 in. orange ball for nose, 1 in. balls for cheeks; flatten cheeks and attach all with damp brush. Shape ½ in. square white teeth and 1¾ in. black log eyebrows; attach with damp brush. Roll black fondant ⅛ in. thick and cut a strip 11 x ¾ in. wide for hat band; position and trim to fit. For candy corn, roll ⅜ in. thick white and orange logs and ¼ in. thick yellow log. Position logs together and roll out ⅛ in. thick. Cut 12-15 pieces using triangle cutter. Brush backs with damp brush and position on hat. Serves 24.

*Note: Combine Orange with a little Red-Red for orange shown. Combine Violet with a little Rose for violet shown.

▲ Bat Bites

Cookie: Halloween 4 Pc. Grippy™ Set, p. 193; Cookie Sheet, Cooling Grid, p. 217

Tip: 3, p. 138

Colors: Black, Leaf Green, Lemon Yellow, Violet, p. 133

Recipe: Color Flow Icing, Roll-Out Cookie, p. 112

Also: Color Flow Mix, p. 132; Parchment Triangles, p. 137; Tricks 'N Treats Party Bags, p. 191

Tint dough Leaf Green/Lemon Yellow combination. Roll out dough and cut bat cookies; bake and cool. Prepare color flow; tint ¾ of recipe black, ¼ violet. Outline cookie with tip 3 and full-strength color flow (p. 120); fill in with thinned color flow using parchment bag with opening cut to size of tip 3. Let dry. Place cookies in party bags. Each serves 1.

◀ Circle of Sorcery

Conjure up a spooky sweet table with ease! Our bobbling ghost toppers guard easy to decorate cupcakes while a shadowy color flow witch hovers above a simple, colorful cake.

Pan: 8 x 3 in. Round, p. 147; Standard Muffin, p. 149
Tips: 1M (2110), 2, 16, p. 138-139
Colors: * Orange, Red-Red, Leaf Green, Lemon Yellow, Violet, Black, p. 133
Recipe: Buttercream, Color Flow Icings, p. 112
Also: 2006 Pattern Book (Witch), p. 124; Color Flow Mix, p. 132; Petite Tricks 'N Treats Icing Decorations (3 pks. needed), Ghost Bobbling Toppers, Tricks 'N Treats Baking Cups, p. 191; 8 in. Lollipop Sticks, p. 221; Cake Board, Fanci-Foil Wrap, p. 169; Parchment Triangles, p. 137; waxed paper, toothpick

At least 48 hours in advance: Make color flow witch using pattern (p. 120). Attach lollipop stick to back using full-strength color flow.

Ice 2-layer cake smooth (bake two 2½ in. layers for a 5 in. high cake). Pipe a 1 in. wide band of tip 16 stars at top and bottom edges of cake. On cake side bands, using a toothpick, mark triangle shapes ¾ in. x ½ in. high. Fill in triangles with tip 16 stars. Attach icing decorations with dots of icing. Insert witch in cake top.

Bake and cool cupcakes. Pipe tip 1M swirl on tops; position icing decorations and toppers. Cake serves 20, each cupcake serves 1.

Note: Combine Orange with a little Red-Red for orange shown. Combine Leaf Green and Lemon Yellow for green shown.

▶ Stirring Up Trouble

Pans: Spooky Ghost, p. 190; Sports Ball, p. 153; Cookie Sheet, Cooling Grid, p. 217
Tips: 2A, 3, 4, 5, 12, 16, 352, p. 138-139
Colors: * Leaf Green, Lemon Yellow, Golden Yellow, Violet, Orange, Rose, Black, Red-Red, Christmas Red, p. 133
Recipe: Buttercream Icing, p. 112
Also: Brush Set, p. 129; Piping Gel, p. 132; Plastic Dowel Rods, p. 167; Fanci-Foil Wrap, p. 169, Witch Hat Comfort Grip™ Cutter, p. 193; Butterfly Metal Cutter, p. 214; pretzel rods, scissors, cornstarch

In advance: Make hat and butterfly "shoe" cookies. Roll out dough and cut 1 hat and 1 butterfly cookie. Cut butterfly in half and turn over right side half so that "toes" point in the same direction. Bake and cool.

Ice ghost cake sides and background areas smooth. Pipe tip 4 mouth and eyes (smooth with finger dipped in cornstarch). Outline and pipe in tip 4 pupils and tip 3 teeth. Outline body and head with tip 4; fill in with tip 16 stars. Build up nose and arm with tip 16 stars. Pipe tip 16 zigzag sleeve trim and belt. Add tip 16 pull-out star hair. Pipe tip 5 dot mole. Cut one pretzel rod to 4½ in. and one to 6 in. long. Position on each side of hand area. Outline hands with tip 4; build up with tip 16 stars. Cover hat cookie with tip 16 stars. Add tip 16 zigzag hat band and tip 5 buckle. Cut a dowel rod to 3½ in. long and attach hat with buttercream; insert in cake. Cut 2 dowel rods to 7½ in. long for legs; mark a 3 in. stocking area on one and 3½ in. on the other. Cover stocking areas with tip 16 stars in ½ in. wide stripes. Outline and pipe in shoe cookies with tip 5 (pat smooth with finger dipped in cornstarch). Attach shoes to legs with icing; insert legs in cake. Outline and pipe in tip 5 shoe tongues. Ice half ball cake smooth and position on foil-wrapped

board. Pipe tip 2A outline rim. Spatula stripe icing bag (p. 107) using orange and red icings; fill bag with yellow icing and pipe tip 352 pull-out leaf flames. For witch's brew, tint piping gel and icing in Leaf Green/Golden Yellow combination. Fit bag with tip 12, then brush inside of bag with piping gel; fill bag with icing and pipe balls for brew. Position cauldron next to witch. Witch serves 12; cauldron serves 6.

Note: Combine a little Rose with Violet for violet shown. Combine Leaf Green and Golden Yellow for green shown. Combine Red-Red and Christmas Red for red shown in flames.

▲ The Boys of Winter

Pan: Bite-Size Gingerbread Boy, p. 194

Tips: 5, 7, 10, p. 138

Fondant: White Ready-To-Use Rolled Fondant (24 oz. needed), Primary Colors Fondant Multi Pack, p. 126; Cutter/Embosser, p. 131; Brush Set, p. 129; Rolling Pin, Roll & Cut Mat, p. 130

Also: Confectionery Tool Set, p. 131; Cake Release, Pastry Brush, p. 135; 1 pk. (14½ oz.) gingerbread cake and cookie mix

Brush pan with Cake Release. Prepare mix following package directions; pour batter into pan. Bake at 350°F for 15 minutes. Let cool and unmold. For hats, roll red and green fondant into 2 in. high cones. Roll out white fondant ⅛ in. thick; cut a ⅛ in. wide strip and attach to red hat in a spiral with damp brush. Cut polka dots with narrow end of tip 10; attach with damp brush. For pompoms, roll ½ in. balls; insert hat. Indent fluffy texture with large end of veining tool. For brim, cut a 2 x ⅛ in. wide strip and attach with damp brush; indent texture as for pompom. Roll a ¾ in. long strip for mouth. Using narrow ends of tips, cut tip 7 eyes and cheeks, tip 5 nose, tip 10 buttons; attach all with damp brush. For scarf, cut ⅛ x 2½ in. long strip; wrap around neck; for scarf ends, cut a 2 in. long strip and fold under first piece. For bow tie, cut ½ in. triangles; attach with damp brush. Cut knot with narrow end of tip 10; attach with damp brush. Mix makes 20; each cake serves 1.

▶ High-Voltage Christmas

In every town there's one house people have to see lit up for Christmas. This year, make it yours—this dazzling candy-covered gingerbread family house that will add sparkle throughout the season.

Cookie: Pre-Baked Ultimate Gingerbread House Kit (includes house and tree gingerbread pieces, icing mixes, bags and tips, mini red/green/white candies, mini jellies, jelly rings, cherry sours, spearmint leaves, red and green pinwheel mints)* p. 199

Colors: Lemon Yellow, Kelly Green, Red-Red, p. 133

Recipes: Grandma's Gingerbread, Royal Icing (optional, if extra icing is needed), p. 112

Also: 2006 Pattern Book (Peaked Door), p. 124; Round Cut-Outs™, p. 128; Meringue Powder (optional), p. 132; Angled Spatula, p. 137; candy canes, hollow center fruit candies, mini candy-coated chocolates, spice drops, candy fruit slices, sugar cones, toothpick, small plastic ruler, 17 x 19 x ½ in. thick foamcore board or triple-thick cardboard wrapped with foil

In advance: Make trees. Stack 2 or 3 cones for taller trees, use single cones for others. Working from bottom, pipe rows of tip 12 elongated bead branches. After piping each row of beads, flatten slightly by running spatula over top of beads. Overlap rows of beads as you work toward top. Attach mini candies and spice drop halves to trees; add tip 5 pull-out snow. Let dry overnight. Prepare gingerbread and cut 9 head cookies (3 used on back) using medium Cut-Out. Bake and cool.

Assemble house following kit directions. Using toothpick, mark 2 in. square side and top front windows and 3 in. square bottom front window; mark door and door window using pattern. Ice door and windows smooth with spatula. Pipe outline panes on door window using tip 5 from kit. For front windows, cut fruit slices lengthwise in half and attach with icing for shutters. Pipe tip 5 outline curtains on bottom front window. Attach mini chocolates around all windows and for doorknob. Attach stacked jelly ring, hollow center candy and mini chocolate above all windows and door. Attach spice drop halves above windows and candy cane ledges below. Pipe tip 5 seams at house corners; attach mini chocolates. Ice roof smooth; pipe tip 5 pull-out icicles on eaves and chimney. Attach cherry sours and mini jelly halves on roof. Attach pinwheel mints on eaves, mini jelly halves and candy canes on chimney and jelly rings at roof peak. Decorate gingerbread heads. Pipe hair and facial features with tip 5. Attach heads in windows.

Ice base fluffy. Attach jelly ring halves around house and walkway. Attach spice drops and mini candies on alternating rings. Cut spearmint leaves lengthwise in half; position under windows for bushes. Position trees.

***Note:** In addition to those included in kit, you will need extra pinwheel mints and jelly rings, about 12 oz. each.

Two days in advance: Make ears for elf. Tint 20 oz. of fondant copper; roll out ¼ in. thick and cut 4 leaves using largest Cut-Out; reserve remaining copper fondant. Using medium leaf Cut-Out, cut centers from 2 leaves. Turn over one leaf and one open-center leaf for opposite ear. Attach open-center leaf to whole leaf with damp brush. Trim off an angled slice at wider end of leaf to create a straight edge where ear will meet head. Let dry for one day. Attach sticks to ears with thinned fondant adhesive. Let dry for one day.

On both cakes, trim off top corners of hat, holly and eye areas; on elf cake, trim off nose area. Position cakes on foil-covered, double-thick cake boards. Prepare for rolled fondant (p. 111). Cover elf cake with reserved copper fondant. For Santa cake, tint 24 oz. of fondant Red-Red/Christmas Red combination, 8 oz. copper, and a 1 in. ball black. Reserve remaining white fondant. Cover Santa face area with copper fondant; smooth. Roll out white fondant ¼ in. thick and cut beard area; position on cake. Using large and small ball tools from set, imprint swirls in beard. For hats, roll out red or green fondant ¼ in. thick and cut an 11 x 18 in. high triangle; trim off approximately 1 in. from point to accommodate pompom and gather into folds. Position on cake, folding top to side. For elf hat, roll out red fondant ⅛ in. thick and cut polka dots using smallest Round Cut-Out. Attach to hat with damp brush. With black fondant, cut a 1 x 1½ in. wide

mouth for Santa and a 1¼ in. x 3 in. wide mouth for elf. For both cakes, roll ½ in. ball eyes. Attach features with damp brush. For Santa's mustache, roll two 1¼ x 4 x ½ in. thick white teardrops; bend points up and attach with damp brush. Imprint swirls same as beard. For Santa's eyebrows, roll two 2 x ⅜ in. wide white logs; attach with damp brush. For elf's eyebrows, roll two brown logs, 1½ x ¼ in. wide; attach with damp brush. For elf's hair, roll brown fondant ⅜ in. thick; using large round Cut-Out, cut three ½ in. wide crescent shapes and smooth together at bottom. Imprint layered texture with smallest ball tool and attach with damp brush. For elf's cheeks, roll out rose fondant ⅛ in. thick and cut circles using medium round Cut-Out. Shape elf's tongue from ⅛ in. thick fondant and trim to fit mouth. Attach with damp brush. For elf's nose, roll a 1¼ x 2 in. high cone, bend tip slightly; attach with damp brush. For fur trim on both hats, cut a 1¾ in. x 10 in. x ¾ in. thick white strip, for pompom roll a 2 in. round white ball. Attach pieces with damp brush and imprint texture with large ball tool from set. Insert elf ears. Each serves 12.

*Note: Combine Red-Red with Christmas Red for red shown.

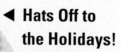

► The Toy Tag Team!

Pan: Step-by-Step Snowman, p. 194

Colors:* Red-Red, Christmas Red, Copper (skin tone), Black. For elf, also use Kelly Green, Brown, Rose, p. 133

Fondant: White Ready-To-Use Rolled Fondant (60 oz. needed for each cake), p. 126; Brush Set, p. 129; Rolling Pin, Roll & Cut Mat, p. 130. For elf, also use Round and Leaf Cut-Outs™, p. 128

Recipe: Buttercream Icing, p. 112

Also: Confectionery Tool Set, p. 131; Double-Thick Cake Boards, Fanci-Foil Wrap, p. 169; 4 in. Lollipop Sticks, p. 221; paring knife

◄ Hats Off to the Holidays!

Pan: Mini Wonder Mold, p. 153

Color: Sky Blue, p. 133

Fondant: White Ready-To-Use Rolled Fondant (24 oz. needed), Fondant Multi Packs in Primary (2 pks. needed) and Neon Colors*, p. 126; Round Cut-Outs™, p. 128; Brush Set, p. 129; Rolling Pin, Roll & Cut Mat, p. 130; Cutter/Embosser, Easy-Glide Fondant Smoother, p. 131

Recipe: Buttercream Icing, p. 112

Also: Confectionery Tool Set, p. 131; 6 in. Cake Circles, Fanci-Foil Wrap, p. 169

Bake and cool cakes. Position on individual foil-covered circles. Prepare for rolled fondant (p. 111). For red hat, cover cake with red fondant; smooth with Easy-Glide Smoother. Roll out white fondant ⅛ in. thick and cut circles using smallest round Cut-Out; attach with damp brush. For purple/blue hat, roll out fondant ⅛ in. thick and cut into ½ in. wide strips; position strips alternately on cake. For green/red hat, dot mark bottom of cake in 2 in. wide sections. Roll out red and green fondant ⅛ in. thick. Cut into 2 in. wide x 3½ in. long sections, taper top end to ¼ in. wide. Position on cake. For pompoms, roll 1½ in. diameter balls of white fondant; attach to cake top with damp brush. For hatbands, roll ¾ in. diameter x 13 in. long logs of white fondant; attach to base of cakes with damp brush. To create fluffy look, insert large end of veining tool in fondant at various angles. Each serves 1.

*Note: Mix ½ pack of noon purplo with 2 oz. of white fondant for purple shown. Mix ½ pack of primary blue with 2 oz. of white fondant and add a little Sky Blue icing color for blue shown.

▼ Playing Reindeer Games

Pan: Long Loaf, p. 149
Cookie: Bell Metal Cutter, p. 214; Cookie Sheet, Cooling Grid, p. 217
Candy: Candy Melts®† in Light Cocoa (2 pks.) and White (1 pk.), p. 218; 6 in. Lollipop Sticks, Primary Candy Color Set, p. 219
Recipes: Roll-Out Cookie, p. 112; Candy Clay, p. 120; favorite crisped rice cereal treats (3 batches needed)
Also: 2006 Pattern Book (Reindeer), p. 124; Parchment Triangles, p. 137; Fanci-Foil Wrap, p. 169; shredded wheat cereal, spice drops, pinwheel mints, cardboard (8 x 20 in.), ⅜ in. wide red ribbon (11 ft. needed), waxed paper, vegetable pan spray, corn syrup

In advance: Prepare Candy Clay for fence and let set overnight.

Roll out dough and cut 9 cookies with bell cutter; cut clapper off bottom, bake and cool. Melt 1 pk. each white and cocoa candy. Using candy colors, tint ¼ cup white candy red, ⅓ cup yellow and ⅓ cup black (combine red and blue candy colors). Add a small amount of white candy to light cocoa to lighten shade.

Place cookies on cooling grid over waxed paper, cover with cocoa candy (p. 120); refrigerate to set. If needed, trim excess candy from sides. Cover pattern with waxed paper and position cookie on face area. For antlers, add a little more white candy to make cocoa candy one shade lighter. Pipe antlers using melted candy in cut parchment bag; follow pattern and be sure to connect antlers to cookie. Pipe ears using the darker cocoa shade used to cover cookie; refrigerate until firm. Pipe inner ears with white candy and hair with yellow candy. Pipe white eyes, black facial features and Rudolph's red nose. Attach lollipop sticks to cookies with melted candy. Tie a 14 in. piece of ribbon into a bow on each stick.

Prepare 3 batches of cereal treats. Spray pan with vegetable pan spray. Pack cereal treat mixture into pan. Unmold onto foil-covered board. Make fence (p. 121). Cut a spice drop in half and attach to each ball on fence posts with melted candy. Insert cookies in loaf. Crush shredded wheat and sprinkle around base of fence; position assorted candies. Treats serve 18; each cookie serves 1.

† Brand confectionery coating.

▶ Skatin' St. Nick

Pan: Petal Set (9 in. pan used), p. 148
Colors: Violet, Orange, Copper (skin tone), p. 133
Fondant: Ready-To-Use Rolled Fondant in White and Pastel Blue (24 oz. each needed), Primary Colors Fondant Multi Pack, p. 126; Fine Tip Primary Colors FoodWriter™ Edible Color Markers, Brush Set, p. 129; Rolling Pin, Roll & Cut Mat, p. 130; Cutter/Embosser, Easy-Glide Fondant Smoother, p. 131
Recipe: Buttercream Icing, p. 112
Also: Gum Tex™, p. 130; Cake Boards, Fanci-Foil Wrap, p. 169; 8 in. Lollipop Sticks, p. 221; Holiday Colorful Cutter Set, p. 197; Tree Stencil-A-Cookie Set, p. 196; 8 in. Tapered Spatula, p. 137

In advance: Make fondant Santa (p. 118).

Prepare 2-layer cake for rolled fondant (p. 111); cover with fondant, smooth with Fondant Smoother. Tint a 2½ in. ball of white fondant orange and another violet. Roll out fondant ⅛ in. thick; cut two trees each in orange, violet, red, and green, using cutter from Holiday Set. Attach to cake sides using damp brush. Roll small balls of yellow fondant and attach to trees. For bottom border, roll white fondant logs ½ in. wide x 4 in. long, taper at each end. Attach at each petal point with damp brush. Roll small white dots to decorate logs and ½ in. balls for between logs; attach with damp brush. Insert fondant Santa into cake top. Serves 14.

◄ Joy Spreads

Pan: Sports Ball (2 needed), p. 153

Fondant: Star and Round Cut-Outs™, p. 128; Cutter/Embosser, p. 131

Recipes: Cheese Onion Round, Spicy Cheddar Spread, Avocado Dip, p. 112

Also: Fresh dill, Colby cheddar cheese slices, mozzarella cheese slices, roasted red peppers, cherry tomatoes, pimiento-stuffed green olives, chives, paring knife

In advance: Prepare recipes and mold overnight in pan halves. Unmold. For Cheese Onion mold (far left), using wavy wheel of Cutter-Embosser, cut three 1 in. wide strips of cheddar. Position at center and sides of mold. Cut two ½ in. wide strips and position between wide strips. Using medium star Cut-Out, cut 5 red pepper stars; position at center of strips. Using smallest round Cut-Out, cut 5 mozzarella circles for each 1 in. wide strip; position. For hanger, cut off the bottom of a cherry tomato, hollow out center and position. Cut a 5 in. strip of chive, cut a slit in top of tomato and insert. For spicy cheddar mold (at bottom), using medium star Cut-Out, cut mozzarella stars; using small star Cut-Out, cut cheddar stars. Position stars, stacking small on medium. Make hanger as above and position. For Avocado mold (at top), cut strips of chive to fit from top to bottom edge; position to form ornament sections. Using medium round Cut-Out, cut circles of cheddar. Position around center of mold, top with an olive slice. Make hanger as above and position. Cut extra cheddar stars using large Cut-Out. Arrange dill on serving platter; position molds and cheddar stars. Each mold makes 25 (appetizer-size) servings.

► It's a House Paté!

Pans: Stand-Up House, p. 152; Cookie Sheet, p. 217

Tip: 5, p. 138

Recipe: Holiday Paté, p. 113

Also: 8 in. Angled Spatula, p. 137; Cake Board, Fanci-Foil Wrap, p. 169; Gingerbread Boys Nesting Cutter Set, p. 197; Disposable Decorating Bags, p. 137; broccoli, parsley, pimiento-stuffed green olives, sliced pimientos, brick cream cheese (8 oz. needed), milk, rye and wheat bread, scissors, plastic wrap

Prepare recipe following directions. Unmold onto a foil-wrapped board cut to size of pan. Beat cream cheese with 2 tablespoons of milk until creamy. Using tip 5 with cream cheese mixture, outline door and windows. Cut pieces of pimiento and position in windows. Pipe zigzag snow-covered window ledges. Add dot doorknob. Cut parsley into small pieces and position stems to form wreath and window arches, attaching with cream cheese mixture. Position pimiento pieces on wreath. Using heavy pressure, pipe an outline bottom border. Position broccoli bushes; pipe snow. Spatula ice roof with cream cheese mixture. Position sliced olives on eaves.

Using smallest Gingerbread Boy cutter, cut bread shapes. Place on cookie sheet and bake in a 400° oven for 8 minutes, until toasted. Position around house. Makes 64 (appetizer size) servings.

▶ Pine Dining

Pan: Iridescents!™ Holiday Tree, p. 194
Recipe: Your favorite potato salad (5-6 lbs. needed)
Also: Cake Board, Fanci-Foil Wrap, p. 169; cherry
tomatoes, fresh parsley, dried parsley flakes,
celery, non-stick vegetable oil cooking spray,
plastic wrap

Prepare potato salad recipe. Spray pan and line
with plastic wrap. Pack pan with potato salad
and chill thoroughly. Unmold. Sprinkle tree with
parsley flakes; garnish with fresh parsley and
cherry tomato halves. Cut celery stalks in
2 in. lengths; position to form tree trunk.
Makes 16 (½ cup) servings.

▲ Christmas Club

Cookie: Nesting Stars Metal Cutter Set, p. 214
Recipe: Favorite ham salad
Also: White bread, American cheese (¼ in. thick), parsley,
pimientos, wooden skewers

Use all but largest cutter to cut 2 of each size bread stars.
Fill each of the 3 star sandwiches with ham salad. Stack
sandwiches, alternating points to create a full tree. Cut
cheese star with smallest cutter. Insert wooden skewer in
bottom of cheese star and through sandwiches. Garnish
with parsley and pimientos. Each serves 1.

◀ The Great Ice-scape

Pans: Soccer Ball, p. 153; Jumbo Muffin, p. 149
Tip: 3, p. 138
Recipe: Cheesy Pesto Spread, p. 112
Also: Tapered Spatula, Disposable Decorating Bags,
p. 137; colossal and medium black olives, shredded
carrots, whipped cream cheese, round crackers,
scissors, paring knife, vegetable pan spray

One day in advance: Prepare spread following recipe
directions. Spray pans with vegetable spray and
line with plastic wrap; fill with mixture. Refrigerate
overnight.

Assemble 3 penguins (p. 117).

Unmold spread from pans; position large mold on
serving dish. Using spatula, smooth ball and score lines
for ice blocks. For door, trim off a small portion from
side of muffin mold; place flat side down next to igloo.

For doorway, hollow out a small portion from front.
Score lines as for large mold. Position penguins around
cheese spread. Makes 80 (2 tablespoon) servings.

◀ Heaven-Sent Holidays

Pans: Butterfly, p. 151; Cookie Sheet, Cooling Grid, p. 149
Tips: 1, 2, 3, 5, 8, 14, p. 138-139
Colors:* Violet, Copper (skin tone), Brown, Rose, Black, Red-Red, p. 133
Recipes: Buttercream Icing, Roll-Out Cookie, p. 112
Also: 2006 Pattern Book (Angel Body, Arms), p. 124; Yellow Colored Sugar, p. 134; 101 Cookie Cutters Set, p. 216; 4 in. Lollipop Sticks, p. 221; Cake Boards, Fanci-Foil Wrap, p. 169; miniature marshmallows, paring knife

Roll out dough; using pattern, cut body and arms. Cut star on wand with smallest star cutter and halo with medium circle cutter from set; trim off ⅓ of circle cookie for halo. Sprinkle halo and star cookies with yellow sugar. Bake and cool all cookies.

Ice cake smooth; outline wing area with tip 5. Pipe tip 2 swirls on cake top. Add tip 8 ball bottom border.

Decorate cookies: Ice inside sleeves smooth. Pipe in mouth with tip 3. Outline sleeves, robe, neck and feet with tip 3; cover angel with tip 14 stars. Pipe tip 3 dot nose, outline eyes and eyebrows; add tip 1 pull-out eyelashes. Pipe tip 14 reverse shell hair. For arm holding wand, attach lollipop stick to hand with icing. Outline fingers with tip 3 and cover both hands with tip 14 stars. Position cookies on cake; prop up arms with mini marshmallows. Attach star to wand and halo to head with icing. Serves 12.

***Note:** Combine Brown and Red-Red for brown shown.

▼ A Chorus for Us

Pans: 18 x 3 in. Half Round, p. 147; Mini Snowman, p. 194
Tips: 2, 3, 5, 8, 10, 12, 47, p. 138-139
Colors: Royal Blue, Christmas Red, Kelly Green, Black, Orange, Rose, Violet, p. 133
Recipe: Buttercream Icing, p. 112
Also: Cake Boards, Fanci-Foil Wrap, p. 169; black shoestring licorice, graham crackers, paring knife, cornstarch

In advance: Make caroling book and snowman arms. For book, cut graham cracker into two 1¼ x 1 in. high pieces. Ice one side smooth; let dry, then ice the other side and let dry. Pipe in top and bottom edges of each piece with tip 5; let dry. For arms, cut licorice into six 2½ in. lengths; for fingers, cut twelve ½ in. lengths. Cut one end of each finger diagonally; attach 2 fingers on diagonal end to each arm with a tip 2 dot. Let dry.

Bake and cool 1-layer half round (2 in. high) and 3 snowman cakes. Ice half round smooth. Spatula ice fluffy snow at bottom of cake. Pipe tip 3 message. For snowman with earmuffs, trim off hat and top of head. Spatula ice snowmen and position on cake. Pipe tip 2 eyes and outline mouths. Add tip 3 pull-out noses, dot cheeks and buttons.

For earmuffs, cut a 3 in. piece of licorice. Pipe a small tip 8 dot on each side of head; insert licorice and overpipe ends with a tip 8 ball. For top hat, pipe tip 12 band hat and tip 8 outline brim. Add tip 5 string hat band. Pipe tip 12 pull-out stocking cap with tip 3 zigzag trim. Add tip 3 dot pompom. On earmuff and stocking cap snowmen, pipe tip 8 outline scarves with tip 2 outline fringe. On top hat snowman, pipe tip 47 band scarf. Insert book pieces, raised so that edges meet in a V-shape; pipe tip 5 outline binding.

Insert arms in earmuff and stocking cap snowmen, trimming as needed. For top hat snowman, cut two 1 in. long licorice shoulder pieces; insert on each side. Trim arms to 1¾ in. long; attach hand portion to book and arm to shoulder with tip 2 dots. Pipe tip 2 and 3 dot snowflakes; add tip 10 ball bottom border. Serves 58.

◄ A Recruit Salutes

Pans: Little Hero, p. 153; Cookie Sheet, Cooling Grid, p. 149

Tips: 2, 3, 6, 16, 21, p. 138-139

Colors: Brown, Royal Blue, Copper (skintone), Red-Red, Kelly Green, Lemon Yellow, Rose, Black, p. 133

Recipes: Roll-Out Cookie, Buttercream Icing, p. 112

Also: 2006 Pattern Book (Hat), p. 124; Wooden Dowel Rod, p. 167; 13 x 19 in. Cake Board, Fanci-Foil Wrap, p. 169; large marshmallows, cornstarch, toothpick

Roll out dough. Using pattern, cut out hat, bake and cool. Outline with tip 3. Pipe in brim with tip 3 (smooth with finger dipped in cornstarch). Cover hat with tip 16 stars. Add tip 21 shell fleur-de-lis; pipe tip 3 dot buttons.

Cut cake board to fit cake with hat; wrap with foil. On cake, cut off fire hose area and right forearm holding hose. Build up area 1 in. below elbow with icing to make straight arm. Ice cake sides and background areas smooth. Outline soldier with tip 3; outline right arm straight down. Pipe in tip 3 eyes and mouth (smooth with finger dipped in cornstarch). Cover face, right hand and clothes with tip 16 stars. Build up nose with tip 16 stars. Pipe in inside of sleeve with tip 3 (smooth with finger dipped in cornstarch). Pipe in shoes with tip 6 (smooth with finger dipped in cornstarch). Pipe tip 6 epaulets; pipe tip 3 pull-out fringe along bottom edge. For candy cane, cut a dowel rod to 9 in. long. Position end in hand area. Cover rod with tip 16 stars. Pipe a tip 6 band for curved area of cane; cover band with tip 16 stars. Outline hand over candy cane with tip 3. Cover left hand with tip 16 stars, overpipe twice for dimension. Pipe tip 2 outline eyebrows. Add tip 16 pull-out star hair. Position marshmallows for hat support; position hat and attach with icing. Pipe tip 21 shell bottom border. Cake serves 12; cookie serves 1.

▼ Fowl Weather Friend

Pan: Star, p. 152

Tips: 2A, 3, 5, 8, 16, p. 138-139

Colors:* Black, Red-Red, Christmas Red, Lemon Yellow, Kelly Green, p. 133

Recipes: Buttercream, Chocolate Buttercream** Icings, p. 112

Also: 2006 Pattern Book (Penguin Head and Legs), p. 124; Cake Board, Fanci-Foil Wrap, p. 169; toothpick, cornstarch

Lightly ice cake with spatula. Trace patterns with toothpick. Build up facial area with tip 8 mounds. Pipe eyes and inside of mouth with tip 8 (smooth with finger dipped in cornstarch). Cover cake with tip 16 stars. Outline beak with tip 5; overpipe to build up (smooth with finger dipped in cornstarch). Pipe tip 16 rosettes for hat trim and pompom. Pipe tip 3 zigzag scarf; add tip 3 pull-out fringe. Pipe tip 2A elongated shell feet. Serves 12.

*Note: Combine Red-Red with Christmas Red for red shown. Add Black Icing Color to chocolate icing for black shown.

**Or use Chocolate Ready-To-Use Decorator Icing, p. 132

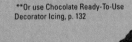

◄ See Snow and Smile

Candy: White Candy Melts®†, p. 218; Garden Candy Color Set, p. 219; Smiley Face Lollipop Mold, p. 220

Cookie: Nesting Snowflakes Cutter Set, p. 197; 8 in. Cookie Treat Sticks, p. 217; Non-Stick Cookie Sheet, p. 146

Also: Parchment Triangles, p. 137; spice drops, black shoestring licorice, candy corn, granulated sugar, waxed paper

Mold face candies without sticks, about ¾ in. deep or just below stick indent line in mold. Refrigerate until firm; unmold. Place second largest snowflake cutter on waxed paper-covered cookie sheet. Fill cutter ³⁄₁₆ in. deep with melted candy, refrigerate until firm; unmold. Using melted candy in cut parchment bag, attach faces to snowflakes; pipe vein lines on snowflakes. Tint portions of melted candy black and pink using candy colors. Pipe eyes, mouth and cheeks using melted candy in cut parchment bags. For noses, trim off yellow area from candy corn; attach with melted candy. For earmuffs, cut two spice drops horizontally in half and cut a 3 in. piece of licorice; attach rounded tops of spice drops to ends of licorice and attach to face with melted candy. For red hat, shape spice drop with a pointed top and a slightly flattened bottom. Pipe hat band and pompom with melted candy; attach to face. For green hat brim, using rolling pin, flatten spice drop on surface sprinkled with granulated sugar; cut in half. For hat, slightly flatten another spice drop and attach to brim with melted candy. For hat band, roll out a yellow spice drop and cut a small strip; attach band to hat and hat to face with melted candy. Attach sticks to backs of snowflakes with melted candy. Each serves 1.

† Brand confectionery coating.

◀ A Real Tree Topper

Pans: 6, 8, 10 x 2 in. Round, p. 148; Mini Ball, p. 153

Tips: 2, 5, p. 138

Color: Kelly Green, p. 133

Candy: Holiday Ornaments Candy Mold, p. 195; White Candy Melts®† (3 pks. needed), p. 218; Decorator Brush Set, Candy Melting Plate, Garden and Primary Candy Color Sets, p. 219; 11¾ in. Lollipop Sticks, p. 221

Recipe: Buttercream Icing, p. 112

Also: Flower Nail No. 7, Parchment Triangles, p. 137; Wooden Dowel Rods, p. 167; spice drops, waxed paper, knife

In advance: Make candy treetop ornament. Using candy colors, tint portions of melted white candy violet and green. For center globe, use mini ball pan to mold 2 violet candy shells (p. 121); refrigerate until firm, unmold. For top and bottom globes, use candy melting plate as mold; make 4 green candy shells, refrigerate until firm and unmold. Mold 32 candy ornaments using painting method (p. 121); refrigerate until firm; unmold.

Ice 2-layer cakes smooth with buttercream and prepare for stacked construction (p. 110). Pipe tip 5 bead bottom borders on all cakes. For tip 2 branches on top borders, make a center string stem and add pull-out string needles; continue piping over side of each cake. Assemble treetop ornament. For top of ornament, press in sides of spice drop to lengthen and insert lollipop stick in bottom. To make holes at top and bottom of ornament globes for threading lollipop stick, heat tip of nail portion of flower nail and melt an opening for lollipop stick on globe halves. Make sure the openings line up on each half. Attach globe halves around lollipop stick with melted candy. Insert spice drop on bottom of stick. Leave 4 in. of stick exposed at bottom of ornament. Trim off remaining stick; insert in cake. Cut spice drops in half, flatten and attach on sides of treetop ornament with melted candy. Attach candy ornaments on cake sides with icing. Serves 60.

▶ Big Name Guests

Pan: Mini Loaf, p. 149

Candy: Primary Candy Color Set, p. 219; White Candy Melts®†, p. 218

Also: Holiday Ornaments Icing Decorations, p. 195; Parchment Triangles, p. 137

Mold candy plaques (p. 121) ⅜ in. deep in pan cavities; refrigerate until firm, unmold. Tint portions of melted candy red and green using colors from set. Using melted candy in cut parchment bag, pipe tree branch and name. Attach icing decoration with melted candy. Each serves 1.

◀ Hang Around for Fun!

Pans: Cookie Sheet, Cooling Grid, p. 217

Tips: 2, 3, 12, p. 138

Colors:* Red-Red, Violet, Rose, Kelly Green, Lemon Yellow, p. 133

Recipes: Roll-Out Cookie, Color Flow Icing, p. 112

Also: 2006 Pattern Book (Ornament Cap), p. 124; Comfort Grip™ Christmas Tree Cutter, p. 197; Comfort Grip™ Cutters in Heart and Round shapes, p. 214; Parchment Triangles,

p. 137; spice drops, granulated sugar, waxed paper, straight pin

In advance: Make 1 ornament cap for each cookie. Using pattern, tip 2 and full-strength color flow, outline cap; flow in with thinned color flow (p. 120). Let dry. For hanging hook, cut a thin layer from spice drop; sprinkle waxed paper with sugar and flatten with finger. Cut out center with small end of tip 12. Attach to back of cap with full-strength color flow. Let dry.

Cut out various shaped cookies; bake and cool. Place cookies on cooling grid over waxed paper. On heart and tree cookies, pipe full-strength color flow borders and let dry, then flow in various colored sections with thinned color flow; let dry. Overpipe scroll design on heart with tip 3 and full-strength color flow. On round cookie, flow in background with color flow and immediately add dots of red and yellow. With pin, pull out star points from yellow dots. Let dry. Attach caps to front of cookies with full-strength color flow. Each serves 1.

***Note:** Combine Violet with a little Rose for violet shown.

† Brand confectionery coating.

▶ Sparkle of the Season

Pan: Mini Holiday Ornament, p. 194

Tips: 3, 5, p. 138

Colors:* Golden Yellow, Red-Red, Christmas Red, p. 133

Also: Vanilla Whipped Icing Mix, p. 132; Disposable
    Decorating Bags, p. 137; strawberry and lime gelatin
    (3 oz. pk. each), non-stick vegetable pan spray

Prepare gelatin flavors following package directions.
Lightly spray pan with non-stick vegetable spray and
fill with gelatin. Refrigerate until firm; unmold. Decorate
with tinted whipped icing. Pipe tip 5 dot and string
ornament hanger on all designs. For lime ornament, pipe
tip 5 pull-out petals and tip 3 dot accents and flower
centers. For strawberry ornament, pipe tip 5 lines and
scrolls. Each serves 1.

***Note:** Combine Red-Red with Christmas Red for red shown.

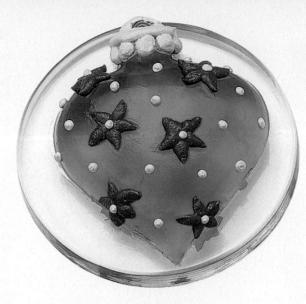

▶ Handling a Tall Order

Cookie: Comfort Grip™ Christmas Tree Cutter, p. 197;
    Cookie Sheet, Cooling Grid, p. 217

Tips: 1, 2, 3, 4, 5, 12, p. 138-139

Colors:* Copper (skintone), Black, Red-Red, Christmas
    Red, Lemon Yellow, Violet, Royal Blue, Kelly Green,
    p. 133

Recipes: Royal Icing, Roll-Out Cookie, p. 112

Also: Square Cut-Outs™, p. 128; Meringue Powder,
    p. 132; 11¾ in. Lollipop Sticks, p. 221; Rolling Pin,
    Roll & Cut Mat, p. 130, paring knife, waxed paper,
    cornstarch, plastic ruler

In advance: Prepare and decorate Santa and gift
cookies. Roll out dough; for each Santa cookie,
cut 1 tree using cutter, 1 large square and 3 medium
squares using Cut-Outs. Trim off extended branch areas
from tree to create a triangular shape. Trim large square
to 1 x 2 in. and medium squares to 1½ x 1 in., 1½ x ¾ in. and
1 x 1 in. Bake and cool all cookies.

Ice Santa and gifts smooth. Pipe tip 3 stripes or dots on
medium gifts, tip 4 stripes on large gift. Pipe tip 4 dot bow

on 1 in. gift. Place Santa on waxed paper. Pipe in tip 12
face (pat smooth with finger dipped in cornstarch). Pipe
tip 5 arms; add tip 12 bead boots. Pipe tip 4 zigzag beard and
fur trim on coat hem. Add tip 2 dot nose, tip 1 string eyes
and dot mouth, tip 3 pull-out moustache. With royal icing,
attach large gift at top of triangle. Pipe tip 4 mittens holding
gift. Build up hat under gift with tip 4 and add tip 3 zigzag fur
trim on hat and sleeves. Let dry overnight.

Remove Santa from waxed paper and attach stick to
back with royal icing, leaving 4 in. extended at bottom.
Attach remaining gifts to stick with royal icing. Let dry.
Each serves 1.

***Note:** Combine Red-Red and Christmas Red for red shown.

▶ Too Pretty To Open

Pan: Dimensions® Gift, p. 194

Tips: 3, 16, p. 138-139

Colors:* Red-Red, Christmas Red, Royal Blue, Kelly
    Green, Lemon Yellow, Golden Yellow, Violet, Rose,
    p. 133

Recipe: Buttercream Icing, p. 112

Also: Round Cut-Outs™, p. 128; Cake Board, Fanci-Foil
    Wrap, p. 169, cornstarch

Ice cake sides, background areas and bow loop
openings smooth. Outline loop openings and ends of
bow with tip 3. Cover bow with tip 16 stars. Imprint
ornaments on cake top using medium Cut-Out. Outline
and pipe in ornaments with tip 3 (pat smooth with finger
dipped in cornstarch). Add tip 3 dot or string designs.
Outline and pipe in ornament holders with tip 3 (pat
smooth with finger dipped in cornstarch). Pipe tip 3
swirls randomly on cake top. Serves 12.

***Note:** Combine Red-Red and Christmas Red for red shown.
Combine Lemon Yellow and Golden Yellow for yellow shown.
Combine Violet and Rose for violet shown.

◄ Love Loud and Clear

Pans: Oval Pan Set (10¾ x 7⅞ in. needed), p. 148; Mini Stand-Up Bear, p. 152

Tips: 3, 5, 8, 13, p. 138-139

Colors: Royal Blue, Violet, Rose, Red-Red, Lemon Yellow, Brown, Black, Copper (skin tone), p. 133

Recipe: Buttercream Icing, p. 112

Also: 2006 Pattern Book (Conversation Bubble), p. 124; Alphabet/Numerals Icing Decorations, p. 184; Sweet Talk Icing Decorations (2 pks. needed), p. 201; Kandy Clay™ Bright Colors Multi-Color Pack, p. 222; 8 in. Lollipop Sticks, p. 221; Cake Board, Fanci-Foil Wrap, p. 169; black shoestring licorice, card stock paper, hot glue gun, toothpick, cornstarch

Knead grape Kandy Clay to soften. For phone, shape into a rectangle ¾ x ¼ x 2 in. high. Insert 1 in. piece of licorice for antenna.

Trim ears, tummy and snout areas off bear cakes. For boy, trim off right arm; for girl, trim off both arms. Position cakes on foil-wrapped boards, cut to fit. Mark division for shirt and pants with toothpick. Build up shoe areas with icing; smooth with finger dipped in cornstarch. Outline and pipe in mouth with tip 3. Cover face and body with tip 13 stars. Attach phones with dots of icing. Build up arms, fingers, nose and ears with tip 13 stars. Pipe tip 3 string eyes. For boy, pipe tip 13 pull-out star hair. For girl, pipe tip 3 string hair and bow.

Ice smooth 2-layer 10¾ x 7⅞ in. oval cake (bake two 1½ in. layers to make a 3 in. high cake). Pipe tip 5 ball top border and tip 8 ball bottom border. Attach icing decorations with dots of icing. Position boy and girl cakes. Trace pattern on card stock paper and cut out conversation bubble. Attach lollipop sticks to back with hot glue. Attach icing decorations with dots of icing. Insert bubble in cake. Serves 28.

▼ Words of Love

Pans: 10½ x 15½ in. Jelly Roll, Cooling Grid, p. 149

Tip: 1, p. 138

Colors:* Rose, Violet, Kelly Green, Lemon Yellow, Golden Yellow, Red-Red, Christmas Red, p. 133

Recipes: Quick-Pour Fondant Icing, p. 111; Buttercream Icing, p. 112

Also: Heart Cut-Outs™, p. 128; Parchment Triangles, 12 in. Angled Spatula, p. 137

Bake and cool 1 in. high cake in jelly roll pan. Cut hearts using largest Cut-Out. Prepare and cover cakes with poured fondant (p. 111); let set. Print tip 1 messages in buttercream. Each serves 1.

*****Note:** Combine Lemon Yellow and Golden Yellow for yellow shown. Combine Violet and Rose for violet shown. Combine Red-Red and Christmas Red for red shown.

▲ Heartfelt Sentiments

Pan: Standard Muffin, p. 149

Tip: 1M (2110), p. 139

Recipe: Buttercream Icing, p. 112

Also: Pink Colored Sugars, p. 134; Sweet Talk Baking Cups, Fun Pix™, p. 201

Pipe tip 1M swirl on cupcakes; sprinkle with sugar. Insert picks in cupcakes. Each serves 1.

▲ Love Scene in Ice Cream

Cookie: Heart Comfort Grip™ Cookie Cutter, p. 202; Cookie Sheet, 10½ x 15½ in. Jelly Roll, p. 149; Cooling Grid, p. 217

Colors:* Rose, Lemon Yellow, Golden Yellow, p. 133

Recipes: French Vanilla Custard Ice Cream (included in The Incredible Ice Cream Machine™ Recipe Booklet), Roll-Out Cookie, p. 112

Also: The Incredible Ice Cream Machine (see Inside Front Cover); 6-Mix Sweetheart Assortment Sprinkle Decorations, p. 202; Red Candy Melts®†, p. 218; Rolling Pin, p. 130; Parchment Triangles, p. 137

Prepare frozen custard recipe and spread 1 in. thick in jelly roll pan; freeze until ready to use.

Divide cookie dough in half; tint yellow and pink. Roll out dough; cut 2 heart cookies for each sandwich. Bake and cool. Using melted candy in cut parchment bag, print message; let set. Cut ice cream hearts with cookie cutter and sandwich between two cookies. Press in sprinkles on sides of sandwiches. Serve immediately or wrap and freeze until ready to serve. Each serves 1.

*****Note:** Combine Lemon Yellow and Golden Yellow for yellow shown.

† Brand confectionery coating.

◄ Romantic Reminders

Cookie: Girl, Boy Plastic Cutters, p. 216; Cookie Spatula, p. 137; Cookie Sheet, Cooling Grid, p. 149

Tips: 2, 3, 4, p. 138

Colors: Royal Blue, Lemon Yellow, Kelly Green, Black, Rose, Copper (skin tone), Brown, p. 133

Recipes: Royal Icing, Roll-Out Cookie, p. 112

Also: Sweet Talk Icing Decorations, p. 201; Rolling Pin, p. 130, Meringue Powder, p. 132; cornstarch

Roll out dough; cut, bake and cool cookies. Outline and pipe in clothes with tip 3 (smooth with finger dipped in cornstarch). Position icing decorations. Pipe tip 4 string arms with tip 3 dot fingers. Add tip 2 dot and string facial features. Pipe tip 3 string or pull-out hair; add tip 2 string hair ribbons or bows. Pipe in tip 3 shoes (smooth with finger dipped in cornstarch). Each serves 1.

► Valentine Assembly Line

Pan: Horseshoe, p. 152

Colors: Lemon Yellow, Violet, Rose, Kelly Green, Brown, Black, Creamy Peach, Copper (skin tone), p. 133

Fondant: White Ready-To-Use Rolled Fondant (72 oz. needed), p. 126; Heart Cut-Outs™, p. 128; Fine Tip Primary Colors FoodWriter™ Edible Color Markers, Brush Set, p. 129; Roll & Cut Mat, Rolling Pin, p. 130; Cutter/Embosser, Easy-Glide Fondant Smoother, p. 131

Recipes: Buttercream Icing, p. 112

Also: Gum-Tex™, p. 130; Confectionery Tool Set, p. 131; Piping Gel, p. 132; 16 in. Cake Circles (3 needed), p. 169; thick uncooked spaghetti, craft knife, ruler, 10 x 2 in. high craft block, cornstarch, cellophane tape

Three days in advance: Make floor using 24 oz. of fondant. Tape 2 cake circles together. Using pan as pattern, trace horseshoe shape, marking 2 in. off on each side of horseshoe ends. Cut out board 2 in. larger than pattern. Cover with fondant; reserve remaining fondant for cherubs. Also in advance: Make fondant cherubs (p. 118) using 10 oz. fondant. Reserve remainder of white for additional features.

Make fondant blocks and hearts. Add 2 teaspoons Gum-Tex to 24 oz. fondant. Divide fondant in 5ths and tint violet, rose, peach, yellow and green. Roll out colors 1⅞ in. thick and cut two each 1½ in. squares in rose, green and yellow and 1 each in violet and peach. Roll out violet and rose ¼ in. thick and cut one 3 x 2 in. rectangle in each. Roll out colors ¼ in. thick and cut at least 15 hearts in each color using medium Cut-Out. Print messages with FoodWriter.

Bake and cool 1-layer cake; trim 2 in. off each end of horseshoe. Prepare cake for rolled fondant (p. 111). Cover cake with fondant; smooth with Fondant Smoother. Position cake on floor. Position cherubs and work area as shown; support cherubs with tiny balls of fondant if needed. Position hearts and fondant blocks. Serves 10.

◀ True Love Truffles

Pans: Sports Ball, p. 153

Tip: 2, p. 138

Candy: Hearts Candy Mold, p. 201; Light Cocoa Candy Melts®† (5 pks. needed), p. 218; Decorator Brush Set, p. 219; 6 in. Lollipop Sticks, p. 221

Recipe: Basic Ganache and Truffles, p. 120

Also: From The Heart Nesting Cutter Set, p. 203; Non-Stick Cookie Pan, p. 146; "Hidden" Pillars, p. 166; Parchment Triangles, p. 137; Cake Boards, Fanci-Foil Wrap, p. 169; waxed paper, plastic ruler, wooden mixing spoon, knife

In advance: Prepare truffles. Mold 30 hearts in candy mold (p. 121). On cookie pan, mold 4 hearts in smallest crinkle cutter from set, filling ¼ in. deep with melted candy. Refrigerate until firm; gently press to release hearts. Attach crinkle hearts to lollipop sticks with melted candy; let set.

Make goblet. For bowl section, make a ¼ in. thick candy shell (p. 121) using ball pan half and 3 pks. of melted candy. For base section, make a 1 in. thick candy plaque (p. 121) using remaining melted candy from shell in ball pan half. Make goblet "stem" (p. 121). Attach heart candies to bowl and base with melted candy. Trim lollipop sticks as needed and insert 2 or 3 truffles on each stick to support crinkle hearts. Brush sticks with melted candy. Position crinkle hearts in bowl and fill bowl with truffles. Each truffle serves 1.

▼ Chocolate Can Charm

Pan: 10 x 2 in. Heart, p. 147, Small Non-Stick Cookie Pan, p. 146

Tips: 10, 127D, p. 138-139

Candy: Light Cocoa Candy Melts®†, p. 218; Truffles Mold, p. 221

Recipe: Chocolate Buttercream Icing, p. 112 (or use 3 pks. Chocolate Ready-To-Use Decorator Icing, p. 132)

Also: Cake Board, p. 169; From The Heart Nesting Cutter Set, p. 203

In advance: Mold 20 truffles (p. 121), filling mold half full. Refrigerate until firm. On cookie pan, mold a ¼ in. deep candy center heart in largest crinkle cutter from set. Refrigerate until firm; gently press to release.

Ice smooth 2-layer heart cake (bake two 1½ in. layers to make a 3 in. high cake). Pipe tip 127D ruffle top border; position truffles and center heart. Pipe tip 10 ball bottom border. Cake serves 24; each truffle serves 1.

▲ Chocolate Lover's Valentine

Pans: 9 in. Heart Springform, p. 200; Cookie Sheet, p. 217

Tip: 21, p. 139

Recipe: Chocolate Cheesecake, p. 113, Chocolate Buttercream Icing, p. 112 (or use Chocolate Ready-To-Use Decorator Icing, p. 132)

Also: 2006 Pattern Book (Candy "C"), p. 124; Parchment Triangles, p. 137; Light Cocoa Candy Melts®† (2 pks. needed), p. 218; cherry pie filling, waxed paper

In advance: Make 30 candy "C" pieces. Place pattern on cookie sheet and cover with waxed paper. Outline pattern using melted candy in cut parchment bag; refrigerate until firm. Carefully peel candy off waxed paper and turn over; outline back of "C"; refrigerate until firm. Make extras to allow for breakage.

Bake and cool cheesecake. Pipe tip 21 shell bottom border. On top of heart, pipe tip 21 shells in a heart shape, 1¼ in. from top edge. Fill inside shell heart with cherry filling. Position "C" candies around cake. Serves 20.

† Brand confectionery coating

▲ Ruffled Rose Romance

Pan: SweetHeart, p. 200

Colors: Rose, Kelly Green, p. 133

Fondant: White Ready-To-Use Rolled Fondant (24 oz. needed), p. 126; Leaf Cut-Outs™, p. 128; Brush Set, p. 129; Rolling Pin, Roll & Cut Mat, p. 130; Shaping Foam, Cutter/Embosser, p. 131

Recipe: Buttercream Icing, p. 112

Also: Confectionery Tool Set, p. 131; Cake Board, Fanci-Foil Wrap, p. 169; cornstarch

Ice smooth 2-layer cake (bake two 1½ in. high layers to make a 3 in. high cake). Tint 8 oz. fondant dark rose, 6 oz. light rose and a 1½ in. ball light green; reserve remainder white. Roll out light rose fondant ⅛ in. thick; cut two 1 x 15 in. long strips. Position strips flat around top border of cake; trim to fit heart shape.

Make 19 ruffled ribbon roses (p. 119) in dark rose. Attach flowers to top edge of cake with damp brush. Roll out light green fondant ⅛ in. thick. Cut 20 leaves using smallest Cut-Out. Place leaves on thin foam and score vein lines with veining tool. Attach with damp brush. Roll out light rose fondant ⅛ in. thick. Cut ¼ in. wide strips; position on cake to form message. Roll ½ in. balls of white fondant and attach to bottom border with buttercream. Serves 12.

▲ Love's Twists and Turns

Cookie: Hearts Cutter Set, p. 203; Cookie Sheet, Cooling Grid, p. 217

Tips: 2, 3, p. 138

Colors:* Rose, Kelly Green, Violet, p. 133

Recipe: Color Flow Icing, p. 112; Roll-Out Cookie, p. 112

Also: Color Flow Mix, p. 132; Rolling Pin, p. 130

In advance: Make cookies. Roll out dough and cut cookies using heart cutter; bake and cool. Cover cookies with thinned color flow (p. 120); let set overnight. Using full-strength color flow, pipe tip 2 swirls on tops and tip 3 dots on sides of cookies; let set. Each serves 1.

***Note:** Combine Violet with a little Rose for violet shown.

▼ Get Right to the Point!

Cookie: Heart Cut-Outs™, p. 128; 6 in. Cookie Treat Sticks, Cookie Sheet, Cooling Grid, p. 217

Tips: 4, 352, p. 138-139

Colors:* Rose, Red-Red, Christmas Red, p. 133

Recipes: Buttercream Icing, Poured Cookie Icing, Roll-Out Cookie, p. 112

Also: Rolling Pin, p. 130; 1 x 1½ in. paper name tags with hole, paring knife, waxed paper, marking pen, 12 in. pink curling ribbon for each cookie

Roll out dough ⅜ in. thick. Using largest Cut-Out, cut 2 hearts for each arrow. Place small ball of dough on cookie sheet; flatten and position cookie treat stick on top. Position heart cookie over stick. Cut 2nd heart into a "V" shape by trimming ½ in. from each side at widest point. Using trimmed off dough, form a ball and insert on opposite end of stick. Position V-shaped piece on top of ball for arrow tail, pressing slightly together to secure. Bake and cool cookies, allowing more baking time for thicker cookies. Cover heart cookie with poured cookie icing (p. 120); let set. On arrow tail, pipe tip 4 center line in buttercream. Add tip 352 pull-out leaf feathers, starting at wide end and working toward narrow end. Write message on name tag and attach to stick with ribbon. Each serves 1.

***Note:** Combine Red-Red and Christmas Red for red shown.

▶ Peeker Cottontails

Pans: 12 x 2 in. Round, p. 148; Cookie Sheet, Cooling Grid, p. 149
Tips: 1, 2, 3, 5, 18, 47, 233, p. 138-139
Colors:* Royal Blue, Kelly Green, Rose, Brown, Red-Red, p. 133
Recipes: Buttercream Icing, Roll-Out Cookie, p. 112
Also: Petite Eggs Icing Decorations (2 pks. needed), p. 205; Plastic
   Nesting Bunny Cookie Cutter Set, p. 207; Rolling Pin, p. 130;
   Cake Circles, Fanci-Foil Wrap, p. 169; cornstarch, toothpick

Roll out cookie dough. Cut 1 bunny using 2nd largest cutter and
2 bunnies using 2nd smallest cutter; bake and cool. Ice cookies
smooth in buttercream. Outline and pipe in inner ears and noses
with tip 3 and mouth and eyes with tip 2 (smooth all with finger
dipped in cornstarch). Pipe tip 1 string whiskers.

Ice 1-layer cake smooth. Mark cake top, 4½ in. from bottom
edge with toothpick. Cover area with tip 47 (ridged side up)
basketweave. Pipe tip 18 rope top border for handle. Add tip 233
pull-out grass on top edge of basket. Attach bunny cookies to
cake with dots of buttercream; pipe tip 5 bead paws. Add tip 233
pull-out grass bottom border and position icing decorations. Cake
serves 20; each cookie serves 1.

***Note:** Combine Brown and Red-Red for brown shown.

◀ Every Hare in Place

Pan: Mini Egg, p. 204
Colors: Rose, Kelly Green, p. 133
Fondant: White Ready-To-Use Rolled Fondant (24 oz. needed), p. 126;
   Oval Cut-Outs™, p. 128; Fine Tip Neon Colors FoodWriter™ Edible
   Color Markers, Brush Set, p. 129; Rolling Pin, Roll & Cut Mat, p. 130
Recipe: Buttercream Icing, p. 112
Also: Cake Board, Fanci-Foil Wrap, p. 169; cornstarch

Divide fondant in 3rds. Tint portions rose, dark rose and green. Roll out
⅛ in. thick and cut outer ears using largest Cut-Out and inner ears using
medium Cut-Out. Attach inner ear to outer ear with damp brush. Let dry
on cornstarch-dusted surface.

Prepare egg cakes for rolled fondant (p. 111) and cover cakes. Using
a ⅛ in. ball of fondant, shape nose and attach with damp brush. Draw
facial features with FoodWriter. Before serving, position cake on ears.
Each serves 1.

◀ Get a Bunny Hug

Pans: 3-D Egg, Mini Egg, p. 204
Tips: 3, 8, 12, p. 138-139
Colors: Rose, Black, p. 133
Recipe: Buttercream Icing, p. 112
Also: Parchment Triangles, p. 137; 16 in. Cake Circles, Fanci-Foil Wrap,
   p. 169; 1 in. wide purple satin ribbon (2 ft. needed), cornstarch

Bake and cool half 3-D egg cake and 3 mini egg cakes. For feet, cut
1 mini egg in half horizontally. For ears, cut 2 mini eggs horizontally,
leaving ⅝ in. high bottom. Position cakes, trimming feet to fit against
curve of body. Trace shape on board, allowing 3 in. for arms and an
additional ¾ in. for each ear. Cut board and wrap with foil; position
cakes. Ice cakes smooth; extend length of ears ¾ in. with icing. Pipe
tip 8 oval eyes with tip 3 oval pupils (smooth with finger dipped in
cornstarch). Outline and pipe in mouth and teeth with tip 3 (smooth
with finger dipped in cornstarch). Build up tip 12 cheeks and tip 8 nose
(smooth nose with finger dipped in cornstarch). Pipe inner ears with
tip 3 (smooth with finger dipped in cornstarch). Pipe tip 12 ball arms and
paws (smooth with finger dipped in cornstarch). Make a purple bow;
attach with icing. Serves 9.

▶ Basket Inspectors

Pan: Standard Muffin, p. 149
Tip: 233, p. 139
Color: Kelly Green, p. 133
Recipe: Buttercream Icing, p. 112
Also: 2006 Pattern Book (Basket Handle), p. 124; Bunnies & Chicks Standard Baking Cups, Icing Decorations, p. 205; White Candy Melts®†, p. 218; Garden Candy Color Set, p. 219; Parchment Triangles, p. 137, Cake Board, p. 169; mini jelly beans, waxed paper

In advance: Make candy handle. Tint melted white candy pink using candy color. Tape pattern on board and cover with waxed paper. Using melted candy in cut parchment bag, pipe connecting dots over pattern line; refrigerate until firm. Carefully remove waxed paper and turn over handle; repeat, piping connecting dots on back. Refrigerate until firm.

Cover tops of cupcakes with tip 233 pull-out grass in buttercream. Attach handle to cupcake with dots of icing. Position icing decoration and jelly beans. Each serves 1.

† Brand confectionery coating.

▼ Falling Into Spring

Pan: Standard Muffin, p. 149
Tip: 233, p. 139
Color: Kelly Green, p. 133
Fondant: White Ready-To-Use Rolled Fondant (24 oz. needed), p. 126; Fine Tip Neon Colors FoodWriter™ Edible Color Markers, Brush Set, p. 129; Rolling Pin, Roll & Cut Mat, p. 130
Recipe: Buttercream Icing, p. 112
Also: Coupler Ring Set, p. 133; Bunnies and Chicks Standard Baking Cups, p. 205; Easter Bite-Size Cutter Set, p. 207; mini jelly beans, cornstarch, craft knife, small plastic ruler

In advance: Make fondant bunny head and limbs. Roll out fondant ⅛ in. thick. Cut out head using cutter from set; cut out feet using back of coupler ring then shape into oval. For arms, cut ¼ x 1 in. strips using craft knife. For hands, flatten a ¼ in. ball of fondant; shape into hands and attach to arms with damp brush. Let dry on cornstarch-dusted surface at least 1 hour. Using FoodWriter markers, draw details on head and feet.

Pipe tip 233 pull-out grass on cupcake tops. Insert head, supporting back with jelly bean. Insert arms and paws, trimming if necessary. Position jelly beans between feet and arms. Each serves 1.

▲ Bow-Tied Bunnies

Candy: Candy Melts®† in White and Light Cocoa (1 pk. each), p. 218; Smiley Face Candy Mold, p. 220; Garden Candy Color Set, p. 219; 6 in. Lollipop Sticks, p. 221
Also: Leaf Cut-Outs™, p. 128; Non-Stick Cookie Sheet, p. 146; Parchment Triangles, p. 137; ⅜ in. wide pink satin ribbon (8 in. needed for each lollipop)

Tint a small portion of melted white candy rose using candy color. Mold face lollipops in white (p. 121). Refrigerate until firm; unmold. For ears, place medium leaf Cut-Out on cookie sheet; fill ¼ in. deep with melted white candy. Refrigerate until firm; gently press on back to release. Repeat for other ear, reversing Cut-Out. Using melted candy in cut parchment bag, pipe facial features and inner ears. Attach ears with melted candy; refrigerate until firm. Tie on bow. Each serves 1.

▶ Grabbing His Garden Gift

Pans: Oval Set (13½ x 9⅞ in. needed), p. 148; 3-D Bunny, p. 204
Tips: 1A, 3, 16, p. 138-139
Colors: Kelly Green, Violet, Rose, p. 133
Fondant: White Ready-To-Use Fondant (24 oz. needed), Pastel Colors Fondant Multi Pack, p. 126; Daisy Cut-Outs™, p. 128; Brush Set, p. 129; Rolling Pin, Roll & Cut Mat, p. 130; Shaping Foam, p. 131
Recipe: Thinned Fondant Adhesive, p. 111; Buttercream Icing, p. 112
Also: Gum-Tex™, p. 130; Confectionery Tool Set, Flower Former Set, p. 131; Dowel Rods, p. 167; Cake Boards, Fanci-Foil Wrap, p. 169; cloth-covered florist wire (three 6 in. lengths needed), brown candy-coated chocolates, pink jelly bean, cornstarch, craft block, drinking straw

At least 48 hours in advance: Make fondant daisies. Tint 4 oz. white fondant violet using violet icing color with a little rose.

Add rose color to pastel pink fondant to deepen color. Add ½ teaspoon Gum-Tex to each 4 oz. fondant. Roll out colors ⅛ in. thick and cut 30 medium and 20 small daisies in various colors using Cut-Outs. On thin foam, soften petals from outside petal tip toward center using medium ball tool from

set. Cup centers of flowers on thick foam using dogbone tool. Roll ⅛ in. to ¼ in. fondant balls for flower centers; flatten slightly and attach with damp brush. Let dry on medium flower formers dusted with cornstarch. **At least 24 hours in advance:** Make 3 flower calyxes. Roll a ½ in. ball of pastel green fondant; shape into a teardrop. Dip florist wire in water and insert in tip of teardrop; flatten top and let dry overnight in craft block. Attach 3 large daisies to bases with thinned fondant adhesive.

Ice 1-layer oval cake smooth. Dowel rod area where bunny will sit. Position bunny cake. Ice inner ears smooth. Outline legs and mouth with tip 3. Build up hands with tip 1A. Cover bunny with tip 16 stars. Add tip 16 rosette tail. Attach candy coated chocolate eyes and jelly bean nose with dots of icing. Attach daisies to cake sides with dots of icing. Thread wired flowers through a 1½ in. piece of drinking straw. Push straw up to align with hand position. Add a 2 in. piece of drinking straw to bottoms of wires for inserting in base cake. Insert flowers in hands. Serves 27.

◀ Pure Egg-stravagance!

Pan: 10 x 2 in. Round, p. 147
Tip: 190, p. 138
Colors: Violet, Kelly Green, p. 133
Fondant: Ready-To-Use Rolled Fondant in White (72 oz. needed) and Pastel Pink (24 oz. needed), Pastel Colors Fondant Multi Pack, p. 126; Leaf Cut-Outs™, p. 128; Brush Set, p. 129; Rolling Pin, Roll & Cut Mat, p. 130; Cutter/Embosser, Easy-Glide Fondant Smoother, p. 131
Recipe: Buttercream Icing, Roll-Out Cookie, p. 112
Also: Hoppy Easter Colored Metal Cutter Set, p. 207; Mini Geometric Crinkle Cutter Set, p. 214; 8 in. Lollipop Sticks, p. 221; 8 in. Cookie Treat Sticks, p. 217; 12 in. Round Silver Cake Base, p. 169; White Candy Melts®†, p. 218; Gum-Tex™, p. 130; Cake Dividing Set, p. 136; Confectionery Tool Set, Flower Former Set, p. 131, Cake Board, p. 169; 1½ in. wide pink satin ribbon (1 yd. needed), cornstarch

Several days in advance: Make fondant handle. Add 1 teaspoon Gum-Tex to 12 oz. white fondant. Roll 2 logs, ⅝ in. thick and 22 in. long; twist together. Brush cookie treat sticks with water and insert on each end. Curve to shape on cornstarch-dusted board and let dry. **Also in advance:** Make fondant leaves. Tint 8 oz. white fondant green; roll out ⅛ in. thick. Cut 50 leaves using medium Cut-Out. Score vein lines using straight-edge wheel from Cutter/Embosser; let dry on large flower formers dusted with cornstarch.

Cut 30 cookies using egg cutter from set; bake and cool. Tint 4 oz. white fondant violet; roll out violet and pastel pink, yellow and blue fondant ⅛ in. thick. Cut egg shapes with cutter. Imprint designs on fondant using wheels of Cutter/Embosser for lines, small end of tip 190 for flowers and parts of mini crinkle cutters for various designs. Attach fondant to cookies with buttercream. Attach lollipop sticks to cookies with melted candy. Prepare 2-layer cake for rolled fondant (p. 111). Cover cake and smooth with Fondant Smoother. Divide cake in 10ths; mark 2 in. down from top edge of cake between division marks. For swags, roll out pink fondant ⅛ in. thick and cut 4 x 3 in. pieces. Gather at ends to form folds; attach at division points with damp brush. Deepen folds using veining tool. Roll ½ in. balls of pink fondant and attach at division points with damp brush. For bottom border, roll 2 logs, ½ in. thick and 30 in. long. Twist together to make rope and attach to cake with damp brush. Insert egg cookies and handle in cake. Attach leaves around eggs with buttercream. Tie bow to handle. Cake serves 28; each cookie serves 1.

† Brand confectionery coating.

▶ The Cool Chicks

Cookie: Easter Cutter Collection, p. 207; Cookie Sheet, Cooling Grid, p. 149
Tips: 2, 3, 4, 102, p. 138-139
Colors:* Orange, Lemon Yellow, Golden Yellow, Violet, Rose, Kelly Green, p. 133
Recipe: Royal Icing, Roll-Out Cookie, p. 112
Also: Rolling Pin, p. 130; Meringue Powder, p. 132, cornstarch

In advance: Make cookies. Roll out dough; cut cookies with chick cutter. Bake and cool. Outline body and beak with tip 2. Pipe in body and beak with thinned royal icing; let set overnight. With full-strength royal icing, pipe tip 4 dot eye and pupil; pipe in tip 4 hat and foot (pat smooth with finger dipped in cornstarch). Add tip 102 ruffle on hat. Pipe tip 4 string hatband and tip 3 bow. Outline wing with tip 4. Each serves 1.

***Note:** Combine Lemon Yellow and Golden Yellow for yellow shown and Violet and Rose for violet shown.

▶ Scrambled Colors!

Pan: Decorated Egg, p. 204
Tips: 12 (4 needed), 18, p. 139
Colors: Kelly Green, Rose, Violet, Lemon Yellow, p. 133
Recipe: Buttercream Icing, p. 112
Also: Disposable Decorating Bags, p. 137; Cake Board, Fanci-Foil Wrap, p. 169; shredded coconut, jelly beans, zip-close plastic bag

Prepare firm-textured batter such as pound cake. Tint ¼ batter each green, rose, violet and yellow. Grease and flour pan. Fill four disposable bags fitted with tip 12 with tinted batter. Randomly pipe dollops of batter in pan, using all batter. Bake cake 50-60 minutes; let cool 10 minutes and level bottom. Unmold cake and let cool completely. Ice smooth. Pipe tip 18 loose zigzags. Position jelly beans. Tint coconut green (p. 117) and sprinkle around cake. Serves 12.

▲ An Egg-cess of Eggs!

Candy: Candy Melts®† in White (2 pks. needed) and Light Cocoa (1 pk. needed), p. 218; Hoppy Easter Lollipop Mold, p. 205; Garden and Primary Candy Color Sets, Decorator Brush Set, p. 219

Also: 2006 Pattern Book (Hutch Door and Windows), p. 124; Bunny Hutch Cookie House Kit (includes pre-baked house, fruit jelly rounds and jelly beans) p. 206; Cake Board, Fanci-Foil Wrap, p. 169; Parchment Triangles, p. 132; 9 x 14 x 1 in. craft block, 1 in. wide pink satin ribbon (5 ft. needed), 24-gauge white florist wire (7 in. long, 24 pieces needed), white florist tape, wafer candy (3-4 rolls needed), shredded coconut, pastel candy-coated chocolate peanuts, jelly beans (additional needed), hot glue gun, small paring knife, zip-close plastic bag

In advance: Mold candies. Reserve ⅔ pk. of white candy for covering base. Tint portions of remainder pink, dark green, violet, yellow and orange and leave 1 portion white. Mold assorted candies without sticks using painting method (p. 121); refrigerate until firm and unmold.

Trim base board from Bunny Hutch Kit to measure 1 in. around hutch. Score door and window patterns with paring knife; pipe in with melted candy. Let set. Pipe curtains, doorknob and door window with melted candy; let set. Attach wafer candy halves for awnings and fruit jelly round halves for window sills using melted candy. Attach wafer candies on roof and eaves with melted candy; let set. Attach wafer candies at roof peak with melted candy; let set.

For base, wrap craft block with foil. Tint reserved white candy light green. Attach decorated hutch to base with melted candy. Cover top of base with melted candy; let set. Attach candies with melted candy; let set. For trees, attach a jelly bean to end of each wire with melted candy; let set. Tape wires together to form trees. Insert end of brush in top of base to make placement holes for trees. Insert trees. Glue ribbon around sides of base; make a bow and glue to base. Tint coconut (p. 117) using candy color and sprinkle in grass area. Position candies.

◄ First Bloom of Spring

Colors: Rose, Violet, Kelly Green, Lemon Yellow, Royal Blue, p. 133

Fondant: White Ready-To-Use Rolled Fondant, p. 126; Cut-Outs™ in Leaf and Garden Shapes, p. 128; Rolling Pin, Roll & Cut Mat, p. 130; Cutter/Embosser, p. 131

Candy: Candy Melts®† in White and Light Cocoa, p. 218; Decorator Brush Set, p. 219; Cordial Cups Mold, 6 in. Lollipop Sticks, p. 221

Recipe: Peanut Butter Filling, p. 121

Also: Clear Vanilla Extract, p. 132; cornstarch, paring knife

One day in advance: Make fondant tulips and leaves. Tint portions of white fondant blue, yellow, green, rose and violet (add a little rose to violet). Roll out tinted fondant ⅛ in. thick. Cut tulips and smallest leaves using Cut-Outs. Use straight-edge wheel of Cutter/Embosser to score vein lines on leaves. Let dry 24 hours on cornstarch-dusted surface. Trim lollipop sticks to 3 in. Tint 1 teaspoon of vanilla green; brush on lollipop sticks to make stems; let dry. Attach tulips and leaves to stems with melted candy; let set.

Combine 3 parts white candy with 1 part cocoa candy. Make candy shells in mold (p. 121); fill shell with Peanut Butter Filling and seal top of shell with candy. Refrigerate until firm; unmold. Make a small hole in center of cordial cup with knife. Insert stems, securing with melted candy. Each serves 1.

◄ Proud Uncle

Pan: Little Hero, p. 153; Cookie Sheet, Cooling Grid, p. 149
Tips: 2, 4, 13, 16, 21, p. 138-139
Colors:* Royal Blue, Red-Red, Christmas Red, Black, Copper (skin tone), p. 133
Recipes: Buttercream Icing, Roll-Out Cookie, p. 112
Also: 2006 Pattern Book (Hat), p. 124; 6 in. Lollipop Sticks, p. 221; Cake Board, Fanci-Foil Wrap, p. 169; small flag decal (4 x 2¼ in.), large marshmallows, cellophane tape, scissors, knife, cornstarch

Roll out dough. Using pattern, cut hat. Bake and cool; set aside. Pipe tip 2 star shapes on hatband; cover remainder of hatband with tip 13 stars. Cover stripes and brim of hat with tip 16 stars.

Trim suspenders and fire hose off cake. Ice sides and background areas smooth. Outline body, clothes and shoes with tip 4. Pipe in eyes, mouth, shirt, inside of jacket tail and sleeves with tip 4 (smooth with finger dipped in cornstarch). Cover shoes, pants, jacket and face with tip 16 stars. Build up nose with tip 16 stars. Overpipe tip 4 dot pupils (smooth with finger dipped in cornstarch). Outline and pipe in tip 4 bow tie and add tip 4 dot knot (smooth with finger dipped in cornstarch). Pipe tip 16 pull-out star moustache and goatee; pipe tip 16 stripe hair. Pipe tip 21 star bottom border. Tape flag decal to lollipop stick and position in hands; insert additional stick at bottom of hands. Outline hands with tip 4 and overpipe with tip 16 stars. Position hat; support with large marshmallows. Cake serves 12; cookie serves 1.

*Note: Combine Red-Red and Christmas Red for red shown.

▲ Popping With Pride

Cookie: Star Comfort Grip™ Cutter, p. 214; Cookie Sheet, Cooling Grid, p. 217
Tips: 2, 4, p. 138
Colors:* Royal Blue, Red-Red, Christmas Red, Black, Copper (skin tone), p. 133
Recipes: Royal Icing, Roll-Out Cookie, p. 112
Also: Round Cut-Outs™, p. 128; Stars and Stripes Party Picks, p. 208; 6 in. Cookie Treat Sticks, p. 217; Meringue Powder, p. 132; black jelly beans, red spice drops, white wafer candies, cornstarch

Roll out dough and cut cookies using medium round Cut-Out™ and star cutter. Bake and cool. Ice face and shirt area smooth (smooth with finger dipped in cornstarch). Pipe tip 2 facial features, hair, beard and goatee. For hat, turn spice drop upside down and pipe tip 2 blue band on bottom (smooth with finger dipped in cornstarch). Attach to wafer candy brim with icing. Pipe tip 2 white stripes on hat and attach to head with icing; set aside. Outline and pipe in jacket and lapels with tip 4 (smooth with finger dipped in cornstarch). Pipe tip 2 stripes on pants. Pipe in tip 2 bow tie. Attach head to body with icing. For shoes, cut jelly beans in half and attach with icing. Pipe tip 2 hands; position flag pick in left hand and overpipe dot fingers; let dry. Attach stick to back of cookie with icing. Let dry. Each serves 1.

*Note: Combine Red-Red and Christmas Red for red shown.

► Making Summer Sizzle

Pan: 10½ x 15½ in. Jelly Roll, p. 149
Fondant: White Ready-to-Use Rolled Fondant (48 oz. needed), Primary Colors Fondant Multi Pack (2 pks. needed), p. 126; Star Cut-Outs™, p. 128; Fine Tip Primary Colors FoodWriter™ Edible Color Markers, Brush Set, p. 129; Cutter/Embosser, p. 131; Rolling Pin, Roll & Cut Mat, p. 130
Recipe: Buttercream Icing, p. 112; Jelly Roll Yellow Sponge Cake, p. 113
Also: Red, Blue Cake Sparkles™, p. 134; Patriotic Foil Fun Pix®, p. 208; Star Nesting Cookie Cutter Set, p. 216; Cake Board, Fanci-Foil Wrap, p. 169

In advance: Roll out red, white and blue fondant ⅛ in. thick. Cut 3 white stars using smallest nesting cookie cutter. Cut 2 red and 1 blue stars using 2nd largest nesting cookie cutter. Let stars dry. Crush Cake Sparkles™ to a finer texture with rolling pin. Brush tops of red and blue stars with water and sprinkle with matching color sparkles.

Bake and cool 3 jelly roll cakes. Fill, roll and prepare each for rolled fondant (p. 111). Cover cakes with fondant. Using Cutter/Embosser, cut out ½ in. wide strips of red and blue fondant; attach diagonally on each cake, about 1¼ in. apart, with damp brush. Using smallest Cut-Out, cut approximately 32 red or blue stars for each cake. Attach small stars between strips with damp brush. Using blue FoodWriter, write message on white stars. Attach white to large colored stars with buttercream; attach to cakes. Insert Foil Pix in cake tops. Position remaining stars around cakes. Each cake serves 12.

▶ Old Glory Custard Cake

It's red, white and blue through and through! Cake batter is tinted before baking; the colorful layers sandwich a sheet of creamy vanilla custard made in our Incredible Ice Cream Machine.

Pan: Stars and Stripes, p. 208
Tips: 16, 21, p. 139
Colors: Red-Red, No-Taste Red, Royal Blue, p. 133
Recipes: Buttercream Icing, p. 112; French Vanilla Custard Ice Cream (included in The Incredible Ice Cream Machine™ Recipe Book)
Also: The Incredible Ice Cream Machine™, (see Inside Front Cover); Cake Board, Fanci-Foil Wrap, p. 169; plastic wrap, sharp knife

Divide cake batter in half; tint blue and red. Separately bake and cool 1 in. high layers, removing carefully from pan. Prepare custard. Line pan with plastic wrap and spread an even 1 in. layer of custard in pan. Freeze until firm.

Position blue cake layer on foil-covered board. Unmold custard and position on top of blue cake layer; trim to fit flush with cake using knife. Position red cake layer on top of custard layer. Ice cake sides smooth with buttercream. Cover star field area with tip 16 blue stars; add tip 21 white stars on top. Pipe tip 21 alternating red and white curving stripes on remainder of cake. Add tip 21 star bottom border. Freeze until ready to serve. Serves 12.

*Note: Combine Red-Red and No-Taste Red for red shown.

▲ Treats at Attention

Pan: Standard Muffin, p. 149
Tip: 1M (2110), p. 139
Cookie: Nesting Stars Metal Cutter Set, p. 214; Cookie Sheet, Cooling Grid, p. 149
Candy: White Candy Melts®†, p. 218; 4 in. Lollipop Sticks, p. 221
Recipes: Buttercream Icing, Roll-Out Cookie, p. 112
Also: Old Glory Baking Cups, p. 208; 3-Mix Patriotic Sparkling Sugars, p. 209; Disposable Decorating Bags, Tapered Spatula, p. 137

Cut cookies using smallest star; bake and cool. Ice cookies smooth. Sprinkle with sparkling sugars. Attach sticks to backs of cookies with melted candy; let set. Pipe tip 1M swirl on cupcake tops. Sprinkle cupcakes with white sparkling sugar. Trim sticks as needed and insert two cookies in each cupcake. Each serves 1.

† Brand confectionery coating.

◀ Covered With Glory

Pan: 8 x 2 in. Round, p. 148
Tips: 12, 13, 16, p. 139
Colors: Royal Blue, Christmas Red, p. 133
Cookie: Nesting Stars Metal Cutter Set, p. 214; Cookie Sheet, Cooling Grid, p. 217
Recipes: Buttercream Icing, Roll-Out Cookie, p. 112
Also: Red, Blue Colored Sugars, p. 134; White Candy Melts®†, p. 218; 11¾ in. Lollipop Sticks, p. 221; Cake Board, Fanci-Foil Wrap, p. 169; Cake Dividing Set, p. 136, white curling ribbon, plastic ruler, toothpick

Ice 2-layer cake smooth. Divide cake into 4ths. Pipe tip 12 outline pole at division marks. Mark 3 in. to the right of each pole for blue field. In each division, starting from bottom of cake, pipe 6 rows of tip 16 stars, alternating red and white rows. Pipe tip 16 blue stars in marked area. Continue piping alternating rows of tip 16 red and white stars to top of cake, ending with red rows. Pipe tip 13 white stars on blue field. Pipe tip 12 ball on top of each flag pole.

Cut cookies using 2 smallest stars; bake and cool. Ice cookies smooth. Sprinkle with sugars. Attach lollipop sticks to backs of cookies with melted candy; let set. Cut 30 in. lengths of curling ribbon. Curl ribbon and tie to lollipop sticks. Insert cookies in cake. Cake serves 20; each cookie serves 1.

Times of Your Life

A cake is a great way to start making your special occasion feel truly special. Sometimes just seeing our dessert ideas can help your entire party décor fall into place. Sprinkle an umbrella look throughout the baby shower with candy and cookie favors and a fun cake. Or roll out the scrolls at the graduation party...cream-filled roll-up cookies and a happy grad clutching his diploma create a great themed look. We're here to inspire you with fondant bouquets for the bride, mini bassinet cakes for the mother-to-be and much more!

Instructions for projects shown on these two pages are on page 70.

Romance in the Rain

Pans: 8, 12 x 2 in. Round, p. 147; Sports Ball Set, p. 153

Tips: 1, 2, p. 138

Color: Leaf Green, p. 133

Fondant: Ready-To-Use Rolled Fondant in White (48 oz. needed) and Pastel Blue (72 oz. needed), Neon Colors Fondant Multi Pack, p. 126; Round Cut-Outs™, p. 128; Brush Set, p. 129; Rolling Pin, Roll & Cut Mat, p. 130; Cutter/Embosser, Easy-Glide Fondant Smoother, p. 131

Recipes: Gum Paste, p. 111; Buttercream and Royal Icings, p. 112

Also: Floral Collection Flower Making Set, Confectionery Tool Set, p. 131; Gum Paste Mix, p. 130; Cake Dividing Set, p. 136; Piping Gel, Meringue Powder, p. 132; Cake Boards, 14 in. Round Silver Cake Base, p. 169; Wooden Dowel Rods, p. 167; ⅝ in. wide white satin-edged ribbon (16 in. needed), ⅜" wide white satin ribbon (51 in. needed), cornstarch

At least 3 days in advance: Make large umbrella cake top (p. 119) and flowers. For flowers, tint 3 oz. portions of white fondant violet, yellow and pink by kneading in ½ in. balls of neon fondant. Roll out colors ⅛ in. thick. Using apple blossom cutter from Flower Making Set, cut 45 yellow and 30 each pink and violet flowers; reserve remaining fondant for umbrellas. Move flowers to thin foam and soften edges with medium ball tool from Confectionery Tool Set. Move flowers to thick foam and cup center with ball tool. Let dry on cornstarch-dusted board. Pipe tip 2 dot centers in royal icing.

Prepare 2-layer round cakes for stacked construction (p. 110). Prepare cakes for rolled fondant (p. 111). Cover cakes with blue fondant; smooth with Easy-Glide Smoother. Position on cake base.

Make cake side umbrellas. Tint 3 oz. of white fondant green using icing color. Roll out green and reserved fondant ⅛ in. thick; cut 2 circles in each color using large Cut-Out. Cut each circle in half and, using wide end of tip 1, cut 4 scallops at bottom edge. Imprint ribs of umbrella with straight-edge wheel of Cutter/Embosser. Attach on cake sides, approximately 1½ in. apart, with damp brush. For tops, roll a small ball; for handles, cut a ⅛ x 2 in. long strip. Attach with damp brush. For bottom borders, roll balls of white fondant from ¼ to ½ in. diameter. Flatten slightly and attach with damp brush, overlapping to resemble clouds. Attach flowers to border with royal icing.

Tie ribbon bow to umbrella cake top handle. Insert umbrella cake top in cake. Using piping gel, pipe tip 1 bead raindrops. Attach ribbon to cake base edge. Serves 60.

The perfect favor: White Tulle Circles (p. 161) filled with Pillow Mints (p. 160), then gathered and tied with Satin Stripe Favor Bands (p. 161).

Love Reigns Supreme

Cookie: Round Comfort Grip™ Cutter, p. 214; Cookie Sheet, Cooling Grid, p. 217

Tips: 1M (2110), 3, 131, p. 138-139

Colors: Kelly Green, Lemon Yellow, Rose, Violet, p. 133

Recipes: Royal Icing, Roll-Out Cookie, p. 112

Also: White Candy Melts®†, p. 218; 11¾ in. Lollipop Sticks, p. 221; Meringue Powder, p. 132; White Tulle Spool, p. 157; 8 x 3 in. high round craft block, ¼ in. wide white ribbon (2 yds. needed), ⅝ in. wide blue ribbon (2¼ yds. needed), 1½ in. white ribbon (2¼ yds. needed), hot glue gun, 22-gauge florist wire (sixty 4 in. pieces needed)

One day in advance: Using royal icing, make 7 tip 131 swirl drop flowers with tip 3 dot centers. Make extras to allow for breakage and let dry. For umbrellas, cut 4 round cookies with cutter. Cut cookies in half; position 7 halves on cookie sheet. Using large end of tip 1M, cut scallops on bottom edge. Bake and cool cookies. Outline cookies and ribs with tip 3 in royal icing; let set, then fill in with thinned royal icing. Let dry overnight.

Attach cookies to lollipop sticks with melted candy. Tie each with a bow made from 10 in. of ¼ in. wide ribbon. Attach flowers to umbrella tops with royal icing. For base, attach strings of white ribbon around craft block with hot glue, attach strips of blue ribbon over white. Cut tulle into 6 in. squares; gather corners of each square and trim to form rounded edges. Twist squares at bottom to form a point and twist a 4 in. piece of wire around to secure. Insert wires into craft block, working from edge to center and covering entire top. Insert cookies on sticks. Each cookie serves 1.

Delightful Downpour

Pan: 10½ x 15½ in. Jelly Roll, Cookie Sheet, Cooling Grid, p. 149

Tips: 2, 349, p. 138-139

Colors: Rose, Kelly Green, Violet, p. 133

Fondant: White Ready-To-Use Rolled Fondant (24 oz. needed), p. 126

Recipes: Quick-Pour Fondant Icing, p. 111; Buttercream Icing, p. 112 or Apricot Glaze, p. 111

Also: Floral Collection Flower Making Set, Confectionery Tool Set, Flower Former Set, p. 131; Round Comfort Grip™ Cutter, p. 214; 4 in. Lollipop Sticks, p. 221; ⅛ in. wide satin ribbon in pink, light green and light violet (10 in. needed for each favor), cornstarch

In advance: Make fondant flowers. Roll out fondant ⅛ in. thick and cut 3 flowers for each cake using forget-me-not cutter from Flower Making Set. Move flowers to thin foam and soften edges with dogbone tool; move to thick foam and cup with small end of dogbone tool. Let dry in small flower formers dusted with cornstarch. Roll small balls for centers and attach with damp brush.

Bake and cool jelly roll cake. Cut individual cakes with cutter; cut each in half. Prepare for poured fondant (p. 111). Follow recipe instructions for covering cakes and let dry. In buttercream, outline cakes and pipe umbrella ribs with tip 2. Attach flowers with buttercream; add tip 349 leaves. Roll a ¾ in. diameter fondant ball and insert at end of lollipop stick. Insert stick in bottom of cake. Using 10 in. pieces of ribbon, tie a matching color bow on each stick. Each serves 1.

† Brand confectionery coating.

Pans: Ring Mold, p. 148; Cookie Sheet, Cooling Grid, p. 149

Tips: 1, 2, 3, 8, 352, p. 138-139

Colors: Copper (skin tone), Rose, Brown, Black, Lemon Yellow, Kelly Green, Orange, p. 133

Fondant: White Ready-To-Use Rolled Fondant (24 oz. needed), p. 126; Flower Cut-Outs™, p. 128; Rolling Pin, Roll & Cut Mat, p. 130; Shaping Foam, p. 131

Recipes: Buttercream and Color Flow Icings, Roll-Out Cookie, p. 112

Also: 2006 Pattern Book (Hairdos, Veil, Face), p. 124; Confectionery Tool Set, p. 131; Gum-Tex™, p. 130; Color Flow Mix, p. 132; Cake Dividing Set, p. 136; Parchment Triangles, p. 137; Tulle Spool (3 yds. needed), p. 157; 12 in. Cake Circles, Fanci-Foil Wrap, p. 169; Circle Metal Cutter, p. 214; White Candy Melts®†, p. 218; 11¾ in. Lollipop Sticks, p. 221; 4 x 3 in. craft block, 22-gauge wire (24 in. needed), 1 in. wide mint green sheer ribbon (24 in. needed per favor), ¼ in. wide white satin ribbon (1½ yds. needed), ¼ in. wide pink satin ribbon (½ yd. needed), craft knife, cornstarch, toothpick

In advance: Make face cookies (at right) and flower cookies (shown below). Roll out dough and cut 5 faces using circle cutter and desired number of flowers for favors using largest Cut-Out. Bake and cool all cookies. Cover faces with skin tone color flow (p. 120). For flowers, outline and flow in with rose color flow and tip 2 (p. 120). Let dry overnight. Add a tip 3 dot center to flowers in full-strength color flow.

Combine 2 teaspoons Gum-Tex with 24 oz. white fondant. Tint 3 oz. each light brown, dark brown, lemon yellow and rose; tint 4 oz. orange. Reserve 8 oz. white. Roll out fondant ⅛ in. thick. Using patterns, cut out hairdos and veil with knife. Attach hairdos to fronts of face cookies and ponytail and veil to backs with full-strength color flow. Using full strength color flow and face pattern, pipe tip 2 string mouth, dot eyes, nose and cheeks (flatten and smooth cheeks with finger dipped in cornstarch). Add tip 3 bead lips and tip 1 string eyelashes. Using smallest Cut-Out, cut 4 rose and 5 white flowers. Move flowers to thick foam and cup centers with medium ball tool from Confectionery Tool Set. Using full-strength color flow, add tip 2 dot centers to flowers, attach white flowers to bride and pink to bridesmaids with full-strength color flow. Attach face and flower cookies to lollipop sticks using melted candy.

Ice ring mold cake smooth in buttercream. Position cake on triple-thick foil-wrapped cake circles. Divide cake into 8ths and mark scallops 1¾ in. from bottom at lowest point. Using smallest Cut-Out, cut 60 white fondant flowers. On thick foam, cup with medium ball tool and add tip 2 dot centers in color flow. Attach at scallop marks with buttercream. Using medium Cut-Out, cut 8 rose flowers, cup with ball tool and add tip 3 dot centers in color flow; attach at scallop points. Pipe tip 352 leaves in buttercream. Add tip 8 ball bottom border.

Cut craft block to fit center of cake; wrap in foil and position. Cut tulle into 6 in. long strips; fold in half and gather together. Wrap wire around gathered folded end and insert into craft block. Insert face cookies in craft block. Cut a 12 in. piece of satin ribbon for each face cookie and tie into a bow around stick. For flower favor cookies, tie green sheer ribbon into a bow around each stick. Cake serves 18; each cookie serves 1.

▼ Wildflower Bouquet

Pans: 6, 10 x 2 in. Square, p. 147

Colors:* Violet, Rose, Kelly Green, p. 133

Fondant: Ready-To-Use Rolled Fondant in White (48 oz. needed) and Pastel Green (24 oz. needed), p. 126; Flower and Leaf Cut-Outs™, p. 128; Green Brush-On Color™, Color Tray, Brush Set, p. 129; Rolling Pin, Roll & Cut Mat, p. 130; Easy-Glide Fondant Smoother, Shaping Foam, p. 131

Recipe: Buttercream Icing, p. 112

Also: Wooden Dowel Rods, p. 167; Confectionery Tool Set, p. 131; "Hidden" Pillars, p. 166; White Candy Melts®†, p. 218; 13 x 19 in. Cake Boards, Fanci-Foil Wrap, p. 169; Candy Melting Plate, p. 219; Gum-Tex™, p. 130; 22-gauge florist wire (50 pieces, 8 in. long needed), florist tape, ruler, pizza cutter or knife, craft block, cornstarch

Two days in advance: Make fondant bow (p. 119). Tint 18 oz. white fondant violet with a little rose; knead in ½ teaspoon Gum-Tex. Roll out ⅛ in. thick. For loops, cut two 4½ x 1 in. strips, let dry following instructions. For bow center, cut a 2¼ x ½ in. strip. Form a loop, brushing ends with water to attach; let dry. Attach center to loops with melted candy. Set aside.

One day in advance: Make fondant flowers and dark green leaves for bouquet (p.119). Combine 19 oz. of pastel green with 6 oz. of white fondant to make light green used for 10 in. cake. Tint 5 oz. of this mixture dark green using Kelly Green icing color and knead in ½ teaspoon of Gum-Tex.

Prepare 1-layer 10 in. cake and 3-layer 6 in. cake (bake two 2 in. layers and one 1 in. layer to create a 5 in. high cake) for stacked construction (p. 110). Prepare cakes for fondant (p. 111); cover and smooth with Easy-Glide Smoother. For top cake, trim hidden pillar to 5 in. and insert into cake. Roll a ¼ in. diameter log and attach around edge of pillar opening with damp brush. Roll out violet fondant ⅛ in. thick and cut 2 medium and 4 small flowers for each side of 6 in. cake using Cut-Outs. Roll small white fondant balls for centers and attach with damp brush. Attach flowers to cake with damp brush. Using Brush-On Color and round brush, paint stems, leaves and grass. For bottom cake, roll out violet fondant ⅛ in. thick and cut ¾ in. wide strips for bottom border; attach with damp brush, blending ends together. Cut two 4 in. long streamers, cut V-shapes in ends and attach with damp brush. Attach bow over streamers with melted candy. Insert a 1 in. ball of fondant in pillars to stabilize wired flowers. Insert flowers and leaves on wires in opening. Serves 27.

***Note:** Combine Violet with a little Rose for violet shown.

▼ Flavorful Favors

Cookie: Cookie Sheet, Cooling Grid, p. 217

Tips: 2, 3, p. 138

Colors:* Violet, Rose, p. 133

Fondant: White Ready-To-Use Rolled Fondant (24 oz. needed), p. 126; Flower Cut-Outs™, p. 128; Rolling Pin, Roll & Cut Mat, p. 130

Candy: White Candy Melts®† (1 pk. needed), p. 218; Garden Candy Color Set, p. 219; 4 in. Lollipop Sticks, p. 221

Recipes: Color Flow Icing, Roll-Out Cookie, p. 112

Also: Tote Favor Containers, p. 160; White Tulle Circles, p. 161; Color Flow Mix, p. 132; Parchment Triangles, p. 137; 1 x 1 x 1¾ in. high craft blocks (1 needed per favor)

Roll out dough and cut 3 cookies per favor using largest Cut-Out. Bake and cool. Tint a portion of color flow violet shade; using tip 2, outline and flow in cookies (p. 120); let dry. Pipe tip 3 dot centers using full-strength color flow; let dry. Attach cookies to lollipop sticks using melted candy. Let set.

Tint a portion of fondant violet; roll out ⅛ in. thick. Cut 2 flowers for each favor, using smallest Cut-Out; attach to tote with melted candy. For flower centers, roll tiny white fondant balls and attach with damp brush. Tint melted white candy green with candy color. Using melted candy in cut parchment bag, pipe stems and leaves on tote. Insert craft block in tote, and position 2 tulle circles, fluffing for a full fan effect. Insert cookies in craft block. Each serves 1.

***Note:** Combine Violet with a little Rose for violet shown.

◀ The Bear Necessities

Pans: Stand-Up Cuddly Bear Set, p. 152; Cookie Sheet, p. 217

Tips: 3, 6, 233, p. 138-139

Colors: Rose, Black, p. 133

Fondant: Pastel Colors Fondant Multi Pack (2 pks. needed), p. 126; Brush Set, p. 129; Rolling Pin, Roll & Cut Mat, p. 130; Cutter/Embosser, p. 131

Recipes: Buttercream Icing, Roll-Out Cookie, p. 112

Also: Baby Cradles, Porcelain Baby Block (3 needed), p. 170; Shower Rattles, Rocking Horses, p. 171; A-B-C and 1-2-3 50-Pc. Cutter Set, p. 216; Piping Gel, p. 132; Tapered Spatula, p. 137; Pillow Mints, p. 160; White Tulle Circles, p. 161; 12 in. Decorator Preferred® Separator Plates (2 needed), 3 in. Grecian Pillars, p. 166; 12 in. Cake Circles, p. 169; waxed paper, plastic wrap, cornstarch, ⅛ in. wide white satin ribbon (12 in. needed for each favor)

One day in advance: Lightly cover top of one 12 in. separator plate with piping gel. Roll out pastel fondant ¼ in. thick and cut sixteen 3 in. squares (4 of each color) with straight-edge wheel of Cutter/Embosser. Imprint squares, some with narrow end of tip 6, others with wavy or ridged wheels of Cutter/Embosser. As each square is imprinted, place on waxed paper, to create a 4 squares high x 4 squares wide quilt formation (cover squares with plastic wrap as you work). When quilt is complete, place a 12 in. cake circle on top, aligning at top and bottom edges. Cut around the circle and position pieces on separator plate, attaching edges with damp brush.

Roll out dough; using alphabet cutters, cut out "BABY" cookies; bake and cool. Roll out pastel fondant ⅛ in. thick and cut "BABY" letters; attach to cookies with piping gel. Reserve remaining fondant.

Bake and cool bear cake using firm-textured batter such as pound cake. Trim off right arm. Build up arm area with buttercream, to align with other arm. Position on fondant-covered separator plate. Ice bottom of feet smooth. Pipe in tip 3 eyes and mouth, tip 6 nose and inside ears (smooth features with finger dipped in cornstarch). Cover bear with tip 233 pull-out fur, omitting arms. Position letter "A" cookie in arm area; using tip 6 and heavy pressure, build up arms and hands to attach letter. Cover arms with tip 233 pull-out fur. Position pillars on plain separator plate; position fondant-covered plate on top. Position remaining letter cookies.

Make 5 rattle, 4 cradle, 4 rocking horse and 3 baby block favors. Place mints in center of tulle circle, lift sides of circle over candy and gather together at center. Tie satin ribbon at gathering point. Place candy bags in blocks or tie to other favor holders. Position favors. Cake serves 12; each cookie serves 1.

▶ A Letter-Perfect Baby

Pan: 2-Mix Book, p. 152

Tips: 2, 4, 225, 349, p. 138-139

Colors:* Lemon Yellow, Rose, Violet, Royal Blue, Kelly Green, p. 133

Fondant: White Ready-To-Use Rolled Fondant (48 oz. needed), Pastel Colors Fondant Multi Pack, p. 126; Round Cut-Outs™, p. 128; Brush Set, p. 129; Rolling Pin, Roll & Cut Mat, p. 130

Recipes: Buttercream and Royal Icings, p. 112

Also: 101 Cookie Cutters Set, p. 216; Baby Blocks Containers, p. 170; Shower Rattles, Sleeping Angels Set, p. 171; Decorating Comb, p. 136; Cake Board, Fanci-Foil Wrap, p. 169; Meringue Powder, Piping Gel, p. 132; 18 x 14 in. foamcore sheet, waxed paper, paring knife

In advance: Using royal icing, make 25 each pink, violet and rose tip 225 swirl drop flowers on waxed paper. Add tip 2 white dot centers. Make extras to allow for breakage and let dry.

Place book cake on same-size board and ice smooth. Comb sides with small-tooth edge of comb. Position cake on foil-wrapped foamcore sheet. Roll out 1 pk. of pink fondant ¼ in. thick. Cut approximately 20 circles using medium round Cut-Out. Cut circles in half and attach to board with piping gel to create scalloped bottom border. Roll out 48 oz. of white fondant ¼ in. thick; position on cake top and trim edges as needed. Roll out pastel fondant ¼ in. thick and cut BABY letters using cookie cutters; attach with damp brush. Print tip 2 messages in matching shades of buttercream. Pipe tip 2 vines around edge of cake top in buttercream. Attach drop flowers with dots of buttercream. Add tip 349 leaves in buttercream. Pipe tip 4 bead bottom border. Attach blocks, angel and rattles with dots of buttercream. Serves 24.

***Note:** Combine Violet and Rose for violet color shown.

◄ Layette On 'Em!

Pans: 6, 10 x 2 in. Round, p. 147

Tips: 1, 1A, p. 138

Colors: Rose, Lemon Yellow, Kelly Green, Royal Blue, Copper (skin tone), p. 133

Fondant: White Ready-To-Use Rolled Fondant (72 oz. needed), Pastel Colors Fondant Multi Pack, p. 126; Cut-Outs™ in Round and People shapes, p. 128; Brush Set, Fine Tip Primary Colors FoodWriter™ Edible Color Markers, p. 129; Rolling Pin, Roll & Cut Mat, p. 130; Cutter/Embosser, Easy-Glide Fondant Smoother, p. 131

Recipe: Buttercream Icing, p. 112

Also: Gingerbread Boy Metal Cookie Cutter, p. 214; 12 in. Round Silver Cake Base, p. 169; Wooden Dowel Rods, p. 167; Cake Dividing Set, p. 136; 6 in. Lollipop Sticks, p. 221

In advance: Make fondant baby (p. 118). Make approximately 80 fondant buttons. Roll ⅜ in. diameter balls of pastel fondant. Flatten and indent center with end of dowel rod. Imprint button holes with narrow end of tip 1. Let dry.

Prepare 2-layer cakes for stacked construction (p. 110). Prepare cakes for rolled fondant (p. 111). Cover cakes with fondant; smooth with Easy-Glide Smoother. Divide 6 in. cake in 4ths and 10 in. cake in 6ths. For clotheslines, roll out yellow fondant ⅛ in. thick. Using straight-edge wheel of Cutter/Embosser, cut ⅛ in. wide strips for clothesline; attach at division points, 1 in. deep. For bows, cut ⅛ x 4 in. long yellow strips; form loops and move tails to opposite sides. Attach bows with damp brush; attach a small ball at center.

For clothes, roll out pastel fondant ⅛ in. thick. Cut booties using shoe Cut-Out; trim off ends. Cut cap using smallest round Cut-Out; trim off bottom. Cut T-shirt using shirt Cut-Out; trim bottom to shorten and cut neckline with small round Cut-Out. Cut 1-piece outfit using shirt Cut-Out; cut neck and leg lines with small round Cut-Out. Cut bib using wide end of tip 1A; cut neckline with narrow end. Attach clothes to clothesline with damp brush. For clothespins, cut thin pieces of copper fondant and attach. For bottom borders, roll a ⅜ in. diameter white rope; attach with damp brush. Attach buttons with buttercream. Add buttercream dots, outlines and scallop details to clothes with tip 1. Insert baby in cake top. Serves 40.

► Eat Neatly

Cookie: Nesting Blossoms Metal Cutter Set, Circle Metal Cutter, p. 214; Cookie Sheet, Cooling Grid, p. 217

Tips: 2, 3, p. 138

Colors: Rose, Royal Blue, p. 133

Candy: Rubber Ducky Candy Mold, p. 173; White Candy Melts®†, p. 218; Primary Candy Color Set, Decorator Brush Set, p. 219

Recipes: Royal Icing, Roll-Out Cookie, p. 112

Also: Disposable Decorating Bags, p. 137; Meringue Powder, p. 132; ¼ in. wide pink or blue satin ribbon (24 in. per cookie needed)

In advance: Make candy. Using candy colors, tint portions of melted candy yellow and orange (with a little red). Mold ducks using painting method (p. 121), filling cavities half full. Refrigerate until firm; unmold. Roll out dough and cut bib using largest blossom cutter; cut neck line using circle cutter. Bake and cool. Using royal icing, outline scallop center of bib, about ¼ to ½ in. from edge, with tip 3. Pipe in with thinned royal icing. Let dry overnight. Pipe tip 3 zigzag border; add tip 3 dots at scallop points. Attach duck candy with royal icing. Pipe tip 2 dots on scallop center. For each cookie, cut a 6 in. length of ribbon; attach ends to cookie with royal icing. Using 18 in. of ribbon, tie a bow at center of neck ribbon. Each serves 1.

† Brand confectionery coating.

▼ Pretty Pin-Ups

Cookie: Cookie Sheet, Cooling Grid, p. 217

Tips: 3, 12, p. 138

Color: Black, p. 133

Fondant: Pastel Colors Fondant Multi Pack, p. 126; Cut-Outs™ in Heart, Oval and Star shapes, p. 128; Rolling Pin, Roll & Cut Mat, p. 130

Recipes: Royal Icing, Roll-Out Cookie, p. 112

Also: Meringue Powder, p. 132; craft knife, cornstarch

In advance: Make fondant shapes. Roll out fondant ⅛ in. thick; cut shapes using medium star, medium heart and large oval Cut-Outs. Cut ovals in half; use narrow end of tip 12 to cut out a notch. Let shapes dry on cornstarch-dusted surface.

Cut out cookies with largest oval Cut-Out; bake and cool. Tint a portion of royal icing gray. Thin remaining icing to pouring consistency. Cover cookies with thinned icing (p. 120); let dry. Pipe tip 3 gray outline. Attach fondant pieces with icing. Each serves 1.

◀ Nursery Rhyme and Rock

Pan: Topsy Turvy, p. 152

Tip: 3, p. 133

Colors:* Royal Blue, Kelly Green, Lemon Yellow, Violet, Rose, p. 133

Fondant: White Ready-To-Use Rolled Fondant (24 oz. needed), Pastel Colors Fondant Multi Pack, p. 126; Cut-Outs™ in Heart, Alphabet/Number and Flower shapes, p. 128; Brush Set, p. 129; Rolling Pin, Roll & Cut Mat, p. 130; Shaping Foam, Cutter/Embosser, Easy-Glide Fondant Smoother, p. 131

Recipe: Buttercream Icing, p. 112

Also: Round Comfort Grip™ Cutter, p. 214; Confectionery Tool Set, p. 131; Cake Boards, Fanci-Foil Wrap, p. 169; 6 in. Lollipop Sticks, p. 221; cornstarch, paring knife

In advance: Make cradle. Roll out yellow fondant ¼ in. thick. Cut a circle using round cutter; trim off ¼ of circle (pie shaped wedge). For ribs of cradle hood, cut three ⅛ in. wide strips using paring knife. Attach to hood with damp brush; trim to fit. For rim, roll and attach a ⅛ x 1½ in. log. For trim, roll ⅛ in. diameter yellow balls and ³⁄₁₆ in. diameter pink balls; attach with damp brush. For bow, roll two ¼ in. diameter balls of blue fondant, shape into beads and flatten for bow loops, attach. Cut 2 streamers ⅛ in. wide x ¾ in. long, attach. For center knot, roll a ³⁄₁₆ in. ball; attach. Place cradle on cornstarch-dusted surface to

dry. Attach 2 lollipop sticks to back of cradle with thinned fondant adhesive (p. 111); let dry. Ice cake tops and sides smooth. Tint 6 oz. of white fondant violet. Roll out fondant ⅛ in. thick; cut strips ⅝ in. wide. Using straight-edge wheel of Cutter/Embosser, imprint lines on strips; position 1¼ in. apart on bottom tier of cake. Roll out pink fondant ⅛ in. thick and cut hearts using small Cut-Out, position on bottom tier. Cut message using letter Cut-Outs; position on middle tier. Roll two ³⁄₁₆ in. balls of fondant and position between words. Roll out pink fondant ¼ in. thick and cut 1 in. wide strips. Imprint diagonal lines ¼ in. apart, with ridged wheel of Cutter/Embosser; position strips on top tier.

Roll out fondant ⅛ in. thick and cut 22 green, 12 yellow, 12 pink, 10 violet and 14 blue flowers using smallest Cut-Out. Place flowers on thick foam and cup centers using medium round ball tool. Roll ⅛ in. diameter balls of white fondant and attach to flower centers. Attach flowers to cake using tip 3 dots of buttercream icing. Insert cradle in cake top. Serves 12.

***Note:** Combine Violet and Rose for violet fondant color shown.

▶ Tweets for the Sweet!

Pan: Baby Buggy, p. 151

Tips: 2, 2A, 3, 4, 6, 12, 13, 44, 102, 103, 352, p. 138-139

Colors: Rose, Lemon Yellow, Royal Blue, Kelly Green, p. 133

Recipes: Buttercream and Royal Icings, Color Flow Icing, p. 112

Also: 2006 Pattern Book (Bluebirds), p. 124; Flower Nail No. 7, p. 137; Flower Former Set, p. 131; Color Flow Mix, Meringue Powder, p. 132; Cake Board, Fanci-Foil Wrap, p. 169; 4 in. Lollipop Sticks, p. 221; Decorator Brush Set, p. 219; uncooked thin spaghetti, waxed paper, cornstarch

At least 2 days in advance: Make color flow bluebirds (p. 120) on waxed paper using pattern and tip 2. When dry, add tip 2 dot eyes with full-strength color flow; let dry. Attach lollipop sticks to backs of bluebirds with full-strength color flow; let dry.

Also in advance: Using flower nail and royal icing on 2 in. waxed paper squares, make 15 tip 102 wild roses (p. 116) with tip 2 dot centers and 6 tip 103 wild roses with tip 3 dot centers. Set all flowers on small flower formers to dry. For flower stem, use thinned royal icing to paint a 1½ in. piece of uncooked spaghetti; let dry on waxed paper. When flowers and stem are dry, attach stem to a tip 102 wild rose and to beak of bird; let dry.

Ice cake sides, bottom of buggy and background areas smooth in buttercream. Pipe tip 44 lattice on bottom of buggy. Outline hood with tip 4 and fill in with tip 13 stars. Pipe tip 2A handle and top buggy rim (smooth rim area with finger dipped in cornstarch). Pipe tip 12 wheel rims with tip 6 spokes; add tip 6 dot hubcap. Attach flowers to bottom border with buttercream; add tip 352 leaves. Attach flowers to edge of hood; insert bluebirds. Serves 12.

◀ Taking Their Sweet Time

Pan: Mini Ball, p. 153

Candy: White Candy Melts®† (at least 3 pks. needed; 1 pk. yields 3-4 umbrella shells in one color), p. 218; Primary and Garden Candy Color Sets, p. 219; 4 in. Lollipop Sticks, p. 221

Also: Newborn Baby Figurines, p. 171; Pillow Mints, p. 160; Parchment Triangles, p. 137; ⅛ in. wide satin ribbon in pink, yellow and green (10 in. needed for each favor), craft knife, white gumballs, waxed paper, warming tray or cookie sheet

Tint candy pink, yellow and green using candy colors. Make umbrella candy shells (p. 121) in pan cavities. Refrigerate for 3-5 minutes to form a ⅛ in. shell, pour out excess candy, smooth top edges and freeze for 15 to 20 minutes. Unmold quickly. Slide shells across warming tray or warm cookie sheet to level bottoms at a slight angle; place on waxed paper. Divide shells in 8ths; using melted candy in cut parchment bags, pipe a line of beads from each division mark to top center. Insert stick in gumball. Attach umbrella to stick with melted candy; let set. Fill umbrella with mints; position figurine. Tie ribbon bow to each stick. Each serves 1.

† Brand confectionery coating.

◀ Bassinet Bliss

Pan: Non-Stick Brioche 6-Pc. Set, p. 146

Tips: 2, 13, p. 133

Fondant: Pastel Colors Fondant Multi Pack, p. 126; Cutter/Embosser, p. 131; Brush Set, p. 129; Rolling Pin, Roll & Cut Mat, p. 130

Recipes: Buttercream and Royal Icings, p. 112

Also: 2006 Pattern Book (Bassinet Hood), p. 124; Confectionery Tool Set, p. 131; Meringue Powder, p. 132; small paring knife

In advance: Using royal icing, make 12 tip 13 star flowers with tip 2 dot centers for each bassinet. Make extras to allow for breakage and let dry. Prepare cakes for rolled fondant by lightly icing with buttercream. Cover cakes with fondant; press in folds with veining tool from set. For hoods, roll out fondant ⅛ in. thick; using pattern, cut out one hood for each bassinet. Attach hood on cake with damp brush. Let set 1 hour before adding flowers. Using buttercream, pipe tip 2 beads at seam line. Attach 13 flowers to each cake with tip 2 dots of icing. Randomly pipe tip 2 dots on bassinet skirt. Each serves 1.

▶ Sunny Side Up!

Pan: 18 x 3 in. Half Round, p. 147

Tips: 1, 3, 8, 12, 127, p. 138-139

Colors: Lemon Yellow, Rose, Royal Blue, Copper (skin tone), p. 133

Cookie: Stars Nesting Metal Cutter Set, p. 214; Cookie Sheet, Cooling Grid, Cookie Spatula, p. 217

Recipes: Buttercream, Royal and Color Flow Icings, Roll-Out Cookie, p. 112

Also: 2006 Pattern Book (Clouds, Umbrella Handle, Head), p. 124; Meringue Powder, Color Flow Mix, p. 132; Fine Tip Primary FoodWriter™ Markers, p. 129; Parchment Triangles, p. 137; Cake Boards, Fanci-Foil Wrap, p. 169; Plastic Dowel Rods, p. 167; ⅞ in. wide yellow satin ribbon and 1 in. wide pink wired ribbon (1 yd. each), waxed paper, paring knife

In advance: Make cookies. Roll out dough; use patterns to cut 4 clouds (reverse pattern for 2), head and umbrella handle. Cut 12 stars using 2nd smallest star cutter. Bake and cool. Set 3 stars aside. Place remaining cookies on cooling grid over waxed paper; cover with thinned color flow (p. 120); let dry overnight. Pipe swirls on clouds using tip 1 and full-strength color flow. Draw faces on iced stars and head with black FoodWriter. On head, pipe tip 3 nose and cheeks in full-strength color flow. Wrap 8 in. of dowel rod with yellow ribbon; leave 4 in. unwrapped to insert in cake. Attach cookie handle to rod with full strength color flow; let dry. Tie on a pink ribbon bow. Set aside. On waxed paper, using royal icing, pipe six tip 127 ruffle garlands 2¾ in. wide x 1½ in. deep; make extras to allow for breakage and let dry. Pipe 7 tip 8 white balls for garland points and 1 tip 12 rose ball, (flattened to 1 in. diameter) for umbrella button. Let dry.

Ice 1-layer cake (2 in. high) smooth in buttercream. Pipe tip 8 bead rib lines on umbrella. Randomly pipe tip 3 dots on cake top. Attach royal icing garlands, balls and button to cake with buttercream. Insert umbrella handle. Ice and stack 3 plain star cookies under head. Position head and add clouds and stars. Cake serves 22; each cookie serves 1.

▼ Future Movers & Shakers!

A bold grad cake gets the nod for our fun bobbling topper and colorful fondant stars on wires. What better occasion than graduation for this kind of color and energy?

Pans: 6 x 3 in., 14 x 2 in. Round, p. 148

Tip: 8, p. 138

Colors:* Lemon Yellow, Golden Yellow, p. 133

Fondant: Pastel Yellow Ready-To-Use Rolled Fondant (24 oz. needed), Primary Colors Fondant Multi Pack, p. 126; Star and Alphabet/Numeral Cut-Outs™, p. 128; Ribbon Cutter/Embosser, p. 127; Brush Set, p. 129; Rolling Pin, Roll & Cut Mat, p. 130

Recipe: Buttercream Icing, p. 112

Also: Female Grad Bobbling Topper, p. 210; Cake Dividing Set, p. 136; Cake Sparkles™ in Red, Yellow, Blue and Green, p. 134; White Candy Melts®†, p. 218; Circle Metal Cookie Cutter, p. 214; Plastic Dowel Rods, p. 167; 6 in., 16 in. (3 needed) Cake Circles, (or use 16 in. foamcore circle, ½ in. thick, for base board), Fanci-Foil Wrap, p. 169, 26-gauge white cloth-covered wire (6 in. lengths, 72 needed), paring knife, cornstarch, craft block

In advance: Make stars on wires. Roll out primary fondant ⅛ in. thick and cut 18 stars in each color using medium Cut-Out. Place on cornstarch-dusted surface. Brush tops with water and sprinkle with matching color Cake Sparkles. Let dry. Bend a hook at end of each wire. Make a teardrop-shaped base for each star, using a ¼ in. ball of matching color fondant. Insert hooked wire into narrow end of teardrop, shape to wire and let dry in craft block. Attach star to base with melted candy. Let set.

Prepare 1-layer 14 in. cake and 2-layer 6 in. cake (bake two 2½ in. layers to create a 5 in. high cake) for stacked construction (p. 110). Assemble cakes on a triple-thick cake board or foamcore base, wrapped in foil. Ice cakes smooth. Divide 6 in. cake into 10ths and 14 in. cake into 6ths. For 6 in. cake, roll out pastel yellow fondant ⅛ in. thick. Using straight-edge cutting wheels and striped embossing wheel from Ribbon Cutter/Embosser, cut 10 strips. Trim to 5 in. long and attach with buttercream at division points. For 14 in. cake, cut dowel rods into six 2 in. lengths; insert at division points, 1½ in. from edge of cake. Pipe tip 8 bead bottom borders on both cakes. Roll ⅜ in. pastel yellow balls and attach with buttercream for top borders. Roll out primary blue, green and red fondant ⅛ in. thick. Cut message using alphabet Cut-Outs; attach with icing. Make 6 groups of wired stars, using 3 stars in each color; twist together at bottom. Insert fondant in dowel rod to stabilize wires. Insert star groups in dowel rods. Roll a 1½ in. log of pastel yellow and wrap around wires at dowel rod opening. For topper base, roll out fondant ½ in. thick and cut a circle with cookie cutter. Position base and topper. Serves 43.

*Note: Combine Lemon Yellow with a little Golden Yellow for yellow shown.

† Brand confectionery coating.

▲ Gen X is Ecstatic!

Pan: Smiley Grad, p. 210

Tips: 4, 16, p. 138-139

Colors:* Royal Blue, Brown, Black, Red-Red, Christmas Red, Lemon Yellow, Golden Yellow, Copper (skin tone), p. 133

Fondant: White Ready-To-Use Rolled Fondant (24 oz. needed), p. 126; Brush Set, p. 129; Rolling Pin, Roll & Cut Mat, p. 130

Recipe: Buttercream Icing, p. 112

Also: Hand Plastic Cookie Cutter, p. 216; Cake Board, Fanci-Foil Wrap, p. 169; paring knife, ⅜ in. wide red ribbon (24 in. needed), 22-gauge wire, cornstarch

Place cake on cut-to-fit foil-wrapped board. Ice background areas smooth. Pipe in tip 4 eyes, mouth and tongue (pat mouth and tongue smooth with finger dipped in cornstarch). Outline cap with tip 4. Cover cap and face with tip 16 stars; build up cheeks, nose, and ears. Pipe tip 16 pull-out star hair, tassel and fringe. Add tip 16 rosette button on cap. For diploma, roll out fondant ⅛ in. thick and cut a 10 x 12 in. piece. Roll up lengthwise to make diploma. Tint portion of fondant skin tone; roll out ⅛ in. thick and cut 2 hands with cutter (reverse cutter for right hand). Attach to diploma with damp brush. Cover hands with tip 16 stars. Wrap ribbon around diploma and tie into a bow. Cut a board to fit diploma, wrap with foil and position diploma. Serves 12.

*Note: Combine Brown and Red-Red for brown shown. Combine Lemon Yellow and Golden Yellow for yellow shown.

◄ Filled With Promise

Try these unique rolled cookies, filled with white chocolate cream, for a graduation dessert that earns high marks.

Cookie: Cookie Sheet, Cooling Grid, p. 217
Tip: 2A, p. 138
Candy: Numerals Mold, p. 220; Red Candy Melts®†, p. 218
Recipes: Tuilles (Cookie Crepes), p. 113
Also: Vanilla Whipped Icing Mix, p. 132; Plastic Dowel Rods, p. 167; Tapered Spatula, Disposable Decorating Bags, p. 137; 1 pk. (3.3 oz.) white chocolate instant pudding mix, ³⁄₁₆ in. wide ribbon (18 in. needed per scroll)

In advance: Make candies. Mold candies (p. 121), filling mold ⅛ in. high; refrigerate until firm and unmold. Make extras to allow for breakage.

Prepare tuille scrolls. For filling, prepare whipped icing mix following package directions; add dry pudding mix and beat. Place filling in decorating bag fitted with tip 2A; fill scrolls. Tie bow around scrolls. Attach number candies with melted candy. Each serves 1.

▼ Beginning a New Chapter

Pans: Graduate, p. 210; Long Loaf, p. 149
Colors:* Royal Blue, Red-Red, Kelly Green, Violet, Rose, Golden Yellow, p. 133
Fondant: White Ready-To-Use Rolled Fondant (72 oz. needed), p. 126; Cutter/Embosser, p. 131; Fine Tip Primary Colors FoodWriter™ Edible Color Markers, Brush Set, p. 129; Rolling Pin, Roll & Cut Mat, p. 130
Recipe: Buttercream Icing, p. 112
Also: 2006 Pattern Book (Graduate Easel), p. 124; Candy Melts®† in White (4 pks. needed) and Light Cocoa, p. 218; Garden and Primary Candy Color Sets, p. 219; Flower Former Set, p. 131; Parchment Triangles, p. 137; Gum-Tex™, p. 130; Cake Boards, Fanci-Foil Wrap, p. 169; heavy-duty aluminum foil, ruler (marked in ⅛ in. increments), cornstarch, cardboard, toothpick

In advance: Make graduate candy plaque and 2 easels (p. 121) using pattern. Make fondant book bindings. Tint 8 oz. of fondant each in blue, red, green and violet; roll out ⅜ in. thick. For 4 large books, cut 5¼ x 2¾ in. strips; for 3 small books, cut 5¼ x 1¾ in. strips. Let large strips dry on

medium flower formers, let small strips dry on small flower formers, all dusted with cornstarch. Cut two 5¼ x 4¼ in. pieces for outer covers of end books; let dry flat on cornstarch-dusted surface. For binding detail, tint 2 oz. of fondant yellow. Roll out ⅟₁₆ in. thick and cut strips in various sizes. Attach to bindings with damp brush, trim to fit; let dry. Print titles using black FoodWriter.

Prepare 2-layer loaf cake (bake two 2½ in. high layers to make a 5 in. high cake) for rolled fondant by icing lightly with buttercream. For pages, roll out 22 oz. of white fondant ¼ in. thick; score lines ⅛ in. apart with straight-edge wheel of Cutter/Embosser. Cut pages into strips in same widths as book bindings and long enough to extend over top and down opposite side of cake; position on cake. For inside book covers, cut matching color fondant strips, ¼ in. wide, long enough to extend over top and down opposite side of cake; brush backs with water and position. Attach bindings to front of cake; use white fondant to fill in gaps between carved bindings and pages, if necessary. Position outer covers. Position candy plaque. Serves 24.

***Note:** Combine Violet with a little Rose for violet shown.

◀ Heaven's Blessings

Pans: Baby Buggy, p. 151; 16 x 2 in. Round, p. 148
Tips: 2, 2D, 3, 5, 12, 127, 131, 224, 349, p. 138-139
Colors: Buttercup Yellow, Moss Green, p. 133
Recipes: Buttercream and Royal Icings, p. 112
Also: Cake Boards, Fanci-Foil Wrap, p. 169; Wooden Dowel Rods, p. 167; Meringue Powder, p. 132; waxed paper, cornstarch

In advance: Using royal icing, make swirl drop flowers on waxed paper. Make 40 tip 2D flowers, 45 tip 131 flowers and 100 tip 224 flowers, all with tip 3 dot centers. Make extras to allow for breakage and let dry. Using thinned royal icing, make 300 tip 2 dots on waxed paper; let dry.

Bake and cool 1 in. high buggy cake and 2-layer round cake (bake two 1½ in. layers to make a 3 in. high cake). Prepare cakes for stacked construction (p. 110). Cut off background areas of buggy cake. In buttercream, ice smooth round cake and wheels, handle area, and upper rim of buggy. Build up hood area with tip 12, piping each section separately (smooth with finger dipped in cornstarch). Pipe tip 12 outline handle. Pipe body of buggy with tip 5 basketweave, piping sections ½ in. apart. Pipe tip 5 outline wheel spokes. Add tip 12 outline wheel rims and ball hubs (flatten hubs and smooth with finger dipped in cornstarch). Pipe tip 127 ruffle on upper rim of carriage. With buttercream, attach tip 224 flowers along top edge of ruffle and tip 131 flower clusters at corner of hood; add tip 2D flowers on wheels. On round cake, pipe tip 12 bead bottom border. Position assorted flowers on border. Add tip 349 leaves. Print tip 3 message. Position buggy cake. Position dots on top and sides of cake. Serves 83.

▶ Day of Dedication

Pan: 12 x 2 in. Round, p. 148
Tips: 2, 3, 129, 131, 233, p. 138-139
Colors:* Kelly Green, Lemon Yellow, Golden Yellow, Rose, Violet , p. 133
Recipes: Buttercream and Royal Icings, Color Flow Icing, p. 112
Also: 2006 Pattern Book (Fence Post, Church, Roof, Cross, Bushes), p. 124; Communion Girl Topper, p. 186; Piping Gel, Color Flow Mix, Meringue Powder, p. 132; 11¾ in. Lollipop Sticks, p. 221; 14 in. Round Silver Cake Base, p. 169; Parchment Triangles, p. 137, waxed paper, cornstarch

In advance: Make color flow fence posts (27 needed), church, roof, cross and bushes (3 of each needed) using patterns (p. 120). Also make a 1½ in. diameter circle base for girl topper in color flow. Make extras of all pieces to allow for breakage and let dry. When dry, attach a lollipop stick to connect cross and church using royal icing. Cut 2 sticks to 8½ in. and attach to church, leaving 3 in. extended to insert in cake. Cut sticks to 3½ in. and attach to bushes, leaving 2 in. extended to insert in cake. Let all dry. Attach roof to church with royal icing; let dry. Using full-strength color flow, outline windows and door with tip 3 (pat smooth with finger dipped in cornstarch). Add tip 3 door and window peaks, window sills and doorstep; pipe tip 2 dots around windows and doors. Using tinted piping gel in cut parchment bags, pipe in stained glass windows. Let set.

Also in advance: Using royal icing, make 35 tip 129 yellow drop flowers and 25 tip 131 rose drop flowers. Add tip 2 dot centers to all. Let dry.

Ice 2-layer cake smooth (bake two 1½ in. layers to make a 3 in. high cake). Position on silver base. Attach fence posts to cake sides, ½ in. apart, with buttercream. Pipe tip 233 pull-out grass bottom border. Insert church and bushes in cake top. Attach drop flowers with buttercream. Position topper with color flow base. Serves 40.

*Note: Combine Lemon Yellow and Golden Yellow for yellow shown.

◄ Beginning His Journey

Pan: Cross, p. 204

Tips: 1, 2, 3, p. 138

Color: Royal Blue, p. 133

Fondant: Ready-To-Use Rolled Fondant in White (24 oz. needed), Pastel Blue and Pastel Green (48 oz. each needed), p. 126; Rolling Pin, Roll & Cut Mat, p. 130; Easy-Glide Fondant Smoother, p. 131

Recipe: Buttercream Icing, p. 112

Also: 2006 Pattern Book (Cross Sections), p. 124; Round Comfort Grip™ Cutter, p. 214; Double-Thick Cake Board (or ½ in. thick foamcore), Fanci-Foil Wrap, p. 169; Gum-Tex™, p. 130; Piping Gel, p. 132; Disposable Decorating Bags, p. 137, paring knife, cornstarch

In advance: Make fondant cross sections. Combine ½ teaspoon of Gum-Tex with 12 oz. of white fondant. Roll out ⅛ in. thick. Using patterns and paring knife, cut section pieces. Using round cutter, cut center circle. Let all pieces dry on cornstarch-dusted surface. Prepare cake board. Cut double-thick cake board or foamcore ¾ in. wider than pan. Wrap with foil, brush with piping gel and cover with green fondant.

Prepare cross cake for rolled fondant by lightly icing in buttercream. Cover cake with fondant; smooth with Fondant Smoother. Position on fondant-covered board. Pipe tip 1 swirls on cake. Add tip 3 bead bottom border. On fondant center circle, pipe tip 2 letters. Attach cross sections to cake top with buttercream. Edge sections with tip 2 beads. Flatten a ball of fondant to 1 in. diameter and ¼ in. thick. Attach with buttercream where cross sections meet. Attach center circle with buttercream. Serves 12.

► Affirming Her Faith

Pan: Cross, p. 204

Tip: 2, p. 138

Fondant: Ready-To-Use Rolled Fondant in White and Pastel Pink (48 oz. each), p. 126; Easy-Glide Fondant Smoother, p. 131; Brush Set, p. 129; Rolling Pin, Roll & Cut Mat, p. 130

Recipe: Buttercream Icing, p. 112

Also: Gum-Tex™, p. 130; Piping Gel, p. 132; 6mm White Pearl Beading*, p. 161; Parchment Triangles, p. 137; cornstarch, non-toxic pastel pink chalk, tea strainer, double-thick cardboard or ½ in. thick foamcore, plastic ruler

At least 1 day in advance: Make fondant ribbon for top of cake. Combine ¼ teaspoon Gum-Tex with 6 oz. white fondant. Roll out ⅛ in. thick. Cut two strips, 2 x 14 in. long. Crimp sections randomly to create a flowing ribbon effect. Position vertical strip on top of pan; trim to fit pan edges, cutting ends on an angle. Pinch vertical strip at center where horizontal strip will cross. Position horizontal strip, wrapping under and over at pinched center of vertical strip. Trim to fit as on vertical strip. Let dry for 1-2 days on cornstarch-dusted surface.

Prepare cake board. Cut double-thick cardboard or foamcore ¾ in. wider than pan. Wrap with foil, brush with piping gel, and cover with pink fondant. Prepare cake for rolled fondant (p. 111). Cover cake with fondant; smooth with Fondant Smoother. Position on fondant-covered board. Using thinned fondant adhesive (p. 111) with water and tip 2, attach beads to bottom border. Grate chalk through tea strainer and brush into crevices of ribbon. Attach ribbon to top of cake with thinned fondant. Serves 12.

* Remove beads and dusted ribbon before cutting and serving.

The Wedding Party

If you have something old, borrowed and blue, we have something new.
Our wedding cake collection builds on tradition with colors, flowers and
presentations that will thrill both you and your guests. Define the day with the
delicate tone of ivory, featured on a 3-tier cake encircled by oval floral ringlets.
Choose a dramatic new flower–plumeria–or a bold color combination
like black and pink. Unveil unique textures like the curtain cake shown here,
with suspended strings which provide a peek into a soft violet backdrop.
It's sheer excitement that can set the tone for your reception.

Instructions for projects shown on these two pages are on page 82.

Dancing On A Cloud

Pans: 8, 12, 16 x 2 in. Round, p. 147
Tips: 2, 10, 16, 18, 103, 352, p. 138-139
Ornament: Always and Forever Musical, p. 162
Recipes: Buttercream and Royal Icings, p. 112
Also: 2006 Pattern Book (Garland Valance), p. 124;
10, 14 in. Decorator Preferred® Separator Plates,
Meringue Powder, p. 132; Cake Dividing Set,
p. 136, 9 in. Baker's Best® Disposable Pillars
with Rings, p. 166; Silver Fanci-Foil Wrap, p. 169;
Flower Nail No. 7, p. 137; triple-thick 18 in. sturdy
cardboard circles, ½ in. thick foamcore board or
cake plate, waxed paper

Several days in advance: Make 30 garland valances
in royal icing. Cover pattern with waxed paper and
fill in area with tip 16 zigzags. Make extras to allow
for breakage and let dry. **Also in advance:** Make 30
tip 103 roses (p. 116) in royal icing; make extras to
allow for breakage and let dry.

If used without cake plate, prepare base using
triple-thick cardboard or foamcore; wrap with foil.
Ice 2-layer cakes smooth and prepare for push-in
pillar construction (p. 110). Divide 8 in. cake in 6ths,
12 in. cake in 8ths and 16 in. cake in 12ths. Pipe tip 18
shell bottom border on all cakes.

At reception: Assemble cakes. Attach garland
valances at division marks, with ends about 1 in.
from edge of cake; press very lightly to attach.
Pipe tip 2 triple drop strings from ¾ to 1½ in. deep
at center of valance and tip 2 double drop strings
from ¾ to 1 in. deep on each side of valance in
royal icing. Add tip 2 dots at string points. Position
a rose at each division point on cake tops. add
tip 352 leaves in buttercream. Position ornament.†
Serves 156.**

A Swirl of Rosettes

Pans: 6, 10, 14 x 2 in. Round, 18 x 3 in. Half Round, p. 147
Tips: 1M (2110), 2, 3, 5, 8, 12, p. 138-139
Ornament: Spring Song, p. 163
Recipes: Buttercream and Royal Icings, p. 112
Also: 8, 12, 16 In. Plates, 7½ in. Twist Logs (3 sets needed), from Crystal Clear Cake Divider Set, p. 165; Meringue Powder, p. 132; Silver Fanci-Foil Wrap, p. 169; Heating Core, p. 147; triple-thick sturdy cardboard or ½ in. foamcore board (20 in. diameter), waxed paper, small ruler, ⅜ in. white satin ribbon (63 in. needed)

One day in advance: On waxed paper-covered board, use royal icing to make 85 tip 1M rosettes with tip 5 dot at center. Make extras to allow for breakage and let dry overnight.

Prepare base using triple-thick cardboard or foamcore; wrap with foil. Ice smooth 2-layer cakes (for 18 in. cake, bake four 2 in. high half rounds to make a 4 in. high cake) in buttercream. Prepare cakes for push-in pillar construction (p. 110). Position 18 in. cake on base. Mark cake sides at 2 in. intervals. At each division mark, pipe alternating tip 2 double and triple drop strings. First string is 1½ in. deep, second string is 2 in. deep, third string is 3 in. deep. Pipe tip 3 dots (not connecting) on each drop string. Attach 1 rosette at each division point with buttercream, extending slightly above cake edge. Pipe a tip 12 dot between each rosette. Add tip 8 ball bottom borders on all tiers. Attach ribbon to side of base board. Position ornament.† Serves 262.**

† Note: Always place a separator plate, or cake board cut to fit, on the cake where you position any figurine or ornament. This protects both the cake and your keepsake. For extra stability, secure your figurine to the plate with double-stick craft tape.

**Note: The top tier is often saved for the first anniversary. The number of servings given does not include top tier.

Eternal Rhapsody

Pans: 8, 12, 16 x 2 in. Square, p. 148

Tips: 2, 3, p. 138

Colors:* Rose, Violet, Leaf Green, Moss Green, Royal Blue, Black, p. 133

Ornament: Our First Dance, p. 163

Recipes: Buttercream and Color Flow Icings, p. 112

Also: 2006 Pattern Book (Panel), p. 124; Color Flow Mix, p. 132; Plastic Dowel Rods, p. 167; Cake Boards, Fanci-Foil Wrap, p. 169; Disposable Decorating Bags, p. 137; 18 in. square base board or foamcore (½ in. thick), waxed paper

Several days in advance: Make color flow panels (p. 120) using pattern. Cover pattern with waxed paper and outline with tip 3 using full-strength color flow in black. Let set 2 hours, then flow in with thinned color flow. Make 12 panels in rose, 16 in green and 20 in violet. Make extras to allow for breakage and let dry. Also in advance: Make 275 tip 2 dots, ⁵⁄₁₆ in. diameter, using thinned color flow icing on waxed paper. Make extras to allow for breakage and let dry.

Ice 2-layer cakes smooth and prepare for stacked construction (p. 110). Pipe tip 2 bead bottom borders. Trim excess waxed paper around panels, leaving back attached. Attach panels on cake sides, about 2 in. apart, using full-strength color flow.†† Attach dots between panels with full-strength color flow. Position ornament.† Serves 200.**

*Note: Combine Rose with a little Violet and Royal Blue for rose shown. Combine Leaf Green with Moss Green for green shown. Combine Violet with a little Rose and Royal Blue for violet shown.

**Note: The smallest tier is often saved for the first anniversary. The number of servings given does not include the smallest tier.

† Note: Always place a separator plate or cake board cut to fit, on the cake before you position any figurine or ornament. This protects both the cake and your keepsake. For extra stability, secure your figurine to the plate with double-stick craft tape.

†† Note: Remove panels before cutting and serving.

Plumeria Promise

Pans: 6 x 3, 8 x 2, 12 x 3 in. Round, p. 147; 10 x 2, 16 x 2 in. Square, p. 148

Tip: 2, p. 138

Colors:* Rose, Kelly Green, Royal Blue, Black, p. 133

Fondant: White Ready-To-Use Rolled Fondant (348 oz. needed), p. 126; Leaf Cut-Outs™, p. 128; Rolling Pin, Roll & Cut Mat, Floral Collection Flower Making Set, p. 131; Brush Set, p.129; Confectionery Tool Set, Easy-Glide Fondant Smoother, p. 131

Ornament: Love's Duet, p. 162

Recipes: Gum Paste Adhesive, p. 111; Buttercream Icing, p. 112

Also: Lily Nail Set, Flower Former Set, p. 137; Flower Spikes, Large (6mm) White Pearl Beading (2 pks. needed), p. 167; "Hidden" Pillars, p. 166; Plastic Dowel Rods, p. 167; Cake Boards, Silver Fanci-Foil Wrap, p. 169; Gum Paste Mix, p. 130; Meringue Powder, p. 132; Heating Core, p. 147; 20-gauge cloth-covered wire (6 in. pieces, 44 needed), ⅜ in. wide black satin ribbon (6 yds. needed), 21½ in. square plywood board, aluminum foil, non-toxic pastel chalk, tea strainer, cornstarch, toothpick

Several days in advance: Make 20 plumeria flowers (p. 119) and 24 leaves using 1 recipe of gum paste. Make extras to allow for breakage. For flowers, tint gum paste rose and roll out ¹⁄₁₆ in. thick. For leaves, tint gum paste green with a little blue and black added; roll out ¹⁄₁₆ in. thick. Cut leaves using tulip leaf cutter from flower making set. Place on thin foam and score vein lines with veining tool. Attach wire to back with adhesive; let dry on large flower formers dusted with cornstarch.

Bake and cool 1-layer 6 in. (3 in. high), 8 in. and 16 in. cakes and 2-layer 12 in. cake (bake two 2½ in. layers for a 5 in. high cake). For bottom tier, bake and cool eight 1-layer 10 in. cakes; stack in twos on foil-wrapped plywood board to form a 20 in. wide x 4 in. high cake. Prepare cakes for stacked construction (p. 110) and rolled fondant (p. 111). Cover cakes in rolled fondant; smooth with Fondant Smoother. Using buttercream, attach ribbon and pearl beading†† to base of each cake. Pipe tip 2 scrolls and dots. Place a small ball of fondant in flower spikes; insert flowers and leaves. Insert spikes in cake. Position ornament.† Serves 332.**

†† **Note:** Remove ribbon and pearls before cutting and serving cake.

A Savage Feast

A kid's birthday is the natural habitat of these wild treats! Decorate the cupcakes, lollipops and cereal treats with Candy Melts® to create an easy, sweet safari.

Dazzling Displays!

Call off the caterer! With our
Cupcakes 'N More™ Dessert Stands
(p. 143), it's easy to create your own
spectacular presentations of party foods.
Their multi-level design lifts your favorite
"finger foods" off the table—raising fun new
decorating options like the jungle scene
shown here. It's the higher profile
your party treats deserve!

In this special section, you'll discover
so many exciting ways to make
Cupcakes 'N More the center of your
celebration. From a tempting buffet of
roll-up sandwiches and exotic appetizers
(p. 104) to a Christmas dessert station filled
with colorful truffles and spritz
cookies (p. 103), we'll show you how
to take your party to new heights.
Look for more Dazzling Displays at
www.wilton.com.

Instructions for projects shown on these two pages are on page 92.

Please see our Product Shops (p. 123-222) for specific decorating items used in this section.

Jungle Gems: Tint white Candy Melts®† with Primary and Garden Candy Colors. Mold candy faces in Melting Plate cavities (p. 120). Unmold on waxed paper and decorate features using melted candy in cut parchment bag; attach to 4 in. lollipop sticks. For trees, pipe a circle of tip 67 leaves in royal icing on large waxed paper-covered flower formers; let dry. Attach leaves to pretzel rod with icing and pipe more leaves on underside. Remove baking cup from cupcakes; turn upside down and cover with melted candy (p. 120); let set, then repeat (1 pk. Candy Melts® will double-coat 4-5 cupcakes). Pipe candy lines on sides using cut bag; let set. Cover tops with tip 352 leaves in buttercream. Insert trees and face pops. Position cupcakes on Standard Cupcakes 'N More Dessert Stand.

Nutty Monkeys: Prepare and cut cocoa crisped rice cereal treats using large and medium round Cut-Outs™. Cut medium round in half; attach to large round for ears with melted candy. Insert 4 in. Lollipop Stick. Pipe features using Peanut Butter Candy Melts® in cut bag (tint portion black using Garden Candy Color Set).

The Party's on Safari: Mold candy plaque (p. 121) bases ⅜ in. deep in Mini Loaf Pan. Follow instructions from Jungle Gems (at left) to make pretzel rod trees. Attach mini marshmallows in corner of plaque with melted candy; insert tree. Lightly coat shredded coconut with melted candy; position around tree. Print name and attach Jungle Animals Topper with melted candy.

Show 'Em a Smile!

Populate your party with smiling faces! That classic yellow fellow from the '70s is back, on lollipop cupcake toppers, cookies and candy stick "candles" for your cake.

A. Gifts and Grins
You choose how to add the fun face toppers! Use our Smiley Faces with Hats Candle Pick Sets (p. 189) or mold your own jolly lollipop faces with fondant hats. If you are making your own faces, work in advance. Make fondant hats following instructions from Clowning 'Round at right. Mold face lollipops with 4 in. Lollipop Sticks and Yellow Candy Melts® in Smiley Face Mold; Tint White Candy Melts® black using Garden Color Set. Pipe in features using black candy in cut bag. Attach hats with candy and add tip 14 pull-out fringe in royal icing. Mold packages in Party Time mold using various colors of candy tinted using Primary and Garden Color sets; attach 4 in. Lollipop Sticks with candy. Using buttercream icing, cover cupcakes with tip 1M (2110) swirl; sprinkle with Rainbow Nonpareils. Trim lollipop sticks as needed and insert candies. Position cupcakes on Standard Cupcakes 'N More Dessert Stand.

B. Merry Men
Tint Roll-Out Cookie (p. 112) dough various colors; cut cookies using Metal Gingerbread Boy Cutter. Trim off heads and replace with yellow heads cut using largest Round Cut-Out™. Thin dough with water; pipe features. Bake and cool cookies.

C. Bright Smiling Faces
In advance: Figure pipe (p. 117) bodies on candy stick "candles" using royal icing and tip 12 for torsos, tip 8 for arms and legs, tip 3 for hands and feet. Attach Smiley Face Candle heads. Pipe tip 3 flame on black licorice wick; pipe tip 3 wax drips on candy stick, insert wick and let dry. Ice 8 x 3 in. cake smooth in buttercream; divide in 8ths and add tip 3 triple drop strings and dots. Pipe tip 21 rosette bottom border. Insert candles.

† Brand confectionery coating.

Every Face in Its Place

Guests won't have to crane their necks to see your decorated cupcakes. The angled holders of our Cupcakes 'N More Stand ensure that your treats won't hide their faces.

D. Happy Unwrapping!

In advance: Make fondant hats following instructions from Clowning 'Round below. Tint White Candy Melts® with Primary and Garden Candy Color Sets. Mold candy faces in Candy Melting Plate (p. 120). Pipe features using melted candy in cut bag; let set. Attach 4 in. Lollipop Stick to back; attach hats and pipe hair using melted candy. Pipe tip 14 pull-out star fringe in royal icing. Mold packages following instructions from Gifts and Grins at left. Using buttercream, cover cupcakes with tip 1M (2110) swirl. Trim lollipop sticks as needed and position candies. Position cupcakes on Standard Cupcakes 'N More Dessert Stand.

E. Faces Of Fun

Mold face lollipops using Funny Faces Candy Making Kit; mold hats using Party Time Mold (p. 220). Pipe hair and facial features and attach hats using melted candy in cut bag. Tie curling ribbon on sticks.

F. Balloon Bunch Bags

Fill Clear Treat Bags with candy-coated chocolates. Insert Circus Balloons toppers and tie with curling ribbon. Tape name tags to balloon stems.

G. Clowning 'Round

In advance: Make fondant hats. Tint portions of white fondant and shape into 1 in. cones; let dry. Draw designs using FoodWriter™ markers in various colors. Mold candy faces in Candy Melting Plate (p. 120). Attach hats and 4 in. lollipop sticks to faces with melted candy. In royal icing, pipe tip 14 pull-out star fringe on hats; let dry. Mold various color candy stars, 1/8 in. deep, using medium Star Cut-Out on Non-Stick Jelly Roll Pan; sprinkle stars with Colored Sugars and let set. Ice half of cupcakes smooth in buttercream; pipe tip 127 ruffle collars and insert clown pops (cut sticks as needed). Cover remaining cupcakes with tip 1M (2110) swirl; sprinkle with colored sugars and position candy star. Position cupcakes on Standard Cupcakes 'N More Dessert Stand.

H. Big Top Place Savers

Mold candy plaque (p. 121) bases 3/8 in. deep in Mini Loaf Pan. For tents, place largest cutter from Nesting House Cutter Set on Non-Stick Cookie Sheet and fill 1/4 in. deep with melted white candy; let set. Pipe details and name with melted candy in cut bag; let set. Cut flags from construction paper and tape to 4 in. Lollipop Sticks. Attach flag to tent and tent to base with melted candy. Position Circus Animal Toppers.

J. Clowns Keeping Cool

Attach balloon to 6 in. Lollipop Stick with curling ribbon. Attach spice drop hands and feet to candy stick arms and legs with melted candy (trim thumb section with paring knife). Insert in scoops of ice cream. Position Small Derby Clown Set head and spice drop halves for buttons; insert balloon.

Please see our Product Shops (p. 123-222) for specific decorating items used in this section.

A Rainbow Glow

The award for "Best Lighting" goes to this pair of shimmering treats: molded gelatin "cupcakes," topped by our Wavy Sparkler Candles and star cookies with a sparkling center of crushed candy.

A

B

A. These "Cupcakes" Shake!
Place baking cups in Standard Muffin Pan and spray with non-stick pan spray. Prepare Gelatin Treats recipe (p. 113) and fill cups just below top edge (sixteen 3 oz. pks. gelatin needed to make 38 desserts); refrigerate until set. Remove cups and set on flattened Mini Baking Cups to hold on stand. Using Vanilla Whipped Icing Mix, pipe tip 1M (2110) swirl on top. Sprinkle with confetti sprinkles from Flowerful Medley Sprinkle Assortment. Insert Rainbow Colors Wavy "Trick" Sparklers Candles and position on Large Cupcakes 'N More Dessert Stand.

B. Stained Glass Gift Cookies
Prepare cookies on sticks (p. 117). Wrap a 6 x 2 in. round craft block with foil. Tie curling ribbon to sticks and insert cookies in craft block. Add curling ribbon to fill out.

Please see our Product Shops (p. 123-222) for specific decorating items used in this section.

C

E

D

Randy

Aaron

Molly

Ice Cream's New Scene

Suddenly the old reliable party sundae doesn't look so "vanilla"! We've served them in tutti frutti-colored candy cups on the Large Cupcakes 'N More Stand, then surrounded them with rice cereal treat cones and candy place cards.

C. A Month of Sundaes

In advance: Mold 38 candy shells in Standard Baking Cups (p. 121) using Candy Melts®† in various colors (tint White Candy Melts® with green and yellow from Primary and Garden Candy Color Sets for green shown). Scoop ice cream into each shell; add Rainbow Jimmies and fudge topping. Using Vanilla Whipped Icing Mix, pipe tip 21 rosette. Position maraschino cherry. Position sundaes on Large Cupcakes 'N More Dessert Stand.

D. Your Own Cone

Press crisped rice cereal treats mixture 1 in. deep into prepared 10½ x 15½ in. Jelly Roll Pan; unmold onto waxed paper. Imprint treats with Ice Cream Cone Plastic Cutter and cut cones with paring knife. Tint White Candy Melts® with Primary and Garden Candy Colors. Cover scoop area with melted candy in cut bag; spread with spatula. Sprinkle with Rainbow Jimmies. Let set.

E. Go For A Dip!

Mold candy plaques (p. 121) ¼ in. deep in Mini Loaf Pan. Tint melted White Candy Melts® blue using Primary Candy Color Set; pipe names using blue candy in cut bag. Attach Ice Cream Icing Decorations with melted candy. Pipe candy on edges of plaque and dip in Rainbow Nonpareils.

† Brand confectionery coating.

A

B

Catch the Highlights!

Candles to burn at both ends—with a hearty party lunch and a brilliant dessert. Start with fun tortilla roll-up sandwiches, with a cheese flame on top. Then enjoy candy-coated cupcakes topped by fondant candles with smiling flames and sparkling stars.

A. Ready For a Blowout Party!

We've made the candles from fondant here—but you can have the same cute look in no time by using our new Chunky Candles (p. 187). If you are making fondant candles (p. 119), work in advance. Bake and cool 38 cupcakes; remove baking cups. Tint portions of White Candy Melts®† using Primary and Garden Candy Color Sets; also melt Pink and Yellow Candy Melts®. Turn cupcakes upside down

and cover with melted candy (p. 120); let set, then repeat (1 pk. of Candy Melts® will double-coat 4-5 cupcakes). Using melted candy, pipe ¼ to ½ in. diameter dots on waxed paper covered board; make approximately 85 dots in each color. Let set. Attach to cupcakes with melted candy. Using buttercream, cover tops of cupcakes with tip 1M (2110) swirls. Sprinkle with Rainbow Nonpareils. Insert candles and position on Large Cupcakes 'N More Dessert Stand.

B. Light Lunch!

Spread 6 in. flour tortillas with softened cream cheese. Place your favorite lunch meats and lettuce in center. Roll up, securing with toothpicks. Cut off ends leaving 4 in. long sections. Cut ¼ in. wide strips of cheese; attach to roll-ups with cream cheese. Insert 4 in. Lollipop Stick in top of roll-up. Cut flame from cheese using medium Leaf Cut-Out™; attach to stick with cream cheese.

Recipe Cards

If you love the look of our Dazzling Displays (p. 90-105), wait until you taste what's on them! Here are a few of the most tempting tastes for your recipe file. Clip and save for your next celebration— and don't forget to show them at their best on the Cupcakes 'N More Dessert Stands (p. 143).

Molten Chocolate Cakes

Chicken Italiano Appetizers

Mini Cheesecakes with Goat Cheese & Sun-Dried Tomato

Molten Chocolate Cakes

Filling:
½ cup Dark Cocoa Candy Melts®*, coarsely chopped
2 tablespoons heavy cream

Heat cream and candy in medium saucepan, whisking until chocolate is melted and smooth. **Do not boil.** Refrigerate until firm. Best made several hours or one day in advance.

Cake:

2 ½ cups semi-sweet chocolate chips   2 tablespoons granulated sugar
½ cup (1 stick) butter   1 teaspoon vanilla
2 tablespoons all-purpose flour   4 eggs, lightly beaten

Preheat oven to 350°F. Spray mini brioche pans with vegetable pan spray. In 2-quart saucepan melt chocolate chips and butter over low heat, stirring constantly, until chocolate is melted, 4-5 minutes. Remove from heat. Stir in flour, sugar and vanilla. Stir in eggs until well mixed. Pour 2-3 tablespoons into each mini pan. Place 1 teaspoon filling in each and top with batter until pan is ⅔ full. Smooth batter to cover filling. Place mini brioches on baking pan. Bake 15-17 minutes or until cake springs back when lightly touched. Cool 5 minutes. Loosen sides gently with spatula; turn out onto serving plates. Serve immediately.

Makes about 1 dozen mini cakes.

*Brand confectionery coating.

Mini Cheesecakes with Goat Cheese & Sun-Dried Tomato

3 packages (12 oz. ea.) refrigerated biscuits
½ pound (8 oz.) goat cheese, crumbled
¼ pound (4 oz.) cream cheese, softened
4 eggs
¼ cup finely chopped fresh basil
½ teaspoon salt (optional)
¼ teaspoon white pepper
½ cup oil-packed sun-dried tomatoes,
   well drained and finely chopped

Preheat oven to 350°F. Break each biscuit apart horizontally into 3 or 4 pieces. Press each piece into bottom and up sides of mini muffin pan cavities. Bake 3-5 minutes or until lightly browned. Cool slightly.

Meanwhile, in food processor or with electric mixer, combine goat cheese, cream cheese, eggs, basil, salt, pepper and ¼ cup tomatoes until smooth and well blended. Spoon into cooled biscuit cups; top with remaining tomatoes. Bake 10-12 minutes or until set. Serve.

Makes about
6 dozen cheesecakes.

Chicken Italiano Appetizers

18 wonton wrappers
½ cup finely chopped red pepper
½ cup finely chopped green onion
2 teaspoons olive oil
2 cups cooked chicken, finely chopped
⅓ cup mayonnaise
2 tablespoons Parmesan cheese
½ teaspoon garlic powder
½ teaspoon onion powder
½ teaspoon oregano
½ teaspoon basil
Salt and pepper to taste

Preheat oven to 400°F. Spray standard muffin pan cavities with vegetable pan spray. Press wonton wrappers into cavities.

In small skillet, cook red pepper and green onion in oil until soft, about 5 minutes. Meanwhile, combine chicken, mayonnaise, cheese and seasonings. Stir in cooked red pepper and green onion. Spoon 3 tablespoons filling into wonton "cup." Bake 7-8 minutes. Serve hot.

Makes 18 appetizers.

Desserts in Disguise

Nothing is as it seems...a party-size cereal treat is dressed up as a layer cake, ice cream sandwiches look like cupcakes and real cupcakes play the role of cherry-topped ice cream sundaes.

C. Pastel Carousel

Bake and cool 23 standard cupcakes; remove baking cups. Tint portions of White Candy Melts® using Primary and Garden Candy Color Sets; also melt Pink Candy Melts®. Turn cupcakes over and cover with melted candy (p. 120); let set, then repeat (1 pk. of Candy Melts® will double-coat 4-5 cupcakes). Using tinted candy and Orange Candy Melts® in cut bags, decorate cupcake sides with swirls, stripes and lines. For dots, pipe ¼ in. diameter circles on waxed paper-covered board; let set, then attach with melted candy. Using buttercream, cover cupcake tops with tip 1M (2110) swirl. Sprinkle with Colored Sugars. Position sour cherry ball candy. Position on Standard Cupcakes 'N More Dessert Stand.

D. Cupcakes & Cream

Cut Roll-Out Cookie Dough (p. 112) with Ice Cream Cone Cutter; trim off bottom. Decorate half the cookies with thinned dough. Using tip 4, pipe plain lines and cover tops with tinted "ice cream." Add Rainbow Nonpareils and bake 6 minutes; add Cinnamon Drop cherry and bake 3 minutes more. Let cool. Lay ½ in. thick slices of ice cream flat. Cut using cone cutter, trim off bottom, and sandwich between plain and decorated cookies.

E. Big Wishes, Little Cakes

Bake and cool 23 standard cupcakes; remove baking cups. Turn cupcakes over and cover with melted White Candy Melts® (p. 120); let set, then repeat (1 pk. of Candy Melts® will double-coat 4-5 cupcakes). Using ½ in. strips of fondant from Primary and Neon Multi Packs, make 5 ribbon roses (p. 119) for each cupcake. Divide cupcake tops in 5ths and attach 2 x ¼ in. fondant strips for garland and roses with melted candy. Attach ⅛ in. diameter rope for bottom border. Wrap bases of Rainbow Lattice Candles with ¼ in. wide fondant strip; attach to cupcakes with melted candy. Position on Standard Cupcakes 'N More Dessert Stand.

F. Saved You A Slice

Mold candy plaques (p. 121) ¼ in. thick in Mini Loaf Pan. Tint melted White Candy Melts® red, orange, pink, yellow and blue using Primary and Garden Candy Color Sets. Mold cake slices in Party Time Mold. Using melted candy in cut bags, pipe names and wavy lines on plaques. Attach confetti sprinkles and cake candies with melted candy.

G. Crunchy Cake

Prepare favorite rice cereal treats recipe and press into 6 x 3 in. round pan. Unmold onto foil-wrapped board. Ice top smooth in buttercream. Pipe tip 21 rosette bottom border; position candy-coated chocolate on each rosette. Divide "cake" in 8ths; pipe tip 3 zigzag garland, 2 in. deep. Position mini candy-coated chocolates on garland. Pipe tip 21 rosettes on "cake" top; insert Rainbow Colors Lattice Candles.

† Brand confectionery coating.

Please see our Product Shops (p. 123-222) for specific decorating items used in this section.

Frilly Flowers

*Lovely fondant loops give these colorful cupcake flowers a 3-D lift. It's a lighter-than-air look
that's picked up in the blossom petit fours and cookie pops.*

A. Puffed-Up Petals
Several days in advance: Make fondant loop petals. Knead 24 oz. white fondant
with 2 teaspoons Gum-Tex™; divide into 4 oz. portions and tint orange, rose, violet,
royal blue and lemon yellow. Roll out ⅛ in. thick and cut 15 strips, 2½ x ⅛ in., for
each cupcake. Fold in half and attach ends with damp brush; let dry. Roll ½ in.
diameter ball flower centers in yellow; flatten slightly and let dry. Ice smooth
23 cupcakes; position loops and attach center with icing. Position on Standard
Cupcakes 'N More Dessert Stand.

B. Baby Blossom Cakes
Bake and cool 1 in. high cake in 10½ x 15½ in. Jelly Roll Pan. Cut flowers using
largest Flower Cut-Out™. Brush cakes with Apricot Glaze (p. 111) and cover in
various colors of Quick-Pour Fondant Icing (p. 111); let set. In buttercream, pipe
tip 3 outline petals with dot centers.

C. Name That Bloom!
Tint Roll-Out Cookie Dough (p. 112) rose and orange. Use cutter and directions from
Flower Stencil-A-Cookie® Set to cut cookies; use stencil to sprinkle design with
Colored Sugar. Bake and cool. Cover 8 in. Cookie Treat Stick with green floral tape,
leaving 2 in. uncovered at one end. Attach uncovered end to cookie with melted
Candy Melts®†. Trace largest Leaf Cut-Out™ on construction paper; cut leaves,
punch a hole in leaf; thread with curling ribbon. Print name; tie tag on stick.

† Brand confectionery coating

**Please see our Product Shops (p. 123-222) for specific decorating items used in
this section.**

Presents with Pizzazz!

Hand cut cakes are coated with pastel poured fondant and topped by delicate royal icing bows. Wrap up the look neatly with candy box favors.

D. A Little Give and Take

In advance: Make teardrop loops using royal icing. Cover loop pattern from 2006 Pattern Book (on p. 42) with waxed paper and pipe 49 tip 3 loops each in violet/rose combination, rose, orange, royal blue, leaf green/lemon yellow combination and lemon yellow; let dry. Several hours in advance: Freeze two 9 x13 in. sheet cakes, 1½ in. high, to make firm for cutting. From one cake, cut 19 rounds using large Cut-Out™. Trim 2nd cake to 1¼ in. high and cut into nineteen 2 in. squares. Prepare 3 recipes of Quick-Pour Fondant Icing (p. 111) and tint portions to match loop colors. Prepare cakes and cover 6 or 7 (38 total) in each color of poured icing; let set. Pipe tip 3 lines and dots in royal icing. Pipe a tip 3 mound on cake tops and insert 7 loops. Position cakes on Large Cupcakes 'N More Dessert Stand.

E. Given with Ribbon

Mold candy shells (p. 121) in cavities of Non-Stick Standard Muffin Pan. Mold candy plaque (p. 121) lids ⅛ in. deep in 3 in. Round Metal Cutter placed on Non-Stick Cookie Pan. Refrigerate until firm; unmold. Fill shell with Pillow Mints. Tie ribbon bow around shell and lid.

F. Candy to Unwrap

Tint portions of White Candy Melts® using Garden Candy Color Set; also melt Yellow and Blue Candy Melts® to mold packages in Gift Truffles Mold using painting method (p. 121). Refrigerate until firm; unmold.

Fun Little Ones

By serving shower cupcakes in place of one big cake, you get to vary your design with all kinds of exciting colors and personalized details. These bedtime babies won't keep you up nights—all decorating is done in easy-to-shape rolled fondant, so it's a breeze to achieve the variety you want.

A. High-Rise Nursery

Ice 23 standard cupcakes smooth in buttercream. For heads, tint 4 oz. of white fondant Copper (skin tone) and roll into 1 in. balls; trim ¼ in. off back to flatten. Roll and attach ⅛ in. fondant ball noses with damp brush; let dry. For pillows, shape 1½ x 1¼ x ¼ in. thick fondant rectangles; indent center. Draw facial features on heads with Black FoodWriter™; attach heads to pillows with damp brush. Pipe tip 6 mound on top half of cupcake and position pillow. For body, roll 1½ x ¾ x ⅜ in. thick fondant log; flatten foot end and position below pillow. Roll out fondant ⅟₁₆ in. thick and cut blanket using pattern from 2006 Pattern Book. Position on cupcake; fold over top edge. Position cupcakes on Standard Cupcakes 'N More Dessert Stand.

B. Baby Bundles

For each favor, gather a White Tulle Circle around 1 oz. of Pillow Mints; tie closed with ⅛ in. wide white satin ribbon. Attach Small Safety Pins, Mini Rocking Horses, Baby Bears or Newborn Baby Figurines with hot glue.

Please see our Product Shops (p. 123-222) for specific decorating items used in this section.

Friends of the Bride

Hosting a shower is all about making people who may never have met feel relaxed and welcome. These cute little cakes really break the ice, with beaming bridesmaids and single-size wedding tiers served in easy reach on the Large Cupcakes 'N More Stand.

C. Bridal Court

Bake 1 in. deep cake in 12 x 18 in. Jelly Roll Pan and 19 cakes, 1½ in. high, in Mini Wonder Mold Pan cavities. Cut 19 cakes from jelly roll using largest Round Cut-Out™. Prepare round cakes for Quick-Pour Fondant Icing (p. 111) and cover. Prepare Mini Wonder Mold cakes for rolled fondant (p. 111). Reserve 6 oz. white fondant; divide 42 oz. in 5 equal portions and tint. Tint 2 oz. of reserved white fondant copper (skin tone). Cover cakes with fondant. Roll out copper fondant ⅛ in. thick and cut 19 heads using People Cut-Out; let dry, then draw features using Black

FoodWriter™. Roll out remaining fondant and cut 30 flowers of each color and 1 in white using smallest Cut-Out™. Cup flowers on thin Shaping Foam using small ball tool from Confectionery Tool Set. Using buttercream, add tip 2 dot centers and tip 349 leaves. Cut fondant bodies using shirt from People Cut-Outs; trim ¼ in. off bottom and fold arms toward center. Let all dry. Pipe tip 2 dots on round cakes. With buttercream, attach clusters of 5 or 6 flowers. Pipe additional tip 349 leaves. For bridesmaids, cut 4 in. Lollipop Sticks to 3 in. and insert into cakes. Attach bodies and heads to stick with royal icing; attach flower to arms. Pipe

tip 2 hair with royal icing. Add tip 2 beads at waist and drop strings at hem in buttercream. Decorate bride same as bridesmaids, then attach a 2 in. white fondant square (1/16 in. thick), gathered at end, for veil with royal icing. Position cakes on Large Cupcakes 'N More Stand.

D. Fancy Favors

Fill 23 White Hexagon Boxes with Mint Drops or other candies. Tie each box with ribbon and bow using 30 in. of ribbon. Position on Standard Cupcakes 'N More Dessert Stand.

Serving Every Season!

With the Cupcakes 'N More Stand, you'll always have the perfect holiday centerpiece! Just fill it with single-size cakes, brownies, cereal treats or cupcakes decorated in seasonal colors to add a festive touch instantly.

A. Easter Ecstasy
Bake and cool two 1 in. high cakes in 10½ x 15½ in. Jelly Roll Pan using firm-textured batter such as pound cake. Cut shapes using Easter Color Metal Cutter Collection. Cover cakes completely with melted Light Cocoa or White Candy Melts®† tinted with Garden Candy Color Set (1 pk. Candy Melts® covers 4 or 5 cakes). Let set on waxed paper. Pipe details using melted candy in cut bag. If needed, attach a Candy Melts® disk on bottom to stabilize. Position on Standard Cupcakes 'N More Dessert Stand.*

B. Gentle As A Lamb
Tint coconut (p. 117); let dry. Position Stand-Up Lamb cake on serving plate. Ice face and rose-tinted inside ears smooth in buttercream. Cover body and head with tip 16 rosettes. Pipe tip 3 string mouth. Attach jellybean nose and candy-coated chocolate eyes with icing. Sprinkle coconut on plate.

C. Who Hopped On Top?
Cover cupcakes with tip 1M (2110) buttercream swirls in various colors; sprinkle with Colored Sugars. Insert Bunny Foil Fun Pix™.

D. Tombstone Tower
Tint Roll-Out Cookie Dough (p. 112) gray using Black Icing Color. Cut tombstones using cutter from 12-Piece Halloween Metal Cutter Set. Using dough thinned with water, outline with tip 2, pipe R.I.P. with tip 1. Bake and cool. Prepare favorite rice cereal treats recipe and press 1 in. thick into 10½ x 15½ in. Jelly Roll Pan. Unmold and cut into 2 in. squares. Ice tops smooth in buttercream; sprinkle with 4-Mix Sprinkle Assortment. Position Ghost Bobbling Toppers and cookies. Position treats on Standard Cupcakes 'N More Dessert Stand.

E. What's Shakin'
Prepare Wilton Gelatin Treats (p. 113) using lime gelatin. Cut shapes using medium cutter from Nesting Ghost Set. Pipe tip 3 features using orange tinted Vanilla Whipped Icing Mix.

F. Eyes Say Surprise!
Cut Roll-Out Cookie Dough (p. 112) using BOO cutter from Spooky Cutter Set. Brush letter B with Orange Icing Color and make bloodshot lines with small amount of Clear Vanilla Extract tinted with icing colors. Tint portions of dough Black and Violet/Rose combination. Using tinted dough thinned with water, outline with tip 3. Bake and cool.

† Brand confectionery coating

Please see our Product Shops (p. 123-222) for specific decorating items used in this section.

G

H

J

The Truffle Tree

Can't you almost taste Christmas? Everyone will gather round to sample our easy Holiday Truffles in Peppermint, Eggnog, Gingerbread and Toffee flavors. Add festive colors here and on the spritz cookies using the Christmas 6-Mix Sprinkle Assortment.

G. Candy Dazzlers
Prepare 4 batches of Holiday Truffles (p. 113) in your favorite flavors. Dip in melted Candy Melts® and cover with White Nonpareils or sprinkles from Christmas 6-Mix Sprinkle Assortment. Position on Standard Cupcakes 'N More Dessert Stand.*

*Note: For added support when stacking stand with many servings, we recommend positioning acetate or cake circles, cut to fit, on each level. Place Doilies on top of acetate or cake circles.

H. Spritz Are Hits!
Fill Comfort Grip™ Cookie Press with your favorite spritz cookie dough. Press cookies onto cookie sheet; top some with Colored Sugars or Nonpareils from Christmas 6-Mix Sprinkle Assortment. Bake and cool. Decorate some cookies with melted Candy Melts® in cut bag, crushed nuts or candy trims.*

J. Gifts That Glitter
Bake and cool 1 in. high cake in 10½ x 15½ in. Jelly Roll Pan. Cut cakes using medium and large Square Cut-Outs™. Cover individual cakes with melted Candy Melts®; refrigerate until firm. Cover with a 2nd coat if needed. Pipe dots and stripes using melted Candy Melts® in cut bag; let set. Attach medium to large square with dots of candy. Tie gold ribbon bow around cakes.

Let the Flavors Mingle

May your parties be filled with interesting people and fascinating flavors! Cupcakes 'N More Stands are the perfect way to let guests taste the variety—the multi-level design keeps every sweet or savory delight organized for easy sampling.

D. Warm & Cool Treats

A hot dessert idea—our rich Molten Chocolate Cakes** (p. 113), flowing with warm chocolate cream in every bite, makes a great partner for cool, creamy Strawberry Mousse (p. 113) in candy shells. Both cakes and shells are made in the elegant Brioche Pan Set and are served on the Standard Cupcakes 'N More Dessert Stand*. Top cakes with a tip 21 rosette in buttercream. Candy shell instructions are on p. 121 (1 pk. of white Candy Melts®† makes 6 to 8 shells).

E. Pastry Panorama

Even when you are in a hurry, your favorite bakery pastries will have homemade flair when served on our Large Cupcakes 'N More Dessert Stand.* From cannoli to cream puffs, everything will be arranged perfectly on this 5-tier scrolled metal tower.

F. A Round of Cheesecakes

Personal-size servings let everyone indulge in their own decorated delight. Choose classic vanilla cheesecake with chocolate crust or our Red Ribbon Cheesecake, with a tart layer of raspberry at the center. Garnish the vanilla cheesecakes with a swirl of Light Cocoa Candy Melts®, piped in a cut bag on waxed paper, and placed in a tip 21 buttercream rosette. Top the raspberry cheesecakes with fresh raspberries, kiwi, currants and mint. Place all cakes on the Standard Cupcakes 'N More Dessert Stand.* The Red Ribbon Cheesecake recipe is on p. 113; for vanilla cheesecake, follow Red Ribbon Cheesecake recipe, omitting raspberries and substituting chocolate crumbs from No-Bake Cheesecake Mix.

† Brand confectionery coating.

**This recipe is a keeper! See the Wilton Recipe Cards in this Yearbook for luscious Molten Chocolate Cakes.

A. Very Tempting Veggies

A great way to add bright color and lighter fare to the celebration! Cut tomatoes, carrots, zucchini, celery, and peppers, then fill with your favorite cheese spread using tip 21. Position on the Standard Cupcakes 'N More Dessert Stand.* You'll find recipes for Herbed Cheese Spread and Goat Cheese and Sun-Dried Tomato Spread on our website, www.wilton.com.

B. The Sandwich Station

Make a tempting variety of mini sandwiches using your favorite breads and fillings. For the Roll-Ups, spread tortillas with softened cream cheese and add assorted meats, cheeses, lettuce and tomato. Roll up and cut into 1 in. lengths. Other sandwiches include roast beef on mini rolls, turkey on white bread with cucumber and lettuce, ham salad on rye with Muenster cheese, ham and cheese on wheat bread with lettuce and egg salad on mini croissants. Garnish with olives, lettuce, shaved radishes, currants and cherry tomatoes and place on Large Cupcakes 'N More Dessert Stand.*

C. Unique Appetizers

Put aside the pigs-in-a-blanket and introduce your guests to these exciting flavors. Spicy Asian Cheeseballs (p. 112) with the kick of wasabi and ginger. Mini Cheesecakes with Goat Cheese and Sun-Dried Tomato** (p. 112), a savory cheese filling baked in flaky biscuits. Or Chicken Italiano Appetizers** (p. 112), featuring wonton wrapper crowns filled with a flavorful sauté of chicken, cheese and vegetables. Serve them all on the Standard Cupcakes 'N More Dessert Stand.*

*Note: For added support when stacking stand with many servings, we recommend positioning acetate or cake circles, cut to fit, on each level. Place Doilies on top of acetate or cake circles.

**Great recipes to clip and save! See the Wilton Recipe Cards in this Yearbook for Chicken Italiano Appetizers and Mini Cheesecakes with Goat Cheese and Sun-Dried Tomato.

Please see our Product Shops (p. 123-222) for specific decorating items used in this section.

Recipes

The cakes, cookies and other desserts in this Yearbook were made using our favorite kitchen-tested recipes. Follow the instructions for decorated desserts that look and taste their best!

ICING RECIPES

Buttercream Icing

½ cup solid vegetable shortening
½ cup butter or margarine [1]
1 teaspoon Clear Vanilla Extract (p. 132)
4 cups sifted confectioner's sugar (about 1 lb.)
2 tablespoons milk [2]

Cream butter and shortening with electric mixer. Add vanilla. Gradually add sugar, one cup at a time, beating well on medium speed. Scrape sides and bottom of bowl often. When all sugar has been mixed in, icing will appear dry. Add milk and beat at medium speed until light and fluffy. Keep bowl covered with a damp cloth until ready to use. For best results, keep icing bowl in refrigerator when not in use. Refrigerated in an airtight container, this icing can be stored 2 weeks. Rewhip before using. Makes 3 cups.

[1] Substitute all-vegetable shortening and ½ teaspoon Wilton No-Color Butter Flavor (p. 132) for pure white icing and stiffer consistency.

[2] Add 2 tablespoons light corn syrup, water or milk per recipe to thin for icing cake.

Chocolate Buttercream Icing

Add ¾ cup cocoa (or three 1 oz. unsweetened chocolate squares, melted) and an additional 1 to 2 tablespoons milk to Buttercream Icing recipe. Mix until well blended. For a unique change of pace, use ⅛ to ¼ teaspoon Wilton Candy Flavors (p. 219) in place of vanilla extract.

Chocolate Mocha Icing: Substitute freshly brewed strong coffee for milk in recipe.

Darker Chocolate Icing: Add 4 more unsweetened chocolate squares (or ¼ cup sifted cocoa powder) and 1 more tablespoon of milk to Chocolate Buttercream Icing.

Snow-White Buttercream Icing

⅔ cup water
4 tablespoons Meringue Powder (p. 132)
12 cups sifted confectioner's sugar (about 3 lbs.)
1¼ cups solid vegetable shortening
¾ teaspoon salt
¾ teaspoon No-Color Almond Extract (p. 132)
¾ teaspoon Clear Vanilla Extract (p. 132)
½ teaspoon No-Color Butter Flavor (p. 132)

Combine water and meringue powder; whip at high speed until peaks form. Add 4 cups sugar, one cup at a time, beating at low speed after each addition. Alternately add shortening and remainder of sugar. Add salt and flavorings; beat at low speed until smooth. Makes 7 cups.

Note: Recipe may be doubled or halved. If halved, yield is 3 ½ cups.

Royal Icing

3 tablespoons Meringue Powder (p. 126)
4 cups sifted confectioner's sugar (about 1 lb.)
6 tablespoons water [3]

Beat all ingredients at low speed for 7-10 minutes (10-12 minutes at high speed for portable mixer) until icing forms peaks. Makes 3 cups.

[3] When using large countertop mixer or for stiffer icing, use 1 tablespoon less water.

Stabilized Whipped Cream Icing

½ pint (1 cup) heavy whipping cream
2 tablespoons confectioner's sugar
2 tablespoons Piping Gel (p. 132)
½ teaspoon Clear Vanilla Extract (p. 132)

Combine whipping cream and sugar in mixing bowl. Whip to soft peak stage. Add Piping Gel and vanilla, then continue to whip until stiff peaks form. Do not overbeat. Makes 1½ to 2 cups.

As an alternative, you can use frozen non-dairy whipped topping or packaged topping mix. Thaw frozen whipped topping in refrigerator before coloring or using for decorating. Use packaged topping mix immediately after preparing. Do not allow either to stay at room temperature, as it becomes too soft for decorating. Store decorated cake in refrigerator until ready to serve.

Heated Wilton Ready-To-Use Decorator Icing (p. 132)

Open icing container, remove foil. Microwave on 50% power for 1 minute; stir. Continue to microwave at 30 second intervals until ready to pour. If a microwave is unavailable, icing container can be heated on a warming tray or in a pan of hot water on a stove.

Classic Whipped Cream for Wilton Dessert Whipper Pro™ (p. 142)

1 pint (2 cups) heavy whipping cream
1 Tablespoon confectioner's sugar

Fill Dessert Whipper Pro™ with well-chilled heavy whipping cream and add confectioner's sugar. Use according to instructions. Makes about 8 cups.

Fluffy Boiled Icing

MERINGUE:
3 tablespoons Meringue Powder (p. 132)
½ cup cold water

SYRUP:
2 cups granulated sugar
¼ cup corn syrup
½ cup water

Beat meringue powder and cold water until stiff, about 4 minutes. In large microwave-safe measuring cup, stir sugar, corn syrup and water. In microwave, bring syrup mixture to a boil (approximately 5 minutes). Cool slightly. Slowly add syrup to meringue mixture while beating on low. Beat on HIGH for 4 minutes until stiff and glossy. Makes 8 cups.

For top of range: Mix sugar, corn syrup and water in 2 quart saucepan. Bring to a boil; cool slightly and follow directions above.

Confectioner's Sugar Glaze

1¼ cups confectioner's sugar
3 tablespoons milk
½ teaspoon Clear Vanilla Extract (p. 132)

Stir milk into sugar. Add vanilla. Drizzle on dessert cakes, muffins and cookies. May be thickened with confectioner's sugar or thinned with milk or other flavored liquids. Makes ½ cup.

Color Flow Icing Recipe (full-strength for outlining)

¼ cup + 1 teaspoon water
4 cups sifted confectioner's sugar (about 1 lb.)
2 tablespoons Color Flow Mix (p. 132)

With electric mixer, using grease-free utensils, blend all ingredients on low speed for 5 minutes. If using hand mixer, use high speed. Color flow icing "crusts"quickly, so keep bowl covered with a damp cloth while using. Stir in desired icing color. Makes approx. 2 cups color flow icing.

THINNED COLOR FLOW

In order to fill an outlined area, the recipe above must be thinned with ½ teaspoon of water per ¼ cup of icing (just a few drops at a time as you near proper consistency). Use grease-free spoon or spatula to stir slowly. Color flow is ready for filling in outlines when a small amount dropped into the mixture takes a count of ten to disappear.

Note: Color flow designs take a long time to dry, so plan to do your color flow piece up to 1 week in advance.

Poured Cookie Icing

This icing dries to a shiny, hard finish. Great to use as icing or to outline and fill in with tip 2 or 3.

1 cup sifted confectioner's sugar
2 teaspoons milk
2 teaspoons light corn syrup

Place sugar and milk in bowl. Stir until mixed thoroughly. Add corn syrup and mix well. For filling in areas, use thinned icing (add small amounts of light corn syrup until desired consistency is reached).

COOKIE RECIPES

Roll-Out Cookies

1 cup unsalted butter, softened
1½ cups granulated sugar
1 egg
1½ teaspoons Clear Vanilla Extract (p. 132)
½ teaspoon No-Color Almond Extract (p. 132)
2¾ cups all-purpose flour
2 teaspoons baking powder
1 teaspoon salt

Preheat oven to 400°F. In mixing bowl, cream butter with sugar until light and fluffy. Beat in egg and extracts. Mix flour, baking powder and salt; add to butter mixture 1 cup at a time, mixing after each addition. Do not chill dough. Divide dough into 2 balls. On a floured surface, roll each ball into a circle approximately 12 in. wide and ⅛ in. thick. Dip cookie cutter in flour before each use. Bake cookies on ungreased cookie sheet 6-7 minutes or until cookies are lightly browned. Makes about 3 dozen cookies. Recipe may be doubled.

Chocolate Roll-Out Cookies

¾ cup butter or margarine, softened
1 cup granulated sugar
2 eggs
1 teaspoon vanilla
3 squares (3 oz.) unsweetened chocolate, melted and cooled
3 cups all-purpose flour
1 teaspoon baking powder

Preheat oven to 375°F. In large mixing bowl, beat together butter and sugar with mixer until light and fluffy. Add eggs and vanilla; mix well. Blend in chocolate. Combine flour and baking powder; gradually add to butter mixture, beating until smooth. Cover and chill until firm, about 1 hour.

Roll dough approximately ⅛ in. thick. Dip cookie cutter in flour before each use. Bake cookies on ungreased cookie sheet 8-10 minutes or until cookies are lightly browned. Remove to rack and cool thoroughly. Makes 2-2 ½ dozen cookies.

Grandma's Gingerbread

5 to 5 ½ cups all-purpose flour
1 teaspoon baking soda
1 teaspoon salt
2 teaspoons powdered ginger
2 teaspoons ground cinnamon
1 teaspoon ground nutmeg
1 teaspoon ground cloves
1 cup solid vegetable shortening
1 cup granulated sugar
1¼ cups unsulphured molasses [4]
2 eggs, beaten

Preheat oven to 375°F. Thoroughly mix flour, soda, salt and spices. Melt shortening in large saucepan. Cool slightly. Add sugar, molasses and eggs to saucepan; mix well. Add 4 cups dry ingredients and mix well.

Turn mixture onto lightly floured surface. Knead in remaining dry ingredients by hand. Add a little more flour, if necessary, to make firm dough.

On a floured surface, roll ¼ in. thick for cut-out cookies. Bake on ungreased cookie sheet. Small and medium-sized cookies for 6-10 minutes, large cookies for 10-15 minutes. Makes 40 medium-sized cookies.

Note: If you're not going to use your gingerbread dough right away, wrap in plastic and refrigerate. Refrigerated dough will keep for a week. Remove 3 hours before using so it softens and is workable.

[4] Substitute 1¼ cups light corn syrup for molasses to make Blonde Gingerbread.

SPECIALTY RECIPES

Mini Cheesecakes with Goat Cheese & Sun-Dried Tomato

3 packages (12 oz. ea.) refrigerated biscuits
½ pound (8 oz.) goat cheese, crumbled
¼ pound (4 oz.) cream cheese, softened
4 eggs
¼ cup finely chopped fresh basil
½ teaspoon salt (optional)
¼ teaspoon white pepper
½ cup oil-packed sun-dried tomatoes, well drained and finely chopped

Preheat oven to 350°F. Break each biscuit apart horizontally into 3 or 4 pieces. Press each piece into bottom and up sides of mini muffin pan cavities. Bake 3-5 minutes or until lightly browned. Cool slightly.

Meanwhile, in food processor or with electric mixer, combine goat cheese, cream cheese, eggs, basil, salt, pepper and ¼ cup tomatoes until smooth and well blended. Spoon into cooled biscuit cups; top with remaining tomatoes. Bake 10-12 minutes or until set. Serve. Makes about 6 dozen cheesecakes.

Chicken Italiano Appetizers

18 wonton wrappers
½ cup finely chopped red pepper
½ cup finely chopped green onion
2 teaspoons olive oil
2 cups cooked chicken, finely chopped
⅓ cup mayonnaise
2 tablespoons Parmesan cheese
½ teaspoon garlic powder
½ teaspoon onion powder
½ teaspoon oregano
½ teaspoon basil
Salt and pepper to taste

Preheat oven to 400°F. Spray standard muffin pan cavities with vegetable pan spray. Press wonton wrappers into cavities.

In small skillet, cook red pepper and green onion in oil until soft, about 5 minutes. Meanwhile, combine chicken, mayonnaise, cheese and seasonings. Stir in cooked red pepper and green onion. Spoon 3 tablespoons filling into wonton "cup." Bake 7-8 minutes. Serve hot. Makes 18 appetizers.

Asian Cheeseballs

(see Unique Appetizers, p.105)

1 package (8 oz.) cream cheese, softened
2 cups (8 oz.) finely shredded Cheddar cheese
2 tablespoons hoisin sauce
1 teaspoon prepared wasabi
½ teaspoon grated ginger
Finely chopped water chestnuts, toasted sesame seeds, chopped nuts or parsley

In food processor, combine cream cheese and Cheddar cheese; process until blended. Add hoisin sauce, wasabi and ginger; process until smooth. Chill until firm. Roll cheese mixture into bite-size balls; roll in water chestnuts, seeds, nuts or parsley. Makes about 48 cheeseballs.

Cheesy Pesto Spread

(see The Great Ice-scape, p. 53)

7 packages (8 oz. ea.) cream cheese, softened
13 oz. goat or feta cheese, at room temperature
1½ cups prepared pesto sauce

Spray Soccer Ball Pan and 1 jumbo muffin cavity with vegetable pan spray; line with plastic wrap. In large bowl, beat cream cheese with electric mixer until creamy. Add goat cheese; continue beating until smooth.

Press about ¾ cup cheese mixture into prepared muffin cup. Press 1 cup cheese mixture onto bottom of soccer ball pan; spread cheese mixture around pan edges to 1½ in. thickness. Spoon pesto sauce into pan. Cover with remaining cheese mixture. Cover with plastic wrap;

refrigerate at least 8 hours or overnight. Unmold onto serving tray. Makes about 80 (2 tablespoon) servings.

Cheese Onion Round

(see Joy Spreads, p. 52)

3 packages (8 oz. ea.) cream cheese, softened
1 envelope dried onion soup mix
½ cup shredded carrots

Spray Sports Ball Pan half with vegetable pan spray; line with plastic wrap. In large bowl, beat cream cheese with electric mixer until creamy. Add onion soup mix and carrots; mix well. Press into prepared pan. Cover with plastic wrap; refrigerate at least 8 hours or overnight. Unmold onto serving tray. Makes about 32 (2 tablespoon) servings.

Spicy Cheddar Spread

(see Joy Spreads, p. 52)

1 package (8 oz.) cream cheese, softened
1 cup sour cream
3 cups (12 oz.) shredded medium Cheddar cheese
1-2 tablespoons chili powder, as desired
½ teaspoon cumin

Spray Sports Ball Pan half with vegetable pan spray; line with plastic wrap. In large bowl, beat cream cheese and sour cream with electric mixer until creamy. Add cheese, chili powder and cumin and continue beating until blended and smooth. Press into prepared pan. Cover with plastic wrap; refrigerate at least 8 hours or overnight. Unmold onto serving tray. Makes about 32 (2 tablespoon) servings.

Avocado Dip

(see Joy Spreads, p. 52)

2 envelopes unflavored gelatin
1 ¼ cups cold water, divided
4 large ripe avocados, finely mashed (about 2 cups)
¾ cup sour cream
¾ cup mayonnaise
½ cup thick and chunky picante sauce or salsa
2 tablespoons lemon juice
1 tablespoon finely chopped onion
1 teaspoon salt

Spray Sports Ball Pan half with vegetable pan spray; line with plastic wrap. Sprinkle gelatin over ½ cup water; let stand 2 minutes until softened. Add remaining water and heat in microwave or saucepan until dissolved, about 2 minutes. Set aside.

In medium bowl, combine avocado, sour cream, mayonnaise, picante, lemon juice, onion and salt; mix well. Add gelatin mixture; mix well. Press into prepared pan. Cover with plastic wrap; refrigerate at least 8 hours or overnight. Unmold onto serving tray. Makes about 32 (2 tablespoon) servings.

Holiday Paté

(see It's a House Paté, p. 52)

3 envelopes unflavored gelatin
¾ cup beef broth
½ medium onion, coarsely chopped
1 clove garlic, minced
2 lbs. liverwurst
2 tablespoons Dijon mustard
1 teaspoon ground nutmeg
4 teaspoons brandy (optional)
1 cup (2 sticks) butter, at room temperature
1 package (8 oz.) cream cheese, softened
Salt and pepper to taste

Spray Stand-Up House Pan with vegetable pan spray; line with plastic wrap. Sprinkle gelatin over broth; let stand 2 minutes until softened. Heat in microwave or in saucepan until dissolved, about 2 minutes. Set aside.

Process onion and garlic in food processor until chopped. Add liverwurst, mustard, nutmeg and brandy; process until smooth. Add cream cheese and butter, process until smooth. Add gelatin mixture and process until blended. Taste for seasonings; add salt and pepper to taste. Place in prepared pan; tap down and smooth top. Chill overnight until firm. To unmold, carefully run small knife around edge of pan; dip pan in warm water 10 seconds. Unmold onto serving plate. Makes 64 (2 tablespoon) servings.

Strawberry Mousse

(see Warm and Cool Treats, p. 104)

1 package (16 oz.) frozen strawberries, thawed
¾ cup granulated sugar
2 envelopes unflavored gelatin
1 ½ cups milk
1 cup heavy whipping cream, whipped

Purée strawberries in blender or food processor. In medium saucepan, combine sugar and gelatin. Stir in milk; stir over low heat until gelatin is completely dissolved, 5-8 minutes. Pour into large bowl, stir in strawberry purée. Refrigerate, stirring occasionally, until mixture mounds slightly. Fold whipped cream into thickened gelatin mixture. Spoon or pipe into candy cups or dessert dishes. Makes about 5 cups mousse.

White Chocolate Mousse

(see A Lively Brew, p. 16)

1 ½ cups heavy whipping cream
2 envelopes unflavored gelatin
6 tablespoons cold water
6 oz. cream cheese, softened
1 cup granulated sugar
½ teaspoon Clear Vanilla Extract (p. 132)
2 ½ cups milk
½ teaspoon lemon juice
2 packages (3.3 oz. ea.) white chocolate flavor instant pudding and pie filling

Whip cream until soft peaks form, set aside. Soften gelatin in cold water; heat in microwave on high, 20-30 seconds until dissolved. Cool. Beat cream cheese and sugar until light and fluffy. Add vanilla, milk and lemon juice; mix well. Add gelatin mixture, stir to combine. Add 2 boxes of pudding mix. Fold in whipped cream. Refrigerate until firm, at least 3 hours or overnight. Recipe may be halved.

Chocolate Cheesecake

Use this recipe for one 9 in. heart cake.

Prepare pans: Fit a cake board into the bottom of the 9 in. springform pan. (Wrap outside of pan with aluminum foil.)

Crust:
1 cup ground pecans
2 cups crushed chocolate cookie crumbs
9 tablespoons butter, melted

Preheat oven to 400°F. Mix ingredients and firmly press mixture into bottom and sides of pan. Bake 6 to 7 minutes; cool before filling.

Batter:
1¾ lbs. cream cheese, at room temperature
⅔ cup granulated sugar
4 eggs
14 oz. Light Cocoa Candy Melts®†, (p. 218), coarsely chopped
1 teaspoon Clear Vanilla Extract (p. 132)
1 ⅓ cups heavy whipping cream

Preheat oven to 350°F. Place cream cheese and sugar in mixing bowl. Using electric mixer, cream mixture until smooth. Add eggs, one at a time, while mixing. Melt Candy Melts following package directions. Cool 7-10 minutes*. Add cooled candy, vanilla and whipping cream to cream cheese mixture. Blend well. Pour batter into prepared pan. Place pan into large ovenproof pan or dish. Pour hot water into large pan until it reaches ½ in. up sides of pan. Bake in center of oven 1¾ to 2 hours. To test for doneness, gently shake pan. The top of cake should move as one solid piece. There should be no soupy movement in center. Cake will set completely when refrigerated. Remove from oven to cool. Refrigerate overnight or for 12 hours.

To Unmold:
Run a straight-edge spatula around edge of pan. Release spring and remove ring. Refrigerate until ready to serve. Cake keeps well in refrigerator, well covered, up to one week.

*It is important that candy be cooled, but still liquid. If too hot, candy will get lumpy when added to batter.

Molten Chocolate Cakes

(see Warm and Cool Treats, p. 104)

Filling:
½ cup Dark Cocoa Candy Melts†,
2 tablespoons heavy whipping cream

Heat cream and candy in medium saucepan, whisking until candy is melted and smooth. **Do not boil.** Refrigerate until firm. Best made several hours or one day in advance.

Cake:
2 ½ cups semi-sweet chocolate chips
½ cup (1 stick) butter
2 tablespoons all-purpose flour
2 tablespoons granulated sugar
1 teaspoon vanilla
4 eggs, lightly beaten

Preheat oven to 350°F. Spray Mini Brioche pans with vegetable pan spray. In 2-quart saucepan melt chocolate chips and butter over low heat, stirring constantly, until chocolate is melted, 4-5 minutes. Remove from heat. Stir in flour, sugar and vanilla. Stir in eggs until well mixed. Pour 2-3 tablespoons into each mini pan. Place 1 teaspoon of filling in each and top with batter. Smooth batter to cover filling. Place mini brioche pan on baking pan. Bake 15-17 minutes or until cake springs back when lightly touched. Cool 5 minutes. Loosen sides gently with spatula; turn out on to serving plates. Serve immediately. Makes about 1 dozen mini cakes.

Red Ribbon Cheesecake

(see A Round of Cheesecakes, p. 104)

5 packages (11.1 oz. ea.) no-bake cheesecake mix, divided
6 ¼ cups milk, divided
1 package (15 oz.) frozen red raspberries, thawed and puréed

Prepare the crust from **2 packages** cheesecake mix; press into the bottom of 13 x 9-inch baking pan. Reserve remaining crumbs for another use.

In large bowl, prepare filling for **4 packages** cheesecake mix according to package directions, using 6 cups milk. Combine puréed raspberries with remaining ¼ cup milk. Prepare remaining **1 package** cheesecake mix following package directions, substituting raspberry mixture for the milk. Spread half the white cheesecake mixture evenly over crust. Top with raspberry cheesecake mixture; spread evenly. Top with remaining white cheesecake mixture. Smooth with metal spatula. Chill at least 2 hours. Cut into squares to serve. Makes about 12 servings.

Jelly Roll Yellow Sponge Cake

(see Making Summer Sizzle, p. 66)

¾ cup sifted cake flour
½ cup granulated sugar
4 eggs, separated
Pinch of salt
½ teaspoon cream of tartar
¾ teaspoon Clear Vanilla Extract (p. 132)

Preheat oven to 400°F. Grease or spray jelly roll pan with vegetable pan spray. Sprinkle well with cake flour. Sift together flour and sugar; set aside. In large bowl, beat egg yolks with mixer until light and fluffy, about 3 minutes. In separate bowl, combine egg whites and salt. Beat with electric mixer until whites begin to foam; add cream of tartar and continue to beat until whites are stiff but moist. Fold ⅓ white mixture into yolk mixture just until blended; spoon yolks over remaining whites. Spoon flour mixture over egg yolks; gently fold together just until there are no streaks of egg white or flour. Spread into prepared pan. Bake 10-12 minutes or until toothpick inserted in center comes out clean. Makes 5 cups batter.

Tuiles

(see Filled With Promise, p. 77)

6 egg whites, room temperature
1 ½ cups confectioner's sugar
1 cup all-purpose flour
12 tablespoons butter, melted
1 teaspoon vanilla extract
Pinch of salt

Preheat oven to 400°F. Spray cookie sheets with vegetable pan spray. In large bowl, beat egg whites, sugar and flour until blended and smooth. Beat in melted butter, vanilla and salt. Preparing 2 cookies at a time, drop 2 tablespoons batter onto cookie sheet, about 6 in. apart. Spread with tapered spatula to form a 4 x 6 in. oval. Bake 6-8 minutes or until edges are golden.

Working quickly, remove cookies with tapered spatula and roll over plastic dowel rod, wrapping from 4 in. side to form 4 in. wide cookies. If cookies become too hard to shape, return cookie sheet to oven for 1-2 minutes to soften slightly. Cool completely. Repeat with remaining dough. Store in airtight container or add filling if desired. Makes about 20 scroll cookies.

Wilton Gelatin Treats

(see These "Cupcakes" Shake, p. 94)

This recipe yields a firmer gelatin, recommended for molding and cutting shapes.

2 packages (3 oz. ea.) flavored gelatin
1 ¼ cups boiling water

Completely dissolve gelatin in boiling water. Lightly spray pan or baking cups with vegetable pan spray. Slowly pour gelatin into pans or cups. Refrigerate until set, at least 3 hours. Unmold.

Peppermint Truffles

(see Candy Dazzlers, p. 103)

1 package (14 oz.) White Candy Melts†, coarsely chopped (p. 218)
½ cup heavy whipping cream
⅛ teaspoon peppermint Candy Flavoring (p. 219)
Red Candy Color (optional, p. 219)
Melted Dark Cocoa, Light Cocoa or White Candy Melts
Crushed peppermint candies

In microwave-safe container or on top of stove, melt Candy Melts with cream. Stir in peppermint flavor and, if desired, a touch of the red color to achieve a light pink. Pour into shallow pan. Refrigerate 1-2 hours or overnight until firm but pliable. Roll into 1 in. ball. Dip in melted candy; roll in crushed candy. Makes about 5 dozen candies.

Eggnog Truffles

(see Candy Dazzlers, p. 103)

1 package (14 oz.) White Candy Melts†, coarsely chopped
¼ cup prepared eggnog
¼ cup heavy whipping cream
¼ teaspoon ground nutmeg
Melted Dark Cocoa, Light Cocoa or White Candy Melts
Christmas Sprinkles Assortment (p. 196)

In microwave safe container or on top of stove, melt Candy Melts with eggnog and cream. Stir in nutmeg. Pour into shallow pan. Refrigerate 1-2 hours or overnight until firm but pliable. Roll into 1-inch balls. Dip into melted candy; roll in sprinkles. Makes about 5 dozen candies.

Gingerbread Truffles

1 package (14 oz.) White Candy Melts†, coarsely chopped
½ cup heavy whipping cream
½ teaspoon ground cinnamon
¼ teaspoon ground ginger
⅛ teaspoon ground cloves
Melted Dark Cocoa, Light Cocoa or White Candy Melts
Christmas Sprinkles Assortment (p. 196)

In microwave-safe container or on top of stove, melt Candy Melts with cream. Stir in cinnamon, ginger and cloves. Pour into shallow pan. Refrigerate 1-2 hours or overnight until firm but pliable. Roll into 1 in. balls. Dip into melted candy; roll in sprinkles. Makes about 5 dozen candies.

Toffee Truffles

1 package (14 oz.) White Candy Melts†, coarsely chopped
½ cup heavy whipping cream
¾ cup toffee baking bits
Melted Dark Cocoa, Light Cocoa or White Candy Melts
Chopped pecans

In microwave-safe container or on top of stove, melt Candy Melts with cream. Remove from heat; let stand 15 minutes. Stir in toffee bits. Pour into shallow pan. Refrigerate 1-2 hours or overnight until firm but pliable. Roll into 1 in. balls. Dip into melted candy; roll in chopped pecans. Makes about 5 dozen candies.

†Brand confectionery coating.

Tip Techniques

Your icing turned out great—now you're ready to learn how to pipe beautiful shapes on your cake. Stars, shells, dots, lines and other techniques are the foundation of your decorating knowledge. We'll tell you step-by-step how to pipe each one, including the angle, pressure and movement to use for a uniform look. With practice, you can build on these basics to create many other impressive designs.

ROUND TIPS

Dot

Pipe dots for flower centers, faces, figure piping and border effects. When making large dots, lift the tip as you squeeze to allow icing to fill out completely.

Practice With: Tip 3
Icing Consistency: Medium
Bag Position: 90°
Hold Tip: Slightly above surface

1. Hold the bag straight up with the tip slightly above the surface. Squeeze the bag and keep point of the tip in icing until the dot is the size you want.
2. Stop squeezing the bag completely before you lift the tip from the dot.
3. Lift tip up and pull away from piped dot.

Ball

An important technique to master, the ball shape makes bold borders and is the first step to learn for figure piping. Vary the basic look by adding stars, dots or spirals on the ball shapes.

Practice With: Tip 9
Icing Consistency: Medium
Bag Position: 90°
Hold Tip: Slightly above surface

1. Squeeze the bag, applying steady even pressure. As the icing begins to build up, raise the tip with it, but keep the tip end buried in the icing.
2. Stop squeezing as you bring the end of the tip to the surface.
3. Lift the tip up and pull away from your piped ball. Use the edge of the tip to shave off any point so that your ball is nicely rounded.

Bead

If you can pipe a shell, you can pipe a bead—the movements are similar. To pipe a bead heart, simply pipe one bead, then a second, joining the tails. Smooth together using a decorator's brush.

Practice With: Tip 5
Icing Consistency: Medium
Bag Position: 45° at 3:00 (9:00)
Hold Tip: Slightly above surface

1. Squeeze as you lift tip slightly so that icing fans out.
2. Relax pressure as you draw the tip down and bring the bead to a point.
3. To make a bead border, start the end of your next bead so that the fanned end covers the tail of the preceding bead to form an even chain.

Cornelli Lace

The lacy design of this freehand technique depends on continuous curving strings that do not overlap or touch.

Practice With: Tip 1 or 2
Icing Consistency: Thin
Bag Position: 90°
Hold Tip: Close to cake so icing attaches without scraping cake with tip and without flattening icing strings

Beginning and ending at edges, pipe a continuous string of icing, curve it up, down and around until area is covered. Make certain strings never touch or cross. Don't leave any loose ends! Stop pressure; pull tip away.

Printing

Practice With: Tip 3 with message press
Icing Consistency: Thin
Bag Position: 45° at 3:00
Hold Tip: Slightly touching surface

You may pipe letters freehand, pipe over a pattern traced with a toothpick, or pipe after imprinting letters with a pattern press. If you are using a pattern press, let icing crust slightly, then imprint the message. With a steady, even pressure, squeeze out a straight line, lifting the tip off the surface to let icing string drop. To prevent tails from forming, be careful to stop squeezing before you touch tip to surface and pull away. Be sure the end of the tip is clean before you go on to another line.

Writing

Practice With: Tip 5
Icing Consistency: Thin
Bag Position: 45° at 3:00
Hold Tip: Slightly touching surface

You may pipe letters freehand, pipe over a pattern traced with a toothpick, or pipe after imprinting letters with a pattern press. If you are using a pattern press, let icing crust slightly, then imprint the message. Steadily squeeze, gliding along the surface in a smooth, continuous motion. Use your arm, not your fingers, to form each line, letter or word. Keep your wrist straight, moving your entire forearm as a single unit. After you begin to master the curves and swings of the letters, lift the tip up slightly as you write. You'll find you have more control if you let the icing draw out slightly over the surface as you write.

Outline

Characters or designs are often outlined first, then piped in with stars or zigzags. Outlines are used for facial features, too. Color Flow plaques are also outlined before icing is flowed into the shape.

Practice With: Tip 3
Icing Consistency: Thin
Bag Position: 45° at 3:00 (9:00)
Hold Tip: Slightly above surface

1. Touch tip to surface. Raise the tip slightly and continue to squeeze.
2. The icing will flow out of the tip while you direct it along the surface.
3. To end, stop squeezing, touch tip to surface and pull away.

Drop Strings

These flowing strings are a beautiful way to adorn the sides of a cake. The trick to making drop strings is to pull the bag toward you as the string drapes down. If you "draw" the string with the tip, you won't achieve a pretty curve and your strings will tend to break. Pipe at eye level to your cake so that strings line up evenly. The Cake Dividing Set (p. 136) is a great help in accurately dividing and marking your cake for even drop strings.

Single Drop Strings

Practice With: Tip 3
Icing Consistency: Stiff
Bag Position: Shoulder level at 4:30 (7:30)
Hold Tip: Lightly touching surface to attach

1. With a toothpick, mark horizontal divisions on cake in the width you desire. Touch tip to first mark and squeeze, pausing momentarily so that icing sticks to surface.
2. While squeezing, pull the bag toward you. Continue squeezing to allow the icing to drape naturally into an arc. Icing will drop by itself—do not move the tip down with the string. The end of the tip should be the same distance from the surface as the width from point to point on your cake.
3. Stop pressure before you touch tip to second mark to end string. Repeat, keeping drop strings uniform in length and width.

Multiple Drop Strings

Try a different color for each row of multiple drop strings—put holiday colors together to really dress up your cake.

To add multiple rows of strings, mark the cake for the deepest row and pipe that row. Return to the first drop string point, squeeze the bag, and drop a string with a slightly shorter arc than in the first row. Join the end of this string to the end of the corresponding string in the first row. Repeat the process for a third row of drop strings above the second.

STAR TIPS

Star

Practice With: Tip 16
Icing Consistency: Medium
Bag Position: 90°
Hold Tip: Between ⅛ and ¼ in. above surface

1. Hold the decorating bag straight up, with the tip between ⅛ and ¼ in. above the surface, while using your other hand to hold the tip steady. Squeeze the bag to form a star. Increasing or decreasing the pressure changes the size of the star.
2. Stop squeezing the bag completely before you lift the tip from the star.
3. Lift the tip up and pull away from piped star.

Pull-out stars add even more dimension to your cake. To make them, hold bag at a 45° angle to surface. As you squeeze out icing, pull tip up and away from cake. When your mound is high enough, stop pressure and pull tip away. Work from bottom to top of area to be covered with pull-out stars.

Star Fill In

Because these close-together stars require so much piping from the same bag, it's a good idea to keep replenishing the icing. Replenish icing when it gets soft or stars will be poorly defined.

Practice With: Tip 16
Icing Consistency: Medium
Bag Position: 90° (straight up)
Hold Tip: ¼ in. above surface

1. Pipe a row of stars evenly and close together, adjusting the tip position slightly each time so that the points of the stars interlock and cover the area without gaps.
2. Pipe a row of stars beneath the first, again adjusting tip position to close any gaps.
3. Continue to fill in entire area.

Zigzag

A quick and popular way to fill in outlined areas, perfect for ribbed sweater and cuff effects. You can use tight zigzags to cover the entire side of your cake—they look great!

Practice With: Tip 16
Icing Consistency: Medium
Bag Position: 45° at 3:00 (9:00)
Hold Tip: Lightly touching surface

1. Steadily squeeze and move your hand in a tight up and down motion.
2. Continue piping up and down with steady pressure. To end, stop pressure and pull tip away. For more elongated zigzags, move your hand to the desired height while maintaining a steady pressure. For a more relaxed look, just increase the width as you move the bag along.
3. Repeat as you move in a straight line with consistent up/down motion.

Zigzag Puff

This is the fluffy look you want for making clouds or smoke and to add dimension as a side border.

Practice With: Tip 17
Icing Consistency: Medium
Bag Position: 45° at 3:00 (9:00)
Hold Tip: Lightly touching surface

1. Begin to pipe with a light pressure, then use heavier pressure toward the center of the puff, then return gradually to a light pressure to form the tapered end.
2. To end each puff, stop pressure and pull tip away.
3. Repeat as you move in a straight line to form a row of puffs.

Shell

Most popular icing technique of all, the shell is the basis for many borders. Lift tip slightly when piping shells to avoid a bumpy look.

Practice With: Tip 21
Icing Consistency: Medium
Bag Position: 45° at 6:00
Hold Tip: Slightly above surface

1. Hold the bag in the 6:00 position so that you can pull the bag toward you. The tip should be slightly above the surface.
2. Squeeze hard, letting the icing fan out generously as it lifts the tip—do not lift the bag. Gradually relax your pressure as you lower the tip until it touches the surface.
3. Stop pressure and pull the tip away, without lifting it off the surface, to draw the shell to a point.
4. To make a shell border, start the end of your next shell so that the fanned end covers the tail of the preceding shell to form an even chain.

Reverse Shell

Opposite-facing shells look spectacular as top and bottom borders and as framed areas on your cake—they add a wonderful motion effect. The look is even fancier finished with a dot or a star at the center of each shell curve.

Practice With: Tip 21
Icing Consistency: Medium
Bag Position: 45° at 6:00
Hold Tip: Slightly above surface

1. As you begin to form a shell, squeeze hard, letting the icing fan out.
2. Form a curve, moving the tip from 9:00 (3:00) to 12:00 to 6:00. Relax pressure and lower the tip, pulling straight toward you at 6:00 to form a tail.
3. Repeat with another shell, curving from 3:00 (9:00) to 12:00 to 6:00.
4. To make a reverse shell border, pipe a chain of swirling reverse shells, with the fan end of each new shell covering the tail of the previous shell. If you are making the border on a round cake, turn the cake as you go so that the back of the bag is at 6:00 and you are working toward yourself

Rope

Finish your piped baskets with pretty edging and handles. Excellent for western or nautical themed cakes. You can make a great-looking rope with star or round tips (or basketweave tips, ridged or smooth side up).

Practice With: Tip 21
Icing Consistency: Medium
Bag Position: 45° at 4:30 (7:30)
Hold Tip: Lightly touching surface

1. Using a steady, even pressure, move the tip in a gentle sideways "S" curve. Stop pressure and pull tip away.
2. Insert tip under the bottom curve of the "S" shape.
3. Squeeze the bag with steady pressure as you pull down, then lift the tip. Move up and over the tail of the "S" as you continue to squeeze and form a hook.
4. Keep spacing as even as possible and "S" curves uniform in thickness, length and overall size. Be sure to tuck the tip into the bottom curve of the previous "S" before you begin squeezing to insure the clean, continuous look of a rope.

e-Motion

These continuous e-shaped loops work best on a bottom border, or as a western lariat. If you have to stop on your border to change positions, push in your tip at the end of the "e" and continue piping to keep a smooth look.

Practice With: Tip 16
Icing Consistency: Medium
Bag Position: 45° at 3:00 (9:00)
Hold Tip: Slightly above surface

1. Starting with bag at a 45° angle, and at bottom edge, squeeze out icing with even pressure, moving tip up to the right…
2. …and around as if writing the letter "e."
3. Repeat to complete the border, using a steady, even pressure. To end, stop pressure, pull tip away. You can vary the look of the e-motion border by making tight e's or stretched e's.

BASKETWEAVE TIPS

Try using different tips to vary the woven effects.

Practice With: Tip 47
Icing Consistency: Medium
Bag Position: 45° at 6:00 for vertical stripes; at 3:00 (9:00) for horizontal bars
Hold Tip: Lightly touching surface, serrated side up

1. Squeeze out a vertical stripe of icing from top to bottom (shown ridged side up).
2. Squeeze out short horizontal stripes of icing across the vertical stripe starting at the top. Spacing between stripes should be the same as the width of the tip opening. Squeeze next vertical stripe over ends of horizontal stripes. Start next set of horizontal stripes by burying the tip under the first vertical stripe.
3. Repeat vertical lines then horizontal lines until you achieve basketweave effect. Each new set should fit between the previous set.

MULTIPLE TIPS

Swirl Drop Flower

The swirled look adds a nice motion effect to the cake. You must squeeze and turn at the same time.

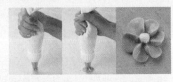

Practice With: Tips 2D, 3; use Large Coupler
Icing Consistency: Use royal icing: medium for flower, thin for center
Bag Position: 90°
Hold Tip: Slightly above surface

1. Turn your wrist in toward you before piping. Hold bag straight up, just touching the surface. You will turn wrist a full twist. Starting with the flat of your knuckles at 9:00 (3:00). As you squeeze out the icing, slowly turn your hand, with knuckles ending at 12:00.
2. Stop squeezing and lift the tip away.
3. Make a tip 3 dot flower center, holding your bag straight up and keeping the tip buried as you squeeze. Stop squeezing, then pull your tip up and away.

Crown Border

Majestic upright shells actually "crown" the top edges and sides of your cake. You can embellish the shell points with dots, stars or strings.

Practice With: Tip 32 or 4B for shell, 4 for dot
Icing Consistency: Medium
Bag Position: Slightly less than 90° at 6:00
Hold Tip: Slightly above surface

1. Start each shell at the top edge of the cake; apply pressure to let the shell build up and curve over the edge of the tier.
2. Relax pressure and move down to draw the shell to a point. Continue piping a row of side-by-side shells over the top edge of your cake.
3. Pipe a tip 4 dot at the end of each shell. Optional: Use tip 3 to pipe double drop strings on shell ends first, then pipe tip 4 dots at shell points.

PETAL TIPS

Ruffle

Everyone loves a ruffle's graceful motion—ruffles always add interest to your cake. Use them as a top border, to frame a plaque or to trim doll dresses and baby bonnets.

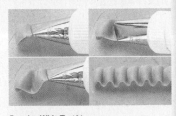

Practice With: Tip 104
Icing Consistency: Medium
Bag Position: 45° at 3:00 (9:00)
Hold Tip: Wide end lightly touching surface with narrow end facing down and away from surface

1. Keep the wide end of your tip touching the cake with the narrow end down. Move wrist up to pull up icing.
2. Move wrist down to complete one curl of the ruffle.
3. Repeat up and down motion.
4. Raise and lower the narrow end as you move around the cake. Repeat this motion for the entire ruffle.

Bow

The bow has many uses. Create a different look by using a different tip: round, star and petal will work.

Practice With: Tip 104
Icing Consistency: Medium
Bag Position: 45° at 6:00
Hold Tip: Wide end touching surface, narrow end straight up

1. With narrow end of tip pointing straight up, squeeze, moving the tip up and around to the left and back to the starting point.
2. Continue around, making a second loop on the right.
3. The two loops will form a figure 8.
4. While holding bag in the same position, return to the center and squeeze out two streamers.

DECORATING WILTON SHAPED CAKES STEP-BY-STEP

When decorating a cake that's simply covered with stars, here are the easy steps involved.

1. Ice sides and other areas smooth per instructions.

2. Outline details.

3. Pipe in facial features, small details.

4. Cover areas with stars, stripes, zigzags or dots.

5. Add message. Edge top and base with borders. Attach flowers or trims.

Flower Making Techniques

Explore beautiful flowers like the sweet pea or carnation, which add lovely color to your cake design. Create the magnificent rose—the most popular icing flower of all. With practice, your flowers will have the just-picked look of real garden flowers.

FLOWER NAIL FLOWERS

Using a Flower Nail

The nail is a revolving platform you hold in your hand to conveniently build roses and other flowers. It allows you to work close up, to turn for easy piping and to remove your completed flowers without damage, to dry.

The key to making the flower on the nail is to coordinate the turning of the nail with the formation of each petal.

Attach a square of waxed paper on the flat surface of the flower nail using a dot of icing. Pipe your flower directly on the waxed paper. Hold the flower nail between the thumb and forefinger of your left (right) hand (use other fingers to support nail) and roll it slowly counterclockwise (clockwise for lefties) as you press out icing with the decorating bag held in the right (left) hand. Your right (left) hand moves in and out, or up and down, as it holds the decorating bag and tip at just the right angle (in most cases 45°) and keeps the icing flowing at an even speed. After piping, slide the waxed paper with flower off the nail to dry.

The Wilton Rose

NOTE: *If you are going to be placing your roses on your cake immediately, waxed paper squares are not needed. To remove finished roses, use the Flower Lifter (p. 137). Slide flower from lifter onto cake, using a spatula.*

Practice With: Tips 104, 12
Icing Consistency: Royal or stiff buttercream
Bag Position: Base 90° (straight up); petals 45° at 4:30 (7:30)
Hold Tip: For base, slightly above nail; for petals, wide end touching base
Flower Nail: #7 (larger roses) or #9 (smaller roses)

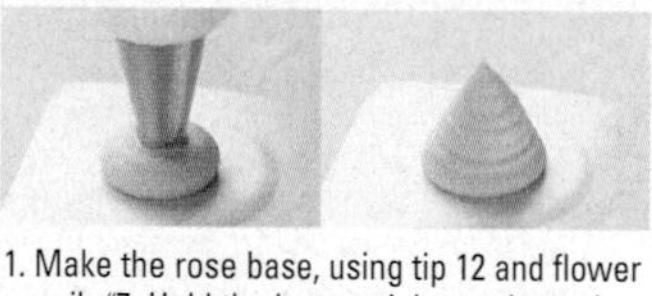

1. Make the rose base, using tip 12 and flower nail #7. Hold the bag straight up, the end of tip 12 slightly above the center of your waxed paper-covered flower nail, which is held in your other hand. Using heavy pressure, build up a base, remembering to keep your tip buried as you squeeze. Start to lift the tip higher, gradually raise the tip, and decrease the pressure.
2. Stop pressure, pull up and lift away. The rose base should be 1½ times as high as the rose tip opening.

3. Make the center bud, using tip 104. Hold nail containing base in your left (right) hand and bag with rose tip 104 in right (left) hand. Bag should be at a 45° angle to the flat surface of the nail and in the 4:30 (7:30) position. The wide end of the tip should touch the cone of the icing base at or slightly below the midpoint, and the narrow end of the tip should point up and angled in over top of base.
4. Now you must do 3 things at the same time: squeeze the bag, move the tip and rotate the nail. As you squeeze the bag, move the tip up from the base, forming a ribbon of icing. Slowly turn the nail counterclockwise (clockwise for lefties) to bring the ribbon of icing around to overlap at the top of the mound, then back down to starting point. Move your tip straight up and down only; do not loop it around the base.
5. Now you have a finished center bud.

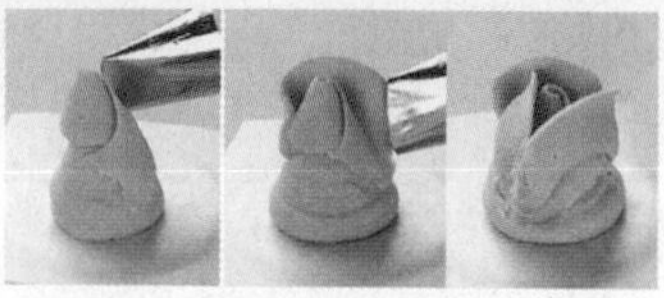

6. Make the top row of 3 petals. Touch the wide end of tip to the midpoint of bud base, narrow end straight up.
7. Turn nail, keeping wide end of tip on base so that petal will attach. Move tip up and back down to the midpoint of mound, forming the first petal.
8. Start again, slightly behind end of first petal, and squeeze out second petal. Repeat for the third petal, ending by overlapping the starting point of the first petal. Rotate the nail ⅓ turn for each petal.

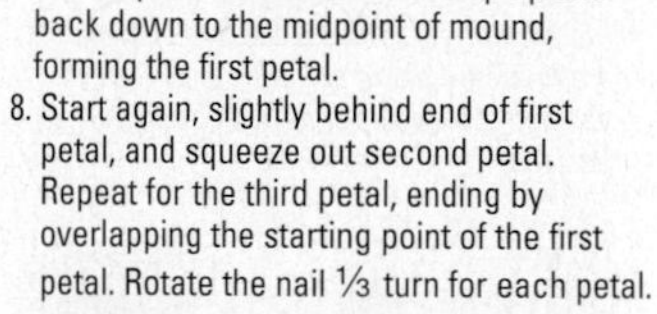

9. Make the middle row of 5 petals. Touch the wide end of tip slightly below center of a petal in the top row. Angle the narrow end of tip out slightly more than you did for the top row of petals. Squeeze bag and turn nail moving tip up, then down, to form first petal.
10. Repeat for a total of 5 petals, rotating the nail ⅕ turn for each petal.
11. The last petal end should overlap the first's starting point.

12. Make the bottom row of 7 petals. Touch the wide end of tip below the center of a middle row petal, again angling the narrow end of tip out a little more. Squeeze bag and turn nail to end of fingers, moving tip up, then down to form first petal.
13. Repeat for a total of 7 petals, rotating the nail ⅐ turn for each petal.

14. The last petal end should overlap the first's starting point.
15. Slip waxed paper and completed rose from nail. This is the completed Wilton Rose.

Rosebud

Finish your petit fours or cupcakes with one pretty rosebud. Made in buttercream, this flat flower can be piped directly on the cake.

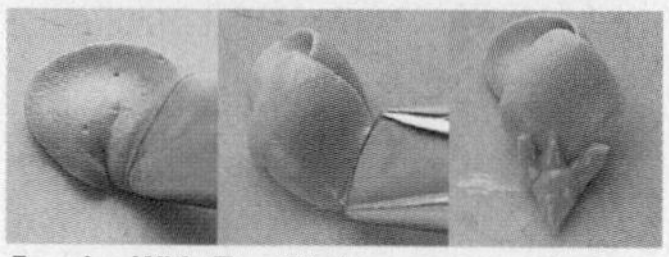

Practice With: Tips 104, 3
Icing Consistency: Stiff consistency buttercream for petals, thin consistency for sepals and calyx
Bag Position: 45° at 4:30 (7:30) for petals; 45° at 6:00 for sepals and calyx

1. Using tip 104, make the base petal. Keep the narrow end of the tip raised up and slightly to the right (left for lefties). While squeezing, move the tip along the surface away from you in a straight line about ¼ in. long. Pause, then continue squeezing as the icing fans out. Returning the tip to the original position and halfway back, start to release pressure, move tip to starting point, stop pressure and pull tip away.
2. Using tip 104, make the overlapping petal. Touch the wide end of the tip to the outside edge of completed petal. The bag is positioned as for the base petal, at 4:30 (7:30); hold it steady in this position until the second petal is completed. As you continue squeezing, the icing will catch the edge of the base petal and roll over it naturally. When the second petal looks complete, stop pressure completely, touch the tip back down to the surface and pull tip away.
3. Using tip 3, make the sepals and calyx. Form the middle sepal first by squeezing and letting icing build up. Lift the bag up and away from the flower. Stop pressure as you pull away to form the point of the sepal. Repeat, making a sepal on the left and right sides. For the calyx, insert tip into the base of the center sepal. Squeeze, letting the icing build up. Slowly draw the tip toward you, relaxing pressure as you move away from the flower. Stop pressure, pull away. You may want to blend the calyx into the stem using a damp brush.

Sweet Pea

One of the fastest, easiest-to-make flowers; works beautifully as part of a floral cascade. Try piping them in variegated shades.

Practice With: Tips 104, 3
Icing Consistency: Buttercream—stiff for petals, thin for calyx
Bag Position: For center petal and calyx 45° at 6:00; for left petal 45° at 4:30; for right petal, 45° at 7:30.
Hold Tip: Wide end touching surface; narrow end straight up

1. Make the center petal. Squeeze the bag and lift the tip slightly off the surface (about ¼ in.) as the icing moves forward and curls. Continue to squeeze without changing position. Relax pressure and return the tip to the surface. Stop squeezing, pull tip away.
2. Make the side petals. Position your bag slightly to the left of the center petal. Follow the same procedure as you did for the center petal—squeeze, and while the petal curls, lift the tip, relaxing your pressure and lowering the tip back to the surface. Stop squeezing and pull away. Repeat for the right side petal, holding the tip to the right of the center petal.
3. Make the calyx with tip 3.

Wild Rose

A pretty year-round flower piped about the size of a flower nail. If you prefer a more cupped shape, increase the angle of the tip. Dry in Flower Formers (p. 137)

Practice With: Tips 103, 1
Icing Consistency: Medium royal icing
Bag Position: For petals 45° at 3:00 (9:00); for center 90°
Hold Tip: For petals, wide end lightly touching center of nail, narrow end pointing out and raised ⅛ in. above nail surface; for centers, slightly above flower
Flower Nail: #7

1. Use tip 103 at a 45° angle. Touch nail with wide end of tip, keeping narrow end just slightly above nail surface. Begin at center of flower nail and squeeze out first petal, turning nail ⅕ turn as you move tip out toward edge of nail. Relax pressure as you return to center of nail, curving tip slightly upward to create a cupped shape. Stop squeezing as wide end touches center of nail and lift up.
2. Repeat step 4 more times.
3. Pipe tiny pull-out dot stamens with tip 1.

Apple Blossom

Pipe apple blossoms about the size of a penny and dry them on Flower Formers (p. 137).

Practice With: Tips 101, 1
Icing Consistency: Stiff royal icing
Bag Position: 45° for petals; 90° for dots
Hold Tip: Wide end touching surface, with narrow end pointed out.
Flower Nail: #7

1. Use tip 101 and hold bag at a 45° angle to flower nail with wide end of tip touching nail center, narrow end pointed out ⅛ in. away from nail surface.
2. Squeeze bag and turn nail as you move tip ⅛ in. out from nail center and back, relaxing pressure as you return to starting point.
3. Repeat procedure to make 4 more petals. Add 5 tip 1 dots for center.

FLORAL GREENERY

Leaves

Practice With: Tips 352, 67, 366
Icing Consistency: Buttercream thinned with corn syrup
Bag Position: 45° at 6:00
Hold Tip: Lightly touching surface; wide opening parallel to surface

Basic Leaf Tip 352 | **Veined Leaf Tip 67** | **Large Leaf Tip 366** Use large coupler

1. Squeeze hard to build up the base and, at the same time, lift the tip slightly.
2. Relax pressure as you pull the tip toward you, drawing the leaf to a point.
3. Stop squeezing and lift away.

FLORAL GREENERY cont.

Vines

Practice With: Tip 3
Icing Consistency: Thin
Bag Position: 45° at 3:00 (9:00)
Hold Tip: Lightly touching surface

1. Touch your tip lightly to the surface as you start to squeeze, then lift slightly above the surface as you draw out the stem.
2. Move tip gently up and down to form "hills and valleys." To end the line, stop squeezing and pull the tip along the surface.
3. Add secondary curved stems, starting at main stem, stopping pressure as you pull to a point.

Attaching Royal Icing Flowers to Wire Stems

On waxed paper square, using royal icing, pipe a dot base with tip 3. Make ⅛ in. hook on end of 4 in. florist wire and insert hook into base. With slightly moistened decorator brush, smooth and taper the icing around the wire. Push other end of wire into a piece of craft block and let dry. Remove waxed paper and attach flower with dots of icing.

Attaching Royal Icing Leaves to Wire Stems

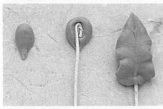

On waxed paper square, using royal icing, pipe a dot base with tip 4. Make a ⅛ in. hook on end of florist wire and insert hook into the dot base. Use tip 352 and pipe a leaf directly on top of wire. Push the other end of the wire into a craft block and let dry. Remove waxed paper square when dry.

Other Decorating Techniques

Combing

Practice With: Icing Sculptor™, Decorating Comb or Triangle, Trim 'N Turn Cake Stand (p. 136)
Icing Consistency: Medium-to-thin buttercream

Cover the cake with a slightly thicker coating of icing so the comb's ridges will not touch the cake. Comb immediately after icing cake, while icing is soft. Using a turntable helps to keep the movement smooth. Use the Icing Sculptor™, Decorating Comb or Decorating Triangle to add different contoured effects to your iced cake. Choose the type of effect you want—wide or narrow—then run that edge around your cake to form ridges. Ridges will be deep or shallow depending on the Icing Sculptor™ blade or the side of Decorating Comb or Triangle you use.

Icing Sculptor™

Select the sculpting blades you want and slide into holder. Press sculptor into iced cake as you rotate cake on turntable. The 64 blades included can create hundreds of different effects! Mix and match between the 14 edge designs to achieve the perfect look for your cake.

Combed Garland

To create a garland, hold comb so that about 4 teeth from the edge are touching the cake at the beginning of garland. Run comb in a curve, positioning so that about 6 teeth are touching cake at the bottom of the garland, then curve back with 4 teeth touching to finish garland. It's important to keep the comb level with the cake surface, so that the ridges created are uniform.

Pattern Press

The trick to uniform designs and steady writing and printing is using a pattern press (p. 142). Simply imprint the press onto all types of icing, including fondant. Use the vine pattern press on cake sides for a beautiful botanical effect.

Practice With: Tips 3, 16
Icing Consistency: Medium
Bag Position: 45° at 3:00
Hold Tip: Slightly above surface

1. Lightly press pattern onto your iced cake to imprint the design.
2. Outline the imprinted design with icing, using the tip of your choice. Change the tip to change the look of each pattern.

Tinting Shredded Coconut

Place desired amount of coconut in plastic bag, add a few drops of color and knead until color is evenly blended. Dry on waxed paper.

Clouds

(see The Crowd's in the Clouds, p. 7)

Use paper towel wide enough to cover width of cake. Tear paper towel in half horizontally to create rough scallops. Place one cut side of paper towel up slightly below top edge of cake and spray Color Mist™ along torn edge. Repeat process, moving towel down 1½ in. each time, until entire surface is covered with cloud effect.

Penguins

(see The Great Ice-Scape, p. 53)

Spread whipped cream cheese on a cracker. Cut ½ in. strips of carrot and position for feet. Fill bag fitted with tip 3 with cream cheese. Trim off bottom of Colossal size olive at hole end to create a flat edge. Fill olive hole with cream cheese. For wings, cut a medium olive lengthwise in half. With scissors, cut 2 "v" shapes in each half; reserve pieces. Attach halves to body with a dot of cream cheese. For head, cut ¼ off a medium olive, at hole end. Fill hole with cream cheese and attach to body. Outline and pipe in face and tummy areas with cream cheese. For eyes, cut 2 small circles from trimmed olive pieces; position. For nose, cut a triangle from carrot; position.

Cookie Flowers

(see Barbie Has Blossomed, p. 32)

Roll out dough. Using Cut-Outs, cut 4 small and 3 large daisies and 6 small and 3 large flowers; bake and cool. Using royal icing, outline cookies with tip 2; pipe in with thinned royal icing in cut parchment bag; let set. Pipe tip 3 dot centers and pull-out stamens using full-strength royal icing; let set. When completely dry, attach wires, cut to various lengths between 6 and 10 in., to cookie backs with melted candy; let set.

Stained Glass Gift Cookies

(see p. 94)

Crush hard candies. Prepare Roll-Out Cookie recipe (p. 112) and line cookie sheet with aluminum foil; spray foil with non-stick pan spray. Cut cookies using 2nd largest cutter from Nesting Metal Star Set; cut out centers with smallest star cutter from set. Place cookies on foil-lined pan and fill open area with crushed candy. Bake 7-8 minutes, until candy is melted and cookies are browned; let cool. Gently peel off foil. With a separate piece of foil, make a small cup and fill with crushed candy; bake 3-4 minutes at 350°. Dip end of 11¾ in. Lollipop Stick in melted crushed candy and attach to back of cookie. Attach candy-coated chocolates to cookies with melted Candy Melts.

Curtain

(See Curtains in Cascade, p. 80)

Following bottom edge of fondant scallops, overpipe 5 tip 3 lines, letting each line dry before piping the next. This will form a ledge for curtain to rest on. Pipe tip 2 vertical curtain lines; let dry. Add tip 2 beads at end of lines and tip 2 drop strings below beads. Pipe tip 1 freehand swirls, dots and bead flowers above fondant scallops.

Strawberry's Flowers

(see Sunny Strawberry Day, p. 32)

Attach some of the flowers below to lollipop stems as directed in cake instructions.

Tulips

Use tip 10 and royal icing to pipe an elongated bead for the center petal. Pipe an elongated bead on the left side of the first bead, pulling tip out to the left. Pipe an elongated bead on the right side of the first bead, pulling tip out to the right. Let dry.

Swirl Flowers

Using royal icing, pipe 1 flower with a tip 10 ball center and 5 flowers with tip 5 ball centers. Using tip 3, pipe swirl on ball. Let dry.

Spiral Flowers

Use tip 10 and royal icing to pipe a cone-shaped closed spiral. In one continuous motion, overpipe spiral and increase in size as you go up. Let dry.

Ice Cream Flowers

Use tip 10 and royal icing to pipe a ball. Using tip 3, pipe icing on top to resemble ice cream topping. Add a tip 3 ball on top for a cherry. Pipe tip 1 pull out dot stem. Let dry.

Dot Flowers

Use tips 3, 4, and 5 to make flowers of various sizes. Use royal icing to pipe center ball. Pipe 5 balls for petals around the center. Let dry.

Figure Piping Techniques

Figure piping is a way to really add personality to your cake. Your figures can be as lifelike or cartoonish as you want them to be. Begin with a base, then add familiar shapes such as dots, balls and strings to give the figure personality.

Dora On Her Unicorn

(see Dora's Only Way to Travel, p. 28)

Using royal icing, pipe tip 6 shirt (smooth with finger dipped in cornstarch). Pipe in tip 2 v-neck on shirt (smooth with finger dipped in cornstarch). Pipe tip 6 outline skirt on unicorn's back (smooth with finger dipped in cornstarch). Pipe tip 6 string arms; position head icing decoration against shirt. Outline and pipe in tip 6 hat; pipe tip 6 pull-out swirl ponytails. Add tip 2 dot hand and fingers.

Smiley Face Candles

(see Bright Smiling Faces, p. 92)

Position a candy stick on waxed paper-covered board and figure pipe using royal icing. Pipe a tip 12 line for torso. Pull out tip 8 arms and legs; add tip 3 ball hands and feet. Attach Smiley Face Candle heads. Let dry.

Fondant/Gum Paste Techniques

Fondant Baby

(see Layette On 'Em, p. 73)

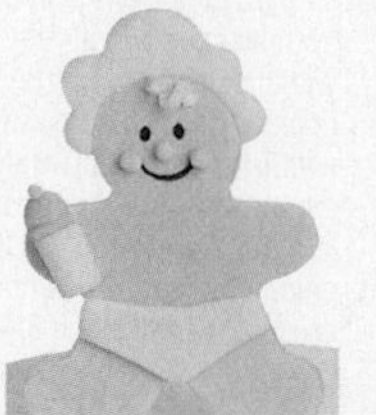

For body, tint a 2 in. ball of white fondant copper; roll out ⅛ in. thick and cut with gingerbread boy cutter.

For diaper, roll out white fondant ⅛ in. thick and cut a triangle shape 1¼ in. deep; attach to body with damp brush. For bonnet, flatten and press 5 small white balls together, forming a larger scallop at center and graduated smaller scallops on sides. Cut opening for head using head of boy cutter. Attach to body with damp brush.

For bottle, roll a ⅜ in. diameter log, cut to ½ in. long. Attach small green balls for top with damp brush; attach bottle to baby. For curl, cut a thin yellow strip; wind around end of brush handle to curl, slide off brush and attach. Draw mouth and eyes with black FoodWriter™. Roll and attach small copper balls for nose and cheeks. Attach baby to lollipop stick with thinned fondant adhesive (p. 111).

Fondant Cherubs

(See Valentine Assembly Line, p. 59)

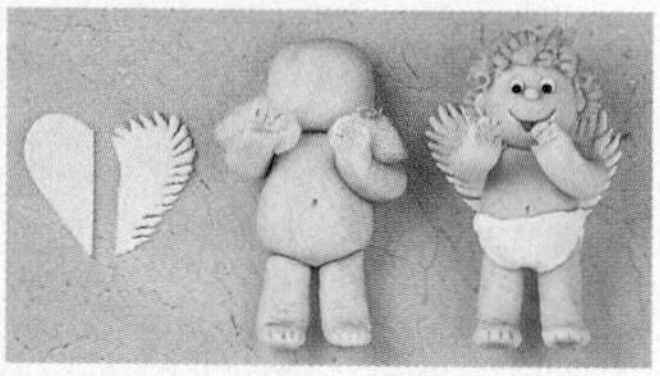

For wings, roll out white fondant ⅛ in. thick. Cut 6 hearts using largest Cut-Out. Cut off left side of heart, starting ¼ in. to left of center point; repeat for right side. Make 3 matching pairs of wings. Cut slits with craft knife and shape into points for feathered effect; let dry on cornstarch-dusted surface.

For cherubs, using copper fondant, roll three 1⅜ in. balls for heads. Insert a 3 in. piece of uncooked spaghetti into each, leaving 2 in. extended. Attach facial features with damp brush: Attach a ⅛ in. ball for nose. Cut mouth with craft knife and use veining tool from confectionery set to shape open mouth. For eyes, flatten 1/16 in. white balls and attach. Tint a ¼ in. ball black; roll and attach tiny balls for pupils. For ears, roll ⅛ in. balls of fondant; flatten, cut in half and attach. Tint ¼ in. ball of fondant rose, shape and attach for tongues. Let heads dry overnight.

When heads are dry, **make bodies**. Roll 2 in. diameter fondant balls and shape into 2 x 1¼ eggs; attach body on spaghetti piece extending from head. For legs, roll two 2 x ½ in. logs for each cherub; bend end over ½ in. for feet. Score toes using veining tool. Push 2 in. piece of uncooked spaghetti through leg and into body. For diaper, cut a 2 x 1 in. white fondant triangle and attach. Support figures against waxed paper-covered craft block to continue assembling.

For curly hair cherub, roll out yellow fondant ⅛ in. thick; cut 1 x 1/16 in. wide strips and wind around spaghetti. Carefully slide off and attach to head with thinned fondant adhesive (p. 111).

For ponytail cherub, cut a 1½ in. yellow piece and attach to head; trim around face. Score lines in hair with veining tool. For ponytail roll a log 1¼ x ½ in. diameter; cut into 3 pieces and attach. Score lines using veining tool. For bow, roll three ⅛ in. white balls; flatten 2 for loops and attach. For bangs, cut a 1¼ x ⅜ in. piece and attach; cut slits with knife. For boy cherub with cowlick, repeat steps for ponytail cherub's hair; use knife to cut slits. Roll a ¼ in. yellow piece for cowlick and attach.

For rolling pin, tint a 1 in. ball of fondant brown and roll a ⅜ in. x 2 in. log; insert a 3½ in. piece of spaghetti for handles and cover with brown fondant. Roll 2 in. x ½ in. logs for arms holding rolling pin, taper ends and bend to form elbow; bend ⅜ in. for hands and cut fingers with knife. Form hands around rolling pin and attach to body with thinned fondant adhesive. Repeat steps for arms holding cutter and FoodWriter™. Attach small heart Cut-Out to hands with thinned fondant. Position FoodWriter™ on shoulder, bend arms in position and attach with thinned fondant adhesive. Attach wings to backs of all cherubs with thinned fondant adhesive; let dry.

Fondant Santa

(see Skatin' St. Nick, p. 51)

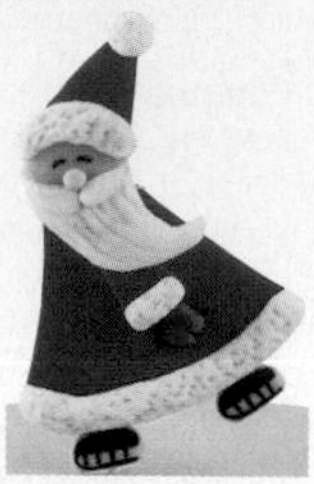

Combine red fondant package with ½ teaspoon Gum-Tex™. Roll out fondant ⅛ in. thick and cut body using tree cutter from stencil set. Trim off tree branch edges to create a bell shaped body.

Cut a triangle hat 1¼ in. high x 1¼ in. wide x ⅛ in. thick. Cut a triangle arm 1¼ in. high x ¾ in. wide x ⅛ in. thick.

For head, roll a ¾ in. diameter copper ball. Flatten to a 1¼ in. circle and attach to body with damp brush. Attach hat and arm with damp brush. For beard, roll a 1½ in. high x 1¼ in. wide x ⅛ in. thick white triangle and shape into a curved triangle. Create texture lines with edge of spatula; attach with damp brush. Roll a ⅛ in. copper ball for nose and two white teardrops for mustache; attach. Roll a log of white fondant for trim and attach to bottom edges of hat, arm and body. Create texture using tip of spatula.

For pompom, roll a ½ in. ball of white fondant, add texture, and attach with damp brush. Shape a small green fondant mitten and attach with damp brush.

For skates, shape 2 pastel blue ovals 1 in. x ½ in., attach with thinned fondant adhesive. Let dry overnight. Add eyes and skate detail with FoodWriter™. Using thinned fondant adhesive, attach lollipop stick to back of Santa, leaving 4 in. extending; let dry.

Girls' Fondant Shapes

(see To Serve Her Majesty, p. 12)

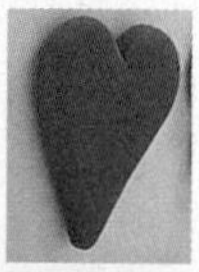

Make 18 various fondant shapes, attaching parts with damp brush.

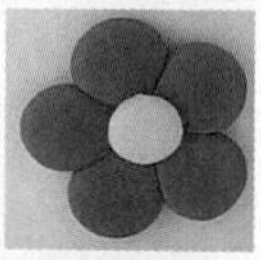

For hearts, roll out neon pink fondant ⅛ in. thick; cut shape.

For flowers, roll five ½ in. balls each in blue and neon orange. Place in a circle and flatten with fingers; attach a ⅜ in. neon yellow ball at center.

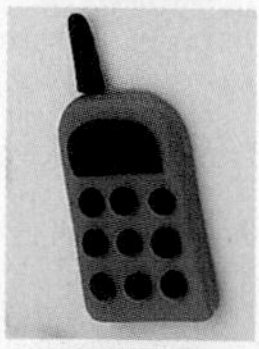

For cell phones, roll out reserved purple fondant ¼ in. thick; cut shape; attach small black ball buttons, dome-shaped screen and log antenna.

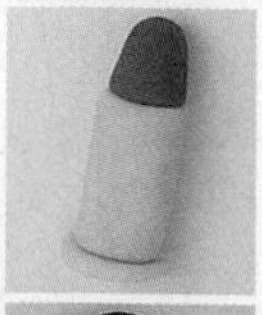

For tube lipstick, roll a ½ x 1 in. pastel pink log body and a ½ in. long neon pink lipstick, rounded at top. Flatten a ½ in. pastel pink ball and attach for base.

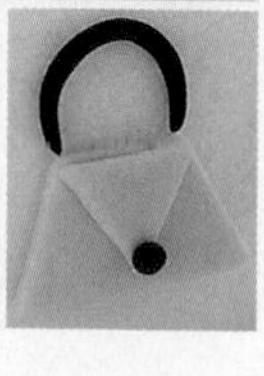

For purse, roll out reserved green fondant ¼ in. thick; cut purse body and flap shapes. Attach black ball button and a 2½ in. log strap.

Fondant Sundaes and Pinwheels

(see Visit the Shortcake Estate, p. 33)

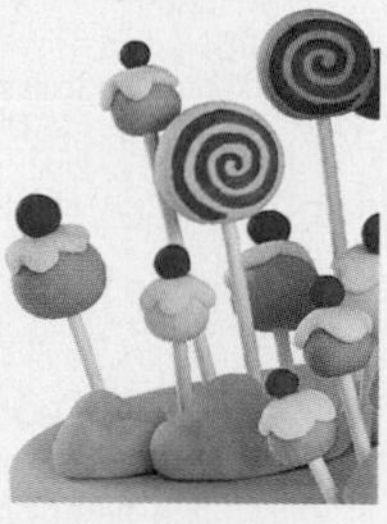

Tint white fondant: 38 oz. yellow (combine Lemon Yellow with a little Golden Yellow), 36 oz. rose (combine Rose with a little Lemon Yellow), 24 oz. green (combine Leaf Green with a little Lemon Yellow), 17 oz. violet (combine Violet with a little Rose), 4 oz. red (combine Red-Red and Christmas Red), 3 oz. Royal Blue; reserve 4 oz. white. Reserve remaining fondant for covering cakes and adding trims.

For sundaes, roll seven ⅝ in. diameter balls and six 1 in. diameter balls; insert lollipop sticks into bottoms. For whipped cream, roll out white fondant ⅛ in. thick and cut a ¾ in. uneven circle. For cherries, roll ¼ in. diameter red balls; attach cream and cherries with damp brush.

For candy pinwheels, roll out white fondant ½ in. thick; cut four 1¼ in. disks; insert lollipop sticks into bottom. Reserve leftover fondant and let sundaes and pinwheels dry overnight in craft block. When dry, draw designs on pinwheels with FoodWriter™ markers.

Fondant Rainbow, Stars, Sun, Hearts, Clouds

(see A Rainbow For Wishing, p. 26, 28)

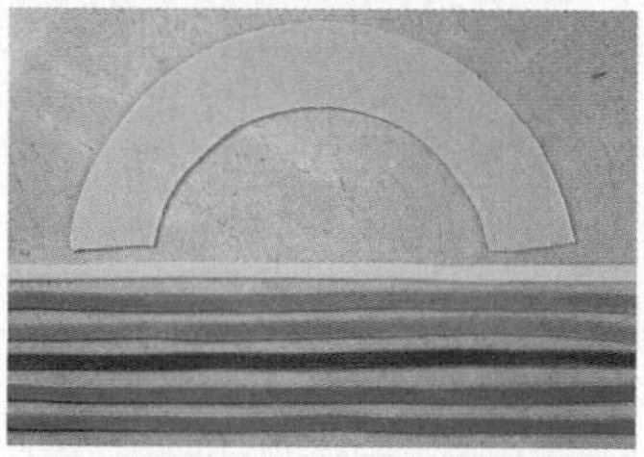

Divide, tint and prepare fondant as follows: Mix 6 oz. pastel blue fondant with ½ teaspoon Gum-Tex™. Tint 9 oz. white fondant yellow; tint 3 oz. each orange, blue, rose, violet and teal. Mix ¼ teaspoon Gum-Tex™ into each of the 3 oz. portions.

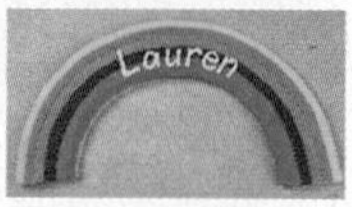

For rainbow, Roll out blue fondant ⅛ in. thick and cut rainbow background using pattern; let dry. Roll out colored fondant ⅛ in. thick and cut ⅜ in. wide x 18 in. long strips for rainbow sections. Attach to background using piping gel, trimming to fit along curve. Trim ends. Using royal icing, pipe tip 3 name.

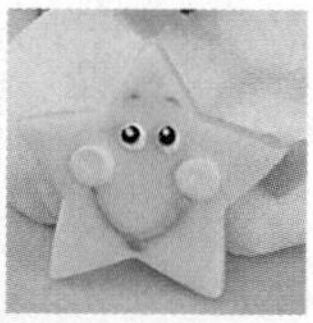

For stars, roll out yellow fondant ¼ in. thick; cut out 2 large, 3 medium, and 15 small stars using Cut-Outs. Using royal icing and patterns, pipe facial features on large and medium stars; pipe in tip 2 dot eyes with tip 1 dot highlights and string eyebrows. Pipe tip 1 string smiles, pipe-in mouths and dot cheeks. Flatten and smooth cheeks with finger dipped in cornstarch. Let dry.

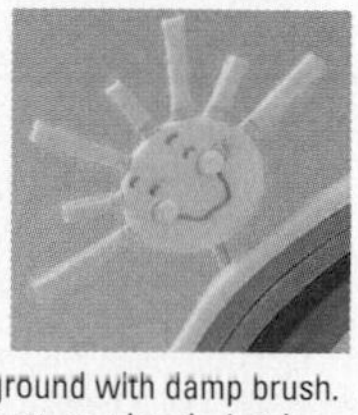

For sun, roll out blue and yellow fondant ⅛ in. thick; cut a sun shape from each using pattern. Trim ⅛ in. off rays of the yellow piece and attach yellow sections to blue background with damp brush. Using royal icing and pattern, pipe tip 1 string eyes, eyebrows and mouth, tip 2 dot cheeks and heart. Let dry.

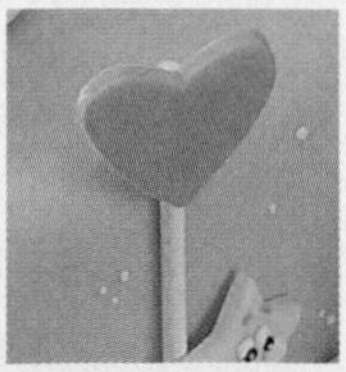

For hearts, roll out violet, green, orange and rose fondant ⅛ in. thick. Using Cut-Outs, cut 1 large violet, 1 each medium green and rose and 6 small orange and rose hearts. Let dry.

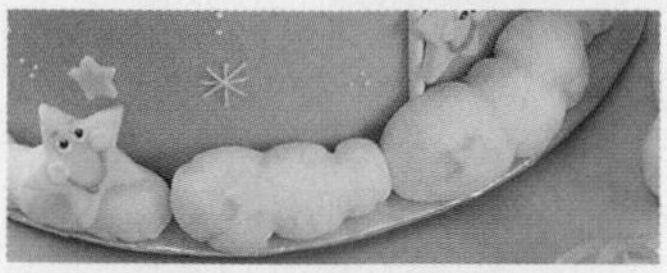

For bottom border clouds, roll white fondant balls ranging from ½ in. to 1½ in. diameter. Group 3 or 4 balls together, roll out additional fondant thin and cover groups of balls. Use the veining tool to sculpt fondant to shape of the balls. Dust outer edge of cake pan with cornstarch and position groups around pans to dry.

For candle base, roll out 1 in. diameter balls of white fondant. Position in a 3 in. diameter circle on waxed paper. Fill in any open areas with ½ in. diameter balls. Roll out fondant thin and cover, trim excess and tuck fondant under. Push candle into top. Let set, then transfer to same-size foil covered board.

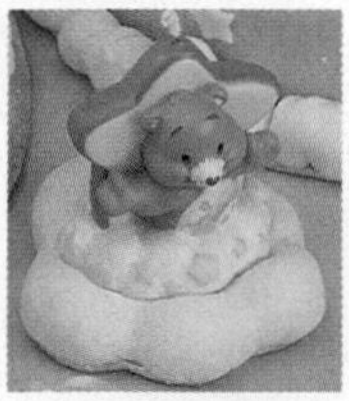

Dora Ponytail

(see Fairytale Dora, p. 29)

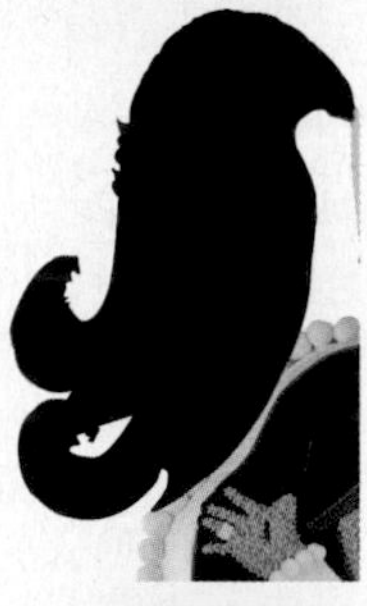

Combine 6 oz. white fondant with ½ teaspoon Gum-Tex. Roll out ⅛ in. thick; using pattern and sharp knife, cut ponytail. Let dry on cornstarch-dusted surface. When dry, pipe tip 17 pull-out hair in buttercream.

Candelabra

(see Every Body's Welcome, p. 42)

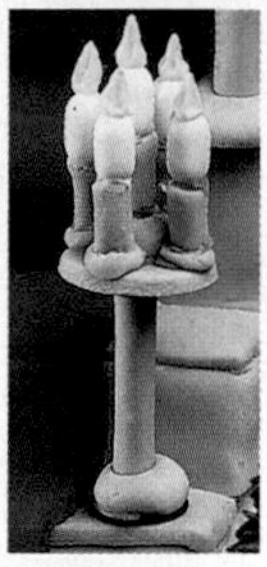

Roll out fondant ⅛ in. thick. Using any tip with a 1 in. diameter bottom, cut 10 candle platform circles; set aside. For candle holders, roll 35 logs, ⅜ in. long x ¼ in. diameter. For candle bases, roll 42 fondant balls, ¼ in. diameter. Attach balls to platform with melted candy tinted gray using black candy color; stack 2 balls for the center candle and position 1 each for 4 outer candles; let set. Attach holders to balls with melted candy; let set. For candles, attach candy-coated oval mints to tops of candle holders with melted candy and let dry overnight. For center pillar, cut 7 lollipop sticks to 3 in. and cover 1¼ in. at top with gray fondant; leave remainder uncovered. Attach stick to bottom of candle platform with melted candy. Let set on sides. In royal icing, pipe tip 15 pull-out star flames on mints.

Staircase and Carpet

(see Every Body's Welcome, p. 42)

To mark staircase: Mark center of 6 in. cake with toothpick. Make another mark 1 in. to the right and score a vertical line to bottom of base cake for right edge of staircase. Mark left edge of staircase with toothpick using these dimensions—top stair is 7½ in. wide, stairs 2 through 6 are 8 in. wide, stair 7 is 9 in. wide, bottom stair is 9½ in. wide. For top of 6 in. cake, cut a 3½ in. circle of gray fondant; attach with damp brush. Each cake will have

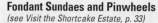

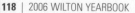

an upper and lower stair. For each upper stair, cut two 1 x ¼ in. deep strips x width of each stair. For each lower stair, cut a rectangle 1 in. high x ¾ in. deep x the width of each stair. For each lower stair you will also need 1 top tread strip (cut 1 in. high x ⅛ in. thick x the width of the rectangle piece) and 1 side wrap strip (cut 1 in. high x ⅛ in. thick and 1½ in. wider than rectangle piece). For upper stair of 6 in.

cake, position strip on cake top, blending with the top fondant circle, and attach with damp brush; attach 2nd strip against cake side. For lower stair on 6 in. cake, attach rectangle at base of cake, then attach side wrap strip to cover front and sides of rectangle with damp brush. Attach top tread strip with damp brush. Follow same procedure for all upper and lower stairs. To fill in gaps on the sides of some upper stairs, you may need to cut and attach a fondant square.

For red carpet, roll out fondant ⅛ in. thick and cut a 12 x 21 in. piece. Brush stairs and cake top with water and position fondant piece, pressing in to conform to stair shape; trim off 1 in. on each end of stairs. For 6 in. cake, roll out gray fondant ⅜ in. thick; cut a ½ in. wide strip for edge of carpet and attach with damp brush.

Umbrella Cake Top
(see Romance in the Rain, p. 70)

Prepare 1 recipe of gum paste. Add 2 oz. of neon yellow fondant to 6 oz. of prepared gum paste. Roll out ⅛ in. thick and cut an 8 in. circle; reserve remaining mixture. Generously dust the outside of one ball pan half with cornstarch and position circle on top. Trim to ¾ in. above bottom of pan. While still on pan, using Cake Dividing Set, divide circle in 12ths. Using large round Cut-Out, cut a scallop between each division, so that edge of Cut-Out just meets division marks, approximately ⅜ in. deep. Let dry on pan for several days.

For handle, cut a dowel rod to 11 in. long. Wrap top 7 in. of rod with reserved gum paste mixture. For curve of handle, roll a log ½ in. thick x 3½ in. long, then flatten to ¼ in. thick x ⅝ in. wide. Shape into a "J" and let dry 48 hours on waxed paper-covered board. Attach curved piece to

side of covered dowel rod with royal icing; let dry. Using 16 in. of ribbon, tie a bow on top of handle. To decorate umbrella, cut ⅛ in. wide x 3 in. long strips of gum paste mixture. Attach from top of umbrella to division points with damp brush. Attach drop flowers at top and division points with royal icing.

Fondant Candles
(see Ready For a Blowout Party!, p. 96)

In advance: Tint 3 oz. portions of fondant in light and dark shades of Rose, Leaf Green, Royal Blue, Orange, Violet mixed with a little Rose and Lemon Yellow mixed with a little Golden Yellow. Tint 6 oz. additional in dark yellow. Roll light shades into 2½ x ⅜ in. diameter log candles; let set overnight. Roll out dark yellow fondant ⅛ in. thick and cut 20 stars using medium Star Cut-Out™ and 20 flames using small Leaf Cut-Out. Moisten end of a 1 in. piece of shoestring licorice and insert for wick. Let dry overnight. Brush stars with water and sprinkle with Yellow Colored Sugar. Draw faces on flames with Black FoodWriter™. Roll out dark shaded fondant ⅛ in. thick and cut 4 x ⅛ in. strips. Wind around candles, attaching with damp brush. Trim away excess at bottom. Using a thin wooden skewer, indent a hole at top of candle; insert flames and stars.

Fondant or Gum Paste Flowers and Leaves On Wires
(see Flowers for La Quinceañera, p. 20, Wildflower Bouquet, p. 71 or Curtains in Cascade, p. 80, 82)

These general instructions will work for flowers and leaves on all 3 cakes. See cake instructions for colors needed; for Wildflower Bouquet, use remaining violet fondant from bow for flowers.

Roll out gum paste ¹⁄₁₆ in. thick or fondant ⅛ in. thick. Cut out flowers using pansy cutter from Floral Collection Flower Making Set for the La Quinceañera cake, pansy and apple blossom cutters for the Curtains in Cascade cake, and the medium Flower Cut-Out™ for the Wildflower Bouquet cake. Soften edges on thin foam using medium ball tool from Confectionery Tool Set; cup center of pansy flowers on thick Shaping Foam (p. 131) using ball tool.

For double flowers, attach apple blossoms inside pansies with gum paste adhesive (p. 111). Let dry in Candy Melting Plate that has been dusted with cornstarch. Roll small balls of white gum paste or fondant and attach for center of flowers using gum paste adhesive or thinned fondant adhesive.

Prepare calyxes on stems using 24 gauge florist wires for gum paste flowers or 22 gauge wires for fondant flowers. For each calyx, roll a ⅜ in. ball, bend end of wire to form a tiny hook, dip into adhesive and insert hook end into ball and shape into teardrop. Attach flower to calyx with a little adhesive. Insert wires into a craft block to dry. Prepare leaves on stems using 26-gauge wire for gum paste leaves and 22-gauge wire for fondant leaves. Roll out gum paste ¹⁄₁₆ in. thick and fondant ⅛ in. thick. For La Quinceañera and Curtains In Cascade leaves, use large rose leaf cutter from Floral Collection Set. Place on thin foam and imprint using veining tool from Confectionery Set. Dip end of wire into gum paste adhesive; attach to back of leaf and pinch leaf onto wire. Let dry on back of small flower former dusted with cornstarch.

For Wildflower Bouquet leaves use small Leaf Cut-Out to cut leaves; attach to wires by brushing back of leaf with water and pinching around wire. Let dry in craft block. Paint these leaves using Brush-on Color and round tip blue; let dry.

Plumeria Flowers
(see Plumeria Promise, p. 89)
Tint gum paste rose and roll out ¹⁄₁₆ in. thick. For each flower, cut 5 petals using large leaf

Cut-Out. Soften edges of wide end of petals on thin foam using medium ball tool. Curl 1 edge of each petal by rolling around a toothpick. Brush pointed ends with gum paste adhesive and lay in a fan position. Roll together to shape flower. Cut hidden pillars into 1½ in. lengths. Shape 3 in. squares of aluminum foil in largest lily nail; remove foil and make an opening in bottom of foil cup. Position flower in foil cup and set in pillar length to dry. To make 20 calyxes, shape ½ in. balls of gum paste into teardrop shapes. Indent wide end with dogbone tool and add hooked wire. Attach to base of each flower with adhesive. Let dry with flower turned upside down on petals. When dry, dust flowers with non toxic chalk which has been grated in tea strainer.

Fondant Ribbon Roses

1. Roll out fondant ⅛ in. thick on Roll & Cut Mat lightly dusted with cornstarch. Cut a strip following dimensions stated in project instructions.

2. Begin rolling lightly from one end, gradually loosening roll as flower gets larger. Fold cut edge under. For ruffled ribbon roses, roll the strip more loosely from beginning to end.

3. Trim flower to desired height with scissors.

Fondant Bows
Nothing says "celebrate" like a cake topped with a lush fondant bow. While the bow looks intricate, it's really just a grouping of fondant strips, folded, wrapped and arranged to create a full effect. When you cut strips with the Fondant Ribbon Cutter/Embosser, you can create bows with richly-textured embossed designs.

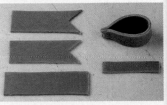

1. Cut strips for bow loops and streamers, using dimensions listed in project instructions. Your bow may use more loops than shown here or it may omit the bow center. Cut ends of streamers in a v-shape; set streamers aside on a cornstarch-dusted surface, which has been covered with waxed paper. Fold strips over to form loops. Brush ends lightly with damp brush. Align ends and pinch slightly to secure. Stuff loops with crushed facial tissue. Let dry.

2. Cut strip for bow center, if needed, following dimensions in project instructions. Wrap strip around the ends of 2 loops, to create a knot look, attaching with damp brush. Or form strip into a loop, attaching ends with a damp brush; let dry, then attach bow loops to bow center with thinned fondant adhesive or melted candy.

3. Attach streamers under loops with damp brush.

Fondant Ovals and Strips
(see Petal Allure, p. 83)
Roll out ivory fondant ⅛ in. thick. Using patterns, cut 8 ovals in each size. Position small ovals on petal sections of 9 in. cake, centering from top edge. Repeat using medium ovals for 12 in. and large for 15 in. cake. Roll out white fondant ⅛ in. thick; using Cutter/

Embosser, cut four 3½ x ¼ in. strips for each 9 in. petal section. Position 1 strip at each petal division; position 3 strips spaced evenly to complete each petal. Repeat, using 6 strips total for each section on 12 in. cake and 8 strips total for 15 in. cake. Trim strips evenly at bottom edge of cake.

COLOR FLOW

Working With Color Flow

1. Trace your design pattern onto parchment paper, then tape paper onto a cake circle or the back of a cookie pan. Cover with waxed paper; smooth and tape. Using tip 2 and parchment bag half-filled with full strength Color Flow, squeeze, pull and drop icing string following pattern outline. Stop, touch tip to surface and pull away. If you will be using the same color to fill in, let outline dry a few minutes until it "crusts." To prevent bleeding of colors, let outline dry 1-2 hours before filling in.

2. Thin Color Flow mixture with water. Cut opening in parchment bag to the size of tip 2. Fill in design with thinned Color Flow.

3. Let decorations air dry thoroughly, at least 48 hours. To remove, cut away waxed paper from board, then turn over and peel waxed paper off the Color Flow piece.

Hint: For curved decorations, dry pieces on flower formers.

To easily remove dried Color Flow, pull waxed paper backing over the edge of a table with one hand, while holding decoration with other hand. Waxed paper will pull off naturally. Or, with dried Color Flow resting on cookie sheet, place cardboard sheet over Color Flow, lift and turn over so that top of decoration rests on cardboard. Lift off waxed paper.

Since any moist icing will break down Color Flow, either position Color Flow decorations on cake shortly before serving or place a piece of plastic wrap cut to fit on area first and position Color Flow on sugar cubes.

Color Flow Scrolled Panel Assembly
(see Life's Inspiration, p. 21)

1. Mark hexagon board with a FoodWriter™ marker: Mark a 10 in. circle at center of board. Mark a 1½ in. vertical line from point of each hexagon; mark ¼ in. from cake at center of each hexagon edge. With ruler, mark a horizontal line starting from ¼ in. mark at each hexagon edge, connecting vertical lines.

2. To attach scrolled panels ¼ in. from 10 in. cakes, pipe a line of full-strength color flow along one horizontal line marking. Attach panel on icing line. Edge panel side with icing and pipe a line on next horizontal line on hexagon board; attach 2nd panel, making sure panels line up. Repeat to attach all panels.

Color Flow Windows
(see Every Body's Welcome, p. 40)

Tint 1 cup royal icing gray (using small amount of black icing color). Make 2 recipes of Color Flow; tint ¾ cup each in royal blue, violet and black, ¼ cup Lemon Yellow/Golden Yellow combination; reserve ½ cup white. Tape copies of patterns to cookie sheets and cover with waxed paper. Outline outer frames in gray royal icing with tip 3; let dry. Flow in windows using thinned Color Flow Icing in cut parchment bags. Flow in yellow moon on Pattern 2. On all windows, flow in blue sky, then white clouds and black ground areas. Quickly flow in violet background. Immediately flow in tree branches using pattern and thinned black Color Flow; pull out edges of branches with toothpick to create smaller branches.

COVERING CAKES AND COOKIES WITH CANDY MELTS®* AND POURED ICINGS

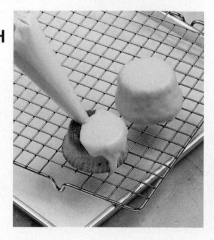

A quick and easy way to give a professional-looking finish to all your baked goods! For Candy Melts®*, melt following package directions. For icings, follow recipe directions to reach pouring consistency. Place cooled cakes or cookies on cooling rack positioned over cookie sheet or pan. Pour or pipe candy or icing on center of item, spreading to edges with a spatula so that candy or icing drips down and covers sides. Let dry.

Candy Making Techniques

USING CANDY MELTS®*

Fast-melting confectionery coating wafers are the key to easy candy making. Smooth texture and great taste make Candy Melts® your most convenient option for molding. Check out all the great colors on p. 218.*

To Melt

Double boiler method: Fill lower pan with water to below level of top pan. Bring water to simmer, then remove from heat. Put Candy Melts in top pan and set in position on lower pan. Stir constantly, without beating, until smooth and completely melted.

Microwave method: In microwave-safe container, microwave 1 package Candy Melts at half power or defrost setting for 1 minute. Stir thoroughly. Continue to microwave and stir at 30 second intervals until smooth and completely melted. Candy Melts may also be melted in a disposable decorating bag. Melt as described above, squeezing bag between heating intervals to blend Candy Melts together. When completely melted, snip off end of bag and squeeze melted Candy Melts into molds. Throw away bag when empty.

Note: Confectionery coating will lose its pouring and dipping consistency if overheated, or if water or other liquid is added. If coating is overheated, add 2 teaspoons hydrogenated vegetable shortening per 14 oz. Candy Melts.

To Mold (1 color candies)

Pour melted candy into clean dry mold; tap lightly to remove air bubbles. Place mold on level surface. Refrigerate until bottom of mold appears frosty or until candy is firm. Pop out candy. For lollipops, fill molds, tap to remove air bubbles, position sticks in mold. Rotate sticks to thoroughly cover with candy so they remain securely in place. Refrigerate to set, pop out lollipops.

To Color

Add Candy Colors (p. 219) to melted Candy Melts®* a little at a time. Mix thoroughly before adding more color. Colors tend to deepen as they're mixed. Pastel colored candies are most appetizing, so keep this in mind.

To Flavor

The creamy, rich taste of Candy Melts®* can be enhanced by adding approx. ¼ teaspoon oil-based Candy Flavor (p. 219) to 14 oz. (one pack) of melted Candy Melts®*. Never use alcohol based flavorings; they will cause candies to harden.

Multicolored Candy
Painting Method

It's easy to mold with different areas of color —just use a decorator brush to "paint" the mold with melted Candy Melts®*. Refrigerate a few seconds until coating hardens, then fill mold to top with melted candy. Remember, only fill in one section of the mold at a time and let harden before adding more colors. Look for other ways to color and flavor your candy in our *Candy Making Beginner's Guide* (p. 124).

Marbleizing Method

1. Separately melt two different colors of Candy Melts®*.
2. Stir colors together, using a lollipop stick to draw lines in mixture. Do not overmix.
3. Quickly spoon or place into molds while mixture is still soft. Tap. Refrigerate until firm; unmold.

Layering Method

Pour melted Candy Melts®* into dry molds to desired height. Refrigerate until partially set. Pour melted contrasting color to desired height. Refrigerate until partially set. Repeat until desired number of layers are formed; refrigerate until firm and unmold.

SPECIALTY TECHNIQUES

Candy Shells

Fill pan or mold to the top edge with melted candy. Tap on counter to remove air bubbles. Let chill in refrigerator for 10-15 minutes or until a ¼ in. shell has formed. Pour out excess candy, smooth top edges with spatula and chill for 15-20 minutes longer. Carefully unmold shells (if you have difficulty removing shells, place in freezer for 2-3 minutes, then unmold). Excess candy can be reheated and reused.

Candy Shells in Baking Cups

1. Add 1 to 2 Tablespoons of melted candy in the bottom of a standard baking cup.
2. Brush candy slightly up sides, about halfway to top, forming an even edge.
3. Refrigerate 5 to 8 minutes. Repeat process if desired, for a thicker shell. Refrigerate until firm. Carefully peel baking cup off candy shell.

Candy Faces
(see Jungle Gems, p. 92, Happy Unwrapping, p. 93 and Clowning 'Round, p. 93)

Make all the faces in the Candy Melting Plate (p. 219); fill cavities with melted Candy Melts®* using a cut decorating bag. Use white Candy Melts®* for zebra, yellow for lion, orange for tiger. For elephant, tint white candy gray using Black from Garden Candy Colors Set. For clowns and kids, tint white candy skin tone using Orange from Primary Candy Color Set or use Light Cocoa Candy Melts®* for ethnic skin tone. Refrigerate until firm and unmold.

Place faces on waxed paper-covered board and decorate facial features using melted candy in cut bag. In addition to colors already used, you will need pink (tint white candy with Pink from Garden Tone Candy Color Set (p. 133).

Elephant

Pipe gray ears, black eyes and mouth; let set. Pull out gray trunk and pipe pink inner ears; let set.

Tiger
Pipe orange dot ears; let set. Pipe pink inner ears and nose; let set. Add black stripes, mouth, eyes and stubble; let set.

Lion
Pipe Light Cocoa mane around head; let set. Pipe yellow dot ears, let set. Pipe pink inner ears and nose; let set. Add black eyes, eyebrows, mouth and stubble; let set.

Zebra
Pipe white dot ears; let set. Pipe pink inner ears; let set. Add black stripes, eyes, nostrils and hair; let set.

Clowns
Pipe black eyes and mouth, pink cheeks and red nose; let set. Add hair in green, red, yellow, blue or orange; let set. Attach fondant hat with melted candy. Add tip 14 pull-out star fringe in royal icing.

Kids
Pipe black eyes and mouth, skin tone or Light Cocoa nose; let set. Add black, yellow or Light Cocoa hair; let set. Attach fondant hat with melted candy. Add tip 14 pull-out star fringe in royal icing.

*Brand confectionery coating.

Candy Plaque Graduate
(see Beginning a New Chapter, p. 77)

1. Tint 1 pk. White Candy Melts®* with blue Candy Color; also tint 6 oz. White Candy Melts®* with 1 to 2 tablespoons of melted Light Cocoa Candy Melts®* to create skin tone, tint 2 oz. yellow with Candy Color, tint 7 oz. of Cocoa Candy Melts®* black with Candy Color. Reserve remaining White and Cocoa Candy Melts®* . Make candy plaque in graduate pan, molding areas in this order: yellow tassel, white diploma, black hair, face and hands, blue cap and gown. Refrigerate to firm each area before starting the next. Cut cardboard to fit inside pan, place over plaque after it is firm.
2. Unmold plaque. Using melted candy in cut parchment bag, pipe white eyes, black pupils and mouth and skin tone nose. Add black message. Let set.
3. Make 2 easels. Using heavy-duty foil, make a dam in the bottom of Long Loaf Pan, to create a 10 in. area for molding. Pour 1 pk. of melted White Candy Melts®* in area; refrigerate until firm, unmold. Let plaque come to room temperature before cutting. Trace easel pattern with toothpick; cut easel with sharp knife. Make base for bottom of plaque. Make a dam in Long Loaf Pan to create a 7½ in. molding area; fill with 1 pk. of melted White Candy Melts®*; refrigerate until firm, unmold. Attach plaque and easels to base with melted candy.

Mickey Candy Plaque Head
(See Birthday Hugs From Mickey, p. 36)

1. Tint melted White Candy Melts®* with a little orange Candy Color to achieve flesh tone used. Fill face portion of pan first, being careful not to fill above round area at top of face; next fill ear portions 1¼ in. thick. Refrigerate until firm.
2. To unmold, cut cardboard to fit inside pan. Before removing from pan, with melted candy, attach lollipop sticks diagonally to support each ear. Let set. Place cardboard in pan and turn over to unmold.
3. Turn plaque right side up. Using royal icing and tip 3, outline and pipe in eyes, nose, mouth and tongue (smooth with finger dipped in cornstarch). Cover ears and head with tip 16 stars.

Strawberry Shortcake Candies
(see Visit the Shortcake Estate, p. 33)

Tint portions of melted white candy pink, green (add a little yellow), orange, brown (mix red and green) light blue (add a little blue); also melt red, white, blue candy from kit. Mold candies on sticks using painting method; refrigerate until firm.

Goblet Stem
(see True Love Truffles, p. 60)

Place a dollop of melted candy on waxed paper covered cake board. Cut (trim) Hidden Pillar to 3½ in. and position upright in candy; refrigerate until firm. Using melted candy in cut parchment bag, fill pillar; tap gently to remove air bubbles. Place in freezer until completely chilled. To remove stem, gently push through pillar with handle of mixing spoon. Level top center of base and bottom center of bowl by sliding over a warm cookie sheet. Attach stem to level area of base with melted candy; let set. Turn bowl open side down and attach stem to level area with melted candy; let set. Using melted candy in parchment bag cut to size of tip 2, pipe beads on edge of bowl and where stem meets base and bowl; let set.

Candy Gift Boxes
(see Given with ribbon, p. 99)

For base of box, using White Candy Melts, mold a candy shell (see instructions this page) ⅛ in. deep in cavity of Non-Stick Standard Muffin Pan. Do not use baking cups. Freeze until firm and unmold.

For lid, place 3 in. Metal Circle Cutter on Non-Stick Cookie Pan or Sheet. Fill ⅛ in. deep with melted white candy; refrigerate until firm and unmold.

Modeling a Candy Clay Rose

Start with the base and mold a cone approx. 1½ in. high from a ¾ in. diameter ball of candy clay. Next, flatten a ⅜ in. ball of candy clay into a circular petal about ¼ in. thick on one side and about the diameter of a dime. Make 4 petals this size. Wrap 1 petal around the point of the cone to form a bud. Now press 3 more petals around the base of the bud. Gently pinch edges of petals. Make 5 more petals using slightly larger balls of candy clay. Flatten, then thin edge with finger and cup petals. Press and attach petals under first row of petals. Continue adding petals, placing them in between and slightly lower than previous row. For a fuller flower, continue adding petals in this manner.

Candy Clay Fence
(see Playing Reindeer Games, p. 51)

Roll out candy clay and cut ½ in. wide strips: four 16 in. long for top and bottom borders in front and back, four 4 in. long for top and bottom borders on sides, 3 in. long for vertical posts and 5 in. long for diagonal posts. With melted candy, attach top and bottom border strips, vertical posts 4 in. apart and diagonal posts to connect vertical posts. Roll a ¼ in. ball of candy clay and attach with melted candy at top and bottom of vertical posts.

CANDY RECIPES

Basic Ganache and Truffles
14 oz. Candy Melts®* (p. 218)
½ cup heavy whipping cream

Chop Candy Melts®* (you can use a food processor). Heat whipping cream in saucepan just to boiling point. Do not boil. Remove from heat and add chopped Candy Melts, stir until smooth and glossy.

Ganache Glaze: If mixture is too thick, add 1 to 2 tablespoons whipping cream. Position cake on wire rack over drip pan. Pour glaze onto center and work out toward edges.

NOTE: Cake may be iced first in buttercream. Let icing set, then pour on ganache glaze. If cake has a perfect surface, no other icing is needed.

Whipped Ganache: Follow recipe above, using 1 cup whipping cream. Allow mixture to set and cool to room temperature (mixture will have the consistency of pudding, this may take 1-2 hours). Whip on high speed with an electric mixer until light and soft peaks form.

Truffles: Add 1 tablespoon liqueur for flavor, if desired. Stir until smooth and creamy. Refrigerate until firm. Roll into 1 in. diameter balls. Can be used as center for dipped candies, served plain or rolled in nuts, coconut or cocoa powder. Store truffles in refrigerator up to 3 weeks. Makes about 2 dozen (1 in.) balls.

Ready-In-Minutes Cocoa Fudge
20 oz. (approximately 4½ cups)
    Dark Cocoa Candy Melts®* (p. 218)
1 can (14 oz.) condensed milk
    (not evaporated)

Melt Candy Melts® in microwave-safe container using microwave on low power. Add milk; stir until blended. Microwave an additional 2 to 3 minutes on medium power; stir until fudge develops a sheen. Pour mixture into buttered 7 x 11 in. non-stick Biscuit/Brownie pan and refrigerate until firm.

Candy "Clay"
14 oz. package of Candy Melts®† (p. 218)
⅓ cup light corn syrup

Melt Candy Melts® following package directions. Add corn syrup and stir to blend. Turn out mixture onto waxed paper and let set at room temperature to dry. Wrap well and store at room temperature until needed. candy clay handles best if hardened overnight.

To Use
Candy clay will be very hard at the start; knead a small portion at a time until workable. If candy clay gets too soft, set aside at room temperature or refrigerate briefly. When rolling out candy clay, sprinkle work surface with cornstarch or cocoa (for cocoa clay) to prevent sticking; roll to approximately ⅛ in. thick.

To Tint
White candy clay may be tinted using Candy Color or Icing Color. Knead in color until well blended.

To Store
Prepared candy clay will last for several weeks at room temperature in an airtight container.

Peanut Butter Filling
(see First Bloom of Spring, p. 65)
1½ Tablespoons butter, softened
½ cup chunky style peanut butter, room temperature
¾ cup sifted confectioner's sugar

Cream butter with peanut butter. Stir in confectioner's sugar, blending well. Add more confectioner's sugar as necessary to make thick enough to form into a ball. Use filling as a candy center for dipping, or as a center between 2 layers of coating. Makes approximately 30 candy centers.

Learn From The Leaders In Cake Decorating!

Celebrating 78 Years

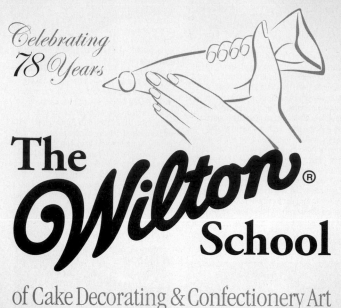

The **Wilton®** School
of Cake Decorating & Confectionery Art

For almost 80 years, The Wilton School has been home to the leading authorities in cake decorating. Today, our curriculum is more extensive than ever, featuring world-class decorating specialists who give students individual guidance in their field of expertise. Whether you are a professional seeking to grow your business or a hobbyist looking to gain new skills for entertaining at home, The Wilton School is the ideal place to enjoy an unforgettable learning experience.

SIGN UP NOW FOR THESE POPULAR COURSES

The Master Course
The world's most comprehensive cake decorating course! In this exciting 2-week class, students learn the skills needed to become a professional cake decorator. Learn 20 borders and 15 flowers, including The Wilton Rose. Decorate with color flow, piping gel and figure piping. Create a floral birthday cake, then design, assemble and decorate a 3-tiered wedding cake with skills learned. Virtually all materials included.

SUPPLEMENTARY CLASSES *Available during the Master Course.*
Confectionery Creations
Master candy making and decorating to expand your business or create incredible gifts using Candy Melts® brand confectionery coating (no tempering needed). Learn to make roses, leaves, ganache, boxes, baskets and more.

Introduction to Sugar Artistry
Start with basic recipes and equipment to become familiar with sugar art, then proceed to spun, pulled, molded and piped techniques. Students create flowers and leaves, a spun sugar cage, ribbons, bows and more that can be used on a cake or as accent decorative pieces.

Introduction to Rolled Fondant
Learn creative ways to work with fondant, including hand-cut and shaped flowers, ribbons and bows. Discover special icing effects on fondant—sponging, crimping and embossing.

EXPLORE OTHER GREAT CLASSES!
Cakes for Catering, Lambeth, Advanced Sugar Artistry, Chocolate Inspirations, Advanced Gum Paste and Fondant, Fondant Art.

1-day Workshops:
Art of Sweet Tables, Holiday Icing Flowers, Holiday Candy Making, Wedding Cake Assembly, Cupcakes by Design and more!

For class schedules, details and enrollment visit **www.school.wilton.com** or call 630.810.2211

Certificate of Approval to operate issued by the Illinois State Board of Education, 100 N. First Street, Springfield, IL 62777.

2006 PRODUCT SHOPS

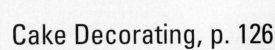

Instructional, p. 124

Cake Decorating, p. 126

Bakeware, p. 145

Wedding Style, p. 154

Wedding Cakes, p. 162

Baby, p. 170

Character, p. 174

Party, p. 184

Seasonal, p. 190

Cookie Making, p. 212

Candy Making, p. 218

Wilton for Kids™, p. 222

Invitation Kits, p. 224

FIND IT FAST… ORDER WITH EASE!

Welcome to the most complete selection of cake decorating products anywhere! Here you'll find all the great Wilton tools, ingredients, accents and more you need to create every design in this Yearbook.

Go ahead and browse! Our shops are conveniently organized to help you find what you need fast. Whether you're decorating a batch of holiday cookies or creating a 3-tiered wedding cake, it's easy to find everything on your list.

When you're ready to buy, we make it a breeze! Charge your order 4 easy ways at your convenience:

PHONE TOLL-FREE
800-794-5866
8:00 am-4:30 pm, Monday-Friday CST
(RETAIL CUSTOMERS ONLY)

FAX TOLL-FREE
888-824-9520
24 HOURS A DAY/7 DAYS A WEEK

ORDER ON-LINE
www.wilton.com
24 HOURS A DAY/7 DAYS A WEEK

MAIL YOUR ORDER
Use the convenient retail order form in this book.

Se Habla Español!
Para mas informacion,
marque 800-436-5778

Instructional

Find inspiration with Wilton how-to books and videos. There's something perfect for your next celebration, from kids' birthday cakes to multi-tiered wedding designs.

Specialty Publications

Cake Decorating Beginner's Guide

With this exciting book, anyone can decorate a fantastic-looking cake the very first time! Wilton, the #1 name in cake decorating, shows beginners everything they need to know, step-by-step. The *Beginner's Guide* makes decorating easy to learn and fun to do for everyone!
• How to bake and ice perfect cakes
• How to mix any color icing with ease
• 15 fantastic cake ideas to decorate in 6 steps or less
• Step-by-step decorating instructions for stars, rosettes, drop flowers and more
Soft cover, 40 pages.
902-R-1232 $3.99

Uses of Decorating Tips

Valuable quick reference and idea book for any decorator. Features five of the most popular decorating tip families and explains what each does. Shows the versatility of many tips by presenting varied cake designs. Soft cover, 48 pages.
902-R-1375 $9.99

Candy Making Beginner's Guide

You'll be amazed at the fantastic candies you can make using this book. The possibilities are endless, using the great selection of Wilton Candy Melts®* and Candy Molds. The *Beginner's Guide* shows you how, step-by-step, so you will make great-looking candies your very first time. It's a great new way to add fun to parties and create impressive gifts. The *Beginner's Guide* has the information you need to start making candy like a pro.
• 20 incredible candy ideas—all made in a few easy steps!
• Easy ways to melt perfectly every time
• Painting color details in candy
• How to make classic creme-filled and dipped candies
• Great candy gift and favor ideas
Soft cover, 40 pages.
902-R-1231 $3.99
*Brand confectionery coating.

2006 Yearbook of Cake Decorating   **NEW!**

The #1 annual decorating book helps you create great cakes and desserts throughout the year! It's the ultimate resource for professional bakers and anyone who wants to serve something special. Over 225 exciting decorating ideas—including cakes for every occasion, holiday candies and cookies, favorite character desserts and more. The Dazzling Displays special section features dozens of incredible ways to decorate and serve individual desserts for everyone at the party. Featuring step-by-step decorating instructions, technique resource guide, product section and website link to more cake designs. Soft cover, 224 pages.
English 1701-R-2038 $10.99
Spanish 1701-R-2040 $10.99

2006 Pattern Book   **NEW!**

Duplicate many of the beautiful cake designs featured in the 2006 Yearbook and on the Wilton website. Includes over 100 decorating outlines to transfer to your cake. Easy-to-follow instructions. Soft cover, 60 pages of patterns.
408-R-2006 $7.99

The Wilton School—Decorating Cakes

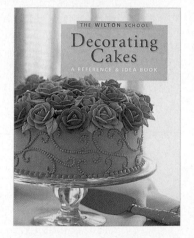

This exciting book presents what Wilton has learned in 75 years of teaching cake decorating, in an easy-to-follow format that reflects today's lifestyles. *Decorating Cakes* is designed to appeal to anyone who wants to make great-looking cakes for families and friends.
• 30 exciting cakes with complete instructions and product listings
• 103 technique instructions, shown step-by-step, including borders, flowers, fondant and more
• Helpful recipes, tip chart, serving and cutting charts, glossary of terms
• In-depth sections on baking cakes, preparing icing, using decorating tips, cutting and transporting cakes
• Product guide, which shows and explains the equipment and ingredients required for decorating
Soft cover, 116 pages.
902-R-904 $14.99

Instructional Videos   **NOW ON DVD!**

How to Make Wedding Cakes

Invaluable lessons on how to design and assemble tiered cakes for weddings, showers, anniversaries and other special occasions. Hints for transporting and serving also included in this 60-minute video. DVD material matches VHS.
DVD 901-R-256 $19.99
VHS 901-R-128 $19.99

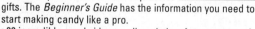

Cake Decorating— Easy as 1-2-3!

Learn how to level and ice a cake perfectly, make simple borders, flowers, leaves and more. 60 minutes. DVD material matches VHS.
DVD 901-R-257 $19.99
VHS 901-R-115 $19.99

How to Make Icing Flowers

Learn how to make roses, Easter lilies, violets, pansies, daisies, poinsettias and more! Five cake designs incorporate all the flowers included in this 60-minute video. DVD material matches VHS.
DVD 901-R-258 $19.99
VHS 901-R-119 $19.99

ORDER TOLL FREE: 800-794-5866

Celebrate! with Fondant

It's the first book to feature fondant done the Wilton way—using our exciting cake designs, step-by-step instructions and convenient fondant products. Celebrate! with Fondant makes fondant cakes easy and fun for everyone. See how to make more than 40 terrific cakes, along with alternate ways to decorate every design and suggestions for the perfect occasions to serve them. Soft cover, 120 pages.
902-R-911 $14.99

NEW!

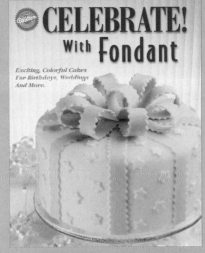

Wedding Publications

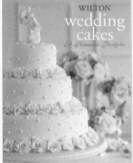

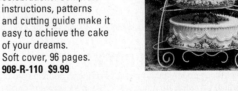

Wilton Wedding Cakes— A Romantic Portfolio

Our exciting new collection of tiered cakes makes the romantic wedding of every bride's dreams a reality. *A Romantic Portfolio* sets the bride's imagination free, with 38 exquisite cakes that express love in many ways. It's all here—beautiful seasonal designs, elegant shapes, classic and contemporary looks. There is a cake for every taste—along with coordinating ornament, favor suggestions and tiered cake accessories.

A Romantic Portfolio will inspire decorators as well as brides. Every design includes step-by-step decorating instructions, product checklists and serving amounts. Used with our comprehensive construction guide, patterns, techniques and recipes, *A Romantic Portfolio* has everything decorators need to recreate each cake to perfection. Soft cover, 144 pages.
902-R-907 $16.99

A Romantic Portfolio and *Wedding Dream Cakes* also include a special pull-out supplement, *My Wedding Planner*. This invaluable booklet is filled with ideas and worksheets to help you organize the perfect wedding in every detail.

Wilton Wedding Dream Cakes

A truly distinctive collection for today's bride, reflecting a new freedom in wedding cake design. More than 45 designs with complete instructions, from elegant classic tiers to colorful cakes with contemporary flair. A special pull-out supplement features ideas from budgeting to floral options.
Soft cover, 128 pages.
908-R-101 $14.99

Wilton Bridal Cakes

A showcase for many favorite wedding cake styles—Victorian, country garden and contemporary. Includes 27 designs, ideal for large or intimate celebrations. Complete instructions, patterns and cutting guide make it easy to achieve the cake of your dreams.
Soft cover, 96 pages.
908-R-110 $9.99

Wilton Party Favors

This exclusive collection is filled with dozens of designs to suit every taste and budget. You'll find a great favor in this book to enhance any wedding, holiday or themed party. Organized to suit the season of the celebration (with an extra section for anniversaries), *Wilton Party Favors* includes all you need to know about making these favors with ease. Step-by-step instructions help you complete a party's worth of favors in just a few hours. A convenient section on favor-making tools and techniques. Plus information on buying the great Wilton products used to make each design. Soft cover, 48 pages.
908-R-119 $14.99

Cake Decorating

Create your greatest cakes with the essentials decorators count on. Time-saving tools.
Precise tips. Quality icings. Plus, the most exciting new products for fondant decorating!

fondant fun!™

Wilton presents the easy system for fondant decorating! Colorful, Ready-To-Use Rolled Fondant. Cut-Outs™ and Cake Stamps™ that create fun shapes. Brush-On Color™ and Icing Writer™ to add vivid designs. Easy-to-use tools that help you roll, cut and color to achieve exciting new decorations!

READY-TO-USE ROLLED FONDANT

Fondant has never been more convenient and fun for decorating! With Wilton Ready-To-Use Rolled Fondant, the color is already mixed in for no kneading, no mess, no guesswork. The 24 oz. (1½ lbs.) package, available in white and pastel colors, covers an 8 in. 2-layer cake plus decorations; the 80 oz. package (5 lbs.), available in white only, covers a 2-layer 6 in., 8 in. and 10 in. round tiered cake plus decorations. Certified Kosher.

1. Roll out.

2. Layer over cake.

3. Trim and decorate.

White
24 oz. (1½ lbs.) Pk.
710-R-2076 $5.99

White
80 oz. (5 lbs.) Pk.
710-R-2180 $19.99

Pastel Pink
24 oz. (1½ lbs.) Pk. 710-R-2181 $7.99

Pastel Blue
24 oz. (1½ lbs.) Pk. 710-R-2182 $7.99

Pastel Yellow
24 oz. (1½ lbs.) Pk. 710-R-2183 $7.99

Pastel Green
24 oz. (1½ lbs.) Pk. 710-R-2184 $7.99

FONDANT MULTI PACKS

Convenient four-pouch assortments of primary, neon, pastel or natural colors are perfect for making multi-colored decorations. The color is already mixed in. . . no kneading, no mess, no guesswork. Great for flowers, borders and fun shapes. The 17.6 oz. package contains four 4.4 oz. packs. Certified Kosher. **$8.99**

Primary Colors
Green, Red, Yellow, Blue
710-R-445

Neon Colors
Purple, Orange, Yellow, Pink
710-R-446

Pastel Colors
Blue, Yellow, Pink, Green
710-R-447

Natural Colors
Light Brown, Dark Brown, Pink, Black
710-R-448

ORDER TOLL FREE: 800-794-5866

Celebrate!® with Fondant

It's the first book to feature fondant done the Wilton way—using our exciting cake designs, step-by-step instructions and convenient fondant products. Celebrate! with Fondant makes fondant cakes easy and fun for everyone. See how to make more than 40 terrific cakes, along with alternate ways to decorate every design and suggestions for the perfect occasions to serve them. Soft cover, 120 pages.
902-R-911 $14.99

NEW!

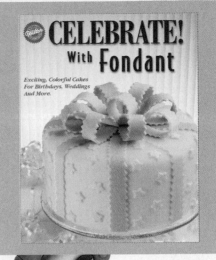

CELEBRATE! With Fondant

Exciting, Colorful Cakes For Birthdays, Weddings And More.

FONDANT RIBBON CUTTER/EMBOSSER SET

NEW!

This easy-to-use tool is the perfect way to add beautiful textured fondant ribbons, stripes and bows to your cake. Just choose the cutting and embossing wheel designs you want, slide the washer, core, wheels and spacers on the roller handle, and roll on top of your fondant. We suggest brushing the assembled roller with shortening for easy release. The perfectly cut ribbon strips are ready to place right on your cake! Produces ribbon widths from ¼ in. to 3¾ in. when combining spacers.

Complete set includes:
• 9 cutting wheels—3 straight, 3 wavy, 3 zigzag
• 8 embossing wheels—4 striped, 4 beaded
• 9 spacers—one ⅓ in., two each ¼, ½, ¾ and 1 in. wide
• Roller handle with detachable core
• Assembly hardware
1907-R-1203 Set/26 $14.99

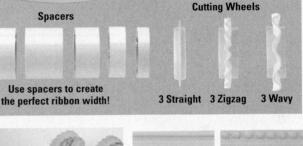

Embossing Wheels

Spacers

Cutting Wheels

4 Beaded 4 Striped

Use spacers to create the perfect ribbon width!

3 Straight 3 Zigzag 3 Wavy

Just Load and Roll!

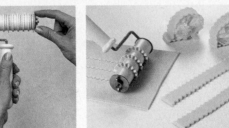

1. Arrange wheels on work surface to create the look you want.

2. Slide wheels and spacers on the roller.

3. Position washer and wing nut on end of roller to secure the wheels.

4. Use a Rolling pin to roll out fondant on your Roll & Cut Mat. Roll the roller over fondant in any direction.

Emboss striped and beaded textures! Cut zigzag, wavy and straight edges!

FONDANT DECORATIVE PUNCH SET

NEW!

Add exciting 3-dimensional decorations in fondant with this easy-to-use tool. In seconds, you can punch out fondant accents with elegant openwork shapes like diamonds and flowers. As you punch, the disk imprints a detailed design that adds a pretty touch of texture to any cake. The comfortable angled handle holds your choice of 8 design disks. Also great for adding fondant detail to cupcakes and cookies. Disks turn to lock into place.
1907-R-1204 Set/9 $8.99

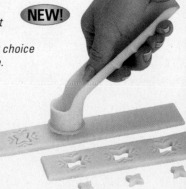

Large Tulip with Leaves **Dutch Blossom** **Paisley with Dots** **Wide Diamond with Scrolls** **Small Tulip with Leaves** **Snapdragon with Leaves** **4-Leaf Clover with Dots** **Narrow Diamond with Scrolls**

fondant fun!™

CUT-OUTS™

With Cut-Outs, it's easy to make fun 3-D shapes for your fondant cakes and cupcakes. Just roll out fondant, press down with Cut-Out and lift away. Remove shapes with a small spatula.

Stainless steel shapes range from ⅝ in. to 2½ in.

- Fast, fun way to brighten any fondant cake!
- Great assortments of shapes for any occasion.
- Perfect for highlighting with Brush-On Color™ or Icing Writer™.

Look what you can do!

1. Layered decorations! Stack cut-out fondant pieces in different sizes and colors.

2. Fondant fill-ins! Use a smaller cut-out to remove the center of your fondant decoration. Fill in with a different color!

3. Cake insets! Cut out shapes from your fondant-covered cake, then replace the pieces with your favorite colors.

NEW!

Oval
417-R-438
Set/3 $2.49

NEW!

Crinkle Shapes
Circle, Square, Triangle, Heart
417-R-444
Set/4 $2.99

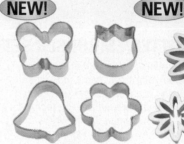

NEW!

Fancy Shapes
Flower, Leaf, Oval, Heart
417-R-445
Set/4 $2.99

NEW!

Garden Shapes
Butterfly, Tulip, Bell, Flower
417-R-443
Set/4 $2.99

NEW!

Daisy
Durable plastic.
417-R-439
Set/3 $2.49

People
417-R-441
Set/6 $3.99

Square
417-R-431
Set/3 $2.49

Round
417-R-432
Set/3 $2.49

Heart
417-R-434
Set/3 $2.49

Star
417-R-433
Set/3 $2.49

Flower
417-R-435
Set/3 $2.49

Funny Flower
417-R-436
Set/3 $2.49

Leaf
417-R-437
Set/3 $2.49

Alphabet/Number
417-R-442 Set/37 $14.99

ORDER TOLL FREE: 800-794-5866

Exquisite Invitations
...you can print at home
Wilton presents beautiful stationery kits for any occasion!

25th

*Loving, caring,
sharing...celebrating!*

*Please join us on our
25th Anniversary
Saturday, November 12, 2012
at 5:00 o'clock in the evening
The Terrace Room*

*Your presence is your gift to
us!
Rita and Thomas Emmanual*

Catherine Murphy
and
Christopher Fitzgerald

Invite you to attend
their marriage
on Saturday, the eighth of
September

Two thousand twelve
at half past three o'clock

St. Patrick's Church
Richmond, Virginia

Reception at 6 o'clock
Old Colonial Country Club

Using our state-of-the-art website,
it's easy to create personalized invitations,
programs, "thank you" cards, and more at a
fraction of the cost of custom stationery.
See p. 224 for more details. Also available at select
retail stores or online at **www.wiltonprint.com**.

PRINT YOUR OWN
at www.wiltonprint.com

Retail Order Form

RETAIL ORDER FORM

Retail Order Form

① SOLD TO: (PLEASE PRINT PLAINLY)

NAME
First   Middle   Last

ADDRESS

CITY   STATE   ZIP

(AREA CODE) DAYTIME PHONE NO. (Required)

E-MAIL

② CREDIT CARD ORDERS
(only payment accepted)   Use Visa, MasterCard or Discover Ca

Fill in the boxes:
Credit Card Number   ☐ **VISA**   ☐ MasterCard

Expiration
Month/Year   Signature

③ How Many	④ Stock Number			⑤ Page	
	1701	R	2038	124	2006

Shipping & Handling Charges (See No. 8)

Orders up to $15.99 . . . . add $7.00
Orders from $16.00-30.99 . . . . add $8.75
Orders from $31.00-40.99 . . . . add $9.75
Orders from $41.00-50.99 . . . . add $11.50
Orders from $51.00-75.99 . . . . add $13.75
Orders from $76.00-100.99 . . . . add $16.75
Orders from $101.00-150.99 . . . . add $20.00
Orders from $151.00 and above . . . . . add $25.00

Enjoy quick delivery!
Wilton orders shipped via United Parcel Service will arrive withi
after we receive them. Please allow 4-6 weeks for orders shippe

ONLY CREDIT CARD ORDERS ACCEPTED

⑦ TOT
⑧ ADI
  NOTI
⑨ STA
⑩ EXF
  Add
  SUE
  ADJ
⑪ ORD

FROM

Name

Address   Apt. No.

City

State   Zip

Caller Service No. 1604
2240 West 75th Street
Woodridge, IL 60517-0750

Will Not Be
Delivered
Without Proper
Postage

Cupcakes 'N More™ Dessert Stands

Easy to assemble!
Just stack each layer of cupcakes onto the locking center rod.

Keeps looking great!
Non-toxic, silver-finished metal has a durable non-chip finish.

Collapsible design!
Stores easily and safely.

Angled holders!
Give the best view of cupcake tops!

Standard
12 in. high x 13 wide.
Holds 23 cupcakes.
307-R-826 $29.99

See the Dazzling Displays section, featuring **Cupcakes 'N More™** starting on p. 90

Large
15 in. high x 18 wide.
Holds 38 cupcakes.
307-R-651 $39.99

So Many Exciting Ways To Serve!

Dessert Tables

Table Centerpieces

Wedding and Shower Party Favors

BRUSH-ON COLOR™

Ready-to-use edible decorating paint adds a vivid finish to fondant shapes! Just pour into the Color Tray (below), then brush on or stamp on your fondant-covered cake. In seconds, you can add brilliant designs in a rainbow of bright colors.
3 oz. bottles.
Certified Kosher.
$2.49

Blue
610-R-922

| **Red** 610-R-920 | **Yellow** 610-R-921 | **Orange** 610-R-923 |
| **Green** 610-R-924 | **Pink** 610-R-925 | **Violet** 610-R-926 |

ICING WRITER™

Squeeze on colorful accents—flowers, swirls, messages and more—with this ready-to-use icing! It's easy to control for precise decorating: Just squeeze the bottle and icing flows easily from the built-in round tip. Trace imprinted shapes made with Cut-Outs or draw dazzling freehand designs. Dries to a smooth, satin finish.
3 oz. bottles.
Certified Kosher.
$2.49

Blue
710-R-2227

| **Red** 710-R-2225 | **Yellow** 710-R-2226 | **White** 710-R-2228 |
| **Green** 710-R-2229 | **Pink** 710-R-2230 | **Violet** 710-R-2231 |

FOODWRITER™ EDIBLE COLOR MARKERS

Use like ink markers to add fun and dazzling color to countless foods. Kids love 'em! Decorate on fondant, color flow, royal icing, even directly on cookies. Brighten everyday foods like toaster pastries, cheese, fruit slices, bread and more. Each set includes five .35 oz. FoodWriter pens. Certified Kosher.

Primary Colors Sets

Yellow Green Red Blue Black

| **Fine Tip** 609-R-100 Set/5 $7.99 | **Bold Tip** 609-R-115 Set/5 $7.99 |

Neon Colors Set

Purple Orange Pink

Light Green Black

Fine Tip
609-R-116
Set/5 $7.99

FINE TIP
BOLD TIP

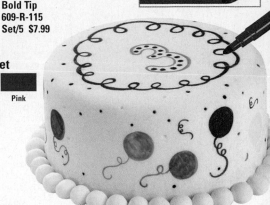

Brush Set

Add a special touch of color to your fondant-covered cake! It's easy and fun with these fine-bristle brushes and Brush-On Color or Icing Writer. Three tip designs—round, square and bevel—help you achieve different painted effects.
1907-R-1207 Set/3 $2.99

Great painting ideas!

1. Use the bevel tip brush to create exciting shading effects.

2. Use the square tip brush for lace-look brush embroidery. Draw design with Icing Writer, then pull outlines toward center with brush.

3. Use the round tip brush to paint pretty free-hand designs.

Color Tray

Become a true fondant artist with this convenient tray! Pour in Brush-On Color (above) and use Cake Stamps (below) or the Brush Set at left to add vivid designs to your fondant cakes.
1907-R-1208 $2.99

Great color ideas!

1. Pour Icing Writer into Color Tray. Dip crumpled paper towel in the color. Test on parchment paper or a paper towel.

2. Lightly press against cake surface.

3. Continue sponging color until surface is covered. If some areas look too light, fill in with a little more color.

CAKE STAMPS™

Stamp colorful designs onto your fondant-covered cakes, cupcakes or cookies—it's easy and fun!

Shapes range from 1 to 1½ in.

• Four exciting stamp sets, each with six lively designs!
• Food-safe, with convenient handles for even imprinting.

1. Fill Color Tray with Brush-On Color. Dip a Stamp into color. Press Stamp on parchment paper or paper towel to get the look just right.

2. Press stamp onto your cake, imprinting the design flat against the surface. Rinse stamp in water whenever you change colors, then dry with paper towel.

3. Continue dipping and stamping until desired design is complete.

Geometric
Star, Square, Square Border, Triangle, Round, Heart
417-R-181
Set/6 $4.49

Romantic
Champagne Glass, Spiral, Dove Left, Dove Right, Bow, Bell
417-R-183
Set/6 $4.49

Nature
Tulip, Bee, 5-Petal Flower, 6-Petal Flower, Butterfly, Leaf
417-R-182
Set/6 $4.49

Baby
Rattle, Bear, Duck, Carriage, Frame, Shoe
417-R-184
Set/6 $4.49

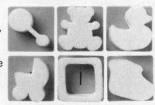

fondant fun! ™

Add shimmering colors!

Make your fondant decorations shine by topping them with a sprinkle of Shimmer Dust™. This finely grained edible glitter gives flowers and greenery an elegant lustre.

1. Brush top of decoration with water.

2. Sprinkle top with Shimmer Dust right from the jar.

3. Shake off excess Shimmer Dust onto a piece of paper. Reserve for use on other designs.

SHIMMER DUST™   NEW!

Give your fondant decorating that added dash of color! Sprinkle on Shimmer Dust —the sparkling color will give your decorations a jolt of excitement your guests will love. Just brush your fondant-covered cake top or fondant Cut-Outs with water and sprinkle lightly over the dampened area.

.47 oz. Certified Kosher.

Elegant
Silver, Gold, Pearl
703-R-212 Set/3 $3.99

Primary
Red, Green, Blue
703-R-210 Set/3 $3.99

Bright
Pink, Yellow, Orange
703-R-211 Set/3 $3.99

ROLLING PINS AND MAT

Roll out and cut fun shapes!

1. Sprinkle Rolling Pin and Roll & Cut Mat with confectioner's sugar.

2. Place fondant on the mat. Roll about ⅛ to ¼ in. thick.

3. Cut pieces with Decorative Punch (p. 127), Cutter/ Embosser (p. 131), or Cut-Outs™ (p. 128).

Wide Glide™ Rolling Pin   NEW!

Its extra-wide, smooth design is perfect for covering cakes with rolled fondant. The non-stick surface makes handling large pieces of fondant easy—just dust the surface with confectioner's sugar and roll out fondant to the size you need, then use the Wide Glide Rolling Pin to lift the fondant from your work surface to the cake. Great for rolling out pastry dough and pie crusts, too.
20 x 1½ in. diameter.
1907-R-1210 $19.99

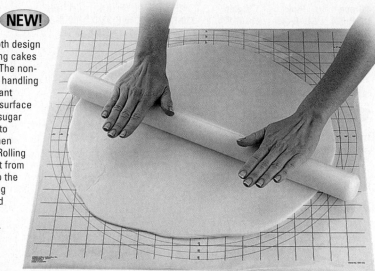

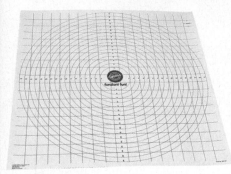

Roll & Cut Mat

For precise measuring, rolling and cutting of fondant or dough. Pre-marked circles for exact sizing. Square grid helps you cut precise strips. Non-stick surface for easy release.
409-R-412 $8.99

Perfect Height™ Rolling Pin

Roll out fondant evenly, at the perfect thickness for easy cutting and shaping, with this non-stick roller. Roll to the perfect ⅛ in. height used for cutting many fondant decorations, using the slide-on guide rings. This rolling pin is easy to handle—just the right size for preparing small amounts of fondant to place on your cake. Perfect for use with Fondant Multi Packs and Cut-Outs™. 9 x 1 in. diameter.
1907-R-1205 Set/3 $5.99

 **NEW!**

FONDANT AND GUM PASTE INGREDIENTS

Glycerin
Stir into dried out fondant, gum paste and icing color to restore consistency. 2 oz. Certified Kosher.
708-R-14 $1.99

Glucose
Essential ingredient for making fondant and gum paste from scratch. Use with Wilton Gum-Tex™. 12 oz.
707-R-107 $3.99

Gum-Tex™
Makes fondant and gum paste pliable, elastic, easy to shape. Flip-top can has a plastic resealable lid. 6 oz.
707-R-117 $7.99

Gum Paste Mix
Just add water and knead. Workable, pliable dough-like mixture molds into beautiful flowers and figures. 1 lb.
707-R-124 $5.99

ORDER TOLL FREE: 800-794-5866

FONDANT TOOLS AND ACCESSORIES

Fondant Shaping Foam **NEW!**

Thick and thin squares are the ideal soft surface for shaping flowers, leaves and other fondant or gum paste cutouts. Use the thin square for thinning petal edges with a ball tool, carving vein lines on leaves and making ruffled fondant strips. Use the thick square for cupping flower centers. Thin: 4 x 4 x ⅛ in. Thick: 4 x 4 x 1 in.
1907-R-9704 Set/2 $2.99

Cutter/ Embosser

Three detachable wheels—straight, wavy and ridged—for cutting and for embossing of patterns on fondant. Light, easy-rolling design cuts at the perfect angle. Comfortable handle also stores wheels.
1907-R-1206 $3.99

Emboss designs in fondant!

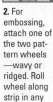

1. To cut strips, attach the straight-edge cutting wheel of the Cutter/ Embosser—just snap the axle into the handle slot. Roll out fondant on the Roll & Cut Mat (at left) using grid marks to determine width. Roll the wheel along a ruler to cut perfect strips.

2. For embossing, attach one of the two pattern wheels—wavy or ridged. Roll wheel along strip in any direction.

3. Wheels create great-looking dots or waves to give your fondant cake terrific texture! Remove strips from mat with angled spatula.

Confectionery Tool Set

Invaluable tools for shaping and imprinting, helping you achieve lifelike fondant or gum paste flowers. Ideal for marking patterns in fondant cakes, shaping marzipan fruits. Includes plastic Dogbone, Umbrella, Shell, Ball and Veining tools.
1907-R-1000 Set/5 $9.99

Flower Former Set

Dry fondant or icing leaves and flowers in a convex or concave shape. Three each of 1½, 2 and 2½ in. wide holders, all 11 in. long.
417-R-9500 Set/9 $5.99

Quick Ease Roller

Makes it easy to prepare small pieces of fondant and gum paste for cutting flowers and designs. Wooden roller fits comfortably in palm of hand.
1907-R-1202 $4.99

Easy-Glide Fondant Smoother

Essential tool for shaping and smoothing rolled fondant on your cake. Works great on top, edges and sides! Shapes fondant to sides of cake so that no puffed areas appear. Trim any excess with a sharp knife. 6¼ in. long x 3¼ in. wide.
1907-R-1200 $4.99

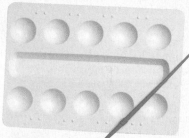

Candy Melting Plate

Great for drying fondant flowers. Microwave-melt up to 11 Candy Melts®* colors at one time for less mess. Plastic with non-slip grip edge. Includes decorating brush.
1904-R-8016 Set/2 $2.99
*Brand confectionery coating.

FONDANT AND GUM PASTE DECORATION SETS

Floral Collection Flower Making Set

Make incredibly lifelike gum paste flowers. Full-color how-to book includes many arranging ideas and step-by-step instructions. Kit includes 24 plastic cutters, 1 leaf mold, 3 wood modeling tools, protector flap, 40-page instruction book and 2 foam squares for modeling.
1907-R-117 Set/32 $19.99
Book only 907-R-117 $9.99

Stepsaving Rose Bouquets Flower Cutter Set

Create gorgeous fondant and gum paste roses and forget-me-nots using cutters and book in this set. Cutters include large and small rose, rose leaf, calyx and forget-me-not.
1907-R-1003 Set/6 $7.99

Floral Garland Cutter/Ejector Set

Quickly and easily cuts and positions fondant or gum paste flowers on cakes. Includes ejector, 5 cutters and instructions.
1907-R-1001 Set/7 $9.99

Icings

All Wilton icings are formulated for decorating as well as taste. That's because Wilton insists on providing you with the perfect consistency icing for decorating. Our quality ingredients mean better results for you.

Creamy White Buttercream Icing Mix

Our convenient mix has the delicious taste and creamy texture of homemade buttercream icing. Use just as you would your favorite buttercream recipe. Makes 1½ to 2 cups. Enough to ice a 1-layer 8 in. cake. Certified Kosher.
710-R-112 $2.99

Vanilla Whipped Icing Mix

Our light, whipped icing is the ideal texture for decorating in an easy-to-make, delicious mix. Just add ice water and it whips up velvety-smooth for icing or decorating. Light and delicate flavor. Makes 4 cups. Certified Kosher Dairy.
710-R-1241 $4.99

Meringue Powder

Primary ingredient for royal icing. Stabilizes buttercream, adds body to boiled icing and meringue. Replaces egg white in many recipes. Resealable top opens for easy measuring. 4 oz. can makes 5 recipes of royal icing; 8 oz. can makes 10 recipes. 16 oz. can makes 20 recipes. Certified Kosher.
4 oz. can 702-R-6007 $4.99
8 oz. can 702-R-6015 $7.99
16 oz. can 702-R-6004 $15.99

NEW! 16 Oz. Can!

Color Flow Mix

Create dimensional flow-in designs for your cake. Just add water and confectioner's sugar. 4 oz. can makes ten 1½ cup batches. Certified Kosher.
701-R-47 $7.49

Piping Gel

Pipe messages and designs or glaze cakes before icing. Use clear or tint with icing color. 10 oz. Certified Kosher.
704-R-105 $3.99

READY-TO-USE DECORATOR ICINGS

NEW! 5 lb. Tub!

Wilton makes the only ready-to-use icing that is the perfect consistency for decorating. The pure white color is best for creating true vivid colors using Wilton Icing Colors. Rich and creamy, with a delicious homemade taste. Certified Kosher.

5 lb. Tub

Ideal thin-to-medium consistency for use in Wilton Method Cake Decorating Classes in a convenient easy-carry tub. Great for spreading on cakes, making borders, messages and more. Contains 10 cups—enough to decorate ten 8 or 9 in. round cake layers.
White 704-R-680 $12.99

1 lb. Can

Ideal stiff consistency for making roses and flowers with upright petals. One 16 oz. can covers two 8 or 9 in. layers or one 9 x 13 in. cake. **$2.49**
White 710-R-118
Chocolate 710-R-119

READY-TO-DECORATE ICING

Anyone can decorate with Wilton Ready-to-Decorate Icing! Brilliant colors and easy-to-use tips make it a breeze to add an exciting finishing touch to treats—without mixing or mess. Just slip one of the four free tips over the nozzle and start the fun. Decorating couldn't be easier!

Colors match Wilton Icing Colors (p. 133). 6.4 oz. Certified Kosher. **$3.49**

Free! 4 decorating tips

Red 710-R-4400	**Green** 710-R-4401	**White** 710-R-4402	**Black** 710-R-4404	**Pink** 710-R-4406
Blue 710-R-4407	**Violet** 710-R-4408	**Yellow** 710-R-4409	**Orange** 710-R-4410	

Four FREE decorating tips included:

Small Round Tip
For dots and outlining

Leaf Tip
For basic and ruffled leaves

Large Round Tip
For writing and printing

Star Tip
For stars, swirls and pretty borders

Flavorings

Decorators trust Wilton flavorings for great taste that won't change icing consistency. Wilton flavors are concentrated— only a drop or two adds delicious taste to icings, cakes, beverages and other recipes.

NO-COLOR FLAVORINGS

Recommended by and used in Wilton Method Classes, these delicious flavors won't change your icing color. Essential for making pure white icings for wedding cakes and maintaining vibrant colors in all your decorating. Certified Kosher.

Clear Vanilla Extract
2 oz.
604-R-2237 $1.99
8 oz.
604-R-2269 $4.99

No-Color Butter Flavor
2 oz.
604-R-2040 $1.99
8 oz.
604-R-2067 $4.99

No-Color Almond Extract
2 oz.
604-R-2126 $1.99

Pure Vanilla Extract
The world's finest vanilla is from Madagascar. Unmatched flavor and aroma to enhance cakes, puddings, pie fillings, custards, salad dressings and more. 4 oz.
604-R-2270 $7.99

ORDER TOLL FREE: 800-794-5866

Tube Icings, Gels

Tube Decorating Icings

The same high quality as our Ready-To-Use Decorator Icing, in a convenient tube. Create flowers, borders and more. Ideal for small areas of color on character cakes. Use with our Tip and Nail Set or Coupler Ring Set and any standard-size Wilton metal tip (not included). Colors match Wilton Icing Colors shown at right. 4.25 oz. Certified Kosher. **$1.79**

Violet 704-R-242	**Pink** 704-R-230	
Red 704-R-218	**Royal Blue** 704-R-248	**Chocolate** 704-R-254
Lemon Yellow 704-R-236	**Leaf Green** 704-R-224	**White** 704-R-200
Orange 704-R-212	**Kelly Green** 704-R-227	**Black** 704-R-206

Coupler Ring Set

Attach Wilton standard size metal decorating tips onto Wilton tube icings to create any technique. 418-R-47306 Set/4 **$1.99**

Tip and Nail Set

Tips easily twist onto Wilton tube icings to create many decorating techniques. Includes Star, Round, Leaf and Petal Tips, Flower Nail. 418-R-47300 Set/5 **$1.99**

Tube Decorating Gels

Add shimmering accents, colorful highlights and sparkle to your decorating with these transparent gels. Create a beautiful stained-glass effect and add distinctive writing and printing. Great for cakes and cookies. Colors match Wilton Icing Colors shown at right. .75 oz. Certified Kosher. **$1.29**

Red 704-R-318	**Orange** 704-R-312	
Pink 704-R-330	**Royal Blue** 704-R-348	
Violet 704-R-342	**Leaf Green** 704-R-324	**White** 704-R-302
Lemon Yellow 704-R-336	**Brown** 704-R-354	**Black** 704-R-306

Tube Icing and Gel Color Chart

Lemon Yellow	Orange	Red	Pink
Violet	**Royal Blue**	**Leaf Green**	**† Kelly Green**
† Chocolate	**Brown**	**White**	**Black**

†Not available in gel.

Icing Colors

Wilton color is made to produce deeper, richer color by adding just a small amount. Our concentrated gel formula helps you achieve the exact shade you want without thinning your icing. You'll find a rainbow of colors, ready to blend together for creating your own custom shades.

*Note: Large amounts of these colors may affect icing taste.

Use No-Taste Red for large areas of red on a cake. When using Black, start with chocolate icing to limit the amount of color needed.

†Daffodil Yellow is an all-natural color. It does not contain Yellow #5. The color remains very pale.

Single Bottles
1 oz. Certified Kosher.
$1.99

Ivory 610-R-208	Daffodil Yellow‡ 610-R-175	Buttercup Yellow 610-R-216	Golden Yellow 610-R-159	Lemon Yellow 610-R-108	Copper (skin tone) 610-R-450	Creamy Peach 610-R-210	Rose Petal Pink 610-R-410	Terra Cotta 610-R-206	Orange 610-R-205
Red-Red* 610-R-906	**Christmas Red*** 610-R-302	**Red (no-taste)** 610-R-998	**Rose** 610-R-401	**Burgundy** 610-R-698	**Pink** 610-R-256	**Violet** 610-R-604	**Delphinium Blue** 610-R-228	**Cornflower Blue** 610-R-710	**Royal Blue** 610-R-655
Sky Blue 610-R-700	**Teal** 610-R-207	**Kelly Green** 610-R-752	**Leaf Green** 610-R-809	**Moss Green** 610-R-851	**Juniper Green** 610-R-234	**Brown** 610-R-507	**Black*** 610-R-981		

Primary 4-Icing Colors Set

Lemon Yellow, Sky Blue, Christmas Red, Brown in .5 oz. jars. Certified Kosher.
601-R-5127 **Set/4 $4.99**

8-Icing Colors Set

Lemon Yellow, Sky Blue, Christmas Red, Brown, Orange, Violet, Pink and Leaf Green in .5 oz. jars. Certified Kosher.
601-R-5577 **Set/8 $9.99**

12-Icing Colors Set

Our most popular collection creates the spectrum of primary colors plus skin tones, teal and burgundy. Lemon Yellow, Teal, No-Taste Red, Brown, Copper (Lt. Skin tone), Violet, Pink, Burgundy, Golden Yellow, Royal Blue, Black, Kelly Green in .5 oz. jars. Certified Kosher.
601-R-5580 **Set/12 $13.99**

White-White Icing Color

Stir in to whiten icing made with butter or margarine. Perfect for wedding cakes. 2 oz. Certified Kosher.
603-R-1236 **$2.99**

Glycerin

Stir into dried out icing color to restore consistency. 2 oz. Certified Kosher.
708-R-14 **$1.99**

Pastel 4-Icing Colors Set

Willow Green, Cornflower Blue, Creamy Peach, Rose Petal Pink in .5 oz. jars. Certified Kosher.
601-R-25588 **Set/4 $4.99**

Garden Tone 4-Icing Colors Set

Buttercup Yellow, Delphinium Blue, Aster Mauve, Juniper Green, in .5 oz. jars. Certified Kosher.
601-R-4240 **Set/4 $4.99**

Color Mist™ Food Color Spray

This easy-to-use spray gives decorators the versatility and dazzling effects of an airbrush in a convenient can! Creates a rainbow of excitement on so many desserts. Use it to transform a plain iced cake with sensational color, add splashes of holiday color to iced cookies and cupcakes. Great for party desserts—highlighting whipped topping or ice cream with color. No mess, taste-free formula; add a little color or a lot.

Colors match Wilton Icing Colors above. 1.5 oz. Certified Kosher. **$2.99**

Red 710-R-5500	Blue 710-R-5501	Yellow 710-R-5502	Green 710-R-5503
Violet 710-R-5504	**Pink** 710-R-5505	**Black** 710-R-5506	**Orange** 710-R-5507

Sprinkles

SPARKLING SUGARS

Put that extra dazzle in your decorating! These easy-pour sugars have a coarse texture and a brilliant sparkle that makes cupcakes, cookies and cakes really shine. 8 oz. bottles. Certified Kosher.
$3.99

White
710-R-992

Lavender/White
710-R-993

Rainbow
710-R-991

SHAPED SPRINKLES

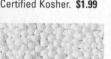

Pour on the fun! Great shapes and colors add a dash of excitement to cakes, cupcakes, ice cream and more.

Plastic shaker bottles for convenient pouring and storing. Certified Kosher. **$1.99**

White Nonpareils
3 oz. bottle
710-R-773

Rubber Ducky Mix
2.5 oz. bottle
710-R-798

Cinnamon Drops
3 oz. bottle
710-R-769

Rainbow Nonpareils
3 oz. bottle
710-R-772

Rainbow Jimmies
2.5 oz. bottle
710-R-776
6.25 oz. bottle
710-R-994 **$3.99**

Chocolate Jimmies
2.5 oz. bottle
710-R-774

COLORED SUGARS

Extra-fine sugar is excellent for filling in brightly colored designs on cakes, cupcakes and cookies. Controlling the flow is easy with the flip-top shaker bottles. 3.25 oz. bottles. Certified Kosher. **$1.99**

Yellow
710-R-754

Pink
710-R-756

Red
710-R-766

Light Green
710-R-752

Blue
710-R-750

Orange
710-R-759

Lavender
710-R-758

Dark Green
710-R-764

Black
710-R-762

ASSORTMENTS

They're so convenient! Assorted fun shapes in an easy-pour flip-top bottle. Top cupcakes, ice cream and other goodies. Certified Kosher.
$4.99

6-Mix

Flowerful Medley
.39 oz. each Confetti, Colorful Leaves, Daisies, Pastel Hearts, .35 oz. Wild Flowers, .32 oz Butterflies.
710-R-4122

Animals and Stars
.39 oz. Fish, .35 oz. each Stars, Dinosaurs, Stars and Moons, Bears, .32 oz. Dolphins.
710-R-4123

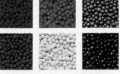

Nonpareils
.5 oz. each Pink, Orange, Green, Red, Yellow, Purple.
710-R-4125

Jimmies
.42 oz. each Pink, Orange, Green, Red, Yellow, Blue.
710-R-4127

4-Mix

Brights Sugars
1.1 oz. each Yellow, Light Green, Lavender, Pink.
710-R-651

Primary Sugars
1.1 oz. each Red, Dark Green, Blue, Yellow.
710-R-650

Cake Sparkles™

Add shimmering color to cakes, cupcakes, cookies and ice cream! Brilliant edible glitter in a great variety of colors is great for stencilling, highlighting messages, snow scenes. .25 oz. Certified Kosher.
$2.89

Silver
703-R-1285

White
703-R-1290

Yellow
703-R-1272

Purple
703-R-1266

Blue
703-R-1314

Red
703-R-1284

Green
703-R-1278

Pink
703-R-1260

Orange
703-R-1308

Black
703-R-1302

Baking Accessories

Bake Easy!™ Non-Stick Spray

For cakes that turn out beautifully every time, start by spraying pans with Bake Easy. This convenient non-stick spray helps your cakes release perfectly with fewer crumbs for easier icing and a flawless look for decorating. Just a light, even coating does the job. Use Bake Easy for all mixes and recipes—cupcakes, brownies, breads and more. Versatile for all types of baking and cooking. 6 oz.
702-R-6018 $2.99

Cake Release

No need to grease and flour your baking pan—Cake Release coats in one step. Simply spread Cake Release lightly on pan bottom and sides with a pastry brush and add batter. Cakes release perfectly without crumbs every time, giving you the ideal surface for decorating. In convenient dispensing bottle. 8 oz. Certified Kosher.
702-R-6016 $3.49

Pastry Brush

Flexible, absorbent bristles for efficient brushing; seamless nylon shaft holds bristles securely. Great for applying Cake Release. 1½ in. wide.
417-R-449 $2.99

Non-Stick Parchment Paper

Use Wilton silicone-treated non-stick parchment to line baking pans and cookie sheets—a non-fat alternative that saves cleanup time. Roll out cookie dough between 2 sheets, dough won't stick and will easily transfer to your cookie sheet. You can even reuse it for the next batch. Oven-safe to 400°F, parchment is great for conventional ovens, microwaves and the freezer. Double roll is 41 square feet, 15 in. wide. Certified Kosher.
415-R-680 $4.99

BAKE-EVEN STRIPS

Cakes bake perfectly level and moist, without cracking, when you wrap these strips around the pan before baking. Oven-safe, instructions and clips included.

Small Set
Two 30 x 1½ in. wide strips, enough for two 8 or 9 in. round pans.
415-R-260 Set/2 $7.99

Large Set
Four strips, 36, 43, 49 and 56 in. long x 1½ in. wide. Enough for one each: 10, 12, 14, 16 in. round pans.
415-R-262 Set/4 $16.99

CAKE STENCILS VARIETY PACK

Our collection of 4 stencil designs gives you several ways to make birthday and everyday cakes more festive. Decorating with stencils is so easy—just place on your iced cake, then sprinkle away with Wilton Cake Sparkles™, add exciting Wilton Sugars in a rainbow of colors or use Color Mist™ food color spray. Also works beautifully with Wilton Rolled Fondant—fill in designs with sugars or decorate with FoodWriter™ markers. Includes Happy Birthday, Flower, Swirl and Heart designs.
417-R-148
Pk./4 $6.99

6-PIECE COVERED MIXING BOWL SET

Perfect for preparing decorating icings—clear lids snap on tight to keep icing the right texture. Includes one each 1, 2 and 3 quart nesting bowls with easy-grip handles and easy-pour spouts for better control. Rubberized base keeps bowls from sliding on countertops. Measurements clearly marked for precise mixing. Dishwasher safe.
417-R-469 Set/6 $12.99

CAKE LEVELERS

Cake Leveler
Make your cake top perfectly level for precise decorating—just place adjustable wire in notches to desired height up to 2 in. and glide through the cake. Makes torting easy, too! For cakes up to 10 in. wide.
415-R-815 $2.99

Large Cake Leveler
Blade easily levels and tortes cakes up to 18 in. diameter. Adjusts up to 3 in. high—just twist feet to lock into notch at desired height then glide the stainless steel blade through your cake.
417-R-1198 $21.99

Decorating Stands

A quality cake stand is a must for easy decorating. Stands lift your cake off the work surface so you can create borders conveniently. And they rotate as well, allowing you to decorate all the way around the cake without straining.

Tilting Cake Turntable

It tilts! Decorate any part of your cake conveniently!

The Tilting Cake Turntable moves to 3 preset angles—12°, 24°, and level—and locks in place, making every decorating technique easier! 6 in. high turntable smoothly rotates in any of the angled positions for effortless decorating of top borders, stringwork, lettering on top and sides of cake, more. Includes lock to prevent rotation. Non-slip base, 12 in. diameter.
307-R-894 **$59.99**

Professional Turntable

Extra strength and effortless turning for decorating tiered wedding cakes. Heavy-duty aluminum stand is 4 ½ in. high with 12 in. diameter plate. Holds cakes up to 16 in. diameter.
307-R-2501 **$59.99**

Revolving Cake Stand

Turns in either direction with easy-rotating ball bearings. 3 in. high, 11 in. diameter plate is white molded plastic. Holds cakes up to 10 in. diameter.
415-R-900 **$11.99**

Trim 'N Turn Cake Stand

Turns smoothly on hidden ball bearings for easy decorating and serving. Flute-edged 12 in. plate is white molded plastic. Holds cakes up to 10 in. diameter.
2103-R-2518 **$7.99**

Decorating Tools

ICING SCULPTOR™

Now your cakes can have an elegant sculpted finish that will give them a beautiful professional look. It's easy with the Icing Sculptor. Just insert any combination of the 64 design blades—mix and match between the 14 sculpting edges to create your favorite customized effects. Then glide the comb over the iced cake sides to create attractive ridges that will beautifully frame your design. Create hundreds of pattern combinations—wide or narrow ridges, dramatic swirls and vertical designs too.

Includes sculptor handle, 64 design blades and complete instructions. This versatile tool has a patent pending.
2104-R-12 Set/66 **$12.99**

So Easy!
Select the sculpting blades you want and slide into handle. Press sculptor into iced cake as you rotate cake on turntable.

So Versatile!
Mix and match between the 14 edge designs on 64 blades to achieve the perfect look for your cake.

Get 8 of each 2-Sided Design Blade

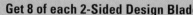

Decorating Comb
Run edge across your iced cake to form beautiful ridges. 12 x 1 ½ in.; plastic.
417-R-156 **$1.49**

Decorating Triangle
Each side adds a different contoured effect to iced cakes. Easy to hold; 5 x 5 in.; plastic.
417-R-162 **$1.09**

Garland Marker
Adjusts to 7 preset widths and varying depths to easily mark perfectly uniform garlands on cake sides. Instructions included.
409-R-812 **$3.99**

Hand & Wrist Support Gloves

Makes decorating and other creative tasks more comfortable! Use whenever you work with your hands. Their exclusive spandex and nylon construction supports vital areas of the hand and wrist to help you work more comfortably, while the breathable fabric reduces perspiration. Hand & Wrist Support Gloves promote circulation and massage muscles to reduce fatigue. Lightweight, fingerless design gives you the freedom of motion you need for all kinds of tasks including computer work, painting, sewing, knitting, quilting, crocheting and more. Machine or hand wash.
417-R-488 Pk./2 **$19.99**

Cake Dividing Set
Measures equal sections of your cake for precise placement of garlands, stringwork and other designs. Cake Dividing Wheel marks up to 16 divisions on cakes up to 20 in. diameter. Garland Marker adjusts to 7 widths. Instructions included.
409-R-806 Set/2 **$8.99**

Practice Board with Patterns Set
Includes stand and 20 full-size patterns. 9 x 6 in.
406-R-9464 **$6.99**

All-Purpose Decorating Gloves
Food-safe disposable gloves keep your hands clean, odor-free and protected in and out of the kitchen. Prevent color stains when tinting fondant, keep fingerprints off homemade candy, eliminate burning of skin when cutting hot, spicy foods. Great when working with craft paint and glue, too. Easy to slip-on, gloves fit either hand.
417-R-1642 Pk./20 **$2.99**

ORDER TOLL FREE: 800-794-5866

Decorating Bags

Featherweight® Decorating Bags

Use these easy-handling bags over and over. Lightweight, strong and flexible polyester will never get stiff. Coated to prevent grease from seeping through. May be boiled; dishwasher safe. Instructions included. Sold singly.

8 in. 404-R-5087 $2.99
10 in. 404-R-5109 $4.49
12 in. 404-R-5125 $5.49
14 in. 404-R-5140 $6.49
16 in. 404-R-5168 $7.99
18 in. 404-R-5184 $8.99

Disposable Decorating Bags

Just use, then toss. Strong, flexible plastic. 12 in. size fits standard tips and couplers. Also perfect for melting Candy Melts®* in the microwave. Instructions included.

2104-R-358 Pk./12 $3.99
2104-R-1358 Pk./24 $6.49

*Brand confectionery coating.

Disposable Decorating Bag Dispenser Box

Now in convenient Value Packs! These dispenser boxes make it easy to pull out one bag at a time, so you can keep your decorating space uncluttered. Instructions included.

2104-R-1273 Pk./50 $12.49
2104-R-1249 Pk./100 $19.99

50 Pack

Parchment Triangles

Make your own disposable decorating bags with our grease-resistant vegetable parchment paper. The professional's choice for convenience and quick bag preparation. Instructions included.

12 in. 2104-R-1206
Pk./100 $5.49

15 in. 2104-R-1508
Pk./100 $5.99

Spatulas

ROSEWOOD

Quality rosewood handle spatulas have been favorites for years. They have strong, flexible stainless steel blades and sturdy handles.

Straight Blade
11 in.; 6 in. blade.
409-R-7695 $4.99
8 in.; 4¼ in. blade.
409-R-6044
$2.99

Angled Blade
12 in.; 6¼ in. blade.
409-R-135 $5.99
8 in.; 4½ in. blade.
409-R-739
$2.99

Tapered Blade
8 in.; 4 in. blade.
409-R-518
$2.99

COMFORT GRIP™

Decorate with greater comfort, more control and less fatigue, thanks to contoured handle with finger pad. Flexible stainless steel blade is perfect thickness for gliding over icing.

Straight Blade
15 in.; 10⅛ in. blade.
409-R-6030 $9.99
11 in.; 6 in. blade.
409-R-6018 $5.99
8 in.;
4½ in. blade.
409-R-6006
$3.99

Angled Blade
15 in.; 9⅞ in. blade.
409-R-6036 $9.99
13 in.; 7¾ in. blade.
409-R-6024 $6.49
8 in.;
4½ in. blade.
409-R-6012
$4.49

Tapered Blade
8 in.; 4 in. blade.
409-R-6003
$3.99

Tip Accessories

Maintain the quality of your Wilton metal decorating tips with these tools.

Tip/Coupler Dishwasher and Storage Bag

Place nylon mesh bag in dishwasher silverware rack for easy tip and coupler cleaning. Tips not included. 5¾ x 6 in.
417-R-1640 Pk./2 $2.99

DECORATING COUPLERS

Couplers make it easy to change decorating tips on the same icing bag.

Standard Coupler
Fits all decorating bags and standard tips.
411-R-1987 $0.59

Large Coupler
Use with large decorating tips and 14 to 18 in. Featherweight Bags.
411-R-1006 $1.49

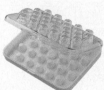

Tip Saver
Restores bent tips to their proper shape; opens clogged tips. Place tip over pointed or cone-shaped end, put on cover and twist back and forth to reshape. Heavy-duty plastic.
414-R-909 $2.79

Tip Covers
Take filled bags along for touch ups—just slip over tip and go. Plastic.
414-R-915 Pk./4 $0.99

Tip Brush
Great for cleaning small tip openings. Plastic bristles. ¼ x 4 in. long.
418-R-1123 $1.39

Tipsaver Cases
Small case holds 26 tips; large case holds 52 tips. Tips not included.
Small 405-R-8773 $5.99
Large 405-R-7777 $7.49

Flower-Making Accessories

Flower Lifter
Easily transfers buttercream flowers from nail to cake without damage. Angled design keeps your hands from touching the cake. Detachable blades for easy cleaning. Plastic. 5¼ in. long.
417-R-1199
$2.99

Flower Nail No. 7
For basic flower making. Provides the control you need when piping icing flowers. Just rotate the nail between your thumb and fingers as you pipe a flower on the head. Stainless steel. 1½ in.
402-R-3007 $1.09

Lily Nail Set
Essential for making cup flowers. Includes ½, 1¼, 1⅝ and 2½ in. diameter cups.
403-R-9444
Set/8 $1.99

Flower Former Set
Dry icing leaves and flowers in a convex or concave shape. Three each of 1½, 2 and 2½ in. wide holders, all 11 in. long.
417-R-9500
Set/9
$5.99

Decorating Tips

All tips work with standard bags and couplers, unless otherwise indicated. Nickel-plated brass. Dishwasher safe.

ROUND TIPS
Outline, lettering, dots, balls, beads, stringwork, lattice, lacework.

 #1 402-R-1 $0.89

#6 402-R-6 $0.89

#2A Smaller version of 1A. 402-R-2001* $1.49

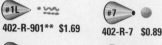 **#1L** 402-R-901** $1.69

#7 402-R-7 $0.89

#1A Bold borders, figure piping. 402-R-1001* $1.69

#1s 402-R-1009 $1.39

#8 402-R-8 $0.89

#230 Fill eclairs and bismarcks. 402-R-230 $1.99

#2 402-R-2 $0.89

#9 402-R-9 $0.89

#55 402-R-55 $0.89

#3 402-R-3 $0.89

#10 402-R-10 $0.89

#57 402-R-57 $0.89

#4 402-R-4 $0.89

#11 402-R-11 $0.89

#301 flat lettering. 402-R-301 $0.89

#5 402-R-5 $0.89

#12 402-R-12 $0.89

DROP FLOWER TIPS
Small (106-225); medium (131-194); large (2C-1G) great for cookie dough.

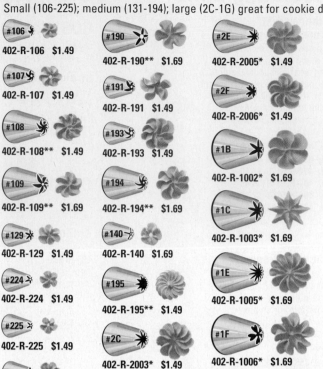

#106 402-R-106 $1.49

#190 402-R-190** $1.69

#2E 402-R-2005* $1.49

#107 402-R-107 $1.49

#191 402-R-191 $1.49

#2F 402-R-2006* $1.49

#108 402-R-108** $1.49

#193 402-R-193 $1.49

#1B 402-R-1002* $1.69

#109 402-R-109** $1.69

#194 402-R-194** $1.69

#1C 402-R-1003* $1.69

#129 402-R-129 $1.49

#140 402-R-140 $1.69

#224 402-R-224 $1.49

#195 402-R-195** $1.49

#1E 402-R-1005* $1.69

#225 402-R-225 $1.49

#2C 402-R-2003* $1.49

#1F 402-R-1006* $1.69

#131 402-R-131 $1.49

#2D 402-R-2004* $1.49

#1G 402-R-1007* $1.69

PETAL TIPS
Realistic flower petals, dramatic ruffles, drapes, swags and bows.

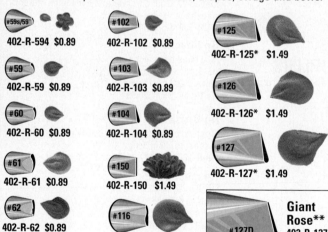

#59s/59 402-R-594 $0.89

#102 402-R-102 $0.89

#125 402-R-125* $1.49

#59 402-R-59 $0.89

#103 402-R-103 $0.89

#126 402-R-126* $1.49

#60 402-R-60 $0.89

#104 402-R-104 $0.89

#127 402-R-127* $1.49

#61 402-R-61 $0.89

#150 402-R-150 $1.49

#62 402-R-62 $0.89

#116 402-R-116* $1.49

#127D Giant Rose** 402-R-1274 $1.69

#64 402-R-64 $0.89

#121 402-R-121* $1.49

#97 402-R-97 $0.89

#123 402-R-123* $1.49

#101s 402-R-1019 $1.39

#124 402-R-124* $1.49

#101 402-R-101 $0.89

BASKETWEAVE TIPS
44, 45 make only smooth stripes; rest of basketweave tips make both smooth and ribbed stripes.

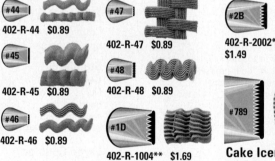

#44 402-R-44 $0.89

#47 402-R-47 $0.89

#2B 402-R-2002* $1.49

#45 402-R-45 $0.89

#48 402-R-48 $0.89

#46 402-R-46 $0.89

#1D 402-R-1004** $1.69

#789 Cake Icer** 409-R-789 $2.99

MULTI-OPENING TIPS
Rows and clusters of strings, beads, stars, scallops.

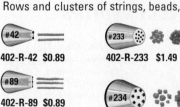

#42 402-R-42 $0.89

#233 402-R-233 $1.49

#235 402-R-235* $1.49

#89 402-R-89 $0.89

#234 402-R-234* $1.69

TRIPLE STAR Triple Star* 402-R-2010 $2.59

#134 402-R-134** $1.69

*Fits large coupler.   **Tip does not work with coupler. Use with parchment or uncut bags only.

ORDER TOLL FREE: 800-794-5866

OPEN STAR TIPS

Star techniques, drop flowers; the finely cut teeth of 199 thru 364 create decorations with many ridges; use 6B and 8B with pastry dough too.

 #13
402-R-13 $0.89

 #21
402-R-21 $0.89

#172
402-R-172** $1.49

 #14
402-R-14 $0.89

#22
402-R-22 $0.89

#1M (2110)
402-R-2110* $1.49

 #15
402-R-15 $0.89

#32
402-R-32 $0.89

#4B
402-R-4400** $1.49

#16
402-R-16 $0.89

#199
402-R-199 $1.49

#6B
402-R-6600** $1.49

 #17
402-R-17 $0.89

#362
402-R-362 $1.49

 #18
402-R-18 $0.89

#363
402-R-363 $1.49

#8B
402-R-8800** $1.69

 #19
402-R-19 $0.89

#364
402-R-364 $1.49

 #20
402-R-20 $0.89

LEFT HANDED TIP SETS

Now left-handers can achieve the same beautiful flowers as right-handed decorators! Nickel-plated brass tips fit standard bags and couplers.

 LEFT-HAND

#59°

#106L

#97L

#107L

#116L

Drop Flower Set
Includes Left tips #106 and #107 for making small swirled flowers.
418-R-613† Set/2 $2.99

Petal Set
Includes Left tip #59° for violets, Left tip #97 for Victorian roses and Left tip #116 for large Wilton roses.
418-R-612† Set/3 $2.99

SPECIALTY TIPS

Shells, ropes, hearts, Christmas trees, ring candle holders!

#98
402-R-98 $0.89

#83
402-R-83 $0.89

#81
402-R-81 $0.89

#347
402-R-347 $1.49

#96
402-R-96 $0.89

#250
402-R-250* $1.69

#136
402-R-136 $1.69

#79
402-R-79 $0.89

#252
402-R-252* $1.69

#77
402-R-77 $0.89

#105
402-R-105 $0.89

#95
402-R-95 $0.89

#78
402-R-78 $0.89

#80
402-R-80 $0.89

LEAF TIPS

So realistic! Ideal for shell-motion borders too.

#65s
402-R-659 $1.39

#65
402-R-65 $0.89

#113
402-R-113* $1.49

#66
402-R-66 $0.89

#67
402-R-67 $0.89

#68
402-R-68 $0.89

#69
402-R-69 $0.89

#115
402-R-115* $1.49

#73
402-R-73 $0.89

#74
402-R-74 $0.89

#75
402-R-75 $0.89

#349/352s
402-R-349 $1.39

#366
402-R-366* $1.69

#352
402-R-352 $1.39

#326
402-R-326 $1.39

Makes leaves for larger flowers.

#70
402-R-70 $0.89

#112
402-R-112** $1.49

CLOSED STAR TIPS

Create deeply grooved shells, stars and fleurs-de-lis.

 #24
402-R-24 $0.89

#29
402-R-29 $0.89

#35
402-R-35 $0.89

 #26
402-R-26 $0.89

#30
402-R-30 $0.89

#133
402-R-133 $0.89

 #27
402-R-27 $0.89

#31
402-R-31 $0.89

#54
402-R-54 $0.89

 #28
402-R-28 $0.89

#33
402-R-33 $0.89

RUFFLE TIPS

Plain, fluted, shell-border, special effects.

#86
402-R-86 $0.89

#353
402-R-353 $1.39

#402
402-R-402* $1.49

#87
402-R-87† $0.89

#340
402-R-340 $1.39

#406
402-R-406* $1.69

#88
402-R-88† $0.89

#401
402-R-401 $1.39

#403
402-R-403** $1.69

#100
402-R-100 $0.89

---

† For left-handers

CAKE DECORATING

Decorating Sets

The Supreme Set

"The Works". Decorate many advanced wedding, floral and basketweave cakes as well as basic cakes. This 53 pc. set includes: metal decorating tips #2, 3, 5, 7, 12, 16, 18, 21, 32, 47, 65, 67, 101, 103, 104, 129, 225 and 352; 24 disposable 12 in. decorating bags, two tip couplers, 5 icing colors (.5 oz. each), one 1 ¼ in. flower nail No. 9; 8 in. angled spatula; storage tray and a 40-page book: *Cake Decorating Beginner's Guide.*

2104-R-2546 Set/53 $29.99

The Deluxe Set

Create many advanced floral cakes and basic wedding cakes. This 37 pc. set includes: metal decorating tips #3, 5, 7, 12, 16, 21, 32, 67, 104 and 225; 18 disposable 12 in. decorating bags, two tip couplers, 4 icing colors (.5 oz. each), one 1 ¼ in. flower nail No. 9, storage tray and a 40-page book: *Cake Decorating Beginner's Guide.*

2104-R-2540 Set/37 $19.99

The Basic Set

A solid foundation set for decorating. This 25 pc. set includes: metal decorating tips #3, 16, 21, 67 and 104; twelve 12 in. disposable decorating bags; two tip couplers; 4 icing colors (.5 oz. each); 1 ¼ in. flower nail No. 9; 12-page instruction booklet.

2104-R-2536 Set/25 $11.99

The Starter Set

Perfect for Wilton character cakes! This 18 pc. set includes: metal decorating tips #3, 16, 21 and 67; 6 disposable 12 in. decorating bags; 2 tip couplers; 5 liquid color packets (.067 fl. oz. each); 10-page instruction booklet.

2104-R-2530 Set/18 $6.99

Tip Sets

Deluxe Tip Set

Includes: 26 metal decorating tips: #2, 4, 7, 13, 16, 17, 18, 30, 42, 46, 47, 61, 65, 66, 67, 74, 78, 97, 98, 101, 102, 103, 104, 106, 107 and 199; 1 ¼ in. flower nail No. 9; tip coupler; plastic tipsaver case.

2104-R-6666 Set/29 $25.99

---

101 Piece Tool Caddy Collection

This convenient caddy contains our most complete collection of tools, colors and flavors for the cake decorator. It's a great way to organize, carry and store the essentials—tips, couplers, colors, spatulas and more. Lift-out tray holds tips, couplers, brushes and colors securely. Upright storage prevents spills and makes it easy to find what you need. Generous storage area keeps books, spatulas, bags and other large supplies neatly organized.

2109-R-861 Set/101 $129.99

Save over $30
Compared to individual prices

Includes These Tools:

- 8 Icing Colors: Golden Yellow, No-Taste Red, Brown, Violet, Pink, Royal Blue, Black, Kelly Green in .5 oz. jars
- 3 Couplers (2 standard, 1 large)
- 2 Tip/Coupler Dishwasher and Storage Bags
- Tip Cleaning Brush
- 24 Disposable 12 in. Decorating Bags
- 3 Professional Reusable Decorating Bags (8, 10 and 16 in.)
- 4 Tip Covers
- Tip Saver
- 1 ½ in. Flower Nail #7
- 3 Spatulas (8 and 13 in. Angled, 8 in. Tapered)
- Flower Lifter
- Garland Marker
- *Decorating Cakes* Book
- 20 All-Purpose Disposable Decorating Gloves
- Practice Board with Patterns
- 2 Bake-Even Strips
- 8 oz. Clear Vanilla and No-Color Butter Flavors
- Cake Leveler
- Quick Ease Roller
- Easy-Glide Fondant Smoother
- Decorating Brush

Plus 18 Tips:

- Round #1, 2, 2A, 3, 12
- Star #16, 18, 21, 32
- Basketweave #48
- Leaf #67, 352
- Petal #102, 103, 104, 125
- Drop Flower #2D
- Cake Icer #789

---

50 Piece Tool Caddy Decorating Set

We've put together the perfect set for beginning and advanced decorators. The generous selection of tips, colors and tools gives you the flexibility to decorate virtually any kind of cake. There's also plenty of room to add new items and and keep everything organized to save you time. Set includes all tools specified as needed in our Course I class.

2109-R-859 Set/50 $54.99

Save $22
Compared to individual prices

Includes These 19 Tips:

- Round #2, 3, 5, 7, 12
- Open Star #16, 18, 21, 32
- Basketweave #47
- Leaf #67, 352
- Petal #101, 103, 104
- Multi-Opening #233
- Drop Flower #225
- Closed Star #133
- Large Drop Flower #2004 (2D)

Plus Tools:

- Tip Brush
- Decorating Brush
- 1 ½ in. Flower Nail #7
- 2 Standard Couplers
- 18 Disposable Bags
- One 10 in. Professional Bag
- 8 in. Angled Spatula
- Four .5 oz. Icing Colors: Lemon Yellow, Christmas Red, Royal Blue, Leaf Green
- Practice Board with stand
- *Cake Decorating Beginner's Guide*

Master Tip Set

Includes 52 metal decorating tips: #1, 2, 3, 4, 6, 7, 12, 13, 16, 17, 18, 22, 24, 27, 30, 31, 32, 42, 45, 46, 47, 48, 54, 59, 61, 65, 66, 67, 68, 69, 70, 73, 74, 78, 96, 97, 98, 101, 102, 103, 104, 106, 108, 109, 123, 124, 129, 134, 136, 195, 199 and 2C; two standard tip couplers; two 1 ¼ in. flower nails No. 9; plastic tipsaver case.

2104-R-7778 Set/57 $44.99

Tool Caddy Only

Lift out tray keeps 48 tips and 12 color jars in easy reach (tips and colors not included). Stores colors upright to prevent spilling.

409-R-860 $24.99

Dessert decorator Pro™

It's easy to add beautiful decorations to any dessert or appetizer in minutes! Designed for comfortable one-hand decorating and effortless tip positioning, this is the most convenient dessert tool you'll ever use.

Create beautiful decorations—shells, stars, rosettes, leaves. The great recipe book included is filled with fabulous ideas to tempt your family and friends: Decorate desserts with elegant whipped cream or icing designs. Dress up pastry shells with dramatic swirls of mousse. Add sophistication to savories with pretty piped cream cheese or seafood spread decorations. With Dessert Decorator Pro, you can do it all!
415-R-850 $29.99

Rotating Cylinder
Just turn to place the tip in the correct position for any decoration.

Ergonomic Design
Easy, comfortable grip for right or left hand. Outer sleeve fits your fingers like a glove.

Stainless Steel Cylinder
Preferred by pastry chefs because stainless won't transfer flavors and it maintains temperature of fillings.

Fits Virtually Any Tip/Coupler
Use with the tips included or with most other Wilton tips.

Pull-Out Plunger
Inner ring pushes filling smoothly through cylinder.

Convenient Thumb Lever
The ideal distance from cylinder for comfortable one-handed decorating.

Durable Construction
Cylinder and plunger are housed in an impact-resistant sleeve for years of great decorating performance.

Easy To Fill and Clean
Most parts detach with ease; wash in warm, soapy water.

DESSERT DECORATOR PRO INCLUDES ALL THIS:

Tips in bag for size reference only. Tips included are shown at left.

| Tip #366 Leaf | Tip #4B Star | Tip #125 Petal | Tip #21 Star | Tip #1M Star | Tip #230 Bismarck |

Six Durable Nickel-Plated Tips
Quality metal tips produce perfectly-shaped decorations every time.

Two Tip Couplers
Two sizes to hold standard (small) and large tips.

Tip/Coupler Dishwasher and Storage Bag
Just place nylon mesh bag with tips and couplers in your dishwasher silverware rack for easy tip and coupler cleaning.

Dessert Pro™ Recipes and Instructions — Livret d'instructions et de recettes

Recipes and Instructions
Includes delicious recipes and easy decorating instructions for elegant desserts and appetizers.

dessert decorator max™

Create sensational decorations for desserts and appetizers in minutes! One easy-to-use tool does it all—tops pies with fancy whipped cream lattice designs, accents deviled eggs with a pretty rosette, decorates party crackers with savory spreads, fills cupcakes with buttercream for the perfect kids' party treat. The complete set includes 6 tips and 2 couplers for making pretty designs like stars, shells, flowers, petals, lattice/basketweave, leaves and more. The Dessert Decorator Max also works with virtually any Wilton tip, giving you complete versatility. Instruction/recipe booklet is filled with easy step-by-step decorating instructions and delicious ideas for sweet and savory foods.
415-R-854 $24.99

Pull-Out Plunger
Inner ring pushes icing through cylinder; cleans easily with soap and water.

Ergonomic Design
Finger-grip barrel is easy to handle in right or left hand.

Convenient Thumb Lever
Lets you hold tool and decorate with one hand.

Easy To Fill and Clean
Parts detach easily; top rack dishwasher safe.

Rotating Cylinder
Places tip in the perfect decorating position with an easy turn.

Basic Dessert Decorator

Give your cakes and pastries a beautiful finishing touch in seconds. The easy-to-control lever helps you fill and decorate all kinds of desserts. Decorating nozzles can pipe stars, rosettes, shells and many other accents. Works great with Wilton Buttercream Icing Mix and Whipped Icing Mix, p. 132.
415-R-825 $10.99

Prepare delicious desserts, toppings, fillings and whipped cream quickly and easily!

The Dessert Whipper Pro makes it easy to add a luxurious look and rich taste to your favorite desserts and drinks! Create the Classic Strawberry Pie with pretty rosettes of fresh whipped cream. Top off sundaes with dollops of chocolate and caramel-flavored cream. Fill cream puffs or cannoli with a rich, creamy center. Or serve cups of hot cocoa crowned with chocolate mint cream.

With the Dessert Whipper Pro, it's a breeze to whip up all these luscious toppings and fillings. Just pour ingredients in the canister, twist on a charger, shake and dispense using the filling or decorating tips. No mess or guessing: everything is perfectly blended in the canister. The easy-press lever with one-hand operation gives you great portion control—anyone can make desserts look great.

Uses iSi charger cartridges, which twist on safely and easily. Complete set includes Dessert Whipper Pro, 10 charger cartridges, 2 decorating tips and recipe booklet.
2104-R-1290 $59.99

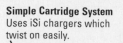

Simple Cartridge System
Uses iSi chargers which twist on easily.

TWO VERSATILE TIPS
Use straight tip for filling, tulip tip for decorating.

Easy-Press Lever
Provides portion control.

iSi Charger Cartridges
2104-R-1447 Set/5 $5.99

Recipe Book Included!
Delicious recipes for maple cream, strawberry whip, chocolate/mocha mousse, peach mousse, cranberry whip and more.

High Yield Design
Produces 5 times the amount of liquid whipping cream poured in!

Brushed Aluminum
Easy to handle and resists smudges.

Wilton

SO EASY TO USE!

1. Fill canister with cream.

2. Twist on a charger.

3. Remove charger, replace cap & shake.

4. Press handle to dispense.

Press Sets

Block Letter Press Set
Includes Best, Happy, Wishes, Anniversary, Birthday, and Congratulations and letter holder. Word height ⅞ in.
2104-R-2077 Set/6 $3.69

Italic Make-Any-Message Press Set
Pretty and sophisticated letters for a custom message. Press words up to 10 ½ in. wide, letters ¾ in. high.
2104-R-2277 Set/58 $7.99

Make-Any-Message Letter Press Set
Imprint the perfect sentiment! Press words up to 10 ½ in. wide, letters ¾ in. high.
2104-R-10 Set/56 $7.99

Decorator Favorites Pattern Press Set
Includes double heart; fleur de lis; medallion; open heart; closed scroll; heart; large, medium and small c-scrolls; crest; double scroll and vine.
2104-R-3160 Set/12 $5.99

Designer Pattern Press Set
Imprints elegant designs for easy overpiping. Includes symmetrical swirl, small and large fleurs de lis, corner flourish, flower, heart bow, scroll and curlicues.
2104-R-3112 Set/8 $5.99

Script Message Press Set
Combine the words Best, Happy, Wishes, Birthday, Anniversary, and Congratulations. Word height ⅞ in.
2104-R-2061 Set/6 $3.69

ORDER TOLL FREE: 800-794-5866

Cupcakes 'N More™ Dessert Stands

Individually decorated cupcakes are the perfect way to add a personal touch to celebrations. Now, with Cupcakes 'N More, you have the perfect way to serve them! The look is fresh and fun, featuring bold silver-finished wire spirals to securely hold each cupcake. The twisting, towering design is perfect for any setting— showers, kids' birthdays, weddings, holidays and more.

See the *Dazzling Displays* section, featuring Cupcakes 'N More™ starting on p. 90

GREAT DISPLAY IDEAS!

Easy to assemble!
Just stack each layer of cupcakes onto the locking center rod.

NEW!

Keeps looking great!
Non-toxic, silver-finished metal has a durable non-chip finish.

Collapsible design
Stores easily and safely.

Angled holders
Give the best view of cupcake tops!

Standard
12 in. high x 13 wide.
Holds 23 cupcakes.
307-R-826 $29.99

Large
15 in. high x 18 wide.
Holds 38 cupcakes.
307-R-651 $39.99

SO MANY EXCITING WAYS TO SERVE!

Dessert Tables

Table Centerpieces

Wedding and Shower Party Favors

ORDER ONLINE: WWW.WILTON.COM

Servers and Savers

THE ULTIMATE 3-IN-1 CADDY™ NEW!

The world's most versatile and safest cake carrier.

- Reversible tray holds 12 standard cupcakes/muffins or 24 minis
- Roomy base holds a 9 x 13 decorated cake when used without tray
- 4 locking latches keep baked goods secure
- Extra-thick walls provide the ultimate protection
- Wide, comfortable handle is easy to grab and go
- Textured base resists scratches when cutting cakes
- Sleek see-through design presents desserts at their best

It's the most convenient way to take along cakes, cupcakes, muffins and more! The Ultimate 3-In-1 Caddy features an exclusive reversible cupcake tray which holds 12 standard or 24 mini cupcakes. Or, remove the tray to carry up to a 9 x 13 in. decorated cake on the sturdy locking base. The see-through cover has higher sides to keep icing flowers and tall decorations protected. You'll also use the caddy at home, to keep pies, cookies and brownies fresh for days after baking. 17.9 x 14.4 x 6.8 in. high.
2105-R-9958 $19.99

Cake Caddy™

Carry decorated desserts with ease! The 6 in. high clear plastic dome has 3 locking latches that hold the base securely in place wherever you go. Convenient handle gives you a firm grip for a safe trip from your car to the party. The elegant base is approximately 13 in. diameter and holds and stores up to 10 in. round cake or pie, cupcakes, cookies and more.
2105-R-9952 $14.99

Cake Dome

An elegant way to display and protect your cake—looks great in any setting. The unbreakable polycarbonate dome gives a clear view of the cake as it rests on the graceful pedestal. The 7 ½ in. high crystal clear dome is the ideal height for multi-layer cakes, angel food, cupcakes and muffins. Pedestal is approximately 12 ½ in. diameter and can be stored inside dome. Holds up to a 10 in. round cake. Instructions and recipes included.
307-R-702 $34.99

Cake Saver

The convenient way to carry decorated cakes! Its generous size accommodates borders and cake top decorations easily. Great for carrying or storing angel food, cheese cakes, pies and layer cakes. Fits a 10 in. round cake with borders or a 12 in. cake without borders. 14 in. round base and 6 in. high cover.
415-R-905 $12.99

Bakeware

Wilton is the #1 bakeware brand in America. From fun novelty shapes for birthday cakes to dramatic cast aluminum styles for elegant desserts, count on Wilton for the best results.

DECORATIVE BAKEWARE

With our non-stick cast aluminum bakeware, anyone can create desserts with elegant shapes and spectacular detail. Heavyweight cast aluminum conducts heat extremely evenly and allows for uniquely sculpted shapes you will be proud to serve. Bake in non-stick cast aluminum as you would in any aluminum pan. Cakes and breads rise high and bake evenly. The premium non-stick surface means foods release perfectly and cleanup is a breeze. Lifetime Warranty.

NEW!

Gift
11 ⅛ in. x 9 ⅝ in. x 1 ½ in. 10 cup capacity;
takes 6 ½ to 7 cups of cake batter.*
2105-R-5027 $27.99

NEW!

Perennial
9 ⅝ in. diameter x 3 ⅛ in. 10 cup capacity;
takes 6 ½ to 7 cups of cake batter.*
2105-R-5031 $27.99

NEW!

Tulip
9 ½ in. diameter x 4 in. 10 cup capacity;
takes 6 ½ to 7 cups of cake batter.*
2105-R-5032 $27.99

Crown of Hearts
11 in. wide x 2 ½ in. 10 cup capacity;
takes 6 ½ to 7 cups of cake batter.*
2105-R-5011 $27.99

6 Cavity Mini Hearts
Each cavity 4 in. x 2 in. 6 cup capacity;
takes 3 to 3 ½ cups of cake batter.*
2105-R-5012 $27.99

Queen of Hearts
9 in. diameter x 3 ¼ in. 10 cup capacity;
takes 6 ½ to 7 cups of cake batter.*
2105-R-5001 $27.99

Cascade
9 ½ in. diameter x 4 ¾ in. 10 cup capacity; takes
6 ½ to 7 cups of cake batter.*
2105-R-1199 $27.99

Belle
9 in. diameter x 3 ¾ in. 10 cup capacity;
takes 6 ½ to 7 cups of cake batter.*
2105-R-1186 $27.99

Marquise
8 ¾ in. diameter x 4 in. 10 cup capacity;
takes 6 ½ to 7 cups of cake batter.*
2105-R-1188 $27.99

*For cakes, fill pans ½ to ⅔ full.

CHECKERBOARD CAKE SET

NEW!

With this unique baking set, you'll create cakes with an exciting multi-colored pattern—there's style in every slice! Baking is easy with the Batter Dividing Ring included. Just place the Dividing Ring in one of the three 9 x 1½ in. pans in the set and follow instructions for adding dark and light colors of batter in the divisions. Repeat for 2 more layers, pouring the dark and light batters in opposite sections for the middle layer. Use the Dividing Ring's easy-lift handles to lift out ring before baking, then stack cakes to form the checkerboard. Enjoy two tastes in one cake—try the Golden Yellow/Chocolate recipe on the package. Great for colorful holiday cakes, too! Three pans feature oversized handles for safe lifting from the oven; each takes 5½ cups batter. Non-stick steel pans; plastic Dividing Ring.
2105-R-9961 Set/4 $12.99

Non-Stick Bakeware

Our premium non-stick bakeware combines superior non-stick performance, serving convenience and elegant design, to provide the highest level of baking satisfaction.

- *Oversized handles for safe lifting of the pan*
- *Pan dimensions permanently stamped into handles*
- *Heavy-duty steel construction prevents warping*
- *Durable, reinforced non-stick coating offers superior release and easy cleanup*
- *10-Year Warranty*

CAKE AND PIE PANS

9 x 1½ in. Round Cake
2105-R-408 $7.99

9 x 9 x 2 in. Square Cake
2105-R-407 $8.99

2105-R-408

11 x 7 x 1½ in. Biscuit/Brownie
2105-R-443 $9.99

13 x 9 x 2 in. Oblong Cake
2105-R-411 $11.99

13 x 9 x 2 in. Oblong Cake w/Plastic Cover
2105-R-423 $15.99

2105-R-411

9 x 1½ in. Pie w/Fluted Edges
2105-R-438 $7.99

MUFFIN AND LOAF PANS

6 Cup Regular Muffin
2105-R-405 $9.99

12 Cup Mini Muffin
2105-R-403 $6.99

12 Cup Regular Muffin
2105-R-406 $13.99

2105-R-405

Large Loaf
9¼ x 5¼ x 2¾ in.
2105-R-402 $7.99

4 Cavity Mini Loaf
5¾ x 3 x 2⅛ in.
2105-R-444 $16.99

2105-R-402

SPRINGFORM PANS

4 x 1¾ in. Round
2105-R-453 $5.49

6 x 2¾ in. Round
2105-R-447 $9.99

9 x 2¾ in. Round
2105-R-414 $13.99

2105-R-435

10 x 2¾ in. Round
2105-R-435 $14.99

4 x 1¾ in. Heart
2105-R-457 $7.99

9 x 2¾ in. Heart
2105-R-419 $16.99

2105-R-419

COOKIE PANS AND SHEETS

Small Cookie
13¼ x 9¼ x ⅝ in.
2105-R-436 $10.99

Medium Cookie
15¼ x 10¼ x ¾ in.
2105-R-412 $11.99

2105-R-412

Large Cookie/Jelly Roll
17¼ x 11½ x 1 in.
2105-R-413 $13.99

Jumbo Air Insulated Sheet
18 x 14 in.
2105-R-422 $19.99

2105-R-422

COOLING GRIDS

10 x 16 in.
2305-R-228
$8.99

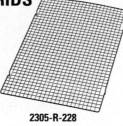
2305-R-228

14½ x 20 in.
2305-R-229
$12.99

13 in. Round
2305-R-230
$9.49

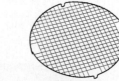
2305-R-230

3-Tier Stackable
15⅞ x 9⅞ in. stackable 3-tier grid.
2105-R-459
$10.99

2105-R-459

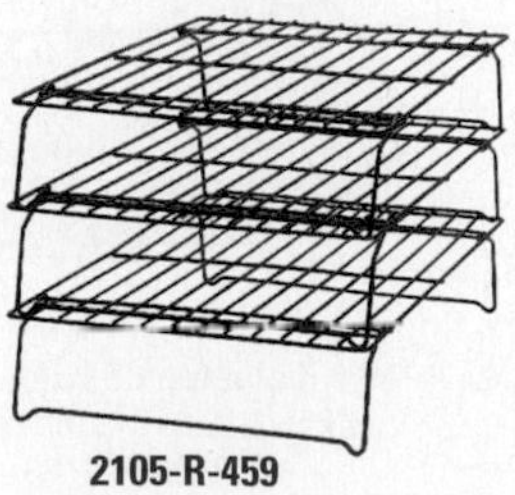

SPECIALTY PANS

Fluted Tube
9¾ x 3⅜ in.
2105-R-416 $13.99

6 Cavity Mini Fluted Tube
4⅛ x 2 in.
2105-R-445 $16.99

2105-R-445

Angel Food
9⅜ x 4¼ in.
2105-R-415 $15.99

14 in. Pizza Crisper
14 x ⅝ in.
2105-R-420 $13.99

2105-R-420

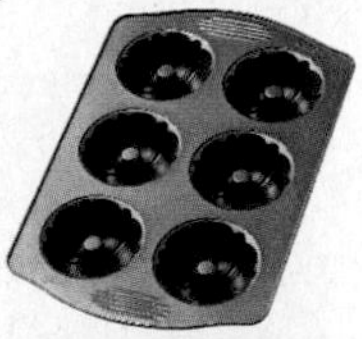

TART/QUICHE PANS

9 x 1⅛ in. Round
2105-R-442 $9.99

11 x 1⅛ in. Round
2105-R-450 $10.99

10 x 1⅛ in. Heart
2105-R-452 $9.99

2105-R-450

Round 3-Pc. Set
8 x 1⅛ in., 9 x 1⅛ in., and 10 x 1⅛ in.
2105-R-451 Set/3 $21.99

Brioche 6-Pc. Set
3¼ x 1¼ in.
2105-R-6762 Set/6 $6.99

2105-R-452

Tartlet 6-Pc. Set
4¾ x 1⅞ x ½ in.
2105-R-6761 Set/6 $6.99

4 in. Tart 4-Pc. Set
4 x ¾ in. with removable bottom.
2105-R-466 $9.99

4 in. Tart/Quiche 6-Pc. Set
4 x ¾ in. with removable bottom.
2105-R-441 $14.99

2105-R-6762

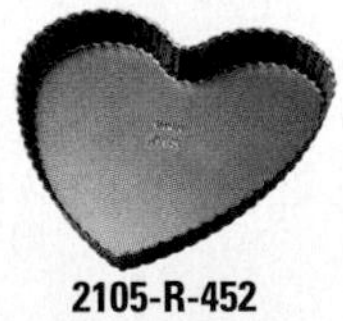

Decorator Preferred®

Professional Aluminum Bakeware

Our most popular bakeware—built with the most features to help decorators bake their best. Compare these benefits to any brand and discover why Decorator Preferred was rated #1 by Good Housekeeping.*

*The May 1999 Good Housekeeping Institute Report rates this Wilton Professional Pan #1 out of 31 different 9 in. round pans.

STRAIGHT SIDES

Bake perfect 90° corners for the precise look wedding cakes require. Ordinary bakeware has rounded corners, giving cakes rounded edges.

GRIP LIP EDGES

Extra-wide rims make heavy filled pans easy to handle.

PURE ALUMINUM

The best material for baking cakes—creates a light, golden brown cake surface, beautiful for decorating.

SUPERIOR THICKNESS

Thicker than ordinary bakeware, built to distribute heat evenly for more consistent baking.

HANDCRAFTED CONSTRUCTION

Sheets and squares are handwelded for excellent detail and durability.

LIFETIME WARRANTY

Superior construction and performance designed and guaranteed to last a lifetime.

ROUNDS

What a selection of sizes—including the hard-to-find 18 in. Half Round, which lets you bake and ice two halves to create one 18 in. round cake.

6 x 2 in.
2105-R-6122 $6.49

8 x 2 in.
2105-R-6136 $7.49

9 x 2 in.
2105-R-6137 $8.49

10 x 2 in.
2105-R-6138 $9.99

12 x 2 in.
2105-R-6139 $11.99

14 x 2 in.
2105-R-6140 $16.99

16 x 2 in.
2105-R-6141 $18.99

6 x 3 in.
2105-R-6106 $7.99

8 x 3 in.
2105-R-6105 $8.99

10 x 3 in.
2105-R-6104 $10.99

12 x 3 in.
2105-R-6103 $13.99

14 x 3 in.
2105-R-6102 $16.99

16 x 3 in.
2105-R-6101 $19.99

**18 x 3 in.
Half Round**
2105-R-6100 $21.99

3-Pc. Round Set
6, 10 and 14 in. diameter x 3 in. deep.
2105-R-6114 Set/3 $34.99

HEARTS

Ultimate heart cake is beautiful for showers, weddings, more!

6 x 2 in.
2105-R-600 $5.99

8 x 2 in.
2105-R-601 $6.99

10 x 2 in.
2105-R-602 $8.99

12 x 2 in.
2105-R-607 $10.99

14 x 2 in.
2105-R-604 $12.99

16 x 2 in.
2105-R-605 $14.99

Contour

Create cakes with an elegant, rounded top edge. This is the perfect shape for positioning rolled fondant. 9 x 3 in. deep.
2105-R-6121 $11.99

Heating Core

Distributes heat to bake large cakes evenly. Recommended for pans 10 in. diameter or larger. Releases easily from cake.
3 ½ x 3 ½ x 4 in. diameter.
417-R-6100 $6.99

SHEETS

Extra-thick aluminum distributes heat efficiently on these large pans.

9 x 13 x 2 in.
2105-R-6146 $15.99

11 x 15 x 2 in.
2105-R-6147 $17.99

12 x 18 x 2 in.
2105-R-6148 $21.99

SQUARES

Perfect 90° corners give you the flawless look necessary for wedding tiers.

8 x 2 in.
2105-R-6142 $9.99

10 x 2 in.
2105-R-6143 $13.99

12 x 2 in.
2105-R-6144 $16.99

Springform Pans

When shopping for a springform pan, you want strong construction and an easy-release design that will let you remove a perfect cheesecake every time. Wilton springform pans are built tough, with strong springlocks that hold up year after year. The removable waffle-textured bottom design keeps crusts from sticking while distributing heat evenly. Springlock releases sides. Aluminum.

6 x 3 in.
2105-R-4437 $10.99

8 x 3 in.
2105-R-8464 $11.99

9 x 3 in.
2105-R-5354 $12.99

10 x 3 in.
2105-R-8465 $12.99

Performance Pans™

The classic aluminum pans—durable, even-heating and built to hold their shape through years of use. We named them Performance Pans because they perform beautifully. These are great all-purpose pans. You'll use them for casseroles, entrees, baked desserts and more. Wilton has sold millions of Performance Pans because decorators and bakers know they can depend on them.

SweetHeart Pan

A gently curving shape gives the classic heart a more romantic flair. Whether you accent it with pretty icing flowers or pair it with bold fondant decorations, this cake will charm guests for birthdays, Mother's Day, Valentine's Day, showers and more. Takes 1 standard mix. 10¼ x 11 x 2 in. Aluminum.
2105-R-1197 $10.99

SQUARES

6 x 2 in.
507-R-2180 $6.49

8 x 2 in. deep
2105-R-8191 $7.99

10 x 2 in.
2105-R-8205 $9.99

12 x 2 in.
2105-R-8213 $13.99

14 x 2 in.
2105-R-8220 $17.99

16 x 2 in.
2105-R-8231 $19.99

ROUNDS

6 x 2 in.
2105-R-2185 $6.49

8 x 2 in.
2105-R-2193 $7.49

10 x 2 in.
2105-R-2207 $8.49

12 x 2 in.
2105-R-2215 $10.99

14 x 2 in.
2105-R-3947 $13.99

16 x 2 in.
2105-R-3963 $16.99

2-Pan Round Set
9 x 2 in. deep
2105-R-7908 $12.49

SHEETS

9 x 13 x 2 in.
2105-R-1308 $10.99

11 x 15 x 2 in.
2105-R-158 $14.99

12 x 18 x 2 in.
2105-R-182 $16.99

Covered Baking Pan

Clear, durable cover makes it easy to transport desserts and keep them fresh at home. 11 x 15 x 2 in.
2105-R-3849 $19.99

PERFORMANCE PANS™ SETS

These are the classic shapes every baker needs. Wilton has them in convenient graduated-size sets, to help you create fabulous tiered cakes or individual cakes in exactly the size you want. Quality aluminum holds its shape for years. Each pan is 2 in. deep, except where noted.

Heart Pan Set

Create the ultimate tiered heart cake—a beautiful way to celebrate showers, weddings and more. Now redesigned for a perfect fit when used with our Decorator Preferred® Heart Separator Plates shown on page 166. Includes 6, 10, 12 and 14 in. pans. Aluminum.
2105-R-606 Set/4 $34.99

Round Pan Set
Includes 6, 8, 10, 12 in. pans.
2105-R-2101 Set/4 $29.99

Round Pan Set, 3 in. Deep
Includes 8, 10, 12, 14 in. pans.
2105-R-2932 Set/4 $39.99

Oval Pan Set
Includes 7¾ x 5⅝ in.; 10¾ x 7⅞ in.; 13½ x 9⅞ in. and 16½ x 12⅜ in. pans.
2105-R-2130 Set/4 $34.99

Square Pan Set
Includes 8, 12, 16 in. pans.
2105-R-2132 Set/3 $39.99

Hexagon Pan Set
Includes 6, 9, 12, 15 in. pans.
2105-R-3572 Set/4 $34.99

Petal Pan Set
Includes 6, 9, 12, 15 in. pans.
2105-R-2134 Set/4 $34.99

Specialty Pans

CLASSIC ANGEL FOOD

If you're looking for a healthy dessert, you can't do better than angel food! It's delicious with a simple fresh fruit topping. Removable inner core sleeve, cooling legs. Aluminum.

7 x 4½ in. deep
Takes ½ standard mix.
2105-R-9311 $12.99

10 x 4 in. deep
Takes 1 standard mix.
2105-R-2525 $15.99

Ring Mold
Turn out spectacular cakes, gelatin molds and more. Takes approx. 1½ standard cake mixes. 10½ x 3 in. Aluminum.
2105-R-4013 $10.99

Fancy Ring Mold
Beautiful sculpted pan, ideal for pound cakes, mousse and more! Takes 1 standard mix. 10 in. diameter x 3 in. Aluminum.
2105-R-5008 $10.99

ORDER TOLL FREE: 800-794-5866

Cookie Sheets and Pans

A warped sheet can ruin a batch of cookies. With Wilton Cookie Sheets, you won't worry about warping. The extra-thick aluminum heats evenly for perfectly browned bottoms. Versatile sheets are great for baking appetizers, turnovers and more.

Aluminum
Extra-thick construction heats evenly for perfectly browned bottoms.

Jumbo 14 x 20 in.
2105-R-6213 $16.99

12 ½ x 16 ½ in.
2105-R-2975
$12.99

Insulated Aluminum
Two quality aluminum layers sandwich an insulating layer of air for perfect browning without burning.
14 x 16 in.
2105-R-2644
$17.99

Jelly Roll and Cookie Pans
Wilton pans are 1 in. deep for fuller-looking desserts.

10 ½ x 15 ½ x 1 in.
2105-R-1269 $11.99

12 x 18 x 1 in.
2105-R-4854 $13.99

Muffin Pans

With so many great Wilton muffin pans to choose from, you'll be making muffins—and cupcakes—more often. You'll love our mini pans for the perfect brunch muffins and the jumbo size pan for bakery-style muffins and cupcakes.

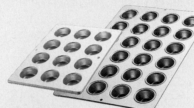

Standard Muffin Pan
Most popular size for morning muffins, after-school cupcakes and desserts. Twelve cups, each 3 in. diameter x 1 in. Aluminum.
2105-R-9310 $15.99

White Standard Baking Cups (shown on p. 184)
Microwave-safe paper. 2 in. diameter.
415-R-2505 Pk./75 $1.49

Mini Muffin Pans
Great for mini cheesecakes, brunches, large gatherings. Cups are 2 in. x ¾ in. Aluminum.
12 Cup 2105-R-2125 $10.99
24 Cup 2105-R-9313 $16.99

White Mini Baking Cups (shown on p. 184)
Microwave-safe paper. 1 ¼ in. diameter.
415-R-2507 Pk./100 $1.49

Jumbo Muffin Pan
Make super-size cupcakes and muffins. Six cups, each 4 x 2 in. Aluminum.
2105-R-1820 $16.99

White Jumbo Baking Cups (shown on p. 184)
Microwave-safe paper. 2 ¼ in. diameter.
415-R-2503 Pk./50 $1.49

Loaf Pans

It's all in the crust. Wilton Loaf Pans bake bread with hearty, crisp crusts and soft, springy centers. Our superior anodized aluminum promotes better browning, resulting in the perfect texture for all your breads.

Petite Loaf Pan
Great for single-size dessert cakes, frozen bread dough. Nine cavities, each 2 ½ x 3 ⅜ x 1 ½ in. Aluminum.
2105-R-8466 $9.99

Mini Loaf Pan
Everyone loves personal-sized nut breads or cakes. Six cavities are 4 ½ x 2 ½ x 1 ½ in. Aluminum.
2105-R-9791 $9.99

9 x 5 in. Loaf Pan
Favorite size for homemade breads and cakes. 2 ¾ in. Aluminum.
2105-R-3688 $6.99

Long Loaf Pan
Legs provide support for cooling angel food cakes, breads or classic cakes. 16 x 4 x 4 ½ in. deep. Aluminum.
2105-R-1588 $13.49

Chrome-Plated Cooling Grids

Sturdy design will never rust. Great selection of popular sizes.

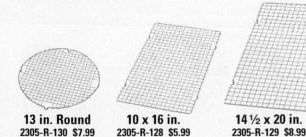

3-Tier Stackable
Use singly or stack to save space while cooling three cake layers or batches of cookies at the same time. Individual grids 13 ½ x 9 ¾ x 3 in. high; stacked grids are 9 ¾ in. high.
2305-R-151 $12.99

13 in. Round
2305-R-130 $7.99

10 x 16 in.
2305-R-128 $5.99

14 ½ x 20 in.
2305-R-129 $8.99

Mini Shaped Pans

Mini Tiered Cakes
One cake mix makes 10-15 mini tiered cakes, perfect for individual wedding, shower and birthday desserts. Six cavity pan is 14 x 10¾ in.; individual cavities are 4 x 4¾ x 1¼ in. deep. Aluminum.
2105-R-3209 $11.99

Mini Embossed Hearts
One cake mix makes 12-18 mini hearts, beautifully scalloped for weddings, showers and brunches. Six cavity pan is 14 x 10¾ in.; individual cavities are 3½ x 3¼ x 1¼ in. deep. Aluminum.
2105-R-3210 $11.99

Mini Fluted Mold Pan
One cake mix makes 12-14 mini fluted molds. Six cavity pan is 14¾ x 9¾ in.; individual cavities are 4 x 1¼ in. deep. Aluminum.
2105-R-2097 $17.99

Mini Bear Pan
One cake mix makes 12-14 mini bears. Six cavity pan is 14½ x 11½ in.; individual cavities are 4⅜ x 4¾ x 1¼ in. deep. Aluminum.
2105-R-4497 $11.99

Mini Train Pan
One cake mix makes 14-16 mini trains. Six cavity pan is 13¾ x 10½ x 1 in. deep; individual cavities are 4¼ x 3¾ x 1 in. deep. Aluminum.
2105-R-4499 $11.99

Mini Star Pan
One cake mix makes 12-14 mini stars. Six cavity pan is 14½ x 11 in.; individual cavities are 4¾ x 1¼ in. deep. Aluminum.
2105-R-1235 $11.99

Wonder Mold Pans

Mini Wonder Mold
Use with Mini Doll Picks for a quartet of party treats. Great with the Wilton Classic Wonder Mold (at right) for a color-coordinated bridal party centerpiece. One cake mix makes 4 to 6 cakes. Pan is 10 x 10 x 3 in. deep. Individual cakes are 3½ x 3 in. Aluminum.
2105-R-3020 $10.99

Mini Doll Picks
4¼ in. high with pick.
1511-R-1019
Pk /4
$5.99

Classic Wonder Mold
Creates an elegant 3-D shape for decorating fabulous dress designs. Use with our Teen Doll Pick to make the doll of your dreams. Pan is 8 in. diameter and 5 in. deep; takes 5–6 cups of firm-textured batter. Heat-conducting rod assures even baking. Kit contains pan, rod, stand, 7 in. brunette doll pick and instructions. Aluminum/plastic.
2105-R-565 $16.99

Teen Doll Pick
Her hair and face are prettier than ever to give your Wonder Mold cakes a realism and sophistication unlike anything you've seen.
7¼ in. high with pick.
$2.99
Brunette
2815-R-101
Blond
2815-R-102

Ethnic Doll Pick
Beautiful face for realistic doll cakes.
7¾ in. high with pick.
2815-R-103
$2.99

ORDER TOLL FREE: 800-794-5866

Novelty Shaped Pans

NEW!

Baby Buggy Pan

These wheels will bring squeals of delight from shower and christening guests. It's a precious carriage design fit for royalty and ready to dress up for colorful cakes or elegant salads and gelatins. One-mix pan is 11¼ x 11¼ x 2 in. deep. Aluminum.
2105-R-3319 **$10.99**

NEW!

Party Hat Pan

When you put on this party hat, you know you're headed for fun! Customize cakes with your favorite colors and fun designs—ideal for molded desserts and salads too. What a great way to cap off any celebration, from birthdays to that New Year's Eve bash! One-mix pan is 10 x 13½ x 2 in. deep. Aluminum.
2105-R-3317 **$10.99**

NEW!

Cupcake Pan

Here's a "cupcake" cake that's big enough for the whole crowd to eat. Bake and decorate it to look like your favorite party cupcake—only bigger! Create endless color and flavor combinations, including the luscious Chocolate Supreme design on the label. One-mix pan is 9¾ x 9½ x 2 in. deep. Aluminum.
2105-R-3318 **$10.99**

NEW!

Lady Bug Pan

These critters are so cute, you'll want them dropping in at all your celebrations. It's a pan that adapts to any environment—try it as a birthday bee, a Valentine love bug or even a friendly fly for that special gardener in your life. One-mix pan is 12 x 10 x 2 in. deep. Aluminum.
2105-R-3316 **$10.99**

Animal Crackers Pan

Make a zoo full of fun animals with this versatile pan! Pick your favorite from the menagerie of critters on the box—pig, cat, giraffe or panda bear—or create a furry face of your own. One-mix pan is 10¾ x 9¼ x 2 in. deep. Aluminum.
2105-R-4945 **$10.99**

Butterfly Pan

A butterfly cake or molded salad is the perfect way to captivate! Go wild with fun colors. One-mix pan is 11 x 8½ x 2 in. deep. Aluminum.
2105-R-2079 **$10.99**

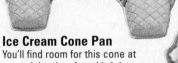

Ice Cream Cone Pan

You'll find room for this cone at any celebration, from birthdays to backyard barbecues. Like a real ice cream cone, create endless flavor and color combinations. One-mix pan is 13¾ x 9¼ x 2 in. deep. Aluminum.
2105-R-2087 **$10.99**

Partysaurus Pan

Our prehistoric party animal is a must-have at all sorts of fun fests—a kid's birthday favorite. One-mix pan is 16 x 10 x 1⅞ in. deep. Aluminum.
2105-R-1280 **$10.99**

Cuddly Lamb Pan

This fleecy friend is the perfect welcome for baby showers, Easter brunches, birthday parties. See the label for 4 great ideas, including a vanilla mousse and a coconut and candy decorated cake. One-mix pan is 11¾ x 8¾ x 2 in. deep. Aluminum.
2105-R-4947 **$10.99**

3-D Rubber Ducky Pan

This bath-time favorite will make the biggest splash for birthdays, baby showers and school celebrations. Five adorable designs included. Two-piece pan takes 5½ cups batter, 9 x 5 x 7 in. high. Aluminum.
2105-R-2094 **$12.99**

Novelty Shaped Pans

Mini Stand-Up Bear Pan Set

Includes baking stand, four clips and instructions. Two-piece pan takes 1 cup of batter; standard pound cake mix makes about 4 cakes. Assembled cakes are 4 x 3 ¼ x 4 ¾ in. high. Aluminum.
2105-R-489 Set/8 $11.99

Stand-Up Cuddly Bear Set

Five decorating ideas on the box! Two-piece pan takes 6 ⅔ cups of firm textured batter. Includes 6 clips, heat-conducting core and instructions. Pan is 9 x 6 ¾ x 8 ⅝ in. high. Aluminum.
2105-R-603 Set/10 $21.99

Huggable Teddy Bear Pan

This classic never hibernates! From birthdays to baby showers to school parties, he's used all year. One-mix pan is 13 ½ x 12 ¼ x 2 in. Aluminum.
2105-R-4943 $10.99

Topsy Turvy Pan

Our topsy turvy "tiered" cake is just the right look for wacky birthdays, wild parties or special occasions. One-mix pan is 10 ¼ x 12 x 2 in. Aluminum.
2105-R-4946 $10.99

One-Mix Book Pan

This open book details life's important chapters—birthdays, baby showers, graduations and more. Five ways to decorate included. 13 x 9 ½ x 2 in. Aluminum.
2105-R-972 $10.99

Two-Mix Book Pan

Serves up to 30. 15 x 11 ½ x 2 ¾ in. Aluminum.
2105-R-2521 $14.99

Stand-Up House Pan

A delightful "welcome home". haunted houses, Easter hutches, Christmas cottages, school houses and dog houses are a few ideas for this pan. Cakes can stand up or lay flat. One-mix pan is 9 x 3 x 8 ¾ in. high. Aluminum.
2105-R-2070 $12.99

Enchanted Castle Pan

Royal treat for little girls' birthdays or any event. Wonderful for molded sugar or ice cream. One-mix pan is 11 ½ x 11 ¾ x 2 in. Aluminum.
2105-R-2031 $10.99

Guitar Pan

Whatever your musical choice, a guitar cake sets the tone for fun at your next party! Celebrate school band concerts, kid and adult birthdays! One-mix pan is 16 ½ x 8 ½ x 2 in. Aluminum.
2105-R-570 $10.99

Star Pan

Brighten birthdays, opening nights, even law enforcement occasions. One-mix pan is 12 ¾ x 12 ¾ x 1 ⅞ in. Aluminum.
2105-R-2512 $10.99

Over The Hill Tombstone Pan

Optimistically mark the passing of one more year. One-mix pan is 13 x 9 ¼ x 2 in. Aluminum.
2105-R-1237 $10.99

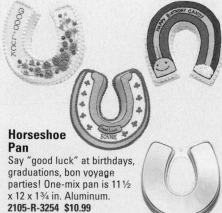

Horseshoe Pan

Say "good luck" at birthdays, graduations, bon voyage parties! One-mix pan is 11 ½ x 12 x 1 ¾ in. Aluminum.
2105-R-3254 $10.99

Sports Ball Pan Set
Use this four-piece set to create a perfect sports cake centerpiece. Includes two 6 in. diameter half-ball pans and two metal baking stands. Each pan half takes 2 ½ cups batter. Aluminum.
2105-R-6506 Set/4 $10.99

Soccer Ball Pan
A great way to reward a season or a game well done! One-mix pan is 8 ¾ x 8 ¾ x 3 ½ in. Aluminum.
2105-R-2044 $10.99

Little Pirate Pan
Cute pirate-in-training design is easy to transform into just about any character. One-mix pan is 9 in. x 14 ¼ in. x 2 in. Aluminum.
2105-R-2078 $10.99

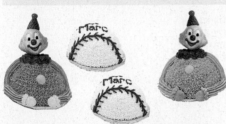

Mini Ball Pan
Ice two mini balls and push together for a 3-D effect. One cake mix makes 10–12 mini balls. Six cavities, each 3 ½ x 3 ½ x 1 ½ in. deep. Aluminum.
2105-R-1760 $10.99

First and Ten Football Pan
Touching down at Super Bowl parties, homecomings, award dinners and much more. One-mix pan is 12 x 7 ¾ x 3 in. deep. Aluminum.
2105-R-6504 $10.99

Little Hero Pan
Bring their favorite figures to life! One-mix pan is 13 ¼ x 6 ½ x 2 in. Aluminum.
2105-R-2077 $10.99

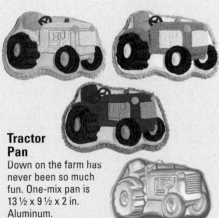

Tractor Pan
Down on the farm has never been so much fun. One-mix pan is 13 ½ x 9 ½ x 2 in. Aluminum.
2105-R-2063 $10.99

Train Pan
Load with delicious cargo! One-mix pan is 14 x 7 ¼ x 2 in. Aluminum.
2105-R-2076 $10.99

Choo-Choo Train Pan Set
Two-piece pan snaps together to create a cake 10 x 4 x 6 in. high. Takes 6 cups batter. Aluminum.
2105-R-2861 Set/2 $11.99

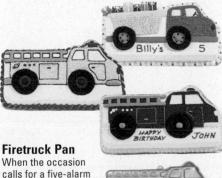

Firetruck Pan
When the occasion calls for a five-alarm celebration. One-mix pan is 15 ½ x 8 ½ x 2 in. Aluminum.
2105-R-2061 $10.99

3-D Cruiser Pan
Bake exciting 3-D cakes, ready to customize for all occasions. One-mix pan is 11 x 6 ¾ x 4 in. high. Aluminum.
2105-R-2043 $10.99

Race Car Pan
Customize it with your favorite colors and racing team identification. One-mix pan is 12 ½ x 9 ½ x 2 in. Aluminum.
2105-R-1350 $10.99

Wedding Style

Wilton has a beautiful selection of products for today's bride. From toasting glasses to garters to favors, we'll help you design the wedding day of your dreams!

Wedding Ensembles

Fulfill your wedding day dreams with the finest coordinated wedding accessories. Nicely presented, a complete collection makes a beautiful gift. Or enjoy the flexibility of choosing individual accessories that personalize the wedding day!

Flower Basket
Held by the flower girl, as she scatters Rose Petals along the bridal path. Petals not included.

Ring Bearer's Pillow
Lovingly carried by the Ring Bearer, this beautiful pillow adds elegance to your wedding ceremony.

Guest Book
The perfect wedding keepsake—guests sign and add their good wishes on your special day.

Guest Pen and Holder
Make signing the guest book easy and elegant.

NEW!

Graceful
Sparkling rhinestone accents.

Sold Separately

Flower Basket	120-R-078	$19.99
Ring Bearer Pillow	120-R-077	$19.99
Guest Pen	120-R-076	$14.99
Guest Book	120-R-079	$19.99

Timeless
Beautiful woven satin ribbon design.

Sold Separately and as a Set

Flower Basket	120-R-604	$19.99
Ring Bearer Pillow	120-R-101	$19.99
Guest Pen	120-R-831	$14.99
Guest Book	120-R-829	$19.99
Complete Set of 4	120-R-460	$69.99

Elegance
Sophistication abounds with tailored satin and ribbon trim.

Sold Separately

Flower Basket	120-R-331	$19.99
Ring Bearer Pillow	120-R-334	$19.99
Guest Pen & Book	120-R-871	$29.99

Eternity
Upscale quilting with floral trim—the essence of bridal chic. Ivory.

Sold Separately

Flower Basket	120-R-339	$19.99
Ring Bearer Pillow	120-R-338	$19.99
Guest Pen & Book	120-R-328	$29.99

Expressions
Lattice ribbon design with delicate floral blooms and ribbon trim.

Sold Separately

Flower Basket	120-R-872	$19.99
Ring Bearer Pillow	120-R-873	$19.99
Guest Pen & Book	120-R-874	$29.99

Traditional
Gleaming white with lace and ribbon trim.

Sold Separately and as a Set

Flower Basket	1006-R-603	$3.99
Ring Bearer Pillow	120-R-100	$15.99
Guest Pen	120-R-804	$14.99
Guest Book	120-R-800	$14.99
Complete Set of 4	120-R-095	$44.99

Radiance
Beautifully designed and crafted with opulent rose blooms and wide organza ribbon trim. Set includes Flower Basket, Ring Bearer Pillow, Guest Pen and Guest Book.
120-R-261 **Set/4 $69.99**

Sold as a Set

Classic
Perfect choice for the bride who appreciates the allure of elegance. Satin with satin ribbon trim. Set includes Flower Basket, Ring Bearer Pillow, Guest Pen and Guest Book.
120-R-472 **Set/4 $69.99**

Sold as a Set

Enchanting
Inspired by the romance of a flower garden, designed in satin with fabric blooms. Set includes Flower Basket, Ring Bearer Pillow, Guest Pen and Guest Book.
120-R-083 **Set/4 $69.99**

Sold as a Set

ORDER TOLL FREE: 800-794-5866

Wedding Day Accessories
UNITY CANDLES & TAPER SETS

NEW!

Graceful
Sparkling rhinestone accents. Unity Candle is 9 in. high x 3 in. diameter; Taper Candles are 10 in. high.
Unity Candle 120-R-461 $24.99
Taper Candles 120-R-463 Set/2 $7.99
Unity Candle and Taper Candles Set
120-R-065 Set/3 $29.99

Ribbon/Rings
Elegant carved detail.

Unity Candle	**Taper Candles**
9 in. high x 2¾ in. diameter.	10 in. high.
120-R-710 $19.99	**120-R-726 Set/2 $4.99**

Silver Candleholder Set
Keepsake-quality set holds the unity candle and tapers for the candle lighting ceremony, then adds the romantic glow of candlelight to your reception table. At home, you'll use the candleholders year-round for special dates, dinner parties and holidays. Silver-plated; ribbon trim. Unity candle holder is 6¼ in. high; holds a pillar candle up to 3¾ in. diameter. Each taper candle holder is 5½ in. high; holds standard size tapers. Candles not included.
120-R-448 Set/3 $34.99

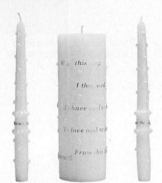

With This Ring
Words of love encircle the candle design. Unity Candle is 9 in. high x 3 in. diameter; Taper Candles are 10 in. high.
120-R-064 Set/3 $29.99

Love, Honor, Cherish
Contemporary lettering. Unity Candle is 9 in. high x 3 in. diameter; Taper Candles are 10 in. high.
120-R-066 Set/3 $29.99

Heart Silver Toasting Glasses and Servers Ensemble
For toasting the bride and groom and cutting the cake. Elegant silver-plated heart design, organza ribbon and pearl trim. Silver–plated. Engrave for a beautiful keepsake.
120-R-232 Set/4 $49.99

TOASTING GLASSES
Beautiful stemware to use at the reception, then at home!

Graceful
Height: 10½ in.
120-R-716 Set/2 $21.99

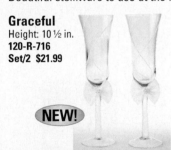

NEW!

Pearl
Height: 9½ in.
120-R-783 Set/2 $21.99

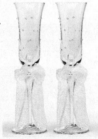

Fluted
Height: 10 in.
120-R-784 Set/2 $21.99

Rosebud
Height: 8⅜ in.
120-R-708 Set/2 $21.99

SERVING PIECES
Quality cake knife and servers will be used again, on special occasions at gatherings with family and friends throughout your married life. Engrave the blades to create beautiful keepsakes.

NEW!

Graceful
Stainless steel blades with acrylic handles.
120-R-718 Set/2 $24.99

Crystal Look
Stainless steel blades with acrylic handles.
120-R-4003 Set/2 $24.99

Silver
Silverplated, with sculpting on handles.
120-R-4004 Set/2 $29.99

Wedding Day Accessories

FLORAL ACCESSORIES

French Rose Wedding Bouquet

Perfect, beautiful blooms to keep or to use during the bouquet toss. Hand-crafted, fine silk flowers with wrapped stem. Bouquet measures approx. 8 ½ in. diameter with 4 in. stem.
120-R-1013
$24.99

White Rose Boutonniere

Perfect for weddings, prom, special occasions
1006-R-694 $4.99

Fresh Look Bouquet Holder

Make bouquets for the wedding party! It's easy to do, using your favorite silk or fabric flowers.
1006-R-611 $7.99

Bouquet Holders

Slip over stems to dress up any bouquet.

White Organza
10 ½ in. diameter.
1006-R-992 $1.99

White Lace
10 ½ in. diameter.
1006-R-604 $1.99

Silver Bouquet Holder

Arrange the bride's favorite flowers in this keepsake holder. Silver-plated. 7 ½ in. long.
120-R-651 $12.99

Flower Petals

Fill the flower girl's basket, scatter on the cake table, decorate favors. Lifelike 2 ½ in. diameter flower petals. Approx. 300 petals in pack.
$9.99

Lavender Hydrangea
1006-R-879

White Rose
1006-R-698

Blush Rose
1006-R-697

Red Rose
1006-R-695

GLOVES

For all celebrations—weddings, prom, parties, Communion and costumes. In white.

Satin Long
Adult
120-R-827
$14.99

Satin Short
Adult
120-R-413
$9.99

Small
Child
120-R-828
$6.99

GARTERS

Buy one to toss, one to keep. Beautifully appointed with lace and ribbon trim.

Tossing

Ribbon, pearl and lace trim.
Blue 120-R-402 $5.99
White 120-R-401 $5.99

Keepsake White

Features engravable silver locket that holds two photos.
120-R-826 $9.99

Beverage Cooler

Great for all celebrations—weddings and showers, even picnics, bbq's, beach parties! Includes Ice bucket, 6 drink glasses with removeable bases, and removable collar to hold the glasses.
120-R-462 $24.99

NEW!

Car Decorating Kit

Eye-catching decorations trim the bride and groom's getaway vehicle with style! Includes: Magnetic "Just Married" sign, window clings, pre-fluffed pom-poms, streamers, balloons. Crafted of weather-resistant materials, reusable (except balloons).
1006-R-483 $14.99

Autograph Mat

Fits 11 x 14 in. frame, holds 5 x 7 in. photo. Includes black pen.
1009-R-508 $5.99

Wedding Day Décor

LIGHTED BRIDAL GARLANDS

Romantic garland adds a soft glow to your wedding ambiance! You'll find so many uses for the ceremony and reception. Drape on pews and line the aisles, place along table edges and around the cake, wrap around pillars. Battery operated (uses 2 D Batteries, not included).

Wedding Bells
8 Ft. Length 1006-R-596 $23.99

Organza Rose
6 Ft. Length 1006-R-584 $23.99

Hydrangea
6 Ft. Length 1006-R-581 $23.99

White Rose
6 Ft. Length 1006-R-350 $23.99

Rose Garland
Non-lighting; roses strung together by organza ribbon. 6 foot length.
1006-R-917 $9.99

Organza Pull-N-Fluff™ Bows
Create stunning bows in 3 easy steps—just pull the strings, tie and fluff! Perfect for weddings, holiday décor, gifts, more. Reusable and dyeable.
Small
6 in. diameter.
1006-R-636 Pk./12 $19.99
Medium
8 in. diameter.
1006-R-637 Pk./12 $29.99
Large
10 in. diameter.
1006-R-635 Pk./12 $39.99

Satin Chair Cover
Distinguish wedding party and special guest seating at your celebration—fits most standard folding and party chairs. Luxurious satin fabric can be dyed using fabric dye to match your colors.
1006-R-131 $9.99

CHAIR WRAPS

Versatile fabric wraps beautifully accent party and reception chairs and more! Place on a table as a lush runner, wrap a large gift, make a magnificent bow. Fabric dye changes this wrap into a perfect-colored accent for your wedding day! 18 in. wide x 12 ft. long.

Organza Beaded
1006-R-382 $9.99

Satin
1006-R-384 $9.99

Tulle Spool
Create beautiful bows and swags, spectacular puffs, even use as ribbon for gift wrap! Simply cut to desired lengths.
6 in. wide x 50 yards long.
1005-R-442 $7.99

NEW!

Iridescent Beaded Garland
⅞ in. diameter beads.
24 ft. length.
1006-R-196 $7.99

Sparkling Ice*
Container size: 1½ in. high x 4½ in. diameter.
1006-R-342 $9.99

*WARNING: CHOKING HAZARD– Small parts. Not intended for children. Not a toy– for decorative use only.

Bubble Machine
Surround your celebration with bubbles! Compact size (4.5 high x 3.75 wide x 7 in. deep) allows for hiding in floral arrangements. Neutral white color. Requires 2 C batteries, not included. Use with Wilton Bubble Solution.
1007-R-8015 $14.99

1 Liter Bubble Solution
1007-R-8016 $4.99

RECEPTION GIFT CARD HOLDERS

Attractively keeps the wedding gift cards together at the reception. Tulle Spool for accents sold at left.

Vertical
16 ½ in. high x 7 in. long x 7 in. deep.
120-R-330 $24.99

Horizontal
12 in. high x 10 in. long x 7 in. deep.
120-R-875 $24.99

Centerpieces

HONEYCOMB PAPER DECORATIONS

Always festive, paper decorations are trendy, fun, and economical too!

NEW!

Sweet Romance
7 ½ in. wide x 9 ⅜ in. high.
120-R-546 $2.99

NEW!

Happy Couple
8 in. wide x 10 ¼ in. high.
120-R-545 $2.99

NEW!

Blossoming Bride
7 in. wide x 9 ¼ in. high.
120-R-841 $2.99

NEW!

See matching place card holders on next page!

Wedding Dress
7 in. wide x 10 in. high.
120-R-547 $2.99

Celebration Tree

NEW!

Use it as a party decoration, displayed on the gift table, and as a centerpiece on reception tables. Easy to assemble. Metal construction. Assembled tree measures approximately 14 in. (high x 11 in. wide. (Favors and decorations shown not included.)
1006-R-571 $9.99

Heart Basket

NEW!

Beautiful heart basket makes a stunning table centerpiece—fill it with flowers, candy, favors, more. Includes a clear liner to securely hold smaller contents. Silvertone metal basket measures 3 ¾ in. high x 5 ⁷⁄₁₆ in. diameter at rim. (Decorations shown not included.)
1006-R-998 $4.99

See matching favor containers on p.160!

Lighted Gazebo

Decorate the gazebo with flowers, greenery, ribbon or tulle. Create one for every table at your reception. Uses 4 AA batteries, not included. 4 ¾ in. deep x 3 ¾ in. long x 8 ½ in. high.
1006-R-223 $19.99

Lighted Arch

What could be more elegant than a centerpiece matched to the celebration? Just add tulle, ribbon, and position your photo or favorite ornament. Uses 4 AA batteries, not included. 3 ½ in. deep x 8 in. long x 10 in. high.
1006-R-222 $19.99

Silver Unlit Arch
1006-R-456 $14.99

Tiered Floral Centerpiece

Create an elegant display for fresh or silk flowers. Use with or without cake. Can be displayed as single tiers. Contains three 2-piece tiers. Tops remove for easy cleaning. Assembly instructions included.
120-R-822 $29.99

Place Cards and Holders

An elegant way to indicate seating arrangements; and a stunning display for photos, special notes and thanks for your guests.

Honeycomb Paper Wedding Dress

Charming place card holder can also display photos, menu, thank you notes. (Place cards not included.)
120-R-842
Pk./6 $5.99

Silver Double Heart Place Cards

Use for every life celebration!
1006-R-752 Pk./40 $2.29

Clip-On Rose

It's easy to add a decorative touch to your reception tables—use on glassware, napkins, place cards, more! Fabric rose measures 3½ in. diameter. (Place cards not included.)
1006-R-467 $1.29

Pedestal

3 in. high x 3¾ in. wide.
1009-R-236 $1.99

Silver Gazebo
Removable roof is slotted to hold place card. 3 in. high x 2½ in. wide. Metal.
1006-R-373 $1.29

Love Potion
Slotted cork holds place card. Includes recipe cards, funnel. 2¾ in. high x 1 in. wide. Glass.
1006-R-352 Pk./6 $5.99

"Glass" Slipper
Heel is slotted to hold place card. 1¾ in. high x 1 in. wide x 2 in. deep. Plastic.
1006-R-370 Pk./12 $5.99

Favor Frames

Insert a favorite photo or use as a place card holder by adding your guest's name. Silver metal.

Fleur-de-lis

2½ in. high x 3½ in. wide.
1006-R-376 Pk/5 $5.99

Single Heart
1 in. high x 1 in. wide.
1009-R-239 $0.99

Favor-Making Kits

Fun and festive kits personalize your favors with ease! Just add candy!

CD Favor Tins

Create personalized CD labels for your celebration using your computer, or hand design. Includes 12 tins, 12 adhesive labels and complete instructions. Just download template from www.wiltonprint.com.
1006-R-391
Pk./12 $24.99

Favor Tins
Create personalized favor tins for your celebration using your computer, or hand design. Includes 12 tins, 12 adhesive labels and strips, complete instructions. Just download template from www.wiltonprint.com.
1006-R-481
Pk./12 $9.99

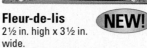

Candle Favors
Add a romantic touch to showers, receptions, every celebration. Includes 12 lightly-scented 4 in. mini candles, and 3 in. candle holders already decorated with white organza bows.
1006-R-643
Pk./12 $14.99

Sweet Things™ Champagne Bottles
Makes 12 favors—includes champagne bottle favor pedestals, ribbon, organza circles and favor tags.
1006-R-227 Pk./12 $14.99

Heart Favor Mega Kits
Makes 24 favors—includes heart containers, tulle circles, ribbon and favor tags.
1006-R-924 Pk./24 $24.99

Goblet Favor Mega Kits
Makes 24 favors—includes goblet containers, tulle circles, ribbon and favor tags.
1006-R-923 Pk./24 $24.99

Drawstring Wrappers
Create 12 cute favors in no time at all! Kit includes pre-assembled drawstring wrapper and favor tags. Just fill and tie.
Pk./12 $12.99
White   1006-R-921
Lavender 1006-R-922

Favor Containers

These beautiful containers hold favors for shower, wedding and anniversary celebrations. Perfect for mints, almonds, potpourri and small gifts.

NEW!

White Wire Rope Heart Basket
3 ½ in. high x 3 in. wide. Metal.
1006-R-687 $1.29

Silver Lace Heart Basket
3 ½ in. high x 3 in. wide. Metal.
1006-R-562 $1.29

Silver Heart Patterned Basket
3 ½ in. high x 3 in. wide. Metal.
1006-R-338 $1.29

Silver Heart Box
2 in. high x 2 in. wide. Metal.
1006-R-169 $1.29

Swan
3 in. high x 1 ½ in. wide x 2 in. deep. Wings are moveable. Acrylic.
1006-R-369 $1.29

Ivory Chest
2 ½ in. high x 2 ¼ in. long x 1 ½ in. wide. Paper.
1006-R-515 Pk./20 $9.99

White Hexagon
2 ½ in. high x 1 ¼ in. long x 2 ½ in. wide. Paper.
1006-R-516 Pk./20 $9.99

Tuxedo
4 in. high. Paper.
1006-R-514 Pk./10 $9.99

Silver Heart Pillow
1 in. high x 3 in. long x 2 ¼ in. wide. Paper.
1006-R-557 Pk./20 $9.99

Heart Tab
2 ¼ in. high x 2 ¼ in. long x 2 ¼ in. wide. Paper.
1006-R-517 Pk./20 $9.99

Champagne Flute
4 in. high x 1 ¼ in. wide. Plastic.
1006-R-193 Pk./12 $5.99

Champagne Glass
Clear. 2 in. high. Plastic.
1006-R-614 Pk./12 $2.49

Tote
4 in. high x 2 ¼ in. wide x 1 ¼ in. deep. Vinyl.
1006-R-372 $1.29

Favor Cake Box
Shaped and decorated like a slice of wedding cake. 20 boxes fit together to form a round cake tier. 4 ¼ in. long x 2 ¾ in. high.
1006-R-629 Pk./20 $6.99

Cake Slice Boxes
5 in. square x 3 ½ in. high.
415-R-955 Pk./5 $3.49

Candy

Trendy and traditional candies make great fillers for favors and candy dishes at showers, weddings, celebrations!

Mini Hearts
12 oz. bag. Fruit flavored. Certified Kosher.
1006-R-797 $3.99

Wedding Message Hearts
10 oz. bag; approximately 90 pieces. Mint flavored.
1006-R-371 $3.99

Candy Bar Molds

Create a sweet memory for your guests, a candy bar featuring a special message.

Molding is easy using Wilton Candy Melts® (p. 218). Present them beautifully in Candy Bar Boxes. Each bar measures 3 ¼ in. wide x 1 ¾ in. tall x ¼ in. deep. 1 design, 4 cavities.
$1.99

Our Wedding
2115-R-1409

Thank You
2115-R-1410

Candy Bar Boxes
The window displays your special message.
Pk./10 $3.99

White
1904-R-1157

Silver
1904-R-1159

Add-A-Message
2115-R-1356

Mint Drops
16 oz. bag. Assorted. Certified Kosher.
1006-R-788 $5.99

Pillow Mints
10 oz. bag. approximately 205 pieces. Assorted. Certified Kosher.
1006-R-858 $3.99

Jordan Almonds
16 oz. bag; approximately 100 pieces. Certified Kosher.
Assorted 1006-R-779 $7.99
White 1006-R-778 $7.99

ORDER TOLL FREE: 800-794-5866

Favors

WEDDING BUBBLES

Celebrate the wedding by showering the newly married couple with shimmering bubbles. It's a fun trend and a great way to wish the bride and groom good luck!

Contains 24 .6 oz. bottles of bubbles with wands. Decorate with Favor Band and Tulle Circles (shown below).
1007-R-8000 Pk./24 $4.99

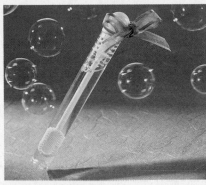

Love Knot Wands
Use after the ceremony or at the reception. 36 wands are packed in a convenient tray for reception table use. Ribbon not included. Each wand contains .16 fl. oz. bubble solution.
1007-R-8017 Pk./36 $9.99

Celebration Bells
Ring for a special kiss after the ceremony and at the reception. Hand to guests exiting the church, and place one at each setting at the reception. Contains 24 bells, poem tags and ties. Bell measures 1¼ in. tall.
Silver 1007-R-8012 Pk/24 $6.49
White 1007-R-8013 Pk/24 $6.49

Favor Accents and Leaves

Romantic accents add sparkling beauty and elegance to favors, table decorations!

Engagement Rings
Use these sparkling favor accents to add beauty to favors, table decorations, centerpieces.
1006-R-115 Pk./12 $1.99

Anniversary Bands
¾ in. diameter.
Pk./48 $1.99
Silver 1006-R-101
Gold 1006-R-100
Pk./288 $6.99
Silver 1006-R-422
Gold 1006-R-421

Rose Flower Spray
8 in. long.
1006-R-507 $1.99

Lily Spray
9 in. long.
1006-R-503 Pk./12 $1.99

White Pearl Spray
8 in. long.
1006-R-506 Pk./12 $2.49

Gold
1⅞ in. long.
1005-R-6518
Pk./144 $3.99
1¼ in. long.
1005-R-6712
Pk./144 $3.49

Silver
1⅞ in. long.
1005-R-6526
Pk./144 $3.99
1¼ in. long.
1005-R-6720
Pk./144 $3.49

Green
2½ in. long leaf, 2½ in. stem.
1005-R-401
Pk./12 $1.49

White
2½ in. long leaf, 2½ in. stem.
1005-R-408
Pk./12 $1.49

Glittered Doves
Coated with non-edible glitter. Do not place directly on cake. 2 x 1½ in.
1006-R-166 Pk./12 $1.99

White Pearl Beading
Molded on one continuous 5-yard strand. Remove pearls before cutting and serving cake.

Small (4 mm)
211-R-1989 $2.99
Large (6 mm)
211-R-1990 $3.99

Satin Stripe Favor Bands
Functional and decorative, a pretty way to accent favors. Use on Drawstring Sachets, Wedding Bubbles bottles and more for an instant decoration. 2 in. wide.
1007-R-8014 Pk./12 $2.99

Sachets and Tulle Circles

Perfect for favors, rose petals, rice, treats, gifts.

Drawstring Sachet Bags
Sheer organza fabric pouch closes with a pull of the ribbons. 3¾ x 4 in.
Pk./12 $5.99

White
1006-R-173
Also available:
4½ x 6¾ in. size.
1006-R-184 Pk./12 $7.99

Platinum
1006-R-925
Gold
1006-R-174
Burgundy
1006-R-178
Red
1006-R-188
Ivory
1006-R-176
Lavender
1006-R-189

White Tulle Circles
Sheer mesh fabric. 9 in. diameter.
1005-R-7897 Pk./25 $2.99

Wedding Cakes

From the keepsake figurine on top, to the impressive stand below,
Wilton has something special just for your wedding cake!

Wedding Figurines

More brides choose Wilton figurines to top their wedding cakes. The rich, sculpted crafting, realistic detailing and romantic designs make these figurines perfect wedding day keepsakes.

Threshold of Happiness
Height: 5 in.
Base: 3¼ x 2 in.
Resin.
202-R-202 $24.99

From This Day Forward
Height: 5 in.
Base: 3¼ x 2 in.
Resin.
202-R-319 $24.99

Always and Forever Petite Embrace
Height: 3¾ in.
Base: 2½ in. diameter. Resin.
202-R-311 $21.99

Bianca
Height: 5½ in.
Base: 3¾ x 3½ in.
Resin.
202-R-207 $24.99

Clear Bianca
Height: 5½ in.
Base: 3¾ x 3½ in.
Acrylic. Perfect on Lighted Revolving Base (sold on p. 163).
202-R-424 $24.99

Always and Forever Musical Ornament
Plays "The Wedding March". Height: 7¼ in.
Base: 4¼ in. diameter.
Resin.
215-R-310 $49.99

IT LIGHTS!

Porcelain Promenade
Height: 6½ in.
Base: 5½ x 3 in. Porcelain.
117-R-508 $29.99

Castle
Lights from within using 2 D batteries (not included).
Height: 7½ in.
Base: 4½ in. Resin.
111-R-2804 $59.99

Just Married
Height: 5 in.
Base: 5 x 3¼ in. Resin.
110-R-864 $44.99

Elegance
Height: 5½ in.
Base: 5 x 3 in. Resin.
110-R-863 $34.99

Forever In Your Eyes
Height: 6 in.
Base: 5 in. diameter. Resin.
110-R-903 $39.99

Horse & Carriage
Height: 4½ in. Base: 7 x 2½ in.
Resin.
110-R-862 $29.99

With This Ring
Height: 4½ in.
Base: 3½ diameter.
Resin.
202-R-313 $24.99

Our Day
Height: 4¾ in.
Base: 2 x 1¾ in.
Poly resin.
Blonde/White Gown
202-R-409 $6.99
Brunette/Ivory Gown
(not shown)
202-R-415 $6.99

Lasting Love
Height: 4½ in.
Base: 2¼ x 1¾ in.
Poly resin.
202-R-302 $6.99
Petite Lasting Love
(not shown)
Height: 3½ in.
Base: 1¾ x 1½ in.
202-R-401 $5.99

Love's Duet
Height: 6 in.
Base: 2½ x 2¼ in.
Poly resin.
202-R-402 $14.99

Ethnic Love's Duet
Height: 6 in.
Base: 2½ x 2¼ in.
Poly resin.
202-R-412 $14.99

ORDER TOLL FREE: 800-794-5866

Our First Dance
Height: 9 ¼ in. Base: 4 ⅝ in. diameter.
118-R-650 $44.99
Couple Only Height: 6 in. Poly resin
202-R-411 $14.99

Always and Forever
Height: 6 ½ in. Base: 7 x 5 in.
118-R-200 $37.99

HUMOROUS WEDDING FIGURINES

Add a lighthearted touch to the celebration. Sure to bring a smile to the face of anyone who has ever planned a wedding!

Now I Have You
Height: 4 ¼ in. Base: 4 ¼ x 3 ¾ in. Resin.
115-R-101 $19.99

The Tiff
Height: 4 in.
Base: 2 ¼ x 2 in. Resin.
115-R-103 $14.99

Ethnic Expression of Love
Height: 7 ¾ in.
Base: 4 ½ in. diameter.
101-R-933 $35.99
Couple Only
Height: 4 ½ in. Base:
2 ¼ x 1 ¾ in. Poly resin.
202-R-306 $6.99

Expression of Love
Height: 7 ¾ in.
Base: 4 ½ in. diameter.
101-R-931 $35.99

Sweetness
Height: 7 ¾ in.
Base: 4 ½ in. diameter.
101-R-153 $29.99

Oh No You Don't
Height: 4 ¼ in. Base: 6 x 3 in. Resin.
115-R-102 $19.99

Liberated Bride
Height: 4 ½ in.
Base: 1 ¼ x 1 ¾ in. Plastic.
2113-R-4188 $5.99

Enduring Love
Height: 5 in. Base: 7 x 5 in. oval.
103-R-235 $35.99

Simple Joys
Height: 8 in.
Base: 4 ½ in. diameter.
103-R-150 $24.99

Reflections
Porcelain couple.
Height: 8 in.
Base: 4 ¾ in. diameter.
117-R-268 $25.99

Spring Song
Height: 9 ½ in.
Base: 4 ⅝ in. diameter.
111-R-2802 $19.99
Kissing Lovebirds
5 ½ in. high.
1002-R-206 $4.99

Petite Spring Song
Height: 7 in.
Base: 3 ¼ in. diameter.
106-R-159 $12.99

Floral Topper
Beautiful handmade flowers, greenery, satin ribbon. White resin base. Height: 5 ¾ in.
Base: 3 ¼ in. diameter
120-R-073 $39.99

Devotion
Height: 7 in.
Base: 4 x 2 ½ in. Ceramic.
111-R-2803 $34.99

Inspirational Cross
Height: 5 ½ in.
Base: 2 x 1 ½ in.
Resin.
202-R-206 $24.99

IT LIGHTS!

Lighted Revolving Base
Select just light, just rotate or both at the same time. Uses 3 AA batteries (not included). Height: 2 in.
Diameter: 5 in.
201-R-453 $24.99

La Quinceañera
Ideal as a cake top decoration or as a favor.
Height: 4 ½ in.
Base: 2 ¾ in. diameter.
203-R-305 $3.99

Anniversary Ornaments

Petite 50th

Height: 5¾ in.
Base: 3¼ in. diameter.
105-R-4273 $9.99

Petite 25th
Silver **105-R-4265 $9.99**

50 Years of Happiness
Height: 10 in.
Base: 4⅝ in. diameter.
102-R-223 $19.99

Ornament Settings and Bases

A beautiful beginning to a cake top ornament you create. Simply add the figurine of your choice, and trim with flowers, fabric tulle and accents.

Romantic Heart
2 pieces, 4⅝ in. diameter
201-R-7332 $2.99

Chapel Windows
Use with base or alone.
6½ x 5 x 1 in. deep.
205-R-3060 $4.99

Gazebo Set
Easy to assemble plastic. 5 x 9 in.
205-R-3061 $4.99

Floral Arch
Height: 10 in.
Base: 4⅝ in. diameter.
210-R-1987 $9.99

WEDDING ATTENDANT FIGURINES
Want to add color? All resin figurines may be personalized using acrylic paint.

Bridesmaid

Height: 4½ in. Resin.
Base: 1½ in. diameter.
203-R-315 $5.99

Groomsman

Height: 4½ in.
Resin. Base: 1½ in. diameter.
203-R-316 $5.99

Ethnic Bridesmaid

Height: 4½ in.
Resin.
Base: 1½ in. diameter.
203-R-318 $5.99

Ethnic Groomsman

Height: 4½ in.
Resin.
Base: 1½ in. diameter.
203-R-317 $5.99

Cake Assembly Sets

Tall Tier Cake Stand

Display your multi-tiered cakes up to 6 tiers high with this majestic stand. Lace-look plates enhance every cake design and hold tiers from 6 to 16 in. diameter. Easier to assemble than pillar construction, the twist-together center columns and strong, interchangeable plates provide sure stability. The optional Lady Windemere-Look 4-Arm Base, sold below, lets you surround up to 3 tiers with multiple small cakes for an even more dramatic presentation.

Basic Set
Includes: 5 twist-apart columns, 6½ in. high; top nut and bottom bolt; 18 in. footed base plate; 8, 10, 12, 14 and 16 in. separator plates (interchangeable, except footed base plate). Plastic.
304-R-7915 Set/13 $45.99

Replacement Parts
Top Column Cap Nut
304-R-7923 $0.79

Bottom Column Bolt
304-R-7941 $0.99

Additional Plates
8 in. **302-R-7894 $3.99**
10 in. **302-R-7908 $4.99**
12 in. **302-R-7924 $5.99**
14 in. **302-R-7940 $8.99**
16 in. **302-R-7967 $11.99**
18 in. **302-R-7983 $14.99**

Additional Columns
6½ in. **303-R-7910 $1.99**
13½ in. **303-R-703 $4.99**
7¾ in. **304-R-5009 $2.99**

Glue-On Plate Legs
Convert 14 or 16 in. separator plate into a footed base plate. Order 6 legs for each plate.
304-R-7930 $0.59

Lady Windemere-Look 4-Arm Base
(For Use With Tall-Tier Stand)
Easily adds 4 base cakes to your tall tier cake. The 4-arm base can be used with any plate from the basic set, except the 18 in. footed base plate. Up to 3 graduated tiers can be added to the center columns. Includes 20 in. diameter 4-arm base with 4 stability pegs and base bolt. Use with 13½ in. column, bottom column bolt and four 12 in. plates, sold above.
304-R-8245 $11.99

Additional Base Bolt **304-R-8253 $0.59**

Crystal-Clear Cake Divider Set
- Sparkling clear twist legs beautifully accent your cake
- Designed for towering cakes from 6 to 14 in. diameter
- An elegant combination with Wilton Crystal-Look accessories

Clear plastic twist legs penetrate cake, rest on plate (dowel rods not needed). Includes 6, 8, 10, 12, 14 and 16 in. plastic separator plates plus 24 legs.
301-R-9450 Set/30 $49.99

Additional Plates
6 in. **302-R-9730 $2.99**
8 in. **302-R-9749 $3.99**
10 in. **302-R-9757 $4.99**
12 in. **302-R-9765 $6.99**
14 in. **302-R-9773 $8.99**
16 in. **302-R-9780 $10.99**

7½ in. Twist Legs
303-R-9794 Pk./4 $3.99

9 in. Twist Legs
Add more height to your tiers.
303-R-977 Pk./4 $4.99

Cake Corer Tube (not shown)
Essential tool easily and neatly removes center from cake tiers when tall tier stand columns are used. Ice cake before using. Serrated edge removes cake center with one push. Cleans easily.
304-R-8172 $1.99

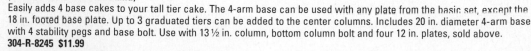

Cake Stands

Stunning Wilton Cake Stands are the perfect way to display your special wedding cake. Take a look—there's one perfectly suited to your wedding cake size and design.

Featured in our Dazzling Displays section, p. 90

NEW!

Standard
Holds 23 cupcakes.
307-R-826
$29.99

Cupcakes 'N More™ Dessert Stands

NEW!

Individually decorated cupcakes are the perfect way to add a personal touch to celebrations. Now, with Cupcakes 'N More, you have the perfect way to serve them! The look is fresh and fun, featuring bold silver-finished wire spirals to securely hold each cupcake. The twisting, towering design is perfect for any setting—kids' birthdays, holidays, weddings, showers, and more. Everyone will love serving themselves—and you'll love presenting your cupcakes, petits fours, candy cups, mini quiches and party favors in the center of the celebration! Easy to assemble, collapsible for easy storage. Holds 38 cupcakes.
Large 307-R-651
$39.99

3-Tier Cake and Dessert Stand

• Beautiful cascading effect with display platforms at 6, 12 and 19 inches high
• Holds cakes up to 8, 10 and 12 inches diameter, also serves appetizers, cookies and candies

Raise your party cakes, petits fours, appetizers and more to dramatic heights. With this 3-Tier Cake and Dessert Stand, creating an elegant tiered display is easier than ever! Set up is easy—the unique design combines the ease of lightweight foam base and 3 foam support plates with the strength and dependability of 3 grooved pillars. Also included are 3 plastic plates with rings on the bottom that insure exact orientation during set-up
304-R-8275 $29.99

Candlelight Cake Stand

• The magic of candlelight heightens the beauty of your cake
• Romantic swirls of scrollwork and hearts
• Great size for smaller weddings

Simple, graceful design reinforced with a crossbar for more support. Sturdy enameled metal design holds up to 40 lbs. Ideal for three stacked tiers supported by a 14 in. separator plate. Stand is 21 ½ in. diameter (13 ¼ in. center cake area) x 5 in. high and uses standard ⅞ in. candles. (Plates and candles not included.)
307-R-871 $34.99

Garden Cake Stand

Our beautiful Garden Cake Stand echoes the wrought-iron look found in many formal gardens. Simply place cakes on plates and set on the stand. Painted metal stand is 23 in. high x 22 in. wide and uses any standard 10 in., 14 in. and 18 in. separator plates. Satellite garden stands sold individually below.
307-R-860 $169.99

Satellite Garden Cake Stand
Painted metal; holds 12 in. separator plate.
307-R-861 $44.99

Scrollwork Cake Stands

• Three graduated stands let you create an elegant flowing presentation
• The cool, captivating look of silver metal, sculpted in graceful curves and scrolls

Presenting a stand design that truly enhances the look of your cake. Its graceful sense of motion begins with a beautiful stepped arrangement which positions three tiers on the cake table in a graceful, flowing fashion. Each stand features magnificent curves and swirls which create a sweeping style and rich texture. Simply place cake on Crystal-Look separator plate (included) and set on the stand. 17 in. stand has crossbar support for added strength. Compatible with any same-sized separator plate.

9 in. diameter x 12 ¼ in. high. Includes 9 in. Crystal-Look separator plate.   307-R-880 $59.99
13 in. diameter x 8 in. high. Includes 13 in. Crystal-Look separator plate.   307-R-882 $69.99
17 in. diameter x 4 ¼ in. high. Includes 17 in. Crystal-Look separator plate.   307-R-884 $79.99

FLOATING TIERS CAKE STAND SETS

• Dramatic illusion of decorated tiers suspended in mid-air
• Back support ideal for adding floral or ribbon treatments
• Great for modest size weddings

Round
Round plates present beautiful tiers. Set includes 17 in. high enamel coated white metal stand, 8, 12, and 16 in. smooth separator plates; instructions.
307-R-825
Set/4 $69.99

Replacement Plates
(Same plates as Crystal-Clear Cake Divider Set.)
8 in. **302-R-9749** $3.99
12 in. **302-R-9765** $6.99
16 in. **302-R-9780** $10.99

Heart
Perfectly sized to heart shaped tiers. Set includes 17 in. high enamel coated white metal stand, 8, 12 and 16 in. Decorator Preferred® Heart separator plates; instructions.
307-R-872
Set/4 $69.99

Replacement Plates
8 in. **302-R-60** $2.99
12 in. **302-R-62** $4.99
16 in. **302-R-64** $8.99

Separator Pillars

Arched Pillars
Grecian-inspired with arched support.
4 ½ in.	303-R-452	Pk./4	$3.99
6 ½ in.	303-R-657	Pk./4	$4.99
13 in.	303-R-9720	Pk./2	$7.99

Lattice Columns
Flattering garden-inspired design.
3 in.	303-R-2131	Pk./4	$2.99
5 in.	303-R-2151	Pk./4	$3.99
13 in.	303-R-2113	Each	$3.99

Roman Columns
Handsome pillars may be used with 16 and 18 in. plates and the Kolor-Flo Fountain (sold on pg. 168).
10 ¼ in.		
303-R-8136	Pk./2	$5.99
13 ¾ in.		
303-R-2130	Pk./2	$6.99

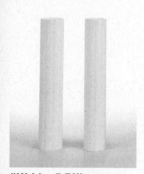

"Hidden" Pillars
Separate cake tiers slightly and create a floating illusion. Pushed into tiers as dowel rods, they fit onto all white separator plates except Tall Tier. Trimmable, hollow plastic. 6 in. high.
303-R-8 Pk./4 $2.99

Grecian Spiked Pillars
Single plate pillars. Wide base for increased stability.
5 in.	303-R-3708	Pk./4	$2.49
7 in.	303-R-3710	Pk./4	$3.49
9 in.	303-R-3712	Pk./4	$4.49

Grecian Pillars
Elegantly scrolled and ribbed.
3 in.	303-R-3606	Pk./4	$2.99
5 in.	303-R-3703	Pk./4	$3.99
7 in.	303-R-3705	Pk./4	$4.99

Baker's Best® Disposable Pillars with Rings
Single plate pillars.
7 in.	303-R-4000	Pk./4	$2.99
9 in.	303-R-4001	Pk./4	$3.49

Crystal-Look Spiked Pillars
Single plate pillars. Double cake circles for extra support.
7 in.	303-R-2322	Pk./4	$4.49
9 in.	303-R-2324	Pk./4	$5.49

Crystal-Look Pillars
Use with Crystal-Look plates (sold at right) and Crystal Bridge and Stairway Set (sold on pg. 167).
3 in.	303-R-2171	Pk./4	$3.49
5 in.	303-R-2196	Pk./4	$4.49
7 in.	303-R-2197	Pk./4	$4.99
*13 ¾ in.	303-R-2242		$3.99

*Sold singly. Use only with 17 in. crystal plate (sold on at right).

Separator Plates

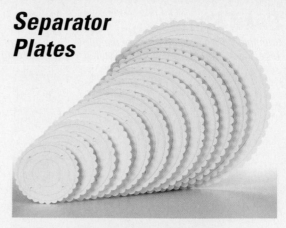

Decorator Preferred® Separator Plates
Our best, strongest separator plates with superior stability, beauty and scalloped edges. Guaranteed non-breakable.

6 in.	302-R-6	$2.29		12 in.	302-R-12	$4.99
7 in.	302-R-7	$2.49		13 in.	302-R-13	$5.49
8 in.	302-R-8	$2.99		14 in.	302-R-14	$5.99
9 in.	302-R-9	$3.49		15 in.	302-R-15	$6.99
10 in.	302-R-10	$3.99		16 in.	302-R-16	$8.99
11 in.	302-R-11	$4.49		18 in.	302-R-18	$11.99

Decorator Preferred® Heart Separator Plates
Perfectly sized to fit Wilton heart pans, for a stunning tiered heart creation. Lovely scalloped edges. Guaranteed non-breakable.

8 in.	302-R-60	$2.99	14 in.	302-R-63	$5.99
10 in.	302-R-61	$3.99	16 in.	302-R-64	$8.99
12 in.	302-R-62	$4.99	18 in.	302-R-65	$11.99

Square Separator Plates
7 in.	302-R-1004	$2.99
9 in.	302-R-1020	$3.99
11 in.	302-R-1047	$4.99
13 in.	302-R-1063	$5.99

Crystal-Look Plates
Wilton Crystal-Look plates have an elegance like no other, with ridged sides that look like cut crystal. Built with the strength and support Wilton is famous for. Use with Crystal-Look pillars (sold at left).

7 in.	302-R-2013	$3.99
9 in.	302-R-2035	$4.99
11 in.	302-R-2051	$5.99
13 in.	302-R-2078	$7.99

*17 in. 302-R-1810 $14.99
*Use only with 13 ¾ in. Crystal-Look pillars (sold at left).

17 in. Crystal-Look Plate and Pillar Set
Ideal style and height for use with fountains (sold on page 168). Contains four 13 ¾ in. pillars and two 17 in. plates. (not shown)
301-R-1387 $45.99

Stairways and Bridges

Bridge the gap between lavish tiers.

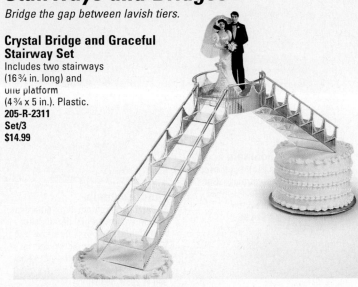

Crystal Bridge and Graceful Stairway Set
Includes two stairways (16¾ in. long) and one platform (4¾ x 5 in.). Plastic.
205-R-2311
Set/3
$14.99

Filigree Bridge and Stairway Set
Includes two stairways (16¼ in. long) and one platform (4¾ x 5 in.). Plastic.
205-R-2109
Set/3
$11.99

Pillar and Plate Sets

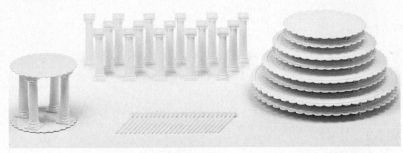

Grecian Pillar and Plate Set
A deluxe money-saving collection for the serious cake decorator. Decorator Preferred® scalloped-edge separator plates and 5 in. pillars. Includes 54 pieces: two each 6 in., 8 in., 10 in., 12 in. and 14 in. plates; 20 Grecian pillars and 24 pegs.
SAVE 27% on set
301-R-8380 $49.99

Roman Column Tier Set
Stately Roman pillars and scalloped-edge plates create beautiful settings for all tiered cakes. Includes 8 pieces: six 13¾ in. Roman columns and two super strong 18 in. round Decorator Preferred® separator plates. Lovely with the Kolor-Flo Fountain (sold on pg. 168).
301-R-1981 $39.99

Arched Tier Set
Dramatic when used with Kolor-Flo Fountain (sold on pg. 168), or Filigree Gazebo Kit (sold on pg. 168). Includes 14 pieces: Six 13 in. arched columns, two super strong 18 in. round Decorator Preferred® separator plates and six angelic cherubs to attach to columns with royal icing or glue.
301-R-1982 $45.99

Classic Separator Sets
Stately Grecian pillars and scalloped-edge plates create beautiful settings for all tiered cakes. Sets include 10 pieces: two Decorator Preferred® plates, four pillars and four pegs.

8 in. Plate Set
8 in. plates; 5 in. pillars
2103-R-256 $7.99

10 in. Plate Set
10 in. plates; 5 in. pillars
2103-R-108 $9.99

12 in. Plate Set
12 in. plates; 5 in. pillars
2103-R-124 $11.99

Dowel Rods and Pegs

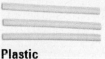

Plastic Dowel Rods
Heavy-duty hollow plastic provides strong, sanitary support for all tiered cakes. Cut with serrated knife to desired length. Length: 12¾ in. Diameter: ¾ in.
399-R-801 Pk./4 $2.49

Wooden Dowel Rods
Cut and sharpen with strong shears and knife. Length: 12 in. Diameter: ¼ in.
399-R-1009
Pk./12 $2.99

Plastic Pegs
Insure that cake layers and separator plates atop cakes stay in place. Pegs do not add support; dowel rod cake properly before using. Length: 4 in.
399-R-762 Pk./12 $1.44

Cake Accents

Romantic accents add a sparkling beauty and elegance to cakes.

White Pearl Beading
Molded on one continuous 5-yard strand. Remove before cutting and serving cake.
Small (4 mm) **211-R-1989 $2.99**
Large (6 mm) **211-R-1990 $3.99**

Scrolls
2¾ x 1¼ in.
1004-R-2801
Pk./24 $2.29

Angel Duet
Fluttering fancies. Each 2 in. high.
1001-R-457 Pk./2 $1.99

Cake Fountains and Accessories

Kolor-Flo Fountain

Professional quality fountain looks spectacular with every tiered cake design. Water cascades dramatically from three levels; simply remove top levels for smaller fountain arrangements. Intricate light system with two bulbs for added brilliance. Use with 14 in. or larger plates, 13 in. or taller pillars for tallest cascade. Coordinates with our 17 in. Crystal-Look Plate and Pillar Set, p. 214. Plastic fountain bowl is 9¾ in. diameter. 110-124 V, AC motor with 65 in. cord. Pumps water electrically. Directions, replacement part information included.
306-R-2599 $109.99

Cascade Set for Kolor-Flo Fountain

Dome shapes redirect water over surface in non-stop streams. Set includes 4 pieces: 2½ in., 4½ in., 8 in., and 11½ in. diameter.
306-R-1172 Set/4 $14.99

Fanci Fountain

Economical fountain in crystal-clear design enhances any tiered cake. Adjustable, smooth water flow. Use with 14 in. or larger plates. Set-up instructions included. Height: 12 in. Diameter: 10 in.
306-R-2000 $69.99

Replacement Parts
Bulb
306-R-1790 $1.79

Cascade Set
306-R-1791 $9.99

Replacement Parts for Kolor-Flo Fountain

Light Bulb
306-R-1053 $5.99

Light Socket
306-R-1045 $5.49

Cascade /Pump Connector
306-R-1088 $3.49

Piston
306-R-1029 $3.99

Floater Switch
306-R-1096 $14.49

Pump/Bulb Bracket
306-R-1037 $3.39

Pump
306-R-1002 $48.99

Bottom Base
306-R-1170 $13.99

Upper Cascade
306-R-1118 $6.99

Middle Cascade
306-R-1126 $8.69

Lower Cascade
306-R-1134 $10.49

Bowl
306-R-1142 $17.99

Fresh Flower Accessories

Crystal-Look Bowl

4½ in. diameter. 1½ in. deep.
205-R-1404 $2.99

Flower Spikes

Fill with water, push into cake, add flowers. Makes cakes safe for insertion of stems or wires. 3 in. high.
1008-R-408 Pk./12 $2.49

Fresh Flower Holders

Insert easily under cake tiers to hold blooms, greenery, pearl sprays, tulle puffs and more. Use with floral oasis to keep flowers fresh.
205-R-8500 Pk./2 $2.99

Flower Holder Ring

Put at base of Kolor-Flo Fountain as shown at left. 12½ in. diameter x 2 in. high. 1¾ in. wide opening; inside ring diameter is 8½ in. Plastic.
305-R-435 $4.99

Construction Settings

Filigree Gazebo Kit

Intricate arch and trellis pieces wrap around Wilton Arched Pillars (not included, sold on p. 166 and 167) to create an elegant garden setting for tiered cakes. Easy assembly—just insert tabs into slots to link pieces. Includes instructions for 3 cake designs.
2104-R-2942 $21.99

Cathedral Cake Kit

Easy-to-assemble set includes: 5 white church pieces, 4 white plastic cake supports, a church window that can be illuminated from within. Opening in tower is 8½ in. high x 2½ in. wide.
2104-R-2940 $15.99

ORDER TOLL FREE: 800-794-5866

Cake Boards and Accents

Your cake will look its best when presented with quality Wilton boards, doilies and ruffled trims.

Cake Boards
Shaped cakes look best on boards cut to fit! Strong corrugated cardboard, generously-sized in rectangular shapes. Perfect for sheet and square cakes. For shaped cakes, use the pan as a pattern and cut out board to fit cake.

10 x 14 in. **2104-R-554 Pk./6 $4.79**
13 x 19 in. **2104-R-552 Pk./6 $5.29**

Cake Circles
Corrugated cardboard for strength and stability.

6 in. diameter **2104-R-64 Pk./10 $3.19**
8 in. diameter **2104-R-80 Pk./12 $4.19**
10 in. diameter **2104-R-102 Pk./12 $5.29**
12 in. diameter **2104-R-129 Pk./8 $5.29**
14 in. diameter **2104-R-145 Pk./6 $5.69**
16 in. diameter **2104-R-160 Pk./6 $6.29**

Silver Cake Bases
Convenient ½ in. thick silver-covered bases are grease-resistant, food-safe and reusable. Strong to hold heavy decorated cakes without an additional serving plate. Perfect for all types of cakes and craft creations.

10 in. Round **2104-R-1187 Pk./2 $6.99**
12 in. Round **2104-R-1188 Pk./2 $7.99**
14 in. Round **2104-R-1189 Pk./2 $9.99**
16 in. Round **2104-R-1190 Pk./2 $11.99**

Show 'N Serve™ Cake Boards
Scalloped edge has the look of intricate lace. Food-safe, grease-resistant coating.

10 in. diameter **2104-R-1168 Pk./10 $4.49**
12 in. diameter **2104-R-1176 Pk./8 $4.99**
14 in. diameter **2104-R-1184 Pk./6 $5.49**
14 x 20 in. Rectangle **2104-R-1230 Pk./6 $5.99**

Ruffle Boards®
Ready-to-use cake board and ruffle in one. Bleached white board and all-white ruffling complement any cake.

8 in. (for 6 in. round cake) **415-R-950 $2.49**
10 in. (for 8 in. round cake) **415-R-960 $2.99**
12 in. (for 10 in. round cake) **415-R-970 $3.99**
14 in. (for 12 in. round cake) **415-R-980 $4.49**
16 in. (for 14 in. round cake) **415-R-990 $5.49**
18 in. (for 16 in. round cake) **415-R-1000 $7.49**

Tuk-'N-Ruffle®
A pretty touch that attaches to edge of your serving tray or board with royal icing or tape.
60 ft. bolt per box.
White **802-R-1008 $14.99**
6 ft. pkg. White **802-R-1991 $2.99**

Fanci-Foil
Serving side has a non-toxic grease-resistant surface. FDA-approved for use with food.
Continuous roll: 20 in. x 15 ft.
White **804-R-191 $7.99**
Gold **804-R-183 $7.99**
Silver **804-R-167 $7.99**

Cake Doilies

Add instant elegance to cake plates, dessert trays, entrée and sandwich servings. Use under table centerpieces and plants, for decorations and crafts, too.

Grease-Proof White
4 in. Round **2104-R-90204 Pk./30 $1.99**
6 in. Round **2104-R-90206 Pk./20 $1.99**
8 in. Round **2104-R-90208 Pk./16 $1.99**
10 in. Round **2104-R-90210 Pk./10 $1.99**
12 in. Round **2104-R-90212 Pk./6 $1.99**
14 in. Round **2104-R-90214 Pk./4 $1.99**
10 x 14 in. Rectangle **2104-R-90224 Pk./6 $1.99**

Silver Foil
4 in. Round
2104-R-90404 Pk./12 $2.49
6 in. Round
2104-R-90116 Pk./18 $2.49
8 in. Round
2104-R-90006 Pk./12 $2.49
10 in. Round
2104-R-90007 Pk./6 $2.49
12 in. Round
2104-R-90412 Pk./4 $2.49

Gold Foil
4 in. Round
2104-R-90304 Pk./12 $2.49
6 in. Round
2104-R-90306 Pk./18 $2.49
8 in. Round
2104-R-90308 Pk./12 $2.49
10 in. Round
2104-R-90310 Pk./6 $2.49
12 in. Round
2104-R-90312 Pk./4 $2.49

Baby

Start planning the party—from pink to blue, and themes in between, this dazzling array of Wilton products will inspire you to make the cutest things for your baby celebration.

Favor Containers

Perfect as favors, filled with candy and treats, and as gift and cake accents.

White Pail Favor
NEW!
Cute container makes a great shower favor—just fill with candy. May also be decorated with paint, markers or other favorite craft supplies. Crafted of food-safe painted metal. Pail measures 2⅛ in. high x 2⅜ in. diameter at rim. Contents shown not included.
1006-R-915 $1.29

Drawstring Sachets

Ready to fill with Jordan Almonds, Rose Petals, Pillow Mints, small gifts. 3¾ in. x 4 in.
Pk./12 $5.99
Pink 1006-R-179
Blue 1006-R-180
Multicolor
3 each pink, blue, yellow, mint green.
NEW!
1006-R-244

Baby Favor Bags
Delightful container for candies, small gifts and other favor treats.
3 x 5½ in. high.
1006-R-362 Pk./12 $7.99

Party Bags
Colorful designs for candy and cookie treats. 20 plastic bags, 20 ties included. 4 x 9½ in.
Pk./20 $1.99
Baby
1912-R-2365
Rubber Duckies
1912-R-1275
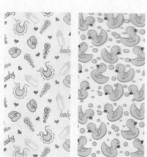

Baby Favor Kits

These kits are the easiest way to create favors for your baby celebration. All components of the kit are included—you add the filler from the selection of Wilton candy and you're done!

Drawstring Wrappers
Create these favors in no time at all—they're pre-assembled! Just fill, tie ribbons, and add favor tag. Candy not included.
Pk./12 $12.99
Pink
1006-R-218
Blue
1006-R-219
White
1006-R-340
NEW!
Multicolor
3 each pink, blue, yellow, mint green. **1006-R-245**

Sweet Things™ Pacifiers
Everything needed to make 6 oh-so-cute favors! Includes pacifier favor pedestals, ribbon, tulle circles, place cards, assembly instructions. Candy not included.
1006-R-531
Pk./6
$9.99

Sweet Things™ Teddy Bears
Everything needed to make 6 adorable favors! Includes teddy bear favor pedestals, ribbon, tulle circles, place cards, assembly instructions. Candy not included.
1006-R-530
Pk./6
$9.99

White Flower Basket
3¾ in. wide x 2 in. high. Metal. Contents shown not included.
1006-R-990 $1.29

Porcelain Baby Block
Letters "B, A, B, Y" on each side. 2 in. wide x 1¾ in. high. Favor and candy not included.
1006-R-324 $2.99

Baby Blocks Containers*
Removable lids for easy filling. Each 1¼ in. high.
2113-R-419 Set/4 $2.99

Pacifier Favor Boxes*
Assembled, decorated and ready to fill with Wilton candies. Each box is 2 in. x 2 in. x 1¼ in. high.
Pk./6 $7.99
Pink 1006-R-330
Blue 1006-R-331
Yellow 1006-R-332

Silver Plated Baby Carriage
With moveable wheels. 3 in. long x 2 in. wide x 3½ in. high.
1006-R-878 $7.99

Baby Cradles
2½ in. high.
Pk./2 $1.99
Pink
2113-R-406
Blue
2113-R-400

Baby Bottles*
Open for easy filling. Pink, lavender, blue, yellow, mint green. 4 in. high; ½ in. diameter opening.
1006-R-696
Pk./6 $5.99

*WARNING: CHOKING HAZARD—Small parts. Not intended for children. Not a toy—for decorative use only.

ORDER TOLL FREE: 800-794-5866

Party Decorations

Add special touches to your celebration.

White Pail Centerpiece **NEW!**

There are so many ways to use these pails for showers and celebrations—as treat holders, centerpieces, more! Add your own creative touch by decorating with ribbon, stickers and accents, then filling with flowers. Add candy, cookies and treats, too —crafted of food-safe painted metal. Pail measures 4¾ in. high x 5⅜ in. diameter at rim. Contents not included.
1006-R-251 $4.99

See matching favor container on p.170!

Lighted Party Garland **NEW!**

Pretty fabric blooms illuminate the baby shower, christening party or the first birthday celebration! 8 ft. long garland has end-to-end connectors and includes 2 replacement bulbs and fuse. 120V, AC, UL listed. For indoor use only.
1008-R-810 $12.99

Favor Accents

Add special touches to your baby favors, gift tie-ons and table decorations.

Baby Bracelets* **NEW!**

Pink, blue, yellow, mint green. 1¼ in. high.
1103-R-56 Pk./6 $2.29

Mini Clothes Pins*
Pink, lavender, blue, yellow, mint green. 1⅜ in. high.
1103-R-27 Pk./20 $1.99

Small Safety Pins*
1½ in. long.
Pk./20 $1.99
Pink **1103-R-21**
Blue **1103-R-26**
Multicolor **NEW!**
Pink, blue, yellow, mint green.
1103-R-42

Mini Baby Bottles*

Pink, lavender, blue, yellow, mint green. 1¼ in. high.
1103-R-16 Pk./20 $1.99

Ethnic Newborn Baby Figurines*
1 in. high.
1103-R-30 Pk./6 $1.99

Newborn Baby Figurines*

1 in. high.
1103-R-62 Pk./6 $1.99

Baby Bears*

1 in. high.
Pk./6 $2.99
Blue **1103-R-7**
Pink **1103-R-8**
Multicolor **NEW!**
Pink, blue, yellow, mint green.
1103-R-46

Rocking Horses

Three blue, three pink. 2½ in. high.
1103-R-28 Pk./6 $3.99

Mini Rocking Horses*

1¼ in. high. Pink, lavender, blue, yellow, mint green.
1103-R-52 Pk./6 $1.99

Shower Rattles*
Pink, lavender, blue, yellow, mint green. 3¾ in. high.
1103-R-29 Pk./6 $2.99

Sleeping Angels Set

A precious pose, one pink and one blue. 2 in. high x 3 in. long.
2113-R-2325 Set/2 $1.99

FAVOR BANDS

Instant decoration for favors, bubbles, gifts. Slip one on to close filled bags and tulle favor puffs, or use to decorate any baby favor.

Baby Bottle

Accented with a cute baby bottle.
Pk./6 $2.49
Pink **1006-R-509**
Blue **1006-R-508**

Baby Pacifier

Accented with a baby pacifier.
Pk./6 $2.49
Pink **1006-R-566**
Blue **1006-R-567**

Multicolor Flower

Accented with satin ribbon. 2 each of yellow, blue, pink, mint green, white, lavender.
1006-R-683 Pk./12 $4.99

*WARNING: CHOKING HAZARD—Small parts. Not intended for children. Not a toy—for decorative use only.

ORDER ONLINE: WWW.WILTON.COM

Candies

Perfect filler for favors, treat bags, candy dishes! Certified Kosher.

Mini Pacifiers
Sweet/tart fruit flavor.
12 oz. bag. Assorted.
1006-R-540 $5.99

Mini Hearts
Sweet/tart fruit flavor.
12 oz. bag. Assorted.
1006-R-797 $3.99

Mint Drops
16 oz. bag. Assorted.
1006-R-788 $5.99

Jordan Almonds
16 oz. bag; approx.
100 pieces.
Assorted 1006-R-779 $7.99
White 1006-R-778

Pillow Mints
10 oz. bag. approx.
205 pieces. Assorted.
1006-R-858 $3.99

Candy Molds

Fun shaped reusable molds celebrate baby over and over again. Making candy is easy to do, complete directions are included! Use Wilton Candy Melts® brand confectionery coating, sold on p. 218.

Baby Bottles
1 design, 6 cavities.
2115-R-1560 $1.99

Baby Shower
4 designs, 11 cavities.
2115-R-1710 $1.99

Mini Baby Icons
5 designs, 20 cavities.
2115-R-1537 $1.99

Baking Accessories
BAKEWARE

NEW!

Baby Buggy Pan
These wheels will bring squeals of delight from shower and christening guests. It's a precious carriage design fit for royalty and ready to dress up for colorful cakes or elegant salads and gelatins. One-mix pan is 11¼ x 11¼ x 2 in. Aluminum.
2105-R-3319 $10.99

Cuddly Lamb Pan
His sweet smile is the perfect welcome for baby showers. See the label for four great decorating ideas. One-mix pan is 11¾ in. x 8¾ in. x 2 in. Aluminum.
2105-R-4947 $10.99

Mini Stand-Up Bear Pan Set
Convenient size for baking cakes and molding candy, ice cream and sugar. 4¾ in. high. Includes 2-piece pan, baking stand, four clips and instructions. Aluminum.
2105-R-489
Set/8 $11.99

Stand-Up Cuddly Bear Pan Set
Five decorating ideas on one box! Two-piece pan takes 6⅔ cups of firm textured batter. Includes 6 clips, heat-conducting core and instructions. Pan is 9½ x 8⅝ in. Aluminum.
2105-R-603 Set/10 $21.99

Huggable Teddy Bear Pan
From birthdays and baby showers to school parties, classic toy shape can be used all year 'round. One-mix pan is 13½ x 12¼ x 2 in. Aluminum.
2105-R-4943 $10.99

BAKING CUPS

Everyone loves the convenience of cupcakes—easy to make, to carry to the party, and simple to serve! Now, you'll make the cutest cupcakes for every baby celebration using Wilton Baking Cups! Also perfect for treats, favors, and as nut or candy cups.

Assorted Pastel
25 pink, 25 blue, 25 yellow. Standard size, 2 in. diameter. Microwave-safe paper.
415-R-394
Pk./75 $1.49

CANDLES

Cute candles brighten the little one's first celebration. Handpainted details, clean-burning design.

Baby Things
Approx. 2 in. high.
2811-R-855
Set/4 $3.49

Soft Colors Candles
From classic to shimmer in yellow, pink, mint and blue.

Shimmer
Shown,
2½ in. high.
2811-R-3664 Pk./8 $1.99

Also available, shown on p. 188:
Rounds
2½ in. high.
2811-R-291 Pk./24 $0.69

Corkscrew
2½ in. high.
2811-R-775 Pk./8 $2.49

Lattice
Shown,
2½ in. high.
2811-R-3657
Pk./8 $1.99

Also available, shown on p. 188:
Tricolor
2½ in. high.
2811-R-782
Pk./10 $1.99

Twist
Shown,
2½ in. high.
2811-R-3661
Pk./8 $2.49

Also available, shown on p. 188:
Party Thins
8 in. high.
2811-R-255
Pk./20 $0.99

Jumbo Crayons
3¼ in. high.
2811-R-292 Pk./8 $1.49

ORDER TOLL FREE: 800-794-5866

Baby Memories

NEW!

Piggy Bank

Whimsical, yet practical, it's a great gift idea and fun accent for baby's room. Cute just as it is, or you can personalize with name and birthdate, pink or blue, or any design you choose. Crafted in ceramic. Has coin slot on top, removable plug on the bottom. 5¾ in. high x 8 in. long.
1009-R-1113 $9.99

Best Wishes Bear

Create a precious keepsake for the new baby. Makes a great shower gift. Includes blue and pink sheer ribbons and pen. 9¼ in. high, holds 4 x 3 in. photo. Fabric covered. Clothespin accents not included.
1009-R-1140 $16.99

Memory Box

Hinged box holds photos outside, precious keepsakes inside. Displays two 3 x 4 in. and two 1 x 3 in. photos. Painted white, ready for you to decorate or simply add photos. 8½ x 8½ in., 2 in. deep.
1009-R-1114 $19.99

Mini Favor Frames

Perfect shower favors, keepsakes, crafts. Hand out instead of cigars! Six different designs per box, each 3 x 3 in. Holds 1½ x 1½ photo. Resin.
1009-R-1131 Pk./6 $12.99

Baby Frame Autograph Mat

Holds a 5 x 7 in. photo, with room for autographs and good wishes of friends and family. Few gifts touch so many like this one! For use in an 11 x 14 in. frame.
1009-R-1106 $5.99

Memory Frame

Create a keepsake for the new baby that becomes a personalized, permanent record! White frame is ready for you to decorate with your own designs, names, etc. 11 x 14 in.
1009-R-1110 $19.99

Rubber Duckies

3-D Cake Pan

This bathtime favorite will make a big splash at baby showers. Five adorable designs included. Two-piece pan takes 5½ cups batter. Aluminum.
2105-R-2094 $12.99

Candles

Handpainted details, clean-burning design. 1½ in. high.
2811-R-9337 Set/6 $3.49

Sprinkles

2.34 oz. plastic shaker bottle for convenient pouring and storing. Certified Kosher.
710-R-798 $1.99

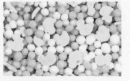

Icon **NEW!** Candles

Highlight your shower theme with candles that feature a fun hand-carved rubber ducky. Instant fun, great size for cupcakes too! 2½ in. high.
2811-R-8419 Pk./10 $1.99

Place Card/ Favor Tag

Tent fold with cutout top.
1006-R-543 Pk./24 $1.99

Favor Box

Fill with candy and tiny treats. Easy to assemble. Size: 2¼ x 3⅛ in. unassembled.
1006-R-545 Pk./24 $6.99

Icing Decorations

Mint-flavored edible sugar shapes to decorate cupcakes, cookies, ice cream and cake. Certified Kosher.
710-R-293 Pk./12 $2.09

Baking Cups

Microwave-safe paper. Standard size, 2 in. diameter.
415-R-378 Pk./50 $1.49

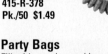

Party Bags

Fill with candy, cookies and other goodies; great for gifts and surprises, too! 20 plastic bags, 20 ties included. 4 x 9½ in.
1912-R-1275 Pk./20 $1.99

Candy Mold

Making candy is easy to do, complete directions are included. Reusable. Use Wilton Candy Melts®† sold on p. 218. 1 design, 6 cavities.
2115-R-1565 $1.99

†Brand confectionery coating.

Character

Wilton helps you make kids feel like stars! We have a great cast of today's favorite faces on fun party products for cakes, cookies and more.

NEW!

Cake Pan

With this pan, kids can enjoy a different *Care Bear* every time! The label includes instructions and patterns for 4 of the most popular "care"acters— it's easy to give *Wish Bear™, Love-A-Lot Bear™, Share Bear™* and *Good Luck Bear™* their distinctive colors and personalities. One-mix pan is 13 x 9½ x 2 in. Aluminum.
2105-R-2424 $11.99

Candle

Handpainted, clean-burning with adorable details. 3 in. high.
2811-R-2424 $3.99

Icing Color Set

Includes four .5 oz. jars of Teal, Blue, Yellow and Orange. Certified Kosher.
**601-R-2424
Set/4 $4.99**

Baking Cups

Standard size, microwave-safe paper. 2 in. diameter.
415-R-2424 Pk./50 $1.69

Icing Decorations

Mint-flavored edible sugar shapes to decorate cupcakes, cookies, ice cream and cake. Certified Kosher.
710-R-2424 Pk./9 $2.29

Treat Bags

Fill with candy, cookies and other goodies; great for gifts and surprises, too! Includes sixteen 4 x 9½ in. bags with twist ties.
**1912-R-2424
Pk./16 $1.99**

Care Bears™ and related trademarks ©2005 Those Characters From Cleveland, Inc. Used under license by Wilton Industries, Inc.

ORDER TOLL FREE: 800-794-5866

Strawberry Shortcake™

Cake Pan
Everyone loves her fun and colorful look! From her bouncy hat to her sweet smile, she adds a "berry" happy touch to the party. One-mix pan is 11¼ x 10 ½ x 2 in. Aluminum.
2105-R-7040 $11.99

Candle
Handpainted, clean-burning with fun details. 3 ¼ in. high.
2811-R-7040 $3.99

Icing Color Set
Includes four 5 oz. jars: Red, Brown, Green and Skin Tone. Certified Kosher.
601-R-7040
Set/4 $4.99

Icing Decorations
Mint-flavored edible sugar shapes to decorate cupcakes, cookies, ice cream and cake. Certified Kosher.
710-R-7041 Pk./9 $2.29

Lollipop Making Kit
Everything you need to make a crop of berry fun pops with *Strawberry Shortcake* and friends! Includes reusable lollipop mold (4 designs, 8 cavities), 10 oz. Candy Melts®* (red, white and blue), 3 disposable decorating bags, 1 decorating brush, 10 lollipop sticks and 10 lollipop bags with ties.
2104-R-7040 $7.99

*Brand confectionery coating.

Fun Pix®
Fun for cupcakes, brownies, ice cream and more. Paper, 3 in. high.
2113-R-7040
Pk./24 $1.29

Baking Cups
Standard size, microwave-safe paper. 2 in. diameter.
415-R-7040
Pk./50 $1.69

Treat Bags
Fill with candy, cookies and other goodies; great for gifts and surprises, too! Includes sixteen 4 x 9 ½ in. bags with twist ties.
1912-R-7040 Pk./16 $1.99

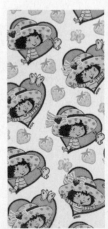

Large Treat Bags
There's more room for fun goodies with this 8 x 8 in. size.
1912-R-7041
Pk./8 $1.99

Barbie™

Cake Pan
Celebration *Barbie* gets the party fun started for your birthday girl. This newest *Barbie* design features pretty pastels, romantic flowers and a fresh, fashionable look that's hers alone. Includes face maker (pictured below). One-mix pan is 9¾ x 13½ x 2 in. Aluminum.
2105-R-8934 $11.99

Face Maker
Place on cake top for the perfect look of Celebration *Barbie*.
504-R-8934
$2.29

Candle
Barbie style makes any cake captivating! Handpainted, clean-burning with colorful details. 3½ in. high.
2811-R-8934 $3.99

Icing Color Set
Includes three .5 oz. jars (Pink, Yellow and Violet), and one .1 oz. jar of White Cake Sparkles™ edible glitter. Certified Kosher.
601-R-8934 Set/4 $4.99

Shaped Sprinkles
Shake up your *Barbie* treats! 4-cell container is convenient for pouring and storing. 2.7 oz. Certified Kosher.
710-R-8901 $5.99

Candy Bar Kit
Everything's included for you to make 8 of the cutest, yummiest candy bars, featuring *Barbie*! Easy and fun —just melt, mold and enjoy. Includes reusable candy bar mold (4 designs, 4 cavities), 10 oz. Candy Melts®* (pink and lavender), 2 oz. candy toppings (Strawberry and Marshmallow) and 8 *Barbie* treat bags with matching stickers to finish these fun gifts.
2104-R-8934 $7.99

Baking Cups
Standard size, microwave-safe paper. 2 in. diameter.
415-R-8934
Pk./50 $1.69

Treat Bags
Fill with candy, cookies and other goodies; great for gifts and surprises, too! Includes sixteen 4 x 9½ in. bags with twist ties.
1912-R-8934
Pk./16 $1.99

*Brand confectionery coating.

SPIDER-MAN

Cake Pan
The Wizard of Webs is back in action, on a pan that will grab every guest! Kids will love the great costume detail. One-mix pan is 9 x 12 x 2 in. Aluminum.
2105-R-5052
$11.99

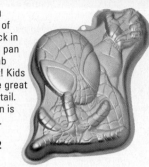

Party Toppers
He's ready to sling his next web on these exciting handpainted toppers. Food-safe plastic to use on cupcakes, brownies, cakes and other treats. 2 ¼ in. high.
2113-R-5052
Set/6 $3.99

Candle
Handpainted, clean-burning with exciting details. 3 ½ in. high.
2811-R-5052
$3.99

Icing Color Set
Includes four .5 oz. jars: Light Blue, Dark Blue, Red and Black. Certified Kosher.
601-R-5052
Set/4 $4.99

Make-a-Cookie-Face Kit
Everything's here for you to decorate 12 fun, colorful cookies starring your favorite web-slinging hero. Includes cookie cutter, 12 sets of *Spider-Man* facial feature icing decorations, 4.25 oz. tube decorating icing, .75 oz. tube decorating gel, recipe and complete instructions.
2104-R-5052 $9.99

Candy Bar Kit
Everything's included for you to make 8 of the coolest, yummiest candy bars, starring *Spidey*! Easy and fun—just melt, mold and enjoy. Includes reusable candy bar mold (4 designs, 4 cavities), 10 oz. Candy Melts®* (red and blue), 2 oz. candy toppings (Toffee and Chocolate) and 8 *Spider-Man* treat bags with matching stickers.
2104-R-5033 $7.99

Icing Decorations
Mint-flavored edible sugar shapes to decorate cupcakes, cookies, ice cream and cake. Certified Kosher.
710-R-5052 Pk./9 $2.29

Baking Cups
Standard size, microwave-safe paper. 2 in. diameter.
415-R-5052
Pk./50 $1.69

Treat Bags
Fill with candy, cookies and other goodies; great for gifts and surprises, too! Includes sixteen 4 x 9 ½ in. bags with twist ties.
1912-R-5052 Pk./16 $1.99

Kandy Clay™† Comic Book Page Activity Kit
Create the yummiest funnies ever— starring *Spider-Man* and made from the modeling clay you can eat! Includes twelve .5 oz. packs of Kandy Clay (Blue Raspberry Blue, Banana Yellow, Hot Fudge Black and Strawberry Red), 2 easy-to-fill Clay Molds for making 10 exciting *Spider-Man* shapes, Sculpting Tool for trimming shapes, complete instructions and Comic Book Board for displaying your *Spider-Man* adventure.
Ages 4 and up.
2104-R-5054 $6.99

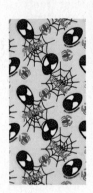

*Brand confectionery coating.

†Brand edible modeling clay.

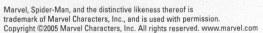
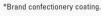

Cake Pan

Everyone's favorite seafaring star will make a big splash at the party. One-mix pan is 13½ x 11¾ x 2 in. Aluminum.
2105-R-5130 $11.99

Mini Treats Cake Pan

Get close-up with your favorite character and create all kinds of exciting single-size desserts. Great for cakes, candy, gelatin and brownies. The pan's intense color makes baking a bubbly good time. One cake mix makes 15 mini cakes. Four-cavity pan is 11 x 9 in.; individual cavities are 3¾ x 3½ x ¾ in. Aluminum.
2105-R-5131 $5.99

Party Toppers

He's surfing your party goodies on these cool handpainted toppers. Food-safe plastic to use on cupcakes, brownies, cakes and other treats. 2 in. high.
2113-R-5130 Set/6 $3.99

Candle

SpongeBob is swimming in loot—giving you a cake to treasure! Handpainted, clean-burning with colorful details. 3½ in. high.
2811-R-5130 $3.99

Edible Cake Decoration Set

Surround the neat-to-eat *SpongeBob* wafer with the edible icing decoration shapes and Happy Birthday message to create instant excitement on any birthday cake.
711-R-5130 Set/20 $2.99

Make-a-Cookie-Face Kit

Decorate 12 colorful cookies that capture *SpongeBob's* bubbly personality. Includes cookie cutter, 12 sets of *SpongeBob SquarePants* facial feature icing decorations, 4.25 oz. tube decorating icing, .75 oz. tube decorating gel, recipe and complete instructions. Certified Kosher.
2104-R-5131 $9.99

Icing Color Set

Includes four .5 oz. jars: Yellow, Red, Blue and Brown. Certified Kosher.
601-R-5130 Set/4 $4.99

Candy Bar Kit

Everything's included for you to make 8 of the yummiest candy bars starring *SpongeBob!* Easy to make—just melt, mold and enjoy. Includes reusable candy bar mold (4 designs, 4 cavities), 10 oz. Candy Melts®* (blue and yellow), 2 oz. candy toppings (Rainbow Big Bits and Marshmallow Big Bits), plus 8 *SpongeBob* treat bags with matching stickers to make fun gifts.
2104-R-5134 $7.99

Lollipop Making Kit

Everything you need to create *SpongeBob* lollipops that will make waves! Includes reusable lollipop mold (4 designs, 8 cavities), 10 oz. Candy Melts®* (Yellow, White and Pink), 3 disposable decorating bags, 1 decorating brush, 10 lollipop sticks and 10 lollipop bags with ties.
2104-R-5130 $7.99

*Brand confectionery coating.

ORDER TOLL FREE: 800-794-5866

Kandy Clay™† Catch The Jellyfish Game Activity Kit

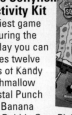

It's the tastiest game ever—featuring the modeling clay you can eat! Includes twelve .5 oz. packs of Kandy Clay (Marshmallow White, Crystal Punch Light Blue, Banana Yellow and Bubble Gum Pink), 2 easy-to-fill Clay Molds for making game pieces, Sculpting Tool for trimming shapes and Game Board for playing the fun "Catch The Jellyfish" game with friends. When the game's over, the eating begins! Ages 4 and up.
2104-R-5140 $6.99

Shaped Sprinkles

4-cell container is convenient for pouring and storing *SpongeBob* (in 2 cells), Flower and Patrick shapes.
2.8 oz. Certified Kosher.
710-R-5131 $5.99

Gummy Candy Making Kit

Kids will have a great time making 16 yummy gummy candies in just minutes! Everything they need is included: reusable mold with 4 exciting *SpongeBob SquarePants* designs, four .7 oz. pouches of Gummy Mix (Lemon, Blue Raspberry, Watermelon and Orange), .7 oz. packet of Sour Sugars for covering gummys, squeeze bottle and funnel. Just add water to the mix, shake, fill mold and pop in your refrigerator. Ages 4 and up.
2104-R-5136 $5.99

Baking Cups

Standard size, microwave-safe paper. 2 in. diameter.
415-R-5130 Pk./50 $1.69

Treat Bags

Fill with candy, cookies and other goodies; great for gifts and surprises, too! Includes sixteen 4 x 9 ½ in. bags with twist ties.
**1912-R-5130
Pk./16 $1.99**

†Brand edible modeling clay.

Cake Pan

Wherever *Dora* goes, it's always "una fiesta"! Discover a world of party excitement with this great pan. One-mix pan is 13¾ x 10 x 2 in. Aluminum.
2105-R-6300 $11.99

Mini Treats Cake Pan

Get close-up with your favorite explorer and create all kinds of exciting single-size desserts. Great for cakes, candy, brownies and gelatin. The pan's intense color makes baking even more fun. One cake mix makes 15 mini cakes.
Four-cavity pan is 11 x 9 in.; individual cavities are 3 ¼ x 5 x ¾ in. Aluminum.
2105-R-6301 $5.99

Party Toppers

Dora is ready to top your delightful party treats! Handpainted, food-safe plastic is great on cupcakes, brownies, cakes and other treats. 2 ¼ in. high.
2113-R-6300 Set/6 $3.99

Candle

Handpainted, clean-burning with colorful details. 3 ¼ in. high.
2811-R-6300 $3.99

Icing Color Set

Includes four .5 oz. jars: Red, Pink, Brown and Skin Tone. Certified Kosher.
**601-R-6300
Set/4 $4.99**

©2005 Viacom International Inc. All Rights Reserved. Nickelodeon, Nick Jr., Dora The Explorer and all related titles, logos and characters are trademarks of Viacom International Inc.

Icing Decorations

Mint-flavored edible sugar shapes to decorate cupcakes, cookies, ice cream and cake. Certified Kosher.
710-R-6300 Pk./8 $2.29

Gummy Candy Making Kit

Kids will have a great time making 16 yummy gummy candies in just minutes! Everything they need is included: reusable mold with 4 exciting *Dora the Explorer* designs, four .7 oz. pouches of Gummy Mix (Grape, Orange, Blue Raspberry and Watermelon), .7 oz. packet of Sour Sugars for covering gummys, squeeze bottle and funnel. Just add water to the mix, shake, fill mold and pop in your refrigerator. Ages 4 and up.
2104-R-6303 $5.99

Baking Cups

Standard size, microwave-safe paper. 2 in. diameter.
415-R-6300 Pk./50 $1.69

Treat Bags

Fill with candy, cookies and other goodies; great for gifts and surprises, too! Includes sixteen 4 x 9 ½ in. bags with twist ties.
1912-R-6300 Pk./16 $1.99

SCOOBY-DOO!

Cake Pan

As usual, *Scooby* gets right next to the food! This fun pan shows him about to put his canines into a big burger. One-mix pan is 10 ½ x 12 x 2 in. Aluminum.
2105-R-3227 **$11.99**

Mini Treats Cake Pan

Get close-up with your favorite character and create all kinds of exciting single-size desserts. Great for cakes, candy, gelatin and brownies. The pan's intense color makes baking even more fun. Four cavity pan is 11 x 9 in.; individual cavities are 3 x 5 ½ x ¾ in. deep. Aluminum.
2105-R-3228 **$5.99**

Party Toppers

Scooby-Doo! is begging for attention on these fun handpainted toppers. Food-safe plastic to decorate cupcakes, brownies, cakes and other treats. 2 ½ in. high.
2113-R-3206 Set/6 **$3.99**

Candle

Handpainted, clean-burning with colorful details. 3 ¾ in. high.
2811-R-3227 **$3.99**

Icing Decorations

Mint-flavored edible sugar shapes to decorate cupcakes, cookies, ice cream and cake. Certified Kosher.
710-R-3206 Pk./9 **$2.29**

Shaped Sprinkles

Shake up your *Scooby-Doo!* treats. Convenient 4-cell container designed for pouring and storing. 2.55 oz. Certified Kosher.
710-R-3207 **$5.99**

Icing Color Set

Includes four .5 oz. jars: Brown, Yellow, Black, Teal. Certified Kosher.
601-R-3206 Set/4 **$4.99**

Candy Bar Kit

Everything's included for you to make 8 of the coolest, yummiest candy bars, starring *Scooby-Doo!* Easy and fun—just melt, mold and enjoy. Includes reusable candy bar mold (4 designs, 4 cavities), 10 oz. Candy Melts®* (Light Cocoa and Yellow), 2 oz. candy toppings (Chocolate and Graham Cracker Crunch) and 8 *Scooby-Doo!* treat bags with matching stickers to complete these fun gifts.
2104-R-3209 **$7.99**

Edible Cake Decoration Set

Surround the fun-to-eat *Scooby-Doo* wafer with the edible icing decorations and Happy Birthday message to create instant excitement on any birthday cake.
711-R-3206 Set/20 **$2.99**

Make-a-Cookie-Face Kit

Everything's here for you to decorate 12 fun, colorful cookies that capture *Scooby's* snack-happy state of mind. Includes cookie cutter, 12 sets of *Scooby-Doo!* facial feature icing decorations, 4.25 oz. tube decorating icing, .75 oz. tube decorating gel, recipe and complete instructions. Certified Kosher.
2104-R-3207 **$9.99**

Lollipop Making Kit

Everything you need to make fun *Scooby-Doo!* lollipops! Includes reusable lollipop mold (4 designs, 8 cavities), 10 oz. Candy Melts®* (Light Cocoa, White and Yellow), 3 disposable decorating bags, 1 decorating brush, 10 lollipop sticks and 10 lollipop bags with ties.
2104-R-3206 **$7.99**

*Brand confectionery coating.

Kandy Clay™† Mystery Machine Puzzle Activity Kit

Kids will love making this puzzle that's also a sweet treat to eat! Includes twelve .5 oz. packs of Kandy Clay (Grape Purple, Orange Orange, Green Apple Green and Blue Raspberry Blue), 2 easy-to-fill Clay Molds for making happy *Scooby-Doo!* shapes, Sculpting Tool for trimming shapes, complete instructions and Puzzle Board for putting clay puzzle pieces together. Ages 4 and up.
2104-R-3228 $6.99

Gummy Candy Making Kit

Kids will have a great time making 16 yummy gummy candies in just minutes! Everything they need is included: reusable mold with 4 fun *Scooby-Doo!* designs, four .7 oz. pouches of Gummy Mix (Green Apple, Grape, Watermelon and Orange), .7 oz. packet of Sour Sugars for covering gummys, squeeze bottle and funnel. Just add water to the mix, shake, fill mold and pop in your refrigerator. Ages 4 and up.
2104-R-3211 $5.99

Baking Cups

Standard size, microwave-safe paper. 2 in. diameter.
415-R-3227
Pk./50 $1.69

Treat Bags

Fill with candy, cookies and other goodies; great for gifts and surprises, too! Includes sixteen 4 x 9 ½ in. bags with twist ties.
1912-R-3227 Pk./16 $1.99

†Brand edible modeling clay.

123 SESAME STREET

Elmo Face Cake Pan
He's sweet, lovable and popular with kids of all ages. One-mix pan is 13 ½ x 10 ½ x 2 in. Aluminum.
2105-R-3461 $11.99

Elmo with Crayons Candle
Elmo brings smiles to the party. Handpainted, clean-burning with colorful details. 3 ½ in. high.
2811-R-3463 $3.99

Icing Decorations
Mint-flavored edible sugar shapes to decorate cupcakes, cookies, ice cream and cakes. Certified Kosher.
710-R-3460 Pk./9 $2.29

Parade Cake Top Set
A fun birthday parade right on your cake. *Cookie Monster, Zoe, Elmo, Big Bird* in food-safe plastic. 1 ½ to 4 in. high.
2113-R-3460 Set/4 $4.99

Baking Cups
Standard size, microwave-safe paper. 2 in. diameter.
415-R-3461
Pk./50 $1.69

Treat Bags
Fill with candy, cookies and other goodies; great for gifts and surprises, too! Includes sixteen 4 x 9 ½ in. bags with twist ties.
1912-R-3461
Pk./16 $1.99

Disney
Winnie the Pooh

NEW!

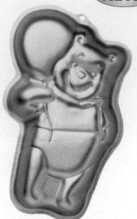

Pooh Cake Pan
He's always ready for a fun party, with his birthday balloon in hand and a happy smile on his face. One-mix pan is 13¾ x 7¾ x 2 in. Aluminum.
2105-R-3100 $11.99

Candles
Pooh is ready for the party. Handpainted, clean-burning with colorful details. 2-3 in. high.
$3.99

Pooh #1 Hunny Pot
2811-R-3102

Pooh and Presents
2811-R-3100

Icing Color Set
Includes four .5 oz. jars: *Pooh* (gold), Red, Green and Black. Certified Kosher.
601-R-3100
Set/4 $4.99

Icing Decorations
Mint-flavored edible sugar shapes to decorate cupcakes, cookies, ice cream and cake. Certified Kosher.
710-R-3100
Pk./9 $2.29

Baking Cups
Standard size, microwave-safe paper. 2 in. diameter.
415-R-3100 Pk./50 $1.69

Treat Bags
Fill with candy, cookies and other goodies; great for gifts and surprises, too! Includes sixteen 4 x 9½ in. bags with twist ties.
1912-R-3100 Pk./16 $1.99

Based on the "Winnie The Pooh" works, by A.A. Milne and E.H. Shepard.
© Disney

ORDER TOLL FREE: 800-794-5866

DISNEY PRINCESS

Cake Pan
Fulfill every little girl's dream of becoming a princess with her very own magical Cinderella cake. One-mix pan is 14 ¼ x 9 ¼ x 2 in. Aluminum.
2105-R-7475 $11.99

Party Toppers
A royally fun way to top party treats. Handpainted, food-safe plastic is great on cupcakes, brownies, cakes and other treats. 2 in. high.
2113-R-7475
Set/6 $3.99

Candle
Wish upon a *Disney* star! Handpainted, clean-burning with colorful details. 3 ½ in. high.
2811-R-7475 $3.99

© Disney

Happy Birthday

Gummy Candy Making Kit
Kids will have a great time making 16 yummy gummy candies in just minutes! Everything they need is included: reusable mold with 4 fun *Disney Princess* designs, four .7 oz. pouches of Gummy Mix (Strawberry, Bubble Gum, Banana and Green Apple), .7 oz. packet of Sour Sugars for covering gummys, squeeze bottle and funnel. Just add water to the mix, shake, fill mold and pop in your refrigerator. Ages 4 and up.
2104-R-7477 $5.99

Icing Decorations
Mint-flavored edible sugar shapes to decorate cupcakes, cookies, ice cream and cake. Certified Kosher.
710-R-7475 Pk./9 $2.29

Shaped Sprinkles
4-cell container for easy pouring and storing. Includes Crown, Heart, Star and Flower shapes. 2.45 oz. Certified Kosher.
710-R-7479 $5.99

Baking Cups
Standard size, microwave-safe paper. 2 in. diameter.
415-R-7475 Pk./50 $1.69

Treat Bags
Fill with candy, cookies and other goodies; great for gifts and surprises, too! Includes sixteen 4 x 9 ½ in. bags with twist ties.
1912-R-7475 Pk./16 $1.99

Icing Color Set
Includes four .5 oz. jars: Blue, Yellow, Pink and Skin Tone. Certified Kosher.
601-R-7475 Set/4 $4.99

DISNEY MICKEY MOUSE

Mickey Face Pan
The world's most beloved mouse goes to the best parties! Easy-to-decorate; loved by all ages. One-mix pan is 10 ½ x 12 x 2 in. Aluminum.
2105-R-3603 $11.99

Mickey with Starburst Candle
Your favorite mouse! Handpainted, clean-burning with colorful details. 3 ½ in. high.
2811-R-3609 $3.99

© Disney

Icing Color Set
Includes four .5 oz. jars: two Black plus *Mickey* Peach and Copper (lt. skin tone). Certified Kosher.
601-R-3603 Set/4 $4.99

Icing Decorations
Mint-flavored edible sugar shapes to decorate cupcakes, cookies, ice cream and cake. Certified Kosher.
710-R-3600 Pk./9 $2.29

Baking Cups
Standard size, microwave-safe paper. 2 in. diameter.
415-R-3610 Pk./50 $1.69

Party

You've written the guest list—now start your decorating list here! From baking cups to candles, cake toppers to treat bags, Wilton has the great-looking designs you want.

Baking Cups

The easiest way to dress up a cupcake! Just put 'em together using Wilton Baking Cups and Icing Decorations in your favorite themes. Ideal for holding candy and nuts, too.

Made of microwave-safe paper unless otherwise noted. Jumbo cups are 2 ¼ in. diameter, standard cups are 2 in. diameter, mini cups are 1 ¼ in. diameter, bon bon cups are 1 in. diameter.

NEW!

Party Hats
Standard 415-R-5365
Pk./50 $1.49

NEW!

Ice Cream
Standard 415-R-121
Pk./50 $1.49

Smiley Faces
Standard 415-R-261
Pk./50 $1.49

Rubber Duckies
Standard 415-R-378
Pk./50 $1.49

Baseball
Standard 415-R-298
Pk./50 $1.49

Football
Standard 415-R-297
Pk./50 $1.49

Soccer
Standard 415-R-296
Pk./50 $1.49

White $1.49
Jumbo
415-R-2503 Pk/50
Standard 415-R-2505 Pk./75
Mini 415-R-2507 Pk./100

Assorted Pastel
25 pink, 25 yellow, 25 blue.
Standard 415-R-394
Pk./75 $1.49

Gold Foil
Wax-laminated paper on foil.
Standard
415-R-206 Pk./24 $1.49
Bon Bon
415-R-306 Pk./75 $1.49

Silver Foil
Standard 415-R-207 $1.49
(24 pure aluminum/24 paper)
Bon Bon 415-R-307 $1.49
(36 pure aluminum/36 paper)

Gold Foil Petite Loaf*
Wax-laminated paper on foil.
415-R-452 Pk./24 $1.49

*Petite Loaf Cups are 3 ¼ x 2 in. and fit Petite Loaf Pan p. 149.

White Petite Loaf*
Microwave-safe paper.
415-R-450 Pk./50 $1.49

Nut and Party Cups
Mini 1 ¼ oz.
415-R-500 Pk./36 $1.69
Standard 3 ¼ oz.
415-R-400 Pk./24 $1.69

Icing Decorations

Wilton Icing Decorations are perfect for topping cupcakes, cookies and ice cream. Mint-flavored edible shapes are Certified Kosher.

NEW!

Happy Birthday with Balloons
710-R-547 Pk./21 $2.09

NEW! **NEW!**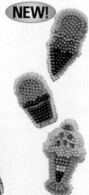

Party Hats
710-R-7205
Pk./12 $2.09

Ice Cream
710-R-7812
Pk./12 $2.09

HAPPY BIRTHDAY
Alphabet/Numerals
710-R-494 Pk./70 $2.09

HAPPY BIRTHDAY
Script Alphabet
710-R-546 Pk./62 $2.09

Rubber Duckies
710-R-293
Pk./12 $2.09

Baseball Mitts
710-R-475
Pk./9 $2.09

Soccer Balls
710-R-477
Pk./9 $2.09

Footballs
710-R-478
Pk./9 $2.09

ORDER TOLL FREE: 800-794-5866

Party Bags

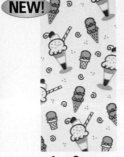

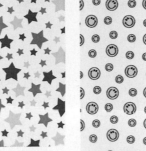

Wrap up cookies, candies, favors and more with color and fun!

Contains 20, 4 x 9 ½ in. bags and 20 twist ties, unless otherwise noted.
Pk./20 $1.99

Clear
(not shown)
1912-R-1240 Pk./25 $1.99

Party Hats
1912-R-4365

Ice Cream
1912-R-3106

Colorful Stars
1912-R-2362

Smiley Faces
1912-R-2361

Rubber Duckies
1912-R-1275

Baby
1912-R-2365

Red
1912-R-2357

Blue
1912-R-2356

Yellow
1912-R-2359

Pink
1912-R-2363

Wedding
1912-R-2364

PIZAZZ

Your treats will be a sensation— bags have a dazzling reflective pattern in 4 bright colors.

Contains 8, 4 x 9 ½ in. bags and 8 twist ties.
Pk./8 $1.99

Silver Pizazz
1912-R-1020

Gold Pizazz
1912-R-1022

Red Pizazz
1912-R-1019

Blue Pizazz
1912-R-1021

Cake Toppers

With Wilton Toppers, a decorated cake is just minutes away! The excellent detail you expect from Wilton is evident in every design.

BOBBLING TOPPERS NEW!

Top off that special cake with these fun bobbling toppers and watch heads turn. There's a fun sports shape for everyone! The food-safe design features hand-painted detail that makes even plain cakes more exciting.

Baseball
2113-R-5242 $3.99

Softball
2113-R-5240 $3.99

Male Soccer
2113-R-5238 $3.99

Female Soccer
2113-R-5239 $3.99

Golfer
2113-R-5237 $3.99

Fisherman
2113-R-5236 $3.99

DOLL PICKS

Teen Doll Pick
Her hair and face are prettier than ever—she'll give your Wonder Mold cakes a realism and sophistication unlike anything you've seen. 7 ¾ in. high with pick. **$2.99**
Brunette 2815-R-101
Blond 2815-R-102
Ethnic 2815-R-103

Mini Doll Pick Set
4 ¼ in. high with pick.
1511-R-1019 Set/4 $5.99

Cake Toppers

Small Derby Clowns Set
2 in. high with pick.
2113-R-2759 Set/6 $1.99

Circus Balloons Set
12 in a bunch, 3 bunches per set, 6 ½ in. high.
2113-R-2366 Set/36 $2.99

Dinosaur Party Set
Reptile revelry!
1 ¾ to 2 ½ in. high.
2113-R-9420 Set/4 $3.99

Musical Light Show Topper
Any birthday cake will become a showstopper when this dazzling decoration is on top! The birthday message flashes brightly while the "Happy Birthday" song is played for everyone to join in. Convenient ON/OFF switch. Requires four AG13 or LR44 Alkaline Button Cell Batteries; 8 batteries included. Each set of 4 batteries lasts for 28 minutes of playing time.
2113-R-3465 $5.99

Tumbling Bears Set
Adorable acrobats,
2 to 2 ½ in. high.
2113-R-9421 Set/4 $3.99

Circus Animals Set
Handpainted performers,
2 ½ to 3 in. high.
2113-R-9422 Set/4 $3.99

Jungle Animals Set
Spectacular safari,
1 ¾ to 3 in. high.
2113-R-2095 Set/4 $3.99

SPORTS THEME

Baseball Set*
Batter, catcher, three fielders and pitcher,
2 ⅛ to 2 ¾ in. high.
2113-R-2155 Set/6 $2.99

Basketball Set*
Includes 1 forward,
2 centers, 3 guards and
1 hoop, 2 ¼ to 4 in. high.
2113-R-2237 Set/7 $2.99

Football Set*
Eight players and two goal posts, 1 ½ to 4 ½ in. high.
2113-R-2236 Set/10 $2.99

Carousel Separator Set
Snaps together fast—sturdy pony pillars and separator plates provide strong support. Set includes four 9 in. high pony pillars and two 10 in. diameter separator plates.
2103-R-1139 Set/6 $12.99

RELIGIOUS

Inspiring decorations that add a beautiful touch to spiritual events.

Inspirational Cross
Polished resin with finely sculpted scroll and bead highlighting.
5 ½ in. high.
202-R-206 $24.99

Soccer Set*
Seven players and two nets,
1 ¾ to 2 in. high.
2113-R-9002 Set/9 $2.99

Golf Set*
Includes 4 ½ in. high golfer plus three each: 2 ½ in. wide greens,
4 in. high flags, 5 in. clubs and golf balls.
1306-R-7274 Set/13 $2.99

Frustrated Fisherman*
4 ½ in. high.
2113-R-2384
$3.49

Communion Girl†
3 ½ in. high.
2113-R-7878
$3.49

Communion Boy†
3 ½ in. high.
2113-R-7886
$3.49

† Designed by Ellen Williams

*CAUTION: Contains small parts. Not recommended for use by children 3 years and under.

Candle Sets

Wilton gives you more choices! Top your cake with candles in the perfect colors—and check out our exciting designs on pages 188-189.

Fiesta
Approx. 1¾ in. high.
2811-R-9345 Set/4 $3.49

Ice Cream
Approx. 2¼ in. high.
2811-R-9349 Set/4 $3.49

Farm
Approx. 1⅝ in. high.
2811-R-9347 Set/4 $3.49

Tropical Fish
Approx. 1½ in. high.
2811-R-9333 Set/4 $3.49

Baby Things
Approx. 2 in. high.
2811-R-855 Set/4 $3.49

Party Time
Approx. 1½ in. high.
2811-R-860 Set/4 $3.49

Take Me Out To The Ballgame
Approx. 2 in. high.
2811-R-9341 Set/4 $3.49

Firefighting
Approx. 1½ in. high.
2811-R-9339 Set/4 $3.49

NEW!

Paper Lanterns
1 in. high.
2811-R-9308 Set/6 $3.49

Smiley Faces
1½ in. high.
2811-R-9351 Set/6 $3.49

SPORTS SETS NEW!

Capture the flavor of the game with these complete cake top sets. Just peel enclosed decals and attach to center theme topper; insert candles in holders, position topper and get ready to have a ball! Each set includes 1 theme topper, 6 candleholders, 10 candles and 1 sheet of decals.

Baseball
2811-R-8425 Set/8 $4.99

Basketball
2811-R-8423 Set/8 $4.99

Football
2811-R-8424 Set/8 $4.99

Hockey
2811-R-8422 Set/8 $4.99

Soccer
2811-R-8421 Set/8 $4.99

Golf
2811-R-8420 Set/8 $4.99

Home Improvement Tools
Approx. 2¼ in. high.
2811-R-9136 Set/5 $3.49

Construction Vehicles
Approx. 1¾ in. long.
2811-R-858 Set/4 $3.49

Race Cars
Approx. 1¾ in. high.
2811-R-9135 Set/4 $3.49

Beach Sandals
⅜ in. high, ⅞ in. long.
2811-R-9352 Set/6 $3.49

Rubber Duckies
1½ in. high.
2811-R-9337 Set/6 $3.49

Margaritas
1¼ in. high.
2811-R-9343 Set/6 $3.49

Champagne Bottles
2 in. high.
2811-R-163 Set/6 $3.49

Beer Cans
1¾ in. high.
2811-R-9326 Set/6 $3.49

PARTY

Candles

RAINBOW COLORS

NEW!

Curly
Twisting, turning fun. 3 in. high.
2811-R-9127
Pk./12 $1.49

NEW!

Candle Holders
Protects cakes and keeps candles secure. Great colors 1 in. high.
2811-R-552
Pk./24 $0.99

CLASSIC

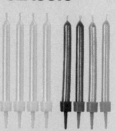

Pearlized
Watch them shimmer from the moment you light them! 2 ½ in. high.
Pk./10 $1.99
White
2811-R-3658
Multicolor
2811-R-3665

Glitter
2 ½ in. high.
Pk./10 $0.99
White 2811-R-248
Pink 2811-R-244
Blue 2811-R-246
Black 2811-R-247

Celebration
2 ½ in. high.
Pk./24 $0.69
White 2811-R-207
Pink 2811-R-213
Red 2811-R-209
Blue 2811-R-210
Black 2811-R-224

Assorted Celebration
Classic spirals in attractive two-tones. 2 ½ in. high.
2811-R-215
Pk./24 $0.69

"Trick"
Blow 'em out —they relight! 2 ½ in. high. Assorted: White, Yellow, Pink, Blue.
2811-R-220
Pk./10 $0.99

Silver and Gold
2 ¼ in. high.
Pk./10 $1.49
Silver 2811-R-9123
Gold 2811-R-9122

Shimmer
2 ½ in. high.
2811-R-3663
Pk./8 $1.99

Lattice
2 ½ in. high.
2811-R-3656
Pk./8 $1.99

Twist
2 ½ in. high.
2811-R-3660
Pk./8 $2.49

Corkscrew
2 ½ in. high.
2811-R-778
Pk./8 $2.49

Tricolor
2 ½ in. high.
2811-R-779
Pk./10 $1.99

Crayons Jumbo
3 ¼ in. high. $1.49
2811-R-226 Pk./8
Regular
2 ½ in. high. $1.49
2811-R-227 Pk./10

Triangle "Trick" Sparklers
2 ½ in. high.
2811-R-278
Pk./9 $0.99

Wavy "Trick" Sparklers
2 ½ in. high.
2811-R-272
Pk./10 $1.99

Rounds
2 ½ in. high.
2811-R-284
Pk./24 $0.69

Party Thins
8 in. high.
2811-R-239
Pk./20 $0.99

HOT COLORS

NEW!

Diamond Dot
2 ½ in. high.
2811-R-551
Pk./20 $1.99

Shimmer
2 ½ in. high.
2811-R-3662
Pk./8 $1.99

Lattice
2 ½ in. high.
2811-R-3655
Pk./8 $1.99

Twist
2 ½ in. high.
2811-R-3659
Pk./8 $2.49

Corkscrew
2 ½ in. high.
2811-R-776
Pk./8 $2.49

SOFT COLORS

Shimmer
2 ½ in. high.
2811-R-3664
Pk./8 $1.99

Lattice
2 ½ in. high.
2811-R-3657
Pk./8 $1.99

Twist
2 ½ in. high.
2811-R-3661
Pk./8 $2.49

Corkscrew
2 ½ in. high.
2811-R-775
Pk./8 $2.49

Tricolor
2 ½ in. high.
2811-R-782
Pk./10 $1.99

Tricolor
2 ½ in. high.
2811-R-779
Pk./10 $1.99

Jumbo Crayons
3 ¼ in. high.
2811-R-282
Pk./8 $1.49

Triangle "Trick" Sparklers
2 ½ in. high.
2811-R-276
Pk./9 $0.99

Wavy "Trick" Sparklers
2 ½ in. high.
2811-R-270
Pk./10 $1.99

Rounds
2 ½ in. high.
2811-R-225
Pk./24 $0.69

Party Thins
8 in. high.
2811-R-237
Pk./20 $0.99

Jumbo Crayons
3 ¼ in. high.
2811-R-292
Pk./8 $1.49

Triangle "Trick" Sparklers
2 ½ in. high.
2811-R-288
Pk./9 $0.99

Wavy "Trick" Sparklers
2 ½ in. high.
2811-R-289
Pk./10 $1.99

Rounds
2 ½ in. high.
2811-R-291
Pk./24 $0.69

Party Thins
8 in. high.
2811-R-255
Pk./20 $0.99

ORDER TOLL FREE: 800-794-5866

NOVELTY

Stars
2811-R-8416

Cupcakes
2811-R-8418

Tombstones
2811-R-8417

Rubber Duckies
2811-R-8419

Stars
2811-R-6325

Smiley Flames
2811-R-6326

Icons
Highlight your party theme with candles that feature a fun hand-carved shape. Instant fun for any celebration, great size for cupcakes, too! 2½ in. high. **Pk./10 $1.99**

Chunkys
Thicker candles to energize any cake! They feature bold textured spirals and a fun hand-carved shape on top. 3¼ in. high. **Pk./4 $3.49**

Musical Candle
Plays "Happy Birthday To You". 4¾ in. high. **2811-R-1231 $3.69**

Longs
Sized right for larger cakes or for making a bold statement on any cake. 5⅞ in. high. **Pk./12 $1.99**

White
2811-R-773

Multicolor
2811-R-777

Over The Hill
The secret of aging is keeping your sense of humor! This Wilton candle helps anyone face those big birthdays with a smile! 2¼ in. high.
2811-R-553 $1.99

Glow Candle Set
Turn out the lights and get ready to serve your cake in a thrilling glow of color. Set of 4 light stick candle holders with candles gives cakes an aura of excitement that lasts up to 6 hours. No batteries needed—the glow starts when you bend the light sticks. Includes 4 each light sticks, connectors and candles. 6½ in. high.
2811-R-6215 Set/12 $4.99

Glow-in-the-Dark
They light up the room even before you light them! These luminous candles will lend an extra touch of fun to any celebration. Assorted colors: white, yellow, green, blue. 2½ in. high.
2811-R-165 Pk./10 $1.99

Slenders
6½ in. high.
2811-R-1188
Pk./24 $0.79

"Trick" Sparklers
Blow 'em out—they relight!
6½ in. high. **Pk./18 $0.99**

Assorted
2811-R-1230

Red and Blue
2811-R-704

NUMERALS

#1
2811-R-9101

Pink #1
2811-R-240

Blue #1
2811-R-241

Festive way to mark age or year. Edged in green unless specified. 3 in. high. **$0.79**

#2	2811-R-9102	#7	2811-R-9107
#3	2811-R-9103	#8	2811-R-9108
#4	2811-R-9104	#9	2811-R-9109
#5	2811-R-9105	#0	2811-R-9100
#6	2811-R-9106	?	2811-R-9110

PICK SETS
Put your celebration message in lights! These bright candle picks are a unique and easy way to pick up the party theme on your cake top. Fun colors are just right for the occasion.

Smiley Faces with Hats
2½ in. high.
2811-R-6327 Set/4 $3.49

Happy Birthday
2811-R-785 Set/15 $1.99

Over The Hill
2811-R-786 Set/13 $1.99

Congratulations
2811-R-787 Set/15 $1.99

3 in. high. Also shown with picks.

Wilton Seasonal

Wilton makes every time of year worth celebrating! With so many fun ways to serve cakes, cookies and other treats, it's easy to let everyone taste the excitement of each season.

HALLOWEEN

Bakeware

Just Batty Pan
A little silly, a little scary—this pan will bring shrieks of delight to your Halloween celebration. See label for fun ideas using brownie and gelatin treat recipes! One-mix pan is 13 x 10½ x 2 in. Aluminum.
2105-R-6411 $7.99

Spooky Ghost Pan
This appetizing apparition will be a welcome vision at all your Halloween happenings—from costume parties at home to celebrations at school. Great for easy-to-decorate cakes and gelatin desserts. One-mix pan is 11½ x 11½ x 2 in. Aluminum.
2105-R-2090 $7.99

Iridescents! Jack-O-Lantern Pan **NEW!**
The perfect holiday pan—this bright, colorful shape is as much fun for serving party treats as it is for baking a great cake! Designed for quick, easy cake decorating. Also ideal for crisped rice cereal treats, molded gelatin, bread dough and more. One-mix pan is 11¾ x 11⅛ x 2 in. Aluminum.
2105-R-2059 $5.99

Stand-Up Jack-O-Lantern Pan
They won't say boo to your 3-D dessert! Ideas and instructions for all skill levels. Two-piece pan is 7 x 5¼ x 6½ in. deep and takes 5 cups of pound cake batter. Aluminum.
2105-R-3150 Set/2 $11.99

Petite Jack-O-Lantern Pan
Make personal petite smiling pumpkins. One mix makes 9-13 dozen jack-o-lanterns. 12 cavities, each 2 x 2 x 1⅛ in. Aluminum.
2105-R-8462 $9.99

Mini Ghost Pan
Create gobs of goblins at one time! One mix makes 9-15 ghosts ready for decorating. 6 cavities, each 4 x 4⅞ x 1⅜ in. Aluminum.
2105-R-3845 $10.99

Jack-O-Lantern Cookie Treat Pan
Create your own cookie blossoms; also great for adding fun shapes to other goodies like rice cereal treats and candy pops. Recipe included. Six-cavity pan, each cavity measures 3¼ x 3¼ x ¼ in. Aluminum.
2105-R-8100 $7.99

Cookie Treat Sticks
6 in. 1912-R-9319 Pk./20 $1.99
8 in. 1912-R-9318 Pk./20 $2.99

Colors & Icings

HALLOWEEN COLOR GUIDE

Orange   Black   Violet   White

Halloween Icing Colors Set
.5 oz. jars of Black and Orange. Certified Kosher.
601-R-3010 Set/2 $2.99

Color Mist™ Food Color Spray
Gives decorators the versatility and dazzling effects of an airbrush in a convenient can! Use it to transform a plain iced cake with sensational color, add splashes of holiday color to iced cookies and cupcakes. No mess, taste-free formula. 1.5 oz. Certified Kosher. **$2.99**
Orange   710-R-5507
Black   710-R-5506
Violet   710-R-5504

FoodWriter™ Edible Color Markers
Use like ink markers to add fun, dazzling color to countless foods. Kids love 'em! Decorate on fondant, color flow, royal icing designs and cookies. Includes Black and Orange markers. .35 oz. Certified Kosher.
609-R-101 Set/2 $3.99

Ready-To-Decorate Icing
Anyone can decorate with Wilton Ready-to-Decorate Icing! Our brilliant colors and four decorating tips make it a breeze to add an exciting finishing touch to treats—without mixing or mess. 6.4 oz. Certified Kosher. **$3.49**
Orange   710-R-4410
Black   710-R-4404
Violet   710-R-4408
White   710-R-4402

Tube Decorating Icing
Tubes can be used with our Tip and Nail Set or Coupler Ring Set (p. 133) and any standard size Wilton metal tip. Colors match Wilton Icing Colors (p. 133). 4.25 oz. Certified Kosher. **$1.79**
Orange   704-R-212
Black   704-R-206
Violet   704-R-242
White   704-R-200

Tube Decorating Gel
Transparent gels are great for writing messages and decorating cakes and cookies. Colors match Wilton Icing Colors (p. 133). .75 oz. Certified Kosher. **$1.29**
Orange   704-R-312
Black   704-R-306
Violet   704-R-342
White   704-R-302

Party

NEW!

Baking Cups
Microwave-safe paper.
Standard size, 2 in. diameter,
Mini size, 1 ¼ in. diameter.
Standard Pk./50 **$1.49**
Mini Pk./75 **$1.49**

Tricks 'n Treats
Standard **415-R-3229**
Mini **415-R-3201**

Just Batty
Standard **415-R-250**

Spooky Ghost
Standard **415-R-371**

FOIL FUN PIX®
Add a shimmering, spooky
touch to cakes, cupcakes,
ice cream and more.
Approx. 3 ½ in. high.
Pk./12 $1.99

Just Batty
2113-R-1346

Party Bags
Colorful Halloween
designs for candy and
cookie treats.
20 plastic bags, 20 ties
included. 4 x 9 ½ in.
Pk./20 $1.99

NEW!

Tricks 'n Treats
1912-R-2479

Just Batty
1912-R-2058

Spooky Ghost
1912-R-1040

Pumpkin
2113-R-713

Icing Decorations
Perfect for topping
cupcakes, cookies and
ice cream. Mint-flavored.
Certified Kosher. **$2.09**

NEW!

Petite Tricks 'n Treats
710-R-456 Pk./12

Just Batty
710-R-273 Pk./9

Petite Ghosts
710-R-3030 Pk./12

Candy **NEW!**

Candy Melts®*
Ideal for all your candy
making—molding, dipping
or coating. Artificially vanilla
flavored unless otherwise
indicated. 14 oz. bag. Certified
Kosher. **$2.50**

Orange	1911-R-1631
Dark Green	1911-R-405
Light Cocoa	1911-R-544
White	1911-R-498
Yellow	1911-R-463
Dark Cocoa	1911-R-358
Chocolate Mint	1911-R-1920
Lavender	1911-R-403

**Jack-O-Lantern
Lollipop Mold**
1 design, 8 cavities.
2115-R-1704 $1.99

**Just Batty
Lollipop Mold**
3 designs, 8 cavities.
2115-R-1411 $1.99

**Spooky Ghost
Candy Mold**
1 design, 8 cavities.
2115-R-1407 $1.99

BOBBLING TOPPERS **NEW!**

Top off that special cake
with these fun bobbling
toppers and watch heads
turn. The food-safe design
features hand-painted
detail that makes even
plain cakes more exciting.
2 ¼ in. high. **Pk./6 $2.99**

Ghost
2113-R-3464

Gummy Making Kit
Kids will have a great
time making 16 yummy
gummy candies in just
minutes! Everything they
need is included: mold
with 4 fun Halloween
designs, four .7 oz.
pouches of gummy mix
(Grape, Lemon, Orange
and Blue Raspberry),
one .7 oz. packet of Sour
Sugars for covering gummys, squeeze bottle and
funnel. Just add water to the mix, shake, fill molds
and pop in your refrigerator. Ages 4 and up.
2104-R-3064 $4.99

Halloween Lollipop Kit
Everything you need to make easy,
fun Halloween treats! Includes one
lollipop mold (3 designs, 8 cavities),
10 oz. Candy Melts® (5 oz. White,
2.5 oz. each Orange and Light
Cocoa), 10 lollipop sticks (8 in.), 10
lollipop bags with ties, 3 disposable
decorating bags and one
decorating brush.
2104-R-1236 $6.99

Pumpkin
2113-R-3463

**See pages 218-221 for more
Wilton candy items.**

*Brand confectionery coating.

HALLOWEEN

JUST BATTY BROWNIE KIT

 NEW!

Go batty with this fun new way to serve brownies! It's easy to make these fudgy favorites, decorated with friendly faces for Halloween. In just 3 easy steps, you'll have 8 terrifying treats to give or gobble with friends. Includes 26 oz. brownie mix, metal bat cutter, 8 sets of Bat face icing decorations. (9 x 13 baking pan and ⅔ cup cold water also needed.)
2104-R-1691 **$7.99**

1 Bake! **2** Cut & Decorate! **3** Serve!

Stencil Sets

STENCIL-A-COOKIE™ CUTTER & STENCIL SETS

Using the fun-shaped stencils and cutter, it's easy to serve cookies with exciting, colorful designs for the season. Just cut cookies, then use the stencils and Cake Sparkles™ or Colored Sugars (shown at right), or Wilton FoodWriter™ Edible Color markers or Color Mist™ Food Color Spray (p. 190) to create dazzling shapes on top after baking. Set includes one metal cutter and two stencils (same design).
Set/3 **$1.99**

Just Batty
2308-R-1413

Jack-O-Lantern
2308-R-1406

Ghost
2308-R-1407

Halloween Cupcake and Cookie Stencils

Turn plain treats into ghoulish goodies with a stenciled Halloween design. Just place one of the fun designs over your baked treat, then sprinkle with Wilton Cake Sparkles™ or Colored Sugars (shown at right) or spray with Color Mist™ Food Color Spray (p. 190). 12 designs.
417-R-497 **$2.99**

Sprinkles

INDIVIDUAL BOTTLES

Shake up your Halloween treats with fun colors and designs. Plastic bottles for convenient pouring and storing. Certified Kosher. **$1.99**

Ghost Mix
2.5 oz. bottle
710-R-767

Halloween Mix
2.5 oz. bottle
710-R-788

Orange Sugar
3.5 oz. bottle
710-R-759

Black Sugar
3.5 oz. bottle
710-R-762

Purple Sugar
3.5 oz. bottle
710-R-758

Sparkling Sugars

A coarse texture and a brilliant sparkle. 8 oz. Certified Kosher. **$3.99**

Orange/White
710-R-572

Lavender/White
710-R-571

Cake Sparkles™

Edible glitter, .25 oz. bottle. Certified Kosher. **$2.89**

Orange
703-R-1308

Black
703-R-1302

Purple
703-R-1266

ASSORTMENTS

4-Mix
.8 oz. Halloween Mix, 1 oz. Halloween Nonpareils, 1.2 oz. each of Black and Orange Sugars. Certified Kosher.
710-R-728 **$4.99**

6-Mix
1 oz. Halloween Mix, 1 oz. Bat Mix, 1.3 oz. Halloween Nonpareils, 1.3 oz. each of Black, Orange and Purple Sugars. Certified Kosher.
710-R-727 **$5.99**

Gingerbread Kits

No baking, just fun! Everything you need is included to make one of 3 great haunted designs.

 **NEW!**

Pre-Baked Halloween Cookie House Kit

This hair-raising Halloween house is easy to build and fun to decorate! Everything's included—pre-baked cookie house pieces, orange and black decorating icing mixes, 2 bat and 2 ghost icing decorations, lots of candy for decorating, 2 decorating tips, 2 decorating bags, cardboard base and complete instructions. House measures 6¾ x 3½ x 7 in. high.
2104-R-2058 **$12.99**

 **NEW!**

Pre-Baked and Pre-Assembled Halloween Cookie House Kit

It's already built so you can get right to the family decorating fun. Everything's included—pre-assembled cookie house, cookie chimney piece, orange and black decorating icing mixes, 2 bat and 2 ghost icing decorations, colorful candy for decorating, 2 decorating tips, 2 decorating bags, cardboard base and complete instructions. House measures 6¾ x 3½ x 7 in. high.
2104-R-2059 **$12.99**

ORDER TOLL FREE: 800-794-5866

Cookie Cutters

COMFORT GRIP™ CUTTERS

These easy-grip cutters with extra-deep sides are perfect for cutting so many favorite foods into spectacular shapes. The cushion grip gives you comfortable control even when cutting thick desserts. Recipe included. Stainless steel sides, 4 ½ x 4 ½ x 1 ½ in. deep. $2.99

NEW!

Witch's Hat
2310-R-630

Pumpkin
2310-R-600

Ghost
2310-R-607

GRIPPY™ CUTTERS

4 Pc. Grippy™ Set
Safe, easy cutting, with a comfortable grip and deep plastic sides. Four shapes include ghost, cat, pumpkin and bat, approx. 3 ½ in.
2311-R-255 Set/4 $3.99

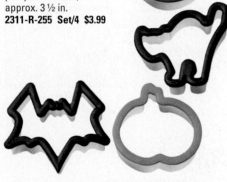

PLASTIC CUTTERS

Child-safe designs mean kids can have a great time helping. And remember all the fun ways to use our cutters—for bread shapes, stencils, sun catchers and so much more. Recipe included.

Spooky Cookie Cutter Set
Favorite frightening shapes, measuring from 3 to 4 ¼ in.
2304-R-9210
Set/10 $3.99

METAL CUTTERS

Put variety in your cookie-making with fun Halloween multi-shape sets. There are styles to please everyone. Recipe included.

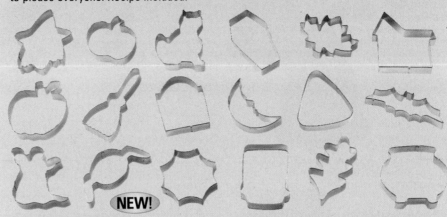

NEW!

Halloween Cutter Set
Set of 18 includes witch, pumpkin, cat, coffin, maple leaf, house, apple, witch's broom, tombstone, moon, candy corn, bat, ghost, spider, spider web, Frankenstein, oak leaf and cauldron, each approx. 3 in. Metal.
2308-R-1131 Set/18 $9.99

NEW!

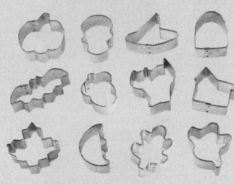

Halloween Mini Cutter Set
Set of 12 includes pumpkin, skull, witch's hat, tombstone, bat, acorn, cat, house, maple leaf, moon, oak leaf and ghost, each approx. 1 ½ in. Metal.
2308-R-1246 Set/12 $4.99

Colorful Cutter Sets
Our metal cutters look great with their bright colors and fun shapes. Perfect for hanging until your next cookie-baking bash.

Halloween Cutter Set
Set of 9 includes bat, ghost, cat, witch, moon, witch's broom, tombstone, house and pumpkin, each approx. 3 to 3 ¾ in. Colored aluminum.
2308-R-2501 Set/9 $9.99

Spooky Shapes Cutter Set
Set of 4 includes moon, pumpkin, witch and ghost, each approx. 3 in. Coated metal.
2308-R-1200 Set/4 $4.49

Nesting Cutter Sets
Create boo-tiful Halloween treats in four sizes. Each cuts neatly and is easy to handle. Sizes from 2 ¼ to 4 ½ in. Metal.
Set/4 $4.49

Ghosts
2308-R-1238

Pumpkins
2308-R-1210

Halloween Mini Cutter Set
Set of 6 includes cat, bat, pumpkin, ghost, moon and skull, each approx. 1 ½ in. Metal.
2308-R-1211
Set/6 $2.99

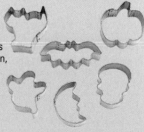

CHRISTMAS

Bakeware

Iridescents! Tree Pan

NEW!

The perfect holiday party pan-this bright, colorful shape is as much fun for serving party treats as it is for baking a great cake! Designed for quick, easy cake decorating. Also ideal for crisped rice cereal treats, molded gelatin, bread dough and more. One-mix pan is 14 x 10 x 2 in. Aluminum.
2105-R-2081 $5.99

DIMENSIONS® DECORATIVE BAKEWARE

With Dimensions non-stick cast aluminum bakeware, anyone can create Christmas desserts with elegant shapes and spectacular detail. Heavyweight cast aluminum conducts heat extremely evenly. Premium non-stick surface for easy release and cleanup. Aluminum.

NEW! **Gift**
11⅛ x 9⅝ x 1½ in.
10 cup capacity.
2105-R-5027 $27.99

NEW!

4 Cavity Mini Snowflakes
11 in. diameter x 2¼ in.
Four 1½ cup cavities;
6 cup total capacity.
2105-R-5028 $27.99

Step-By-Step Snowman Pan

Just bake, ice and decorate. He's also perfect for molding gelatin and ice cream, salads, baking bread and more. One-mix pan is 12 x 9¼ x 2 in. Aluminum.
2105-R-2083 $5.99

Mini Snowman Pan

Bake a blizzard of snowmen! One mix makes 12-18 snowmen, ready for your decorating touch. 6 cavities, each 2⅞ x 4⅝ x 1⅞ in. Aluminum.
2105-R-472 $10.99

Bite-Size Gingerbread Boy Pan

Bake plenty of fun little guys for everyone. One mix makes 24-36 boys. 9 cavities, each 2¾ x 3⅜ x ¾ in. Aluminum.
2105-R-926 $10.99

Petite Christmas Tree Pan

Ideal for bite-size muffins, brownies, tarts or gelatins. One mix makes 7-11 dozen trees. 12 cavities, each 2 x 2½ x ¾ in. Aluminum.
2105-R-8463 $9.99

Mini Holiday Ornament Pan

NEW!

What a dazzling dessert idea! Pretty ornaments in 2 classic shapes make ideal individual servings of cake, molded gelatin, salads, ice cream and more. One mix makes 12-15 ornaments. Six cavities in 4⅞ x 4⅛ x 1¼ in. or 4¼ x 3¾ x 1⅛ in. sizes. Aluminum.
2105-R-9905 $9.99

Cookie Treat Pans

Treats on a stick are so easy; just press dough or rice cereal treat mixture into the pan, insert a cookie stick, then bake, cool and decorate. Each pan makes six individual treats, approx. 4 in high x ½ in. Recipe included. Aluminum. **$7.99**

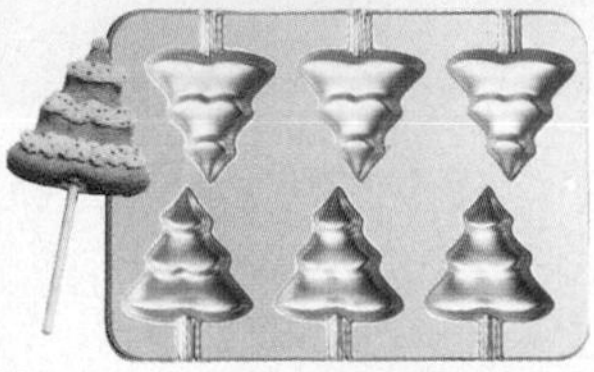

Christmas Tree
2105-R-8101

Snowman
2105-R-8107

Cookie Treat Sticks

6 in.
1912-R-9319
Pk./20 $1.99

8 in.
1912-R-9318
Pk./20 $2.99

Star
2105-R-8102

Colors & Icings

CHRISTMAS COLOR GUIDE

Red   Kelly Green   Leaf Green   White

Holiday Icing Colors Set
.5 oz. jars, Red-Red and Kelly Green. Certified Kosher.
601-R-3011 Pk./2 $2.99

Color Mist™ Food Color Spray
The dazzling effects of an airbrush in a convenient can! Use it to transform a plain iced cake with sensational color, add splashes of holiday color to iced cookies and cupcakes. No mess, taste-free formula. 1.5 oz. Certified Kosher. **$2.99**
Green   710-R-5503
Red   710-R-5500

FoodWriter™ Edible Color Markers

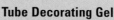

Use like ink markers to add fun, dazzling color to countless foods. Kids love 'em! Decorate on fondant, color flow, royal icing designs and cookies. Includes Green and Red markers .35 oz. Certified Kosher.
609-R-102 Set/2 $3.99

Ready-to-Decorate Icing

Anyone can decorate with Wilton Ready-to-Decorate Icing! Our brilliant colors and four decorating tips make it a breeze to add an exciting finishing touch to treats—without mixing or mess. 6.4 oz. Certified Kosher. **$3.49**
Green   710-R-4401
Red   710-R-4400
White   710-R-4402

Tube Decorating Icing
Can be used with our Tip and Nail Set or Coupler Ring Set (p. 133) and any standard size Wilton metal tip. Colors match Wilton Icing Colors (p. 133). 4.25 oz. Certified Kosher. **$1.79**

Kelly Green 704-R-227
Red   704-R-218
White   704-R-200

Tube Decorating Gel
Transparent gels are great for writing messages and decorating cakes and cookies. Colors match Wilton Icing Colors (p. 133). .75 oz. Certified Kosher. **$1.29**

Leaf Green 704-R-324
Red   704-R-318
White   704-R-302

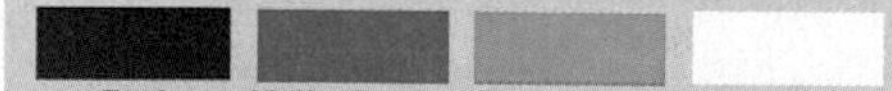

Party

Baking Cups
Microwave-safe paper. Standard size, 2 in. diameter, Pk./50; Mini size, 1¼ in. diameter, Pk./75
$1.49

Holiday Ornaments
Standard 415-R-1204
Mini 415-R-2002

Twinkling Trees
Standard 415-R-476
Mini 415-R-475

Gifts Galore
Standard 415-R-403
Mini 415-R-402

FUN PIX®
Add a fun holiday touch to cakes, cupcakes, ice cream and more. Approx. 3 ½ in. high.
Pk./24 **$1.99**

Party Bags
NEW! Colorful Christmas designs for candy and cookie treats. 20 plastic bags, 20 ties included. 4 x 9 ½ in.
Pk./20 **$1.99**

Shaped plastic bags, 20 ties included. 6 ½ x 7 in.
Pk./20 **$1.99**

Holiday Ornaments
1912-R-3107

Shaped Twinkling Trees
1912-R-1081

Twinkling Trees
1912-R-1082

Gifts Galore
1912-R-1023

Twinkling Trees
2113-R-716

Gifts Galore
2113-R-2311

BOBBLING TOPPERS **NEW!**
Top off that special cake with these fun bobbling toppers and watch heads turn. The food-safe design features hand-painted detail. 2 in. high.
Pk./6 **$2.99**

Icing Decorations
Perfect for topping cupcakes, cookies and ice cream. Mint-flavored. Certified Kosher.
$2.09

Petite Holiday Ornaments
710-R-505 Pk./15

Petite Twinkling Trees
710-R-502 Pk./12

Gifts Galore
710-R-274 Pk./9

Santa
2113-R-2005

Candy **NEW!** **NEW!**

Holiday Ornament Lollipop Mold
4 designs, 9 cavities.
2115-R-1603 **$1.99**

Twinkling Trees Lollipop Mold
1 design, 10 cavities.
2115-R-1406 **$1.99**

Gifts Galore Lollipop Mold
4 designs, 10 cavities.
2115-R-1566 **$1.99**

Candy Melts®*
Ideal for all your candy making —molding, dipping or coating. Artificially vanilla flavored unless otherwise indicated. 14 oz. bag. Certified Kosher.
$2.50

Red	1911-R-499
White	1911-R-498
Dark Green	1911-R-405
Light Cocoa	1911-R-544
Dark Cocoa	1911-R-358
Chocolate Mint	1911-R-1920
Yellow	1911-R-463

BON BON CUPS
Red Foil
415-R-314
Pk./75 **$1.49**

Silver Foil
415-R-307
Pk./72 **$1.49**
(36 pure aluminum 36 paper)

Gold Foil
415-R-306
Pk./75 **$1.49**

Christmas Gummy Making Kit
Kids will have a great time making 16 yummy gummy candies in just minutes! Everything they need is included: mold with 4 fun holiday designs, four .7 oz. pouches of gummy mix (Cherry, Banana, Blueberry and Green Apple), one .7 oz. packet of Sour Sugars for covering gummys, squeeze bottle and funnel. Just add water to the mix, shake, fill molds and pop in your refrigerator. Ages 4 and up.
2104-R-3063 **$4.99**

Christmas Lollipop Kit
Everything you need to make dazzling holiday treats! Includes 1 lollipop mold (3 designs, 9 cavities), 10 oz. Candy Melts® (5 oz. Red, 2.5 oz. each White and Green), 10 lollipop sticks, (6 in.), 10 lollipop bags with ties, 3 disposable decorating bags, 1 decorator brush and complete instructions.
2104-R-1048 **$6.99**

See pages 218-221 for more Wilton candy items.

*Brand confectionery coating.

MINI CUPS
Red/Green
Mixed, glassine paper.
1912-R-1247
Pk./75 **$1.49**

PETITE LOAF BAKING CUPS
For gift breads. Fits Petite Loaf Pan (p.149). Microwave-safe paper. White.
415-R-450 Pk./50 **$1.49**

CHRISTMAS

Christmas Cookie Tree Cutter Kit

Create a beautiful Yule tree as a perfect holiday centerpiece—it's easy and fun! Just bake, stack and decorate. Kit includes 10 star cookie cutters in graduated sizes from small to large, 3 disposable decorating bags, round decorating tip, cookie and icing recipes, baking and decorating instructions for four great designs. Tree measures approx. 8 x 11 in. high.
2104-R-1555 **$7.99**

Cookie and Stencil Sets

NEW!

Holiday Cookie Set

Fun-shaped cutters and colorful sprinkles for sweet Christmas treats. Includes angel, tree, star and gingerbread boy metal cutters and 2 oz. Red and Green Sugars, 1.5 oz. Snowflake Mix, 2 oz. Christmas Nonpareils, 1.5 oz. Gingerbread Boy Mix amd 2 oz. White Nonpareils. Certified Kosher.
2109-R-5392
Set/10 $12.99

Holiday Cupcake and Cookie Stencils

Turn plain treats into holiday visions. Just place one of the fun designs over your baked treat, then sprinkle with Wilton Cake Sparkles™ or Colored Sugars (shown at right) or use FoodWriter™ Edible Color Markers or Color Mist™ Food Color Spray (p. 194). 12 designs.
417-R-492 **$2.99**

Sprinkles
INDIVIDUAL BOTTLES

Shake up your holiday treats with fun colors and designs. Plastic bottles for convenient pouring and storing. Certified Kosher. **$1.99**

NEW!

Candy Cane Mix 2.5 oz. bottle 710-R-990	**Snowflake Mix** 2.5 oz. bottle 710-R-797	**Christmas Tree Mix** 2.5 oz. bottle 710-R-792

Cinnamon Drops 3 oz. bottle 710-R-769	**Chocolate Jimmies** 2.5 oz. bottle 710-R-774	**Red Sugar** 3.25 oz. bottle 710-R-766	**Dark Green Sugar** 3.25 oz. bottle 710-R-764

Sparkling Sugars

Easy-pour sugars have a coarse texture and brilliant sparkle. 8 oz. Certified Kosher. **$3.99**

Red/ White 710-R-998   **Green/ White** 710-R-997

Cake Sparkles™

Edible glitter, .25 oz. bottle. Certified Kosher. **$2.89**

Red 703-R-1284   **Green** 703-R-1278   **White** 703-R-1290

ASSORTMENTS

4-Mix
Includes .75 oz. Christmas Tree Mix, 1 oz. Christmas Nonpareils, 1.1 oz. Dark Green and Red Sugars. Certified Kosher.
710-R-729 **$4.99**

6-Mix
Includes 1 oz. Christmas Tree Mix, 1 oz. Christmas Jimmies, 1 oz. Gingerbread Boy Mix, 1.3 oz. Christmas Nonpareils, 1.3 oz. Dark Green and Red Sugars. Certified Kosher.
710-R-734 **$5.99**

STENCIL-A-COOKIE™ CUTTER & STENCIL SETS

Using the fun-shaped stencils and cutter, it's easy to serve cookies with exciting, colorful designs for the season. Just cut cookies, then use the stencils and Cake Sparkles™ and Colored Sugars (shown above) or Wilton FoodWriter™ Edible Color Markers or Color Mist™ Food Color Spray (p. 194) to create dazzling shapes on top after baking. Sets include one metal cutter and two stencils (same design). **Set/3 $1.99**

Tree 2308-R-1408   **Snowman** 2308-R-1409   **Gingerbread Boy** 2308-R-1410

Cookie Cutters
COPPER CUTTERS

The warmth and beauty of copper make these cutters ideal for adding that decorative touch to your kitchen. These heirloom-quality copper cutters have smoothly rolled edges for that finishing touch.

Holiday Cutters
Each approximately 5½ in. diameter.
$6.99

Snowflake
2308-R-3079

Snowman
2308-R-3081

Gingerbread Boy
2308-R-3001

Christmas Tree
2308-R-3000

Star
2308-R-3002

COMFORT GRIP™ CUTTERS

These easy-grip cutters with extra-deep sides are perfect for cutting so many favorite foods into spectacular shapes. The cushion grip gives you comfortable control even when cutting thick desserts. Recipe included. Stainless steel sides, 4½ x 4½ x 1½ in. deep.
$2.99

Santa Hat
2310-R-640

NEW!

Mitten
2310-R-639

Christmas Tree
2310-R-604

Gingerbread Boy
2310-R-602

Snowman
2310-634

Star
2310-R-631

GRIPPY™ CUTTERS

4 Pc. Grippy™ Set
Safe, easy cutting, with a comfortable grip and deep plastic sides. Four shapes include stocking, tree, star and gingerbread boy, each approx. 3½ in.
2311-R-256
Set/4 $3.99

PLASTIC CUTTERS

Individual Cookie Cutters
Great shapes for end-of-year celebrations!
3 x 4 in. high.
$0.69

Christmas Tree
2303-R-132

5-Pt. Star
2303-R-135

METAL CUTTERS & SCOOP

Put variety in your cookie-making with fun Christmas multi-shape sets. There are styles to please everyone. Recipe included.

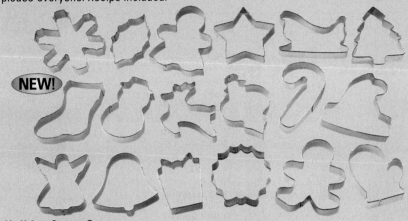

NEW!

Holiday Cutter Set
Snowflake, holly leaf, gingerbread girl, star, sleigh, tree, stocking, snowman, reindeer, ornament, candy cane, Santa hat, angel, bell, gift, wreath, gingerbread boy and mitten, each approx. 3 in. Metal.
2308-R-1132 Set/18 $9.99

NEW!

Holiday Mini Cutter Set
Star, angel, gingerbread girl, stocking, candy cane, ornament, teddy bear, bell, holly leaf, tree, gingerbread boy and sleigh, each approx. 1½ in. Metal.
2308-R-1250 Set/12 $4.99

Colorful Cutter Sets
Our metal cutters look great with their bright colors and fun shapes. Perfect for hanging on the tree until your next cookie-baking bash.

Holiday Cutter Set
Candy cane, gingerbread girl, stocking, angel, star, bell, snowman, tree and gingerbread boy, each approx. 3 to 3¾ in. Colored aluminum.
2308-R-2500 Set/9 $9.99

Jolly Shapes Cutter Set
Stocking, star, tree and candy cane, each approx. 3 in. Coated metal.
2308-R-1201 Set/4 $4.49

Nesting Cutter Sets
Bake your favorite holiday shapes in four fun sizes! Quality metal cuts neatly and is easy to handle. Sizes from 5 to 2½ in.
Set/4 $4.49

NEW!

Houses
2308-R-1251

Snowflakes
2308-R-1244

Gingerbread Boys
2308-R-1239

Holiday Mini Cutter Set
Bell, gingerbread boy, holly leaf, tree, candy cane and angel, each approx. 1½ in.
2308-R-1214 Set/6 $2.99

Holiday Red Cookie Scoop
Festive color and convenient design come together to make holiday baking more fun! Scoops and releases approx. 1 Tbsp. of dough with ease. Dishwasher safe plastic.
417-R-320
$2.49

CHRISTMAS
Cookie Presses

COMFORT GRIP™
Cookie Press

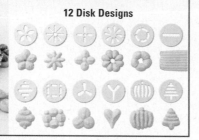

Experience a classic press that is truly comfortable. Its ergonomic handle feels great in your hand—the easy-squeeze action releases perfectly shaped dough. Clear barrel takes the guesswork out of refilling. Fluted bottom raises press off the cookie sheet for better-defined shapes.

Includes 12 cookie disks in a variety of shapes and our classic spritz recipe.
2104-R-4011 Set/13 $12.99

12 Disk Designs

Cookie Pro™ ULTRA

Internal Spring-Loaded Piston for exceptional reliability and efficient pressing.

Pump Action for greater efficiency and ease of use.

Ergonomically-Designed Comfort Grip™ Handle helps you press comfortably even when making large batches of cookies.

Side Grips prevent hands from slipping.

Heavy-Duty Construction of cast aluminum and stainless steel.

Finger-Grip Disk Ring for easy changing of disks.

Easy to use, easy to store—everything you want in a cookie press. Pump-action design lets you press dozens of cookies comfortably. Handle folds over for compact storage. Includes 10 aluminum disks and an attachable storage case. Recipes included.
2104-R-4010 Set/12 $24.99

No More Missing Disks! Storage case attaches to cookie press when not in use.

Space Saving Design Unique flip-over handle for easy and compact storage.

10 Disk Designs

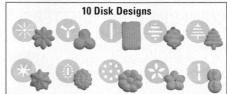

COOKIE MASTER™ Plus
Cordless Cookie Press

Our cordless cookie press is so powerful and easy to operate, you'll use it all year to create cookies, appetizers, desserts and more. Exclusive patented reverse action means there's no need to take press apart for refilling. Ergonomic design is shaped to fit in your hand for excellent comfort.

Includes 12 aluminum disks in classic and seasonal shapes, 4 accent tips for decorating and filling and 2 bonus recipe booklets—sweet and savory. Uses 4 AA batteries, not included.
2104-R-4008 Set/19 $39.99

12 Disk Designs

4 Accent Tips

cookie max™ cookie press

MAXimum Control
Pump action dispenses a perfect cookie every time. 1 click of the plunger equals 1 cookie.

MAXimum Comfort
Soft cushioned pump handle reduces hand fatigue.

MAXimum Efficiency
Recessed plunger disk eliminates backflow—dough won't clog!

MAXimum Fun!
Makes 12 favorite shapes—easy instructions and 3 delicious recipes included.
2104-R-4003 Set/13 $17.99

12 Disk Designs

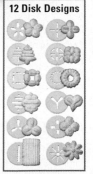

Bakeware
RECIPE RIGHT® NON-STICK

Built with all the right qualities for better baking results. Pan dimensions are embossed on handles for easy reference. Heavy-gauge construction means pans spread heat evenly and won't warp. Non-Stick coating provides exceptional quick release and easy cleanup. 5 year warranty. Aluminum.

15 in. x 10 in. Cookie Sheet
2105-R-967 $4.49

12 Cup Muffin Pan
2105-R-954 $5.49

24 Cup Mini Muffin Pan
2105-R-914 $8.99

Bake Easy!™ Non-Stick Spray

This convenient non-stick spray helps your baked goods release perfectly. Just a light, even coating does the job. Use Bake Easy for all mixes and recipes—cookies, muffins, cupcakes, brownies, breads and more. Versatile for all types of baking and cooking. 6 oz.
702-R-6018 $2.99

Gingerbread Kits

Pre-Baked Ultimate Gingerbread House Kit

 NEW!

Get ready for the ultimate gingerbread experience! This house is so huge, with tons of icing and colorful candy, that everyone can have a great time building and decorating to celebrate the holiday season. Everything you need is inside—pre-baked house pieces, two pre-baked trees, 3 packages of decorating icing mix, 2 decorating bags and 2 nickel-plated tips, boy and girl icing decorations, loads of candy for decorating and complete instructions for assembling and decorating. House measures 10¾ x 9 x 11¾ in. high.
2104-R-1353 $39.99

Pre-Baked Gingerbread Tree Kit

NEW!

This brightly-decorated tree would look so festive on your holiday table—and it's great fun for the whole family to build and decorate. Just stack ready-made star cookies, decorate with icing and candy and add the star icing decoration tree top! Includes 14 gingerbread cookies, white and green icing mix, 3 gift and 1 star icing decorations, multi-colored candies, 2 decorating tips and 2 decorating bags and complete instructions. Tree measures 5½ x 8¼ in. high.
2104-R-2621 $9.99

Pre-Baked Gingerbread House Kit

No baking—get right to the fun of assembling and decorating your festive gingerbread house. Kit includes pre-baked gingerbread house sections, decorating icing mix, assorted candies for decorating, decorating bag and tip, cardboard base and complete instructions with great decorating ideas. House measures 5¼ x 5½ x 4¾ in. high.
2104-R-1537 $9.99

Pre-Baked and Pre-Assembled Gingerbread House Kit

The easiest-to-use gingerbread kit we've ever made! Pre-baked and pre-assembled so the family can get right to the fun of decorating. Kit includes assembled house with cardboard base, decorating icing, candies, decorating bag and tip and complete instructions with great decorating ideas. House measures 5½ x 5½ x 4½ in. high.
2104-R-1516 $12.99

Pre-Baked Gingerbread House Kit

Real gingerbread pieces are ready to assemble and decorate (without the mess of baking). Kit includes pre-baked gingerbread pieces, decorating icing, assorted candies, decorating bag and tip, cardboard base and complete instructions with great decorating ideas. House measures 8 x 7 x 6½ in. high.
2104-R-1509 $12.99

HANUKKAH

Cookie

Hanukkah Cutter Set
Includes Torah, menorah, 6-point star and dreidel, each approx. 3 in. Colored metal.
2308-R-1262
Set/4 $4.49

6-Point Star Cookie Cutter
3 x 4 in. high.
2303-R-122 $0.69

Sprinkles

Plastic bottles for pouring and storing. 3.25 oz. Certified Kosher. **$1.99**

Blue Sugar	Yellow Sugar
710-R-750	710-R-754

Candy

Hanukkah Candy Kit
Everything you need to make easy, fun Hanukkah treats! Includes 10 oz. Light Cocoa Candy Melts®*, Hanukkah candy mold (6 designs, 13 cavities), 25 gold foil squares (4 x 4 in.), 2 disposable decorating bags and 5 mesh coin bags. Complete instructions. Certified Kosher.
2104-R-1328 $6.99

Cake Sparkles™
Edible glitter, .25 oz. bottle. Certified Kosher. **$2.89**

Blue	Yellow	White
703-R-1314	703-R-1272	703-R-1290

Hanukkah Lollipop Mold
5 designs, 10 cavities.
2115-R-1405
$1.99

Candy Melts®*
Ideal for all your candy making—molding, dipping or coating. Artificially vanilla flavored unless otherwise indicated. 14 oz. bag. Certified Kosher.
$2.50

Blue	1911-R-448	Light Cocoa	1911-R-544
Yellow	1911-R-463	Dark Cocoa	1911-R-358
White	1911-R-498	Chocolate Mint	1911-R-1920

*Brand confectionery coating.

See pages 218-221 for more Wilton candy items.

Colors & Icings

HANUKKAH COLOR GUIDE

Blue	Yellow	White

Color Mist™ Food Color Spray
The dazzling effects of an airbrush in a convenient can! Use it to transform a plain iced cake with sensational color, add splashes of holiday color to iced cookies and cupcakes. No mess, taste-free formula. 1.5 oz. Certified Kosher. **$2.99**

| Blue | 710-R-5501 |
| Yellow | 710-R-5502 |

Ready-to-Decorate Icing
Anyone can decorate with Wilton Ready-to-Decorate Icing! Our brilliant colors and four decorating tips make it a breeze to add an exciting finishing touch to treats—without mixing or mess. 6.4 oz. Certified Kosher. **$3.49**

Blue	710-R-4407
Yellow	710-R-4409
White	710-R-4402

Tube Decorating Icing
Tubes can be used with our Tip and Nail Set or Coupler Ring Set (p. 133) and any standard size Wilton metal tip. Colors match Wilton Icing Colors (p. 133). 4.25 oz. Certified Kosher. **$1.79**

Blue	704-R-248
Yellow	704-R-236
White	704-R-200

Tube Decorating Gel
Transparent gels are great for writing messages and decorating cakes and cookies. Colors match Wilton Icing Colors (p. 133). .75 oz. Certified Kosher. **$1.29**

Blue	704-R-348
Yellow	704-R-336
White	704-R-302

VALENTINE

Bakeware

DIMENSIONS® DECORATIVE BAKEWARE

With Dimensions non-stick cast aluminum bakeware, anyone can create Valentine desserts with elegant shapes and spectacular detail. Heavyweight cast aluminum conducts heat extremely evenly. Premium non-stick surface for easy release and cleanup. Aluminum.

Mini Heart (shown)
Each heart is 4 x 2 in. Six 1 cup cavities.
2105-R-5012 $27.99

Also available, shown on p. 145.

Queen Of Hearts
9 in. x 3¼ in. 10 cup capacity.
2105-R-5001 $27.99

Crown Of Hearts
11 x 2½ in. 10 cup capacity.
2105-R-5011 $27.99

9 in. Non-Stick Heart Pan
Your classic heart cake will release perfectly from this non-stick pan. Cleanup is easy too. 9 x 2¼ in. Non-stick steel.
2105-R-410 $10.99

Heart Springform Pans
Create elegant Valentine cheesecakes with these easy-releasing non-stick pans. Springlock sides, removable bottom for easy serving. Non-stick steel.

4 x 1¾ in. Mini
2105-R-457
$7.99

9 x 2¾ in.
2105-R-419
$16.99

Heart Tart Pan
Create luscious desserts and entrees with classic fluted edges. Non-stick; removable bottom.
10 x 1 in.
Non-stick steel.
2105-R-452 $9.99

Heart Pans
For graceful expressions of love on Valentine's Day or anytime, in just the size you need.
2 in. Aluminum.

12 in.
2105-R-607
$10.99

9 in.
2105-R-5176
$7.49

6 in.
2105-R-600
$5.99

SweetHeart Pan
Its gently curving shape gives the classic heart a more romantic flair. Whether you accent it with pretty icing flowers or pair it with bold fondant decorations, this cake will charm guests for birthdays, Mother's Day, Valentine's Day, showers and more. One-mix pan is 10¼ x 11 x 2 in. Aluminum.
2105-R-1197 $10.99

Mini Embossed Heart Pan
Beautiful scalloped shapes with raised centers to decorate with fruit or whipped cream. One mix makes 12-18 hearts. 6 cavities, each 3½ x 3⅜ x 1¼ in. Aluminum.
2105-R-3210 $11.99

Mini Heart Pan
Great size for petit fours, individual brownies and more. One mix makes 12-18 hearts. 6 cavities, each 3⅝ x 3½ x 1 in. deep. Aluminum.
2105-R-11044 $10.99

Petite Heart Pan
Bite-size muffins, brownies and cookies will win hearts. One mix makes 10-15 dozen hearts. 12 cavities, each 1¾ x 1⅝ x ½ in. Aluminum.
2105-R-2432 $9.99

Colors & Icings

VALENTINE COLOR GUIDE

| Red | Pink | Violet | White |

Valentine Icing Colors Set
Red-Red and Pink in .5 oz. jars. Certified Kosher.
601-R-5570 Set/2 $2.99

Color Mist™ Food Color Spray
Gives decorators the versatility and dazzling effects of an airbrush in a convenient can! Use it to transform a plain iced cake with sensational color, add splashes of holiday color to iced cookies and cupcakes. No mess, taste-free formula. 1.5 oz. Certified Kosher. $2.99
Red 710-R-5500
Pink 710-R-5505
Violet 710-R-5504

FoodWriter™ Edible Color Markers

Use like ink markers to add fun, dazzling color to countless foods. Kids love 'em! Decorate on fondant, color flow, royal icing designs and cookies. Includes Pink and Red markers .35 oz. Certified Kosher.
609-R-103 Set/2 $3.99

Ready-to-Decorate Icing
Anyone can decorate with Wilton Ready-to-Decorate Icing! Our brilliant colors and four decorator tips make it a breeze to add an exciting finishing touch to treats—without mixing or mess.
6.4 oz. Certified Kosher. $3.49
Red 710-R-4400
Pink 710-R-4406
Violet 710-R-4408
White 710-R-4402

Tube Decorating Icing
Tubes can be used with our Tip and Nail Set or Coupler Ring Set (p. 133) and any standard size Wilton metal tip. Colors match Wilton Icing Colors (p. 133). 4.25 oz. Certified Kosher. $1.79
Red 704-R-218
Pink 704-R-230
Violet 704-R-242
White 704-R-200

Tube Decorating Gel
Transparent gels are great for writing messages and decorating cakes and cookies. Colors match Wilton Icing Colors (p. 133). .75 oz. Certified Kosher. $1.29
Red 704-R-318
Pink 704-R-330
Violet 704-R-342
White 704-R-302

ORDER TOLL FREE: 800-794-5866

Party

Baking Cups
Microwave-safe paper.
Standard size, 2 in. diameter,
Mini size, 1¼ in. diameter.
Standard Pk/50 $1.49
Mini Pk/75 $1.49

Sweet Talk
Standard 415-R-516
Mini 415-R-471

Hearts Remembered
Standard 415-R-274
Mini 415-R-268

Hearts
Standard 415-R-210
Mini 415-R-310

Party Bags
Colorful Valentine
designs for candy
and cookie treats.
20 plastic bags,
20 ties included.
4 x 9½ in.
Pk./20 $1.99

NEW!

Red Party Bags
Pk./20 $1.99
1912-R-2357

Sweet Talk
1912-R-3105

Hearts Remembered
1912-R-1292

Hearts
1912-R-1269

FUN PIX® NEW!
Add a fun touch to cakes,
cupcakes, ice cream and
more. Approx. 3½ in. tall.
Pk./12 $1.99

Icing Decorations
Perfect for topping
cupcakes, cookies
and ice cream.
Mint-flavored.
Certified Kosher. **$2.09**

NEW!

Sweet Talk
710-R-365 Pk./9

Hearts Remembered
710-R-824 Pk./18

Bon Bon Cups
Wax-laminated paper on
red foil. 1¼ in. diameter
415-R-314 Pk./75 $1.49

Sweet Talk
2113-R-2319

Candy NEW!

Sweet Talk Candy Mold
5 designs, 20 cavities.
2115-R-1435 $1.99

Heart Lollipop Mold
2 designs, 8 cavities.
2115-R-1709 $1.99

Roses and Buds Lollipop Mold
3 designs, 9 cavities.
2115-R-1708 $1.99

Hearts Candy Mold
1 design, 15 cavities.
2115-R-1712 $1.99

Valentine Lollipop Kit
Everything you need to make easy,
fun Valentine treats! Includes
1 Valentine lollipop mold (3 designs,
6 cavities), 10 oz. Candy Melts®*
(5 oz. Red, 2.5 oz. each Pink and
White), 10 lollipop bags with ties,
10 lollipop sticks (6 in.),
3 disposable decorating bags,
decorator brush and
complete instructions.
2104-R-1070 $6.99

CANDY MELTS®*
Ideal for all your candy
making—molding, dipping or
coating. Artificially vanilla
flavored unless otherwise indicated.
Certified Kosher. 14 oz. bag. $2.50
Red 1911-R-499
Pink 1911-R-447
White 1911-R-498
Light Cocoa 1911-R-544
Dark Cocoa 1911-R-358
*Brand confectionery coating.

See pages 218-221 for more Wilton candy items.

VALENTINE
Cookie Stencils

HEART STENCIL-A-COOKIE™ CUTTER & STENCIL SET

Using the fun-shaped stencils and cutter, it's easy to serve cookies with exciting, colorful designs for the season. Just cut cookies, then use the stencils and Cake Sparkles™ and Colored Sugars (shown at right) or Wilton FoodWriter™ Edible Color Markers or Color Mist™ Food Color Spray (p. 200) to create dazzling shapes on top after baking. Sets include one metal cutter and two stencils (same design).
2308-R-1401
Set/3 $1.99

Sweetheart Cupcake and Cookie Stencils

Turn plain treats into visions of love. Just place one of the fun designs over your baked treat, then sprinkle with Wilton Cake Sparkles™ or Colored Sugars (shown at right) or spray with Color Mist™ Food Color Spray (p. 200). Five designs.
417-R-1208 $2.49

Sprinkles
INDIVIDUAL BOTTLES

Shake up your Valentine treats with fun colors and designs. Plastic bottles for convenient pouring and storing. Certified Kosher. **$1.99**

Hearts Mix
2.5 oz. bottle
710-R-854

Kisses Mix
2.5 oz. bottle
710-R-855

Red Sugar
3.25 oz. bottle
710-R-766

Pink Sugar
3.25 oz. bottle
710-R-756

Lavender Sugar
3.25 oz. bottle
710-R-758

Sparkling Sugars

Easy-pour sugars have a coarse texture and brilliant sparkle. 8 oz. Certified Kosher. **$3.99**

Red/ White
710-R-367

Pink/ White
710-R-366

Cake Sparkles™

Edible glitter, .25 oz. bottle. Certified Kosher. **$2.89**

Red
703-R-1284

Pink
703-R-1260

Purple
703-R-1266

Cookie Pans

Heart Giant Cookie Pan

Create a giant-sized pan cookie or brownie in a heart shape that will be a big hit. Ideal for refrigerated dough and brownie mix. Recipe included. Pan is 11½ x 10½ x ½ in. deep. Aluminum.
2105-R-6203 $5.99

Heart Cookie Treat Pan

Just press cookie dough into pan, insert a cookie stick, then bake, cool and decorate. Create your own cookie blossoms for that special someone; also great for adding fun shapes to other goodies like rice cereal treats and candy pops. Each pan makes 6 individual treats, 3½ in. x ¼ in. Aluminum.
2105-R-8104 $7.99

Cookie Treat Sticks
6 in. 1912-R-9319 Pk./20 $1.99
8 in. 1912-R-9318 Pk./20 $2.99

ASSORTMENTS
4-Mix

Contains .75 oz. Heart Mix, 1 oz. Sweetheart Nonpareils, 1 oz. each Pink and Red Sugars. Certified Kosher.
710-R-730 $4.99

6-Mix Assortment

Contains 1 oz. Kisses Mix, 1 oz. Heart Mix, 1.3 oz. Sweetheart Nonpareils, 1.3 oz. each Pink, Red and Lavender Sugars. Certified Kosher.
710-R-738 $5.99

Cookie Cutters

COMFORT GRIP™ CUTTER

This easy-grip stainless steel heart with extra-deep sides is perfect for cutting many favorite foods into heart shapes. The cushion grip gives you comfortable control even when cutting into thick desserts. Recipe included.
4½ x 4½ x 1½ in. deep.
2310-R-616 $2.99

PLASTIC CUTTERS

Nesting Hearts Cutter Set
Great for cookies, imprinting patterns in icing, cutting bread shapes and more. Sizes from 1¼ to 4⅛ in.
2304-R-115
Set/6 $2.99

Heart Cutter
3 x 4 in.
2303-R-100 $0.69

Cookie Cutters

COPPER CUTTERS

The warmth and beauty of copper make these cutters ideal for displaying and adding that decorative touch to your kitchen. These beautiful, heirloom-quality copper cutters have smooth rolled edges for that finishing touch. Recipe included.

Heart and Hand Cutter Set

A lovely way to display your devotion. Hand is 4¾ x 3¾ in., heart is 1⅝ x 1¾ in. Solid copper.
2308-R-3075 Set/2 $6.99

Heart Cutter

Beautiful solid copper cutter with deep sides. Great decorative piece, too. 5½ in. wide.
2308-R-3040 $6.99

METAL CUTTERS

Put variety in your cookie-making with fun Valentine multi-shape sets. There are styles to please everyone.

Valentine Cutter Collection
Vivid Valentine colors bring a touch of romance to cookie-baking. Great variety of heart, hugs and kisses designs. Sizes range from 1 to 5 in. Colored aluminum.
2308-R-2502 Set/9 $9.99

From The Heart Nesting Cutter Set

Nesting metal cutters give you a choice of sizes, with two crinkled shapes. Largest cutter is approximately 5 in.
2308-R-1203 Set/4 $4.49

Hearts Cutter Set
Love comes in all shapes and sizes. Includes seven different heart cutter designs from stylized to traditional. Sizes range from 1½ to 3 in.
2308-R-1237 Set/7 $4.99

Heart Cutter
Quality metal cuts neatly and is easy to handle. 3 in. wide.
2308-R-1003 $0.69

ST. PATRICK'S DAY

Shamrock Pan
Make it a lucky day for everyone! Celebrate St. Patrick's Day with this fun symbol of joy and celebration. Also great for school parties, birthdays, sports celebrations and much more. One-mix pan is 11¾ x 2 in. Aluminum.
2105-R-185 $7.99

Shamrock Baking Cups
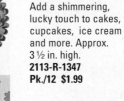
Microwave-safe paper. Standard size 2 in. diameter.
415-R-357 Pk./50 $1.49

Shamrock Party Bags

20 plastic bags, 20 twist ties included. 4 x 9½ in.
1912-R-2233 Pk./20 $1.99

Shamrock Icing Decorations

Sugar-flavored edible shamrocks. Certified Kosher.
710-R-286 Pk./9 $2.09

Shamrock Metal Cookie Cutter

Quality metal cuts neatly and is easy to handle. Approx. 3 in.
2308-R-1011 $0.69

NEW!
Shamrock Foil Fun Pix®

Add a shimmering, lucky touch to cakes, cupcakes, ice cream and more. Approx. 3½ in. high.
2113-R-1347 Pk./12 $1.99

NEW!
Shamrock Lollipop Mold

1 design, 5 cavities.
2115-R-1545 $1.99

4-Leaf Clover Cookie Cutter

Cut cookies, sandwiches, use as party favors and in crafts. 3 in. wide.
2303-R-134 $0.69

EASTER
Bakeware

Step-By-Step Bunny Pan NEW!

Just what you need to get springtime celebrations hopping—just bake, ice and decorate! He's also perfect for molded gelatin, ice cream, salads and more. One-mix pan is 9 ¾ x 14 x 2 in. Aluminum.
2105-R-2074 **$5.99**

3-D Bunny Pan

Sure to get everyone's attention at your holiday brunch and beyond. Instructions for 5 different decorating ideas included. Two-piece pan is 7 ¼ x 7 x 4 ¾ in. Pan takes 4 ½ cups of pound cake batter. No heating core needed. Aluminum.
2105-R-2042 **Set/2 $11.99**

Cuddly Lamb Pan NEW!

You'll find a flock of useful ideas for this fleecy friend. His sweet smile is the perfect welcome for baby showers, Easter brunches, birthday parties. See the label for four great ideas. One-mix pan is 11¾ x 8 ¾ x 2 in. Aluminum.
2105-R-4947 **$10.99**

Stand-Up Lamb Pan

A gentle symbol of springtime. This 3-D lamb will charm everyone at your Easter table. Instructions included. Two-piece pan is 10 x 4 ½ x 7 in. high and takes 6 cups of pound cake batter. Aluminum.
2105-R-2010 **Set/2 $11.99**

Cross Pan

Truly inspiring for holidays, Christenings and other religious occasions. Bevel design is excellent for rolled fondant. Instructions included. One-mix pan is 14 ½ x 11 ⅛ x 2 in. Aluminum.
2105-R-2509 **$7.99**

Decorated Egg Pan

Great for molded desserts as well as cakes. Decorating instructions for five different designs included. One-mix pan is 9 x 11 x 3 ½ in. Aluminum.
2105-R-174 **$7.99**

3-D Egg Pan

Hatch a great Easter centerpiece! Two-piece pan takes just one cake mix. Includes 2 ring bases for level baking of each half. Each half is 9 x 6 x 2 ¾ in. Aluminum.
2105-R-4793 **Set/4 $11.99**

Mini Egg Pan

Make colorful place markers for the holiday table. One mix makes about 24-36 eggs. 8 cavities, each 3 ¼ x 2 ½ x 1 in. Aluminum.
2105-R-2118 **$10.99**

Mini Bunny Pan

Bake 6 treats quick as a bunny! One mix makes about 12-16 bunnies. 6 cavities, each 4 ⅜ x 3 ⅛ x ½ in. Aluminum.
2105-R-4426 **$10.99**

Colors & Icings
EASTER COLOR GUIDE

Pink | Violet | Yellow | Green/Leaf Green | White

Easter Icing Colors Set

Lemon Yellow and Violet in .5 oz. jars. Certified Kosher.
601-R-5571 **Set/2 $2.99**

Color Mist™ Food Color Spray

Gives decorators the versatility and dazzling effects of an airbrush in a convenient can! Use it to transform a plain iced cake with sensational color, add splashes of holiday color to iced cookies and cupcakes. No mess, taste-free formula. 1.5 oz. Certified Kosher. **$2.99**

Pink	710-R-5505
Violet	710-R-5504
Yellow	710-R-5502
Green	710-R-5503

FoodWriter™ Edible Color Markers

Use like ink markers to add fun and dazzling color to countless foods. Kids love 'em! Decorate on fondant, color flow, royal icing designs and cookies. Includes Pink and Lavender markers. .35 oz. Certified Kosher.
609-R-104 **Set/2 $3.99**

Ready-to-Decorate Icing

Anyone can decorate with Wilton Ready-to-Decorate Icing! Our brilliant colors and four decorating tips make it a breeze to add an exciting finishing touch to treats—without mixing or mess. 6.4 oz. Certified Kosher. **$3.49**

Pink	710-R-4406
Violet	710-R-4408
Yellow	710-R-4409
Green	710-R-4401
White	710-R-4402

Tube Decorating Icing

Tubes can be used with our Tip and Nail Set or Coupler Ring Set (p. 133) and any standard size Wilton metal tip. Colors match Wilton Icing Colors (p. 133). 4.25 oz. Certified Kosher.
$1.79

Pink	704-R-230
Violet	704-R-242
Yellow	704-R-236
Leaf Green	704-R-224
White	704-R-200

Tube Decorating Gel

Great for writing messages and decorating cakes and cookies. Colors match Wilton Icing Colors (p. 133). .75 oz. Certified Kosher.
$1.29

Pink	704-R-330
Violet	704-R-342
Yellow	704-R-336
Green	704-R-324
White	704-R-302

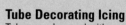

ORDER TOLL FREE: 800-794-5866

Party

Baking Cups

Microwave-safe paper. Standard size, 2 in. diameter, Mini size, 1¼ in. diameter,
Standard Pk/50 $1.49
Mini   Pk/75 $1.49

 NEW!

Bunnies & Chicks
Standard 415 R 515
Mini 415-R-472

Decorated Eggs
Standard 415-R-354

Assorted Pastel
25 pink, 25 yellow, 25 blue.
Standard 415-R-394 Pk./75 $1.49

Party Bags

NEW!

Colorful Easter designs for candy and cookie treats. 20 plastic bags, 20 ties included. 4 x 9 ½ in.
Pk./20 $1.99

FUN PIX®

Add a fun touch to cakes, cupcakes, ice cream and more. Approx. 3 ½ in. tall.
Bunny 2113-R-2318 Pk./12 $1.99

 **NEW!**

Bunnies & Chicks
1912-R-3104

Decorated Eggs
1912-R-1258

Icing Decorations

NEW!

Perfect for topping cupcakes, cookies and ice cream. Mint-flavored. Certified Kosher.
$2.09

Bunnies & Chicks
710-R-368 Pk./12

Petite Eggs
710-R-528 Pk./12

Candy

**Lil' Bunnies
Mini Candy Mold**
4 designs, 12 cavities.
2115-R-1544 $1.99

**Hoppy Easter
Lollipop Mold**
8 designs, 9 cavities.
2115-R-1718 $1.99

Candy Melts®*

Ideal for all your candy making—molding, dipping or coating. Artificially vanilla flavored unless otherwise indicated. 14 oz. bag. Certified Kosher. **$2.50**

Pink	1911-R-447
Lavender	1911-R-403
Yellow	1911-R-463
Blue	1911-R-448
White	1911-R-498
Chocolate Mint	1911-R-1920
Light Cocoa	1911-R-544
Dark Cocoa	1911-R-358

*Brand confectionery coating.

Easter Lollipop Kit

Everything you need to make easy Easter basket treats in fun egg, bunny and chick shapes! Includes 1 Easter lollipop mold (3 designs, 6 cavities), 10 oz. Candy Melts®* (5 oz. Pink, 2.5 oz. each Yellow and White), 10 lollipop bags with ties, 10 lollipop sticks (6 in.), 3 disposable decorating bags and decorator brush.
2104-R-1071 $6.99

Easter Eggs
Candy Mold Set

Make festive candy or sugar eggs in 3 sizes. Includes 2-pc. egg molds: small (3 x 2¼ x 2 ½ in.), medium (4 ¼ x 3 x 3 ¼ in.) and large (5 x 4 x 3 ¾ in.), instructions.
2114-R-1215 $4.99

See pages 218-221 for more Wilton candy items.

SEASONAL

EASTER

Stencil Sets

STENCIL-A-COOKIE™ CUTTER & STENCIL SETS

Using the fun-shaped stencils and cutter, it's easy to serve cookies with exciting, colorful designs for the season. Just cut cookies, then use the stencils and Cake Sparkles™ and Colored Sugars (shown at right) or Wilton FoodWriter™ Edible Color Markers or Color Mist™ Food Color Spray (p. 204) to create dazzling shapes on top after baking. Sets include one metal cutter and two stencils (same design).
Set/3 $1.99

Egg
2308-R-1412

Bunny
2308-R-1411

Flower
2308-R-1403

Easter Cupcake and Cookie Stencils
Turn plain treats into spring sensations with a stenciled Easter design. Place one of the fun designs over your baked treat, then sprinkle with Wilton Cake Sparkles™ or Colored Sugars (shown at right) or spray with Color Mist™ Food Color Spray (p. 204). Five designs.
417-R-1219 $2.49

Cookie Pan

Bunny Cookie Treat Pan
Just press cookie dough into pan, insert a cookie stick, then bake, cool and decorate. Create your own cookie gifts for that special someone; great for adding fun shapes to other goodies like rice cereal treats and candy pops. Each pan makes 6 individual treats, 3 ½ x 2 ¾ x ¼ in. deep. Aluminum.
2105-R-8106 $7.99

Cookie Treat Sticks
6 in. 1912-R-9319 Pk./20 $1.99
8 in. 1912-R-9318 Pk./20 $2.99

Sprinkles

INDIVIDUAL BOTTLES

Shake up your Easter treats with fun colors and designs. Plastic bottles for convenient pouring and storing. Certified Kosher.
$1.99

Bunny/Ducks Mix
2.5 oz. bottle
710-R-870

Soft Pink Sugar	Soft Lavender Sugar	Soft Yellow Sugar	Soft Green Sugar
3.25 oz. Bottle	3.25 oz. Bottle	3.25 oz. Bottle	3.25 oz. Bottle
710-R-896	710-R-897	710-R-895	710-R-898

Sparkling Sugars
Easy-pour sugars have a coarse texture and brilliant sparkle. 8 oz. Certified Kosher. **$3.99**

Pink/White	Lavender/White	Yellow/White
710-R-369	710-R-371	710-R-370

ASSORTMENTS

4-Mix
Includes 1 oz. Lt. Green Sugar, 1 oz. Yellow Sugar, 1 oz. Springtime Nonpareils and .75 oz. Bunnies and Ducks Mix. Certified Kosher.
710-R-736 $4.99

6-Mix
Includes 1 oz. Bunny and Ducks Sprinkle Mix, 1 oz. Egg Sprinkle Mix, 1 oz. Springtime Mix, 1.3 oz. Lavender, Pink and Green Sugars. Certified Kosher.
710-R-740 $5.99

Gingerbread

Pre-Baked and Pre-Assembled Bunny Hutch Cookie House Kit
Imagine how much fun the kids will have decorating this house! It's the perfect springtime project and a cute centerpiece for your Easter table. So hop to it— everything is included: a pre-baked, pre-built house, white and lavender decorating icing mixes, candies, pre-made icing decorations, two cookie bunny ears, two decorating bags and tips, cardboard base and complete instructions with great decorating ideas. House measures 5 ½ x 5 ¼ x 6 in. high.
2104-R-1594 $12.99

ORDER TOLL FREE: 800-794-5866

Cookie Cutters

COMFORT GRIP™ CUTTERS

These easy-grip stainless steel cutters with extra-deep sides are perfect for cutting so many favorite foods into seasonal shapes. The cushion grip gives you comfortable control even when cutting thick desserts. Recipe included.
4 ½ x 4 ½ x 1 ½ in. deep.
$2.99

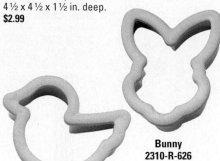

Chick
2310-R-625

Bunny
2310-R-626

METAL CUTTERS

Put variety in your cookie-making with fun Easter multi-shape sets. There are styles to please everyone. Recipe included.

Easter Cutter Collection

Springtime colors add a fresh look to your kitchen and fun to your baking. Lamb, chick, tulip, flower, bunny, egg, butterfly, bunny face, and carrot cutters are approx. 3 in. Colored aluminum.
2308-R-2503 Set/9 **$9.99**

Easter Mini Cutter Set

Butterfly, daisy, tulip, bunny face, chick and bunny, each approx. 1 ½ in. Metal.
2308-R-1209
Set/6 **$2.99**

Hoppy Easter Colored Metal Cutter Set

Springtime favorites in pastels of the season. Tulip, egg, butterfly and bunny. Coated metal. Each approx. 3 ½ in.
2308-R-1207 Set/4 **$4.49**

GRIPPY™ CUTTERS

NEW!

4 Pc. Grippy™ Set

Safe, easy cutting, with a comfortable grip and deep plastic sides. Four shapes include egg, butterfly, flower and bunny and measure approx. 3 ½ in.
2311-R-258 Set/4 **$3.99**

PLASTIC CUTTERS

Child-safe design means kids can have a great time helping. And remember all the fun ways to use our cutters—for bread shapes, stencils, sun catchers and so much more.

Individual Cutters

Child-safe plastic, approx. 3 x 4 in.
$0.69

Cross
2303-R-141

Duck
2303-R-148

Egg
2303-R-119

Easter Egg Canister Cutter Set

A fun and convenient egg canister holds a collection of Easter cutters for holiday cookies. Ten cutters, each approx. 3 ½ in.
2304-R-95 Set/10 **$5.99**

Easter Bite-Size Cutter Set

Bunny, chick, tulip, egg and bunny face shapes, each approx. 1 ½ in.
2303-R-9319 Set/5 **$2.49**

Nesting Bunnies Cutter Set

Great for cookies, imprinting patterns in icing, cutting bread shapes and more. Sizes from 1 ¼ to 4 ⅛ in.
2303-R-9270 Set/4 **$2.99**

COMMUNION

Cross Pan

Beveled design is excellent for rolled fondant. Instructions included. One-mix pan is 14 ½ x 11 ⅛ x 2 in. Aluminum.
2105-R-2509
$7.99

TOPPERS

Inspirational Cross

Beautifully designed sculpted resin. 5 ½ in. high.
202-R-206
$24.99

Communion Girl*
3 ½ in. high.
2113-R-7878 **$3.49**

Communion Boy*
3 ½ in. high.
2113-R-7886 **$3.49**

*Designed by Ellen Williams.

PATRIOTIC
Bakeware

Stars and Stripes Pan
Decorate a grand old flag cake perfect for that July 4th cookout. Accent Old Glory with Piping Gel and fresh summer fruit. One-mix pan is 13 x 9 x 2 in. Aluminum.
2105-R-183 **$7.99**

Star Pan
Your colorful star cake will set off sparks on the 4th and brighten parties all year long. One-mix pan is 12 ¾ x 1 ⅞ in. Aluminum.
2105-R-2512 **$10.99**

Mini Star Pan
Personal-size desserts make everyone feel like a star. One mix makes 12-16 stars. 6 cavities, each 4 ¾ x 1 in. Aluminum.
2105-R-1235 **$11.99**

Party

Baking Cups
Microwave-safe paper. Standard size, 2 in. diameter.
Pk./50 **$1.49**

NEW!

Old Glory
415-R-1262

Party Bags
Colorful Patriotic designs for candy and cookie treats. Pack contains 20 plastic 4 x 9 ½ in. bags and 20 twist ties.
Pk./20 **$1.99**

NEW!

Old Glory
1912-R-3056

Icing Decorations
Perfect for topping cupcakes, cookies and ice cream. Mint-flavored. Certified Kosher. **$2.09**

Patriotic Flags
710-R-726 Pk./9

PARTY PICKS
Many decorative uses.

Stars and Stripes
3 in. high.
2113-R-704
Pk./40 **$1.29**

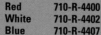

Patriotic Stars
415-R-381

Patriotic Stars
1912-R-1254

Patriotic Stars
710-R-942 Pk./21

Patriotic Foil Pix
Looks like a dazzling fireworks display on your holiday treats! Great for cakes, cupcakes. 4 in. high.
2113-R-712 Pk./12 **$1.99**

Candles

Beer Cans
1 ¾ in. high.
2811-R-9326
Set/6 **$3.49**

Red and Blue Sparklers
6 ½ in. high.
2811-R-704
Pk./18 **$0.99**

Colors & Icings
PATRIOTIC COLOR GUIDE

Red | **White** | **Blue**

Color Mist™ Food Color Spray
Gives decorators the versatility and dazzling effects of an airbrush in a convenient can! Use it to transform a plain iced cake with sensational color, add splashes of holiday color to iced cookies and cupcakes. No mess, taste-free formula.
1.5 oz. Certified Kosher. **$2.99**
Red   710-R-5500
Blue   710-R-5501

Tube Decorating Gel
Transparent gels are great for writing messages and decorating cakes and cookies. Colors match Wilton Icing Colors (p. 133). .75 oz Certified Kosher. **$1.29**
Red   704-R-318
White   704-R-302
Royal Blue   704-R-348

Ready-to-Decorate Icing
Anyone can decorate with Wilton Ready-to-Decorate Icing! Our brilliant colors and four decorating tips make it a breeze to add an exciting finishing touch to treats—without mixing or mess.
6.4 oz. Certified Kosher. **$3.49**
Red   710-R-4400
White   710-R-4402
Blue   710-R-4407

Tube Decorating Icing
Tubes can be used with our Tip and Nail Set or Coupler Ring Set (p. 133) and any standard size Wilton metal tip. Colors match Wilton Icing Colors (p. 133).
4.25 oz. Certified Kosher. **$1.79**
Red   704-R-218
White   704-R-200
Royal Blue   704-R-248

Cookie Pan

Star Cookie Treat Pan
Just press cookie dough into pan, insert a cookie stick, then bake, cool and decorate. Create cookie stars, rice cereal treats and candy pops. Pan makes 6 individual treats, 3 ½ in. diameter x ¼ in. Aluminum.
2105-R-8102 **$7.99**

Cookie Treat Sticks
6 in. 1912-R-9319 Pk./20 **$1.99**
8 in. 1912-R-9318 Pk./20 **$2.99**

CUPCAKES 'N MORE™ DESSERT STANDS

Easy to assemble!
Just stack each layer of cupcakes onto the locking center rod.

Keeps looking great!
Non-toxic, silver-finished metal has a durable non chip finish.

Collapsible design
Stores easily and safely.

Angled holders
Give the best view of cupcake tops!

Individually decorated cupcakes are the perfect way to add a personal touch to celebrations. Now, with Cupcakes 'N More, you have the perfect way to serve them! The look is fresh and fun, featuring bold silver-finished wire spirals to securely hold each cupcake. The twisting, towering design is perfect for any setting—showers, kids' birthdays, weddings, holidays and more.
Large 15 in. high x 18 in. wide. Holds 38 cupcakes.
307-R-651 $39.99

Featured in our Dazzling Displays section, p. 90

Standard
12 in. high x 13 in. wide. Holds 23 cupcakes.
307-R-826 $29.99

Sprinkles
INDIVIDUAL BOTTLES
Plastic bottles for convenient pouring and storing. Certified Kosher. **$1.99**

Patriotic Sprinkle Sparks
2.5 oz. bottle 710-R-940

Patriotic Mix
2.5 oz. bottle 710-R-786

Red Sugar
3.25 oz. bottle 710-R-766

Blue Sugar
3.25 oz. bottle 710-R-750

Cake Sparkles™
Edible glitter, .25 oz. bottle. Certified Kosher. **$2.89**

Red
703-R-1284

Blue
703-R-1314

ASSORTMENTS

3-Mix Sparkling Sugar **NEW!**
Includes 2.8 oz. each Blue and White, Red and White and White Sparkling Sugars. Certified Kosher.
710-R-914 $5.99

6-Mix
Includes 1 oz. each Red and Blue Jimmies and Patriotic Mix, 1.3 oz. each Red and Blue Sugar and .85 oz. Patriotic Sprinkle Sparks. Certified Kosher.
710-R-656 $5.99

Star Comfort Grip™ Cutter
This easy-grip stainless steel cutter with extra-deep sides is perfect for cutting so many favorite foods into star shapes. The cushion grip gives you comfortable control even when cutting into thick desserts. Recipe included.
4 ½ x 1 ½ in. deep.
2310-R-605 $2.99

Cookie
COOKIE STENCIL SETS

Stencil-A-Cookie™ Cutter & Stencil Set
Using the fun-shaped stencils and cutter, it's easy to serve cookies with exciting, colorful designs for the season. Just cut cookies, then use the stencils and Cake Sparkles™ and Colored Sugars (shown above) or Wilton FoodWriter™ Edible Color Markers (p. 129) or Color Mist™ Food Color Spray (p. 208) to create dazzling shapes on top after baking. Sets include one metal cutter and two stencils (same design).
2308-R-1405 Set/3 $1.99

Patriotic Cupcake and Cookie Stencils
Turn plain treats into American classics with a stenciled patriotic design. Just place one of the fun designs over your baked treat, then sprinkle with Wilton Cake Sparkles™ or Colored Sugars (shown above) or spray with Color Mist™ Food Color Spray (p. 208). Five designs.
417-R-131 $2.49

COOKIE CUTTERS

Star Metal Cookie Cutter
Quality metal is clean-cutting and easy to handle. 3 in.
2308-R-1008
$0.69

Stars Nesting Metal Cutter Set
A parade of small to large stars to create fun cookies for the 4th or all year long. Sizes from 5 to 2 ½ in.
2308-R-1215 Set/4 $4.49

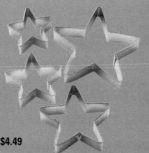

Nesting Stars Cutter Set
1 ⅝ to 4 ⅝ in.
2304-R-704
Set/6 $2.99

GRADUATION

Bakeware

Smiley Grad Pan
Our grinning grad is a smart choice to honor any student who's made the grade—boy or girl, kindergartner to collegian. One-mix pan is 10 ¼ x 12 x 2 in. Aluminum.
2105-R-2073 $7.99

Graduate Pan
Honor male or female grads! One-mix pan is 14 ½ x 8 ¼ x 2 in. Aluminum.
2105-R-1800 $7.99

Party

Baking Cups
Microwave-safe paper. Standard size, 2 in. diameter.
Pk./50 $1.49

Smiley Grad
415-R-294

Icing Decorations
Perfect for topping cupcakes, cookies and ice cream. Mint-flavored. Certified Kosher. $2.09

Petite Smiley Grad
710-R-503
Pk./12

Graduation Cap
710-R-473
Pk./9

NEW!

Grad Fun Pix®
Add a fun touch to cakes, cupcakes, ice cream and more. Approx. 3 ½ in. tall.
2113-R-717
Pk./12 $1.99

Topping Off Success Pan
Decorate in your grad's school colors. One-mix pan is 14 ¾ x 11 ¾ x 2 in. Aluminum.
2105-R-2038 $7.99

Book Pans
Books detail any of life's important chapters, including graduation. Aluminum.

Two-Mix Book Pan
11 ½ x 15 x 2 ¾ in. Serves up to 30.
2105-R-2521 $14.99

One-Mix Book Pan
13 x 9 ½ x 2 in.
2105-R-972 $10.99

Party Bags
Colorful grad designs for candy and cookie treats. 20 plastic bags, 20 ties included. 4 x 9 ½ in.
Pk./20 $1.99

CANDLES

Smiley Grad
1912-R-1130

Candle Set
3 caps, 3 diplomas, ½ to 2 in. high.
2811-R-1800
Set/6 $3.49

Champagne Bottles
2 in. high.
2811-R-163
Set/6 $3.49

Toppers

BOBBLING TOPPERS

Top off that special cake with these fun bobbling toppers and watch heads turn. The food-safe design features hand-painted detail.
Pk./6 $3.99

Female Grad
2113-R-462

NEW!

Male Grad
2113-R-461

Graduation Toppers
Capture the day's excitement with our beautifully-detailed plastic toppers on a special cake. Approx. 4 ¼ in. high.

Female Graduate
2113-R-1821 $1.99

Male Graduate
2113-R-1823 $1.99

Glowing Graduate (girl)
2113-R-1833 $1.99

Successful Graduate (boy)
2113-R-4549 $1.99

Graduation Caps Set
Great party favors or cake toppers, 2 in. high.
Set/2 $1.99
White 2113-R-1800
Black 2113-R-1801

Colors & Icings

GRADUATION AND AUTUMN COLOR GUIDE

Color Mist, Ready-to-Decorate Icing, Tube Decorating Icing and Tube Decorating Gel use the standard spectrum of Wilton colors.

Color Mist™ Food Color Spray
The dazzling effects of an airbrush in a convenient can! Use it to transform a plain iced cake with sensational color, add splashes of holiday color to iced cookies and cupcakes. No mess, taste-free formula. 1.5 oz. Certified Kosher. $2.99

Blue	710-R-5501
Red	710-R-5500
Yellow	710-R-5502
Green	710-R-5503
Violet	710-R-5504
Pink	710-R-5505
Black	710-R-5506
Orange	710-R-5507

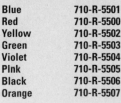

Ready-to-Decorate Icing
Anyone can decorate with Wilton Ready-to-Decorate Icing! Our brilliant colors and four decorating tips make it a breeze to add an exciting finishing touch to treats—without mixing or mess. 6.4 oz. Certified Kosher. $3.49

Blue	710-R-4407
Red	710-R-4400
Yellow	710-R-4409
Green	710-R-4401
Violet	710-R-4408
Pink	710-R-4406
Black	710-R-4404
Orange	710-R-4410
White	710-R-4402

Tube Decorating Icing
Tubes can be used with our Coupler Ring Set or Tip and Nail Set (p. 133) and any standard size Wilton metal tip. Colors match Wilton Icing Colors (p. 133). 4.25 oz. Certified Kosher. $1.79

Royal Blue 704-R-248	Leaf Green 704-R-224	Black 704-R-206
Red 704-R-218	Kelly Green 704-R-227	Orange 704-R-212
Lemon Yellow 704-R-236	Violet 704-R-242	White 704-R-200
	Pink 704-R-230	Chocolate 704-R-254

Tube Decorating Gel
Transparent gels are great for writing messages and decorating cakes and cookies. Colors match Wilton Icing Colors (p. 133). .75 oz. Certified Kosher. $1.29

Royal Blue 704-R-348	Leaf Green 704-R-324	Black 704-R-306	White 704-R-302
Red 704-R-318	Violet 704-R-342	Orange 704-R-312	Brown 704-R-354
Lemon Yellow 704-R-336	Pink 704-R-330		

AUTUMN

Pumpkin Pie Pan
Holds one 15 oz. can of pumpkin pie filling. Use for apple, peach and cherry pies, too! Ideal for ready-to-bake pie crusts.
9 x 1½ in. Aluminum.
2105-R-3970
$6.99

Sprinkles

INDIVIDUAL BOTTLES
Plastic bottles for convenient pouring and storing. Certified Kosher. **$1.99**

Leaves Mix
2.5 oz. bottle
710-R-787

Red Sugar
3.25 oz. bottle
710-R-766

Dark Green Sugar
3.25 oz. bottle
710-R-764

Cake Sparkles™
Edible glitter, .25 oz. bottle. Certified Kosher.
$2.89

Red
703-R-1284

Dark Green
703-R-1278

Orange
703-R-1308

Yellow
703-R-1272

ASSORTMENT
6-Mix
Includes 1.3 oz. each Yellow, Red, Orange and Light Green Sugar, 1 oz. Leaves Mix and Chocolate Jimmies. Certified Kosher.
710-R-751 $5.99

Candy

Pumpkins Candy Mold
1 design, 11 cavities.
2115-R-1558 $1.99

Candy Melts®*
Ideal for all your candy making—molding, dipping or coating. Artificially vanilla flavored unless otherwise indicated. Certified Kosher. 14 oz. bags. **$2.50**

Red	1911-R-499	Dark Green	1911-R-405
Light Cocoa	1911-R-544	Dark Cocoa	1911-R-358
Orange	1911-R-1631	Chocolate Mint	1911-R-1920
Yellow	1911-R-463	White	1911-R-498
		Peanut Butter	1911-R-481

*Brand confectionery coating.

Peanut Butter
1911-R-481

See pages 218-221 for more Wilton candy items.

Autumn Icing Colors Set
.5 oz. jars of Golden Yellow and Orange. Certified Kosher.
601-R-5583
Set/2 $2.99

Party

Baking Cups
Microwave-safe paper. Standard size, 2 in. diameter. **Pk./50 $1.49**

Harvest
415-R-512

Party Bags
Colorful Autumn designs for candy and cookie treats. 20 plastic bags, 20 ties included.
4 x 9½ in.
Pk./20 $1.99

Harvest
1912-R-1288

Icing Decorations
Wilton Icing Decorations are perfect for topping cupcakes, cookies and ice cream. Mint-flavored. Certified Kosher. **$2.09**

Petite Leaves
710-R-230 Pk./12

Leaves
710-R-3003 Pk./12

Cookie

Autumn Cupcake and Cookie Stencils
Turn plain treats into visions of the season with a stenciled Autumn design. Just place one of the fun designs over your baked treat, then sprinkle with Wilton Cake Sparkles™ or Colored Sugars (shown at left) or spray with Color Mist™ Food Color Spray (p. 210). Five designs.
417-R-1207 $2.49

COPPER CUTTERS
The warmth and beauty of copper make these cutters ideal for displaying. Beautiful, heirloom-quality solid copper cutters have smooth rolled edges for that finishing touch.
Each approx. 5½ in. **$6.99**

Oak Leaf
2308-R-3077

Pumpkin
2308-R-3078

Maple Leaf
2308-R-3045

Apple
2308-R-3076

COMFORT GRIP™
Easy-grip stainless steel cutters with extra-deep sides. Great for cutting, cushioned plastic grip gives comfortable control. Recipe included. Approx. 4½ x 4½ x 1½ in. deep. **$2.99**

Oak Leaf
2310-R-633

Maple Leaf
2310-R-632

Pumpkin
2310-R-600

METAL CUTTERS

Leaves and Acorns Nesting Metal Cutter Set
Graduated acorns, oak and maple leaves, (3 each). 1¾ to 3¾ in. Recipe included.
2308-R-2000 Set/9 $5.99

Harvest Mini Metal Cutter Set
Six shapes: oak leaf, maple leaf, apple, pumpkin, elm leaf and acorn, each approx. 1½ in. Recipe included.
2308-R-1217 Set/6 $2.99

Cookie Making

Wilton has just what you need to make cookies fun! Easy-to-use presses, colossal cutter sets, fun stencils, colorful icings and unique toppings sure to create unforgettable cookies!

Cookie Presses

Wilton has four great ways to press cookies—the best selection of feature-packed presses anywhere! From our Comfort Grip™ Press, designed for easy handling and filling, to our powerful cordless Cookie Master™ Plus, spritz cookie-making has never been easier!

COOKIE MASTER™ Plus

Cordless Cookie Press

Distinctive Cookies **Snacks & Appetizers** **Desserts & More!**

Our cordless cookie press is so powerful and easy to operate, you'll use it all year to create cookies, appetizers, desserts and more. Exclusive patented reverse action means there's no need to take press apart for refilling. Ergonomic design is shaped to fit in your hand for excellent comfort.

Includes 12 aluminum disks in classic and seasonal shapes, 4 accent tips for decorating and filling and 2 bonus recipe booklets—sweet and savory. Uses 4 AA batteries, not included.
2104-R-4008 Set/19 $39.99

Cordless, Battery Operated —
No cord means no need to be near an outlet.

Patented Reverse Action —
No need to take press apart to refill—just press a button.

Ergonomic Design —
Shaped to fit your hand for excellent comfort and ease of use. Sealed buttons keep food out.

Unique Dough Guard™ —
Keeps the dough away from the motor.

See-Through Barrel —
Check progress and see how much dough is left.

Fluted Bottom —
Raises press off of the cookie sheet for well-formed designs.

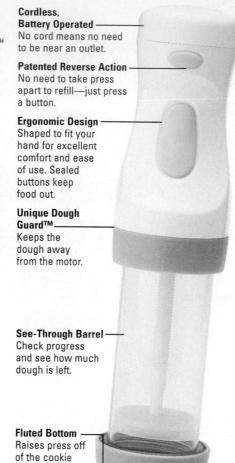

Twelve Disk Designs

Twelve aluminum disks in classic & seasonal shapes let you create distinctive snacks, appetizers, cookies, desserts and pastries.

Four Accent Tips

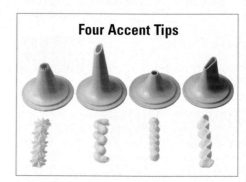

Four multi-purpose accent tips make it easy to fill pastries, garnish appetizers and decorate elegant desserts.

COMFORT GRIP™
Cookie Press

Experience a classic press that is truly comfortable. Its ergonomic handle feels great in any hand—the easy-squeeze action releases perfectly shaped dough. The clear barrel takes the guesswork out of refilling. Fluted bottom raises the press off the cookie sheet to help you create better shapes.

Includes 12 plastic disks in a variety of shapes plus our classic spritz recipe.
2104-R-4011 Set/13 $12.99

Twelve Disk Designs

Cookie Pro™ ULTRA

Easy to use, easy to store—everything you want in a cookie press. Pump-action design lets you press dozens of cookies comfortably. Handle folds over for compact storage.

Includes 10 aluminum disks in an attachable storage case. Recipes included.
2104-R-4010 Set/12 $24.99

Pump Action
For greater efficiency and ease of use.

Space Saving Design
Unique flip-over handle for easy and convenient storage.

Internal Spring-Loaded Piston
For exceptional reliability and efficient pressing.

Ergonomically-Designed Comfort Grip™ Handle
Helps you press comfortably even when making large batches of cookies.

Side Grips
Keep hands from slipping.

Heavy-Duty Construction
Cast aluminum and stainless steel.

Finger-Grip Disk Ring
Makes changing disks easy.

No More Missing Disks!
Storage case attaches to cookie press when not in use.

Ten Disk Designs

Ten Disk Designs Included!
Long-lasting aluminum disks are dishwasher safe.

cookie max™ cookie press

Discover the cookie press that takes convenience and comfort to the max! With the Cookie Max™, you'll see the difference from the first batch. An easy pump action gives you more control—one click of the plunger equals one perfect cookie, every time. The handle is cushioned for a sure, comfortable grip. The see-through barrel and raised bottom let you see the cookie and your remaining dough as you press. No clogging, easy cleaning.

Includes 12 plastic disks in favorite shapes, easy instructions and 3 delicious recipes.
2104-R-4003 Set/13 $17.99

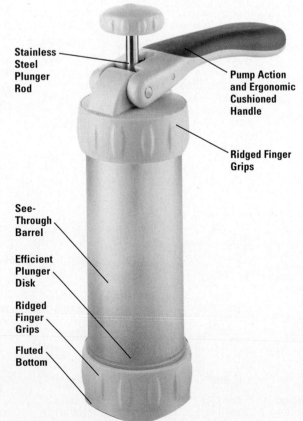

Stainless Steel Plunger Rod

Pump Action and Ergonomic Cushioned Handle

Ridged Finger Grips

See-Through Barrel

Efficient Plunger Disk

Ridged Finger Grips

Fluted Bottom

Twelve Disk Designs

Cookie Cutters

These versatile designs are sure to spark your creativity!

COMFORT GRIP™ CUTTERS

Easy-grip stainless steel cutters with extra-deep sides are perfect for cutting so many favorite foods into spectacular shapes. Ideal for brownies, biscuits, sandwiches, sheet cakes, cheese, crispy rice treats, fudge and much more. The cushion grip gives you comfortable control even when cutting into thick desserts. Recipe included. Each approximately 4 x 4 x 1¾ in. **Each $2.99**

Star
2310-R-605

Teddy Bear
2310-R-609

Round
2310-R-608

Square Crinkle
2310-R-611

Heart
2310-R-616

Butterfly
2310-R-614

Flower
2310-R-613

Daisy
2310-R-619

METAL CUTTER SETS

Multi-piece sets add variety. Built to last, they cut cleanly and release easily. Recipe included.

Basic
Geometric, crinkle diamond, heart, half moon, star and flower. Each approx. 3 in.
2308-R-1235
Set/6 $4.99

Animals
Horse, dove, lion, duck, pig and cat. Each approx. 3 in.
2308-R-1236
Set/6 $4.99

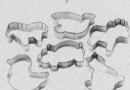

Hearts
Seven different heart cutter designs from stylized to traditional. Sizes range from 1½ to 3 in.
2308-R-1237
Set/7 $4.99

Bug Buddies
Butterfly, caterpillar, bee, ladybug, dragonfly and spider. Each approx. 3 in.
2308-R-1245 Set/6 $4.99

Nesting From The Heart
Two crinkled and two smooth. Largest is approx. 5 in.
2308-R-1203
Set/4 $4.49

Nesting Stars
For holidays and more! Largest is approx. 5 in.
2308-R-1215
Set/4 $4.49

Nesting Blossoms
Pretty flowers in four sizes. Largest is approx. 5 in.
2308-R-1204
Set/4 $4.49

Mini Romantic
Butterfly, heart, bell, crinkled heart, tulip, and blossom. Each approx. 1½ in.
2308-R-1225
Set/6 $2.99

Mini Noah's Ark
Horse, ark, elephant, bear, giraffe and lion. Each approx. 1½ in.
2308-R-1206
Set/6 $2.99

Mini Geometric Crinkle
Square, circle, heart, diamond, oval and triangle. Each approx. 1½ in.
2308-R-1205
Set/6 $2.99

METAL CUTTERS

The classic metal cutter was Grandma's favorite but she never had all these fun shapes! Metal cutters from Wilton are built to last through years of cookie making; they cut cleanly and release with ease. Each shape is approximately 3 in. **Each $0.69**

Star
2308-R-1008

Gingerbread Boy
2308-R-1002

Bear
2308-R-1009

Heart
2308-R-1003

Fish
2308-R-1017

Cross
2308-R-1018

Daisy
2308-R-1007

Acorn
2308-R-1020

Maple Leaf
2308-R-1021

Oak Leaf
2308-R-1013

Butterfly
2308-R-1015

Chick
2308-R-1000

Bell
2308-R-1006

Circle
2308-R-1010

Shamrock
2308-R-1011

ORDER TOLL FREE: 800-794-5866

SOLID COPPER CUTTERS

The warmth and beauty of copper make these cutters ideal for displaying and adding that decorative touch to your kitchen after baking cookies. These beautiful, heirloom-quality copper cutters have smoothly rolled edges for that finishing touch. Each approximately 5 ½ in. across. **Each $6.99**

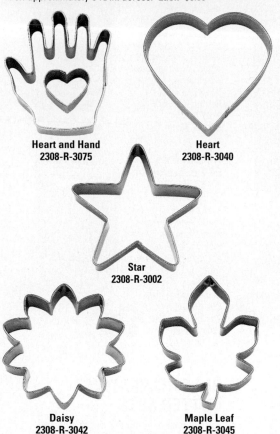

Heart and Hand
2308-R-3075

Heart
2308-R-3040

Star
2308-R-3002

Daisy
2308-R-3042

Maple Leaf
2308-R-3045

Ice-A-Cookie®

Instant fun for all your cookies! The soft, squeezable pouch is easy to handle and the patented snip tip and screw-on decorating cap help you control the flow—use the snip tip for icing cookies and the cap for decorative lines and designs. Delicious vanilla-flavored white icing dries to a smooth, satin finish. Draw fun shapes, messages, decorate with Cake Sparkles™ (not included) and more! Each 10.59 oz. pouch decorates approximately two dozen 3 in. round cookies. Certified Kosher.
710-R-416 $3.99

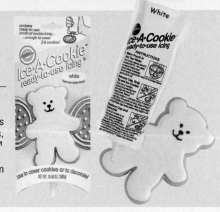

FoodWriter™ Edible Color Markers

Use like ink markers to add fun and dazzling color to countless foods. Kids love 'em! Decorate on cookies, fondant, color flow and royal icing designs. Brighten everyday foods like toaster pastries, cheese, fruit slices, bread and more. Each set includes five .35 oz. FoodWriter pens. Certified Kosher.

PRIMARY COLORS SETS

Yellow Green Red Blue Black

Fine Tip
609-R-100
Set/5 $7.99

Bold Tip
609-R-115
Set/5 $7.99

NEON COLORS SET

Purple Orange Pink Light Green Black

Fine Tip
609-R-116
Set/5 $7.99

FINE TIP
BOLD TIP

STENCIL-A-COOKIE™ CUTTER & STENCIL SETS

Using the fun-shaped cutter and stencil, it's easy to serve cookies with exciting, colorful designs. Just cut cookies, then use the stencil and Wilton FoodWriter™, Cake Sparkles™, Colored Sugars or Color Mist™ Food Color Spray (each sold separately) to create dazzling shapes on top after baking. Cookies look great iced with Wilton Ice-A-Cookie® sold above. Set includes one metal cutter and two stencils (same design). Each shape approximately 4 x 4 in.
Set/3 $1.99

Heart
2308-R-1401

Butterfly
2308-R-1402

Flower
2308-R-1403

Star
2308-R-1405

Cookie Cutters

PLASTIC COOKIE CUTTER SETS

101 Cookie Cutters!

With this set, you're covered! Make cookies featuring popular holiday and theme shapes like sports, flowers, animals and more. Or use the complete alphabet and numeral collections included to create the perfect cookie message. Great for cutting all kinds of food into fun shapes—perfect for crafting, too. Average cutter size approx. 3 ½ x 3 ½ in. Recipe included.
2304-R-1000 Set/101 **$14.99**

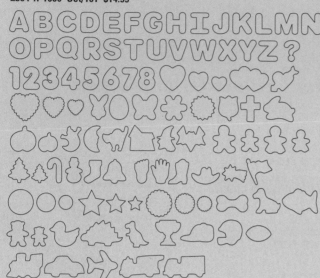

A-B-C and 1-2-3 50-Pc. Cutter Set

Complete alphabet and numeral collection, great for cookies, brownies, gelatin treats, learning games, crafts and more. Average cutter size approx. 3 ½ x 3 ½ in. Recipe included.
2304-R-1054
Set/50 **$8.99**

Animal Pals 50-Pc. Cutter Set

Everyone will go wild for cookies, foods and crafts made with this menagerie of favorite animal shapes. Shapes include fish, dog, cat, birds, butterflies, reptiles and more. Average cutter size approx. 3 ½ x 3 ½ in. Recipe included.
2304-R-1055
Set/50 **$8.99**

PLASTIC COOKIE CUTTERS

With our large variety of brightly-colored cutter shapes, the making is as much fun as the eating! Child-safe design means kids can help.
Each approx. 3 in. x 4 in. **Each $0.69**

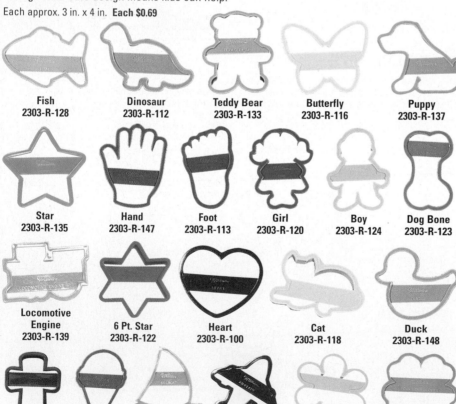

Fish 2303-R-128	Dinosaur 2303-R-112	Teddy Bear 2303-R-133	Butterfly 2303-R-116	Puppy 2303-R-137
Star 2303-R-135	Hand 2303-R-147	Foot 2303-R-113	Girl 2303-R-120	Boy 2303-R-124	Dog Bone 2303-R-123
Locomotive Engine 2303-R-139	6 Pt. Star 2303-R-122	Heart 2303-R-100	Cat 2303-R-118	Duck 2303-R-148
Cross 2303-R-141	Ice Cream Cone 2303-R-111	Sailboat 2303-R-129	Airplane 2303-R-101	Flower 2303-R-117	Four-Leaf Clover 2303-R-134

PLASTIC NESTING CUTTER SETS

Your favorites in child-safe, graduated shapes. Discover all the fun ways to use our cutters—for bread shapes, stencils, sun catchers and so much more.

Teddy Bear
From cub to grizzly size! 1 ¾ to 6 ⅜ in. tall.
2304-R-1520
Set/4 **$2.99**

Blossom
Create pretty blooms with plastic cutters in sizes from 1 ⅛ to 4 ½ in.
2304-R-116
Set/6 **$2.99**

Heart
Great for tracing valentines! 1 ½ to 4 ⅛ in.
2304-R-115
Set/6 **$2.99**

Star
For crafts, cookies or patterns in your iced cake. 1 ⅝ to 4 ⅝ in.
2304-R-111
Set/6 **$2.99**

ORDER TOLL FREE: 800-794-5866

Cookie Bakeware and Accessories

COOKIE TREAT PANS

Cookie treats on a stick are so easy! Just press cookie dough into pan, insert a cookie stick, then bake, cool and decorate. Create your own cookie blossoms for that special someone; also great for rice cereal treats and candy.

Recipe included. Each pan makes 6 individual treats, 3½ in. x ¼ in. deep. Aluminum. **Each $7.99**

Star
2105-R-8102

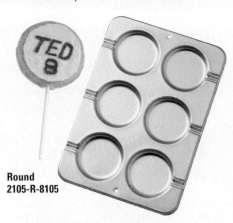

Round
2105-R-8105

Blossom
2105-R-8109

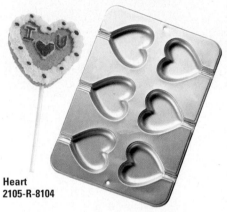

Heart
2105-R-8104

Cookie Treat Sticks
For fun cookie pops.
6 in. 1912-R-9319
Pk./20 $1.99
8 in. 1912-R-9318
Pk./20 $2.99

Clear Party Bags
4 x 9½ in. Each pack contains 25 bags and 25 ties.
1912-R-1240
Pk./25 $1.99

GIANT COOKIE PANS

Our Giant Cookie Pans help you create a jumbo pan cookie in a shape that will be a big hit for any occasion. Specially designed for one package of refrigerated dough, they are also great for brownies and pizza!

Each shape is approximately ¾ in. deep and can be used with recipes that call for a standard 13 x 9 in. pan. Aluminum. **Each $5.99**

Round
2105-R-6201

Heart
2105-R-6203

ORDER ONLINE: WWW.WILTON.COM

COOKIE SHEETS

Wilton Cookie Sheets are extra thick aluminum to heat evenly for perfect, evenly-browned bottoms.

Aluminum
Extra-thick construction.
Jumbo 14 x 20 in.
2105-R-6213 $16.99
12½ x 16½ in.
2105-R-2975 $12.99

Insulated Aluminum
Two quality aluminum layers sandwich an insulating layer of air for perfect browning without burning.
16 x 14 in.
2105-R-2644 $17.99

COOLING GRIDS

Chrome-Plated
Sturdy design will never rust.
13 in. Round
2305-R-130 $7.99
10 x 16 in.
2305-R-128 $5.99
14½ x 20 in.
2305-R-129 $8.99

Non-Stick
Cookies and cakes won't stick with our slick non-stick coating.
13 in. Round
2305-R-230 $9.49
10 x 16 in.
2305-R-228 $8.99
14½ x 20 in.
2305-R-229 $12.99

3-Pc. Stackable Chrome-Plated
Use singly or stack to save space while cooling three batches of cookies at the same time. Individual grids are 13½ x 9¾ x 3 in. high; stacked grids are 9¾ in. high.
2305-R-151 $12.99

See p. 145-153 for the full line of Wilton Bakeware.

COOKIE SPATULA

Stainless steel spatula with riveted rosewood handle.
417-R-470 $3.99

SUGAR CRYSTALS

Brighten up plain cookies fast with our colorful decorating sugars. Just sprinkle these extra-fine sugars on cookies before baking. Controlling the flow is easy with our flip-top shaker bottle. Certified Kosher.
Each $4.99

Brights 4-Mix
Contains 1.1 oz. each: Pink, Yellow, Light Green, Lavender.
710-R-651

Primary 4-Mix
Contains 1.1 oz. each: Red, Dark Green, Blue, Yellow.
710-R-650

Candy Making

Let Wilton show you how great candy can be! Use our Candy Melts®* and molds for beautiful candy in 3 easy steps—just melt, mold and serve.

Candy Melts®*

Versatile, creamy, easy-to-melt wafers are ideal for all your candy making—molding, dipping or coating. Their delicious taste can be varied by adding our Candy Flavors.

Light and Dark Cocoa are all natural, cocoa flavor; colors are artificially vanilla flavored. 14 oz. bag. Certified Kosher. **$2.50**

Peanut Butter	Dark Cocoa	Light Cocoa	Chocolate Mint	Lavender	Pink
1911-R-481	1911-R-358	1911-R-544	1911-R-1920	1911-R-403	1911-R-447

Yellow	Orange	Blue	Red	Green	White
1911-R-463	1911-R-1631	1911-R-448	1911-R-499	1911-R-405	1911-R-498

Kids' Candy Making Kits

It's a whole new way for kids to have fun with candy! Imagine a pizza with the works, a treat-filled treasure chest or a revved-up race car, all made of delicious candy. Now imagine your favorite kids having a blast making these treats come to life. Wilton kits make it easy and fun for anyone to melt, mold and assemble a great looking candy project.

Kits include easy-to-follow instructions that stress safe candy making with help from an adult. All kits include 2 reusable molds, Candy Melts®* in assorted colors, melting bags and instructions; plus other contents as noted below. Recommended for ages 8 and above. **$9.99**

 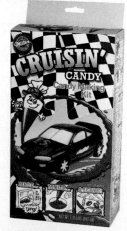   

Treasure Chest
Swashbuckling fun! Create a bounty of fun jewels in a cool candy chest. Includes decorating brush and 19.5 oz. Candy Melts®.
2104-R-1196

Cruisin' Candy
Your pit crew will love putting this candy racecar together! Includes decorating brush and 22.5 oz. Candy Melts®.
2104-R-1197

Flower Fancy
Mold flowers on "stem" sticks. Includes 10 green lollipop sticks, decorating brush, cardboard wrap-around fence and 15 oz. Candy Melts®.
2104-R-1069

Pizza Chef
Toppings look great—there are even two delivery boxes for fun gifting. Includes 20 oz. Candy Melts®.
2104-R-1065

Funny Faces
Create loony lolli-people! Includes 6 lollipop sticks, decorating brush and 20 oz. Candy Melts®.
2104-R-1067

*Brand confectionery coating.

ORDER TOLL FREE: 800-794-5866

Candy Making Tools

Squeeze Bottles

Melt candy with ease, then fill your mold without mess! Our convenient bottles are available in three sizes so you can melt the right amount of Candy Melts®* you need. Melt candy right in the bottle, then squeeze out into molds. Great way to store and reheat leftover candy.

Mini	**Regular**	**Large**
6 oz.	12 oz.	16 oz.
1904-R-1166	1904-R-1189	1904-R-1167
Pk./2 $1.99	$1.69	$1.99

Candy Melting Plate

Microwave-melt up to 11 Candy Melts®* colors at one time with less mess! Plastic with non-slip grip edge. Includes decorating brush.
1904-R-8016 $2.99

Metal Dipping Set

Professional-quality stainless steel with wooden handles. 8¾ in. long.
1904-R-925
Set/2 $9.99

Candy Dipping Set

Easy-handling spoon and fork, each 7¾ in. long.
1904-R-800
Set/2 $2.99

Decorator Brush Set

Plastic, durable bristles, easy-to-hold handle.
2104-R-9355
Set/3 $1.49

Easy-Pour Funnel

Push-button controls flow of candy. 5 x 4 in. diameter, nylon.
1904-R-552 $3.99

Candy Thermometer

Precise measurement essential for preparing hard candy, nougat, more.
1904-R-1200 $14.99

Candy Wraps and Boxes

Your homemade candy deserves a beautiful presentation. Wilton has everything you need to wrap and package your candy like a pro. Designed to keep candies fresh, protected and attractive for gift giving.

Candy Gift Boxes

For attractive gift giving and stay-fresh storage.

1 lb. White Candy Boxes. Pk./3 $2.49
1904-R-1172

½ lb. Candy Boxes. Pk./3 $1.99

White	Red
1904-R-1150	1904-R-1152
Gold	Silver
1904-R-1151	1904-R-1153

Candy Cups

Crisply-pleated, just like professionals use. White glassine-coated paper.

1¾ in. Diameter.
1912-R-1245 Pk./75 $1.49

1 in. Diameter.
1912-R-1243 Pk./100 $1.49

Candy Bar Boxes

Designed to hold candies made in our Candy Bar Molds (p. 221), the window displays your special message.
Pk./10 $3.99

White
1904-R-1157

Silver
1904-R-1159

Gold Elastic Ties

Pre-tied with a bow. Use with Candy Gift Boxes.
1904-R-1186 Pk./5 $1.49

Candy Box Liners

Padded paper liners cushion candy and prevent breakage. Use with ½ lb. Candy Gift Boxes.
1904-R-1191 Pk./4 $1.49

Foil Wrappers

Bright, shiny coverings for candy and lollipops! 4 x 4 in. squares.
Pk./50 $1.99

Gold
1904-R-1197

Silver
1904-R-1196

Red
1904-R-1198

Truffle Boxes

An elegant look, with a lock-close top that forms a perfect "bow." Holds 2-3 pieces of candy.
Pk./4 $1.99

White
1904-R-1154

Silver
1904-R-1155

Gold
1904-R-1156

Candy Color and Flavoring Sets

Primary Candy Color Set

Concentrated oil-based colors blend easily with Candy Melts®. Includes Yellow, Orange, Red and Blue in .25 oz. jars. Certified Kosher.
1913-R-1299 Set/4 $3.99

Garden Candy Color Set

Create pretty pastel colors! Concentrated oil-based colors blend easily with Candy Melts®. Includes Pink, Green, Violet and Black in .25 oz. jars. Certified Kosher.
1913-R-1298 Set/4 $3.99

Candy Flavoring Set

Add your favorite. Includes Peppermint, Cherry, Cinnamon and Creme de Menthe in .25 oz. bottles.
1913-R-1029 Set/4 $5.49

Novelty Candy Molds

More fun shapes and greater detail make Wilton Candy Molds the world's favorite way to create candy. Look at the variety! You can do it all, from exciting kids' party treats to elegant wedding and shower favors. Molding and coloring couldn't be easier when you use Candy Melts®*. Look for terrific design ideas and molding instructions on every mold package.

NEW!

NEW!

Ice Cream
3 designs, 9 cavities.
2115-R-4367 $1.99

Summer Fun
5 designs, 11 cavities.
2115-R-1741 $1.99

Alphabet
26 designs, 26 cavities.
2115-R-1563 $1.99

Numerals
10 designs, 10 cavities.
2115-R-1564 $1.99

Stars
1 design, 12 cavities,
2115-R-1554 $1.99

Party Time Lollipop
6 designs, 8 cavities.
2115-R-1516 $1.99

Seashells
5 designs, 11 cavities.
2115-R-1561 $1.99

Smiley Face Lollipop
1 design, 9 cavities.
2115-R-1715 $1.99

Roses in Bloom
1 design, 10 cavities.
2115-R-1738 $1.99

Roses and Buds Lollipop
3 designs, 9 cavities.
(4 lollipop).
2115-R-1708 $1.99

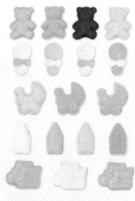

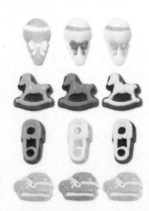

Wedding Shower Lollipop
5 designs, 10 cavities.
(4 lollipop).
2115-R-1711 $1.99

Baby Bottles Lollipop
1 design, 6 cavities.
2115-R-1560 $1.99

Rubber Ducky
1 design, 6 cavities.
2115-R-1565 $1.99

Mini Baby Icons
5 designs, 20 cavities.
2115-R-1537 $1.99

Baby Shower
4 designs, 11 cavities.
2115-R-1710 $1.99

ORDER TOLL FREE: 800-794-5866

Candy Bar Molds

*Create a sweet memory for your guests . . .
a candy bar featuring your special message.*

Molding is easy using Candy Melts®* (p. 218). Present them beautifully in Candy Bar Boxes (below). Each candy bar measures 3 ¼ x 1 ¾ x ¼ in. deep. Mold has 1 design, 4 cavities. **$1.99**

**Add-A-Message
2115-R-1356**

**Our Wedding
2115-R-1409**

**Thank You
2115-R-1410**

Candy Bar Boxes
Designed to hold candies made in our Candy Bar Molds (above), the window displays your special message.
Pk./10 $3.99

**White
1904-R-1157**

**Silver
1904-R-1159**

Classic Candy Molds

Wilton has a great selection of traditional shapes for creating elegant gift assortments and party trays. From luscious filled candies to popular mint patties, these well-defined molds help you turn out perfect candy every time.

Peanut Butter Cups
1 design, 10 cavities.
2115-R-1522 **$1.99**

Deep Heart Truffles
1 design, 7 cavities.
2117-R-100 **$1.99**

Truffles
1 design, 12 cavities.
2115-R-1521 **$1.99**

Roses
3 designs, 12 cavities.
2115-R-1713 **$1.99**

Gift Truffles
1 design, 13 cavities.
2115-R-1728 **$1.99**

Mint Discs
1 design, 16 cavities.
2115-R-1739 **$1.99**

Cordial Cups
Mold a candy "glass" to serve dessert liqueurs! Or, fill with whipped cream and float in your cocoa or coffee. 1 design, 6 cavities.
2115-R-1535 **$1.99**

Dipped Spoons Mold
Turn an ordinary cup of coffee into a mocha delight! Use with the Dipped Spoons Kit at right or use your own spoons, along with Wilton Candy Melts®* and Candy Flavors, to create candy-coated spoons that stir in flavor. Contains mold (1 design, 6 cavities) and instructions.
2115-R-1722 **$1.99**

Accessories

Create the perfect pop with sticks in every size, cool colors too! Clear wrappers make giving easy.

Rainbow Lollipop Sticks
Add pizzazz to your pops! Food-safe plastic sticks; 5 each red, yellow, blue and green. Not for oven or microwave use. 4 in.
1912-R-9316 Pk./20 **$1.99**

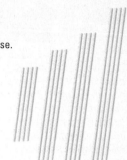

Lollipop Sticks
Sturdy paper sticks in 4 sizes. Not for oven use.
4 in.
1912-R-1006
Pk./50 **$1.99**
6 in.
1912-R-1007
Pk./35 **$1.99**
8 in.
1912-R-9320
Pk./25 **$1.99**
11 ¾ in.
1912-R-1212
Pk./20 **$3.99**

Lollipop Wrapping Kit
Cover your candy lollipops and special treats for gift-giving! Contains 18 sticks, (4 in.) 18 bags, 18 twist ties.
1904-R-1193 **$1.99**

Clear Treat Bags
Let your fun candy and cookie treats show through! 3 x 4 in.
1912-R-2347
Pk./50 **$2.69**

Dipped Spoons Kit
Candy-coated spoons are a delight to make, use or give. Use with the Dipped Spoons Mold at left, plus your favorite Candy Melts®* and Candy Flavors. Includes 6 plastic spoons, 6 bags, 6 twist ties and instructions.
1904-R-1192 **$1.99**

*Brand confectionery coating.

for Kids™

Help kids see how much fun the kitchen can be! Let 'em loose with these kid-safe kits—they'll have a blast making their own yummy fun-shaped cakes and candies. Kids can't go wrong because every kit has step-by-step instructions that make success a sure thing!

No-Bake Cake!™

No oven needed...just add water!

Easy as...

1 Add water and stir batter! 2 Fill mold and watch cake rise! 3 Add icing and sprinkles!

It's the cake every kid loves to make! With No-Bake Cake! Kits, there's no oven, no baking—you just mix the batter, pour in the mold and watch your cake rise before your eyes! In 15-20 minutes, cakes will be ready to ice and decorate in a fun design—or just eat if you can't wait. Use the mold again and again, with the convenient No-Bake Cake! Mix Refill Packs. Ages 4 and above.

COMPLETE CAKE KITS

All kits include 2 cake mixes (yellow and artificially-flavored chocolate), decorating bag and easy instructions for making and decorating the cakes and mixing the icing. 5.5 oz.

ALL NEW!

Cupcake
Also includes 6-cavity cupcake mold, yellow icing mix and rainbow sprinkles. Makes 12 cupcakes.
2104-R-8920 $5.99

Heart
Also includes 4 x 3⅛ x ½ in. deep heart cake mold, light pink icing mix and white sprinkles. Makes 2 heart cakes.
2104-R-8919 $5.99

Teddy Bear
Also includes 4 x 3 x ½ in. deep bear cake mold, white icing mix and artificially-flavored chocolate sprinkles. Makes 2 bear cakes.
2104-R-8918 $5.99

No-Bake Cake!™ Mix Refill Packs
Use these cake mixes with our No-Bake Cake Molds. Each pack includes 3 (1.5 oz.) mixes to make 18 cupcakes or 3 cakes. 4.5 oz. Pk./3 **$4.99**

Chocolate (artificially-flavored) **2104-R-8915**

Yellow 2104-R-8916

GUMMY!

Easy as 1•2•3...

Mix   Shake   Mold

Kids will have a wild time making gummy dinosaurs, flowers, and more with Wilton for Kids kits and gummy mixes. Just follow the easy steps to make great-tasting gummys in 10 minutes! Ages 4 and above.

Gummy Mix Flavors
Add fun new flavors to your Gummy Making Kit and keep the gummy fun going! Each package includes five pouches (.7 oz. each)—enough to make 20 pieces of gummy candy, complete instructions. New Refill Pack includes one pouch each Green Apple, Blue Raspberry, Grape and Strawberry flavors (.7 oz. each) and one pouch (.7 oz. each) of Sour Sugar. Artificial flavors. **$3.99**

Grape 1911-R-303	Strawberry 1911-R-309	Refill Pack 1911-R-329
Green Apple 1911-R-305	Blue Raspberry 1911-R-320	

GUMMY-MAKING KITS

Everything's included to make 16 gummys or 8 lollipops. **$4.99**

Each kit includes:
- Mold with 2-4 fun shapes, mixing bottle and funnel.
- 4 gummy mixes (.7 oz. each) in assorted artificial flavors.
- 1 packet of Sour Sugar (.7 oz.) for covering gummys.
- Lollipop kits include 8 lollipop sticks.
- Easy instructions.

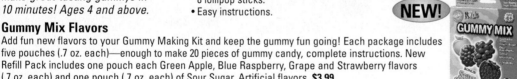

NEW! **Race Day Lollipop 2104-R-7504**

NEW! **Sweet Stuff Lollipop 2104-R-7505**

Glam Girl 2104-R-1616

Creepy Critters 2104-R-1617

Dinosaurs 2104-R-1620

NEW!

Gummy Sour Sugar
Add a sour kick to your gummy flavors! Includes five pouches (.7 oz. each)—enough to cover 80 pieces.
1911-R-1930 $3.99

Look for more fun Gummy Kits and Kandy Clay Kits featuring kids' favorite characters on pages 177-183.

Kandy Clay™

The Modeling Clay You Can Eat!

It's the krazy, kolorful kandy kids can make into any shape! Roll it, shape it and stretch it into anything they can imagine—monsters, jewelry and more. When they're done, they'll have a sweet treat to eat! Here are the kits and kandy kids need to play with Kandy Clay. Ages 4 and above.

KANDY CLAY ACTIVITY KITS

Each theme kit includes all the colorful, yummy candy needed to create great shapes to play with and eat!

Kits contain 12 Kandy pouches (.5 oz. each) in assorted artificial flavors, plus sculpting tool and complete instructions unless otherwise noted. **$5.99**

Kandy Clay Multi-Color Packs
Get creative—grab the flavors and colors you love to add to your Kandy Clay shapes! Each pack includes twelve .5 oz. packages. Artificial flavors. **$3.99**

Rings 'N Things
Includes food-safe string.
2104-R-5030

Monster Madness
Includes cardboard window gift box.
2104-R-5021

Primary Colors
Includes: Blueberry Blue, Green Apple Green, Lemon Yellow, Marshmallow White, Cherry Red, Chocolate Brown.
1911-R-335

Bright Colors
Includes: Blue Raspberry Blue, Lime Green, Orange Orange, Marshmallow White, Watermelon Hot Pink, Grape Purple.
1911-R-333

ORDER TOLL FREE: 800-794-5866

INDEX

Now You Can Print
at www.wiltonprint.com

Introducing the new Wilton Print-Your-Own Stationery Program—the perfect way to announce any special celebration! Complete kits are ready to personalize, print and mail! All invitation kits are crafted of acid-free and lignin-free paper.

Mr. and Mrs. John W. Smith
request the honour of your presence
at the marriage of their daughter
Caroline Grace
to
Mr. William James Jones
on Saturday, the eighth of September
two thousand and twelve
at 6 o'clock in the evening
Museum of Art
Chicago, Illinois

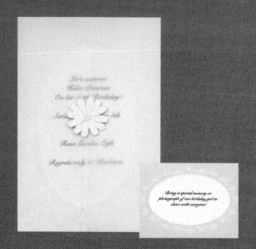

Dream Day
Includes:
25 Invitations and
Mailing Envelopes,
25 Reply Cards
and Envelopes,
25 Paper Flowers
with Adhesive
Backing, 3 Test
Sheets.
1008-R-528
Set/25 $24.99

Portrait of Love
Includes:
25 Invitations and
Mailing Envelopes,
25 Reply Cards
and Envelopes,
25 Mini Frames
with Adhesive
Backing, 25 Mini
Frame Inserts,
3 Test Sheets.
1008-R-529
Set/25 $24.99

**Keeping
with Tradition**
Includes:
50 Invitations and
Mailing Envelopes,
50 Reply Cards and
Envelopes, 3 Test
Sheets.
1008-R-520
Set/50 $24.99
Also available in
Ivory
1008-R-521
Set/50 $24.99

**Joined
Together**
Includes:
50 Invitations and
Mailing Envelopes,
50 Reply Cards and
Envelopes, 3 Test
Sheets.
1008-R-522
Set/50 $24.99
Also available in
Ivory with Gold
1008-R-523
Set/50 $24.99